W9-BUV-175

The Economist
BUSINESS
TRAVELLER'S
GUIDES

JAPAN

The Economist BUSINESS *TRAVELLER'S* GUIDES

JAPAN

PRENTICE HALL PRESS

NEW YORK

This edition published in the United States and Canada in 1987 by
Prentice Hall Press
A division of Simon & Schuster, Inc.
Gulf + Western Building
One Gulf + Western Plaza
New York, New York 10023

PRENTICE HALL PRESS is a trademark of Simon & Schuster, Inc.

Guidebook information is notoriously subject to being outdated by changes to telephone numbers and opening hours, and by fluctuating hotel and restaurant standards. While every care has been taken in the preparation of this guide, the publishers cannot accept any liability for any consequences arising from the use of information contained herein.

Where opinion is expressed it is that of the author, which does not necessarily coincide with the editorial views of The Economist newspaper.

The publishers welcome corrections and suggestions from business travellers; please write to The Editor, *The Economist Business Traveller's Guides*, 40 Duke Street, London W1A 1DW, United Kingdom.

Series Editor Stephen Brough
Editor Rick Morris
Designers Mel Petersen, Alistair Plumb

Consultant travel editor Lesley Downer
Contributors Martin Bloom, Ray Granger, Michael Houser, John Breen, Michael Scott

Library of Congress Cataloging-in-Publication Data
The Economist business traveller's guide. Japan.
Includes index.
1. Japan – Description and travel – 1945 – Guide-books. 2. Business travel – Japan – Guide-books. 3. Japan – Commerce – Handbooks, manuals, etc.
I. Economist (London. England)
DS811.E26 1987 915.2'0448
87–1746
ISBN 0–13–234907–8

Maps and diagrams by Eugene Fleury
Typeset by SB Datagraphics, Colchester, England
Printed in Italy by Arnoldo Mondadori, Verona

Contents

Glossary 6
Using the guide 7
Introduction 8

The Economic Scene
Resources 10
The nation's finances 14
International trade 16

The Industrial Scene
Industry and investment 18
Shipbuilding 20
Heavy chemicals 21
The car industry 22
Consumer electronics 24
Computers 25
Automation 26
Communications 28
New materials 30
Biotechnology 31
Top ten companies 32
Foreign presence 34

The Political Scene
The government of the nation 36
Party politics 38
The reins of power 40
International alignments 42
National security 43

The Business Scene
Government and business 44
Power in business 46
The business framework 48
Employment 52
Financial institutions 56
The banks 57
The markets 59
Other sources of finance 61
Insurance 62
The law 63
Accountants 68
Advertising 70
Market entry 72
Distribution 75

Business Awareness
The Japaneses at work 76
Corporate hierarchies 78
Women in business 79
Business meetings 80
Dressing for business 84
Invitations, hospitality and gifts 85
The business media 88

Cultural Awareness
A historical perspective 89
Important events in Japanese history 92
Beliefs, attitudes and lifestyles 93
Education 96
Language 98
Japanese phrases 99
Manners and conversation 102

City by City
Introduction 106
Tokyo 108
Fukuoka 148
Hiroshima 158
Kita-Kyushu 166
Kobe 170
Kyoto 178
Nagoya 192
Osaka 202
Sapporo 216
Yokohama 226

Planning and Reference
Entry details 234
Climate 234
Holidays 235
Information sources 235
Money 235
Getting there 236
Getting around 236
Hotels 238
Restaurants 242
Bars 244
Understanding sake 244
Shopping 245
Local information 245
Crime 246
Embassies 246
Health care 247
Communications 248
International dialling codes 249
Conversion charts 250
Background reading 251
Index 252

Glossary

AGM Annual General Meeting. A yearly meeting of company shareholders with their directors.
ASEAN Association of Southeast Asian Nations. An economic and trade association.
Article 65 A legal provision which maintains a strict separation between banks and securities dealers.
Diet The Japanese parliament.
gaijin Literally "outside person". The Japanese word for a foreigner.
GATT General Agreement on Tariffs and Trade. Over 100 countries are signatories.
GNP Gross national product.
G5 Abbreviation for Group of Five. Its members are: Britain, France, Japan, the USA and West Germany.
IMF International Monetary Fund.
Invisible trade Exports and imports of services, such as banking, insurance and foreign travel.
JETRO Japan External Trade Organization. A Japanese government agency whose main function now is to help foreign firms wishing to export to Japan.
JNR Japan National Railways.
JNTO Japan National Tourist Organization.
JTB Japan Travel Bureau.
KDD Kokusai Denshin Denwa. Japan's international telecommunications authority.
Keidanren Japan's leading business organization, equivalent to Britain's CBI.
keiretsu gaisha A large industrial group whose many companies are generally based around a trading company and a major bank.
LDP Liberal Democratic Party. Japan's leading political party.
meishi A business card.
MITI Ministry of International Trade and Industry. One of the legendary powers behind Japan's postwar economic renaissance and still a force to be reckoned with.
M2 One of the definitions of money supply used by governments when determining monetary policy.
nemawashi Literally "to dig around the root of a tree to prepare it for transplanting." *Nemawashi* is a process of consultation designed to produce a consensus, and is frequently used in both Japanese companies and society at large.
NTT Nippon Telegraph and Telephone Corporation. Japan's major domestic telecommunications authority.
OECD Organization for Economic Cooperation and Development.
Plaza Agreement An agreement reached in Japan, in September 1985, by finance ministers of the Group of Five countries. It has had the effect of revaluing the Japanese yen against major world currencies.
rationalization Getting rid of unnecessary equipment, personnel, etc, often following a merger.
ramping Artificial boosting of share prices.
ringi-sho An intra-office memorandum to obtain the approval of all concerned for a proposed course of action.
samurai The Japanese warrior caste that formed the aristocracy from the 11th to the 19th centuries.
senmon shosa A trading company specializing in a particular product area.
shogun A military commander. The shoguns became military dictators who effectively ruled until 1867.
shunto The annual "spring wages offensive" when representatives of management and unions agree pay rises for the year.
sogo shosa The 13 largest Japanese general trading companies.
tatami A straw floor-mat. It is also used as a unit of square measurement: 1 tatami = $1{\cdot}62\ m^2$.
TIC Tourist Information Centre.
TSE Tokyo Stock Exchange.
zaibatsu Prewar industrial groups which were disbanded during the US Occupation but have re-emerged in somewhat different form.
zaikai A collective term for Japan's powerful top businessmen.
Note: For definitions of Japanese cuisine see *Planning and reference.*

Using the guide

The Economist Business Traveller's Guide to Japan is an encyclopedia of business and travel information. If in doubt about where to look for specific information, consult either the Contents list or the Index.

City guides

Each city guide follows a standard format: information and advice on arriving, getting around, city areas, hotels, restaurants, bars, entertainment, shopping, sightseeing, sports and fitness, and a directory of local business and other facilities such as secretarial and translation agencies, couriers, hospitals with 24-hour accident and emergency departments, and telephone-order florists. There is also a map of the city centre locating recommended hotels, restaurants and other important addresses.

For easy reference, all main entries for hotels, restaurants and sights are listed alphabetically.

Abbreviations

Credit and charge cards
AE American Express; CB Carte Blanche; DC Diners Club; MC Mastercard (Access); V Visa.

Figures Millions are abbreviated to m; billions (meaning one thousand million) to bn. Trillions are used to mean one thousand billion.

Publisher's note

The Economist Business Traveller's Guides have been prepared for the international marketplace. This particular volume provides first and foremost practical information for any businessperson travelling in Japan. The general background information and analysis of the Japanese economy, politics, society and business structure are also helpful to people doing business *with* Japan even if they are conducting it from overseas.

Price bands (yen)
Price bands are denoted by symbols (see below). These correspond approximately to the following actual prices at the time of going to press. (Although the actual prices will inevitably go up, the relative price category is likely to remain the same.)

Restaurants
(a complete evening meal including drink but excluding tax at 10% and service at 10%)

¥	up to Y4,000
¥¥	Y4,000 to Y8,000
¥¥¥	Y8,000 to Y12,000
¥¥¥¥	Y12,000 to Y16,000
¥¥¥¥¥	over Y16,000

Hotels
(one person occupying a single room, excluding tax at 10% and service at 10%)

¥	up to Y8,000
¥¥	Y8,000 to Y12,000
¥¥¥	Y12,000 to Y16,000
¥¥¥¥	Y16,000 to Y20,000
¥¥¥¥¥	over Y20,000

INTRODUCTION

For all the reams of articles, stacks of books and reels of film produced about it, Japan remains one of the world's least understood and, surprisingly, most unloved countries. It is common knowledge that Japan has experienced a man-made miracle, growing out of the rubble of 1945 to become the second strongest economy in the non-communist world. In 1986 Japan's national per capita income overtook that of its postwar occupier, the United States. Yet conventional answers to such questions as how Japan achieved its present strength, what makes it tick, what, if any, are its aims, and even how sophisticated are its society and economy are laden with myth and misunderstanding.

For their part, the Japanese themselves remain inward-looking and clannish, despite the fact that every year Japan's influence on the world increases. Its exports are everywhere, its multinationals are building factories overseas and employing thousands of Westerners. In the 1980s it took over from the Arab countries as the nation investing the most money overseas each year. It is home to the world's biggest banks, securities houses, shipbuilders, steelmakers and consumer electronics firms. Even its politicians are, reluctantly, making more confident and prominent appearances on the world stage.

Rags to riches

Japan's path to modernity is usually dated from 1945. This is misleading. The foundations of modern Japan were laid from 1868, after the American navy and European traders had forced Japan to re-open itself to the world for the first time in over two centuries. It was Japan's victory over Russia in 1905 that first shocked the West into taking this Asian country seriously as a military and industrial force.

In the years up to the war, Japan absorbed modern capitalism and technology rapidly in the belief that industrial strength was the best means to guarantee survival. Big industrial groups became established, including such now-familiar names as Mitsubishi, Mitsui and Sumitomo. However, amid the depressed world economy of the 1930s, Japan's pursuit of industrial growth was mixed with domestic poverty and insecurity to yield militarism and colonial ambition.

Defeat in the Pacific War (1941–45), combined with postwar land reform, eradicated the country's feudal aristocracy and much of its class system, as well as any military or colonial ambitions. This left Japan free to concentrate on domestic economic growth and enabled a new generation of entrepreneurs – Akio Morita of Sony and Soichiro Honda among them – to rise alongside the restructured industrial groups.

The Japan that grew so rapidly in the next two decades was run by many of the same politicians and industrialists as before the war. There was continuity as well as change. The labour force was highly literate, thanks to the spread of mass education in the 1930s, and cheap because so many of the population were still peasant farmers. Factors such as these gave a potential for growth, although fresh ingredients were needed to ensure that it was achieved.

Among these ingredients, two stand out. One was the achievement of industrial peace after a turbulent patch in the 1950s. Big firms traded the offer of job security ("lifetime employment") in return for moderate, productivity-linked wage claims.

The other ingredient is governmental guidance and control. Leadership by the celebrated Ministry of International Trade and Industry (MITI) and the Ministry of Finance amounted to less than the "Japan Inc" that Westerners like to imagine, but was important, nevertheless. The ministries, however, have never been able to countermand opposition from business. Industries were protected against foreign competition in the 1950s and 1960s, but fierce competition was the rule at home. The ministries' most important roles have been as an intermediary between firms and as a think tank. In the 1970s and 1980s, as trade protection and control of import licences have disappeared, so have many of the ministries' powers.

More open than it looks

"Japan Inc" is a powerful myth, but a myth nevertheless. Concerted thinking was, indeed, responsible for arguably Japan's greatest success in the past three decades: the speed with which its economy and industry adjusted to the two oil-price hikes. But it certainly no longer means that the country is a closed shop to foreign business.

Japan is a hard place for foreigners to do business, but, as one of the world's largest and most lucrative consumer markets, it is worth the effort. Painstaking research is the watchword – exactly the Japanese technique when exporting to foreign markets. The firms that have fared best in Japan have been those that adapted their methods to local needs and have built a Japanese work force on Japanese lines: with job security, a family atmosphere and the sense that the firm is there for the employees, as well as for the shareholders. The likelihood is that Japan will gradually become an easier place in which to do business. Since the country's current-account surplus promises to be durable, the strong yen of the mid-1980s is likely to stay, making imports more competitive. Despite the inward-looking instincts of the ordinary Japanese, the Liberal Democratic government appears to appreciate that Japan ought to have fewer trade barriers than other countries, not more.

The Liberal Democrats are secure in power, having won a record majority in July 1986. The internationalist wing of the party is in the ascendant, which suggests that preserving good economic and military relations with the West will remain a priority. After all, insular or not, Japan has little choice: China is poor and has a stop-go economy, the Soviet Union is hostile and still occupies four Japanese islands. Japan depends too much on the Western world to want to go its own way.

The Economic Scene

Resources

Japan's four main islands and 4,000 smaller ones make up only 0.3% of the world's land mass – an area slightly smaller than California or Sweden – yet accommodate nearly 3% of the world's population. Despite hurricanes and earthquakes, a lack of land and geographical isolation, Japan has become Asia's only fully industrialized economy. Mount Fuji, an inactive volcano rising 3,777m, presides over forested mountain ranges that cover over 70% of Japan's land area. Housing, industry and farming huddle on the coastal flatlands, principally in central-southern Honshu. The country's buoyant economy is almost totally dependent on imported fuel and raw materials.

Islands and regions

Japan's 1,860 mile/2,995km-long chain of islands stretches from the 24th parallel, off Taiwan, north to the 45th parallel, just below the USSR's Sakhalin Island.

Hokkaido is Japan's least populated island. Once a haven for outcasts, in the last century it has developed agriculture, leisure and beer-brewing. Just to the north are the disputed Kurile Islands, some of which have been occupied by the Soviets since 1945.

Honshu is where 80% of Japanese live, the majority concentrated in the plains of *Kanto* (Tokyo) and *Kansai* (Kyoto-Osaka), which have distinctive business cultures. Major ports and airports are in Honshu.

Shikoku is a comparative backwater, primarily devoted to agriculture and little visited by foreigners.

Kyushu has a subtropical climate, and its people are reputedly the most outgoing. Bullet Train services to Hakata, near Fukuoka (which has a major airport), have aided the growth of Japan's Silicon Valley.

The Ryukyus were returned to Japan only in 1972, having been occupied by the USA since World War II, and are the poorest of all Japan's regions. These islands have a hybrid population and several are uninhabited; Okinawa is a major staging base for the US Air Force.

Raw materials

Although 40% of GDP is derived from manufacturing, Japan is deficient in virtually all key industrial minerals and depends heavily on imports from the USA, Canada, Australia and the ASEAN countries. It has no aluminium or nickel and imports over 95% of the iron ore, tin and copper (as well as most of the lead and zinc) its factories need.

Energy

Japan is the world's largest importer of coal, natural gas and oil. It is almost totally dependent on other countries for oil, and imported 1.2bn barrels in 1985. More than 70% comes from the Middle East, nearly 20% from Southeast Asia; imports from China are rising steadily and now constitute 7%. Japan supplies only 8% of its natural gas and 19% of its coal needs.

Until nuclear fusion becomes a commercial reality in the next century, the contribution of local energy sources will be limited to 20%, mainly from hydroelectricity and nuclear fission, as well as limited geothermal and solar sources. Government policy is to reduce oil dependence to 50–60%, in favour of solid fuel, natural gas and local energy, and to diversify sources of supply.

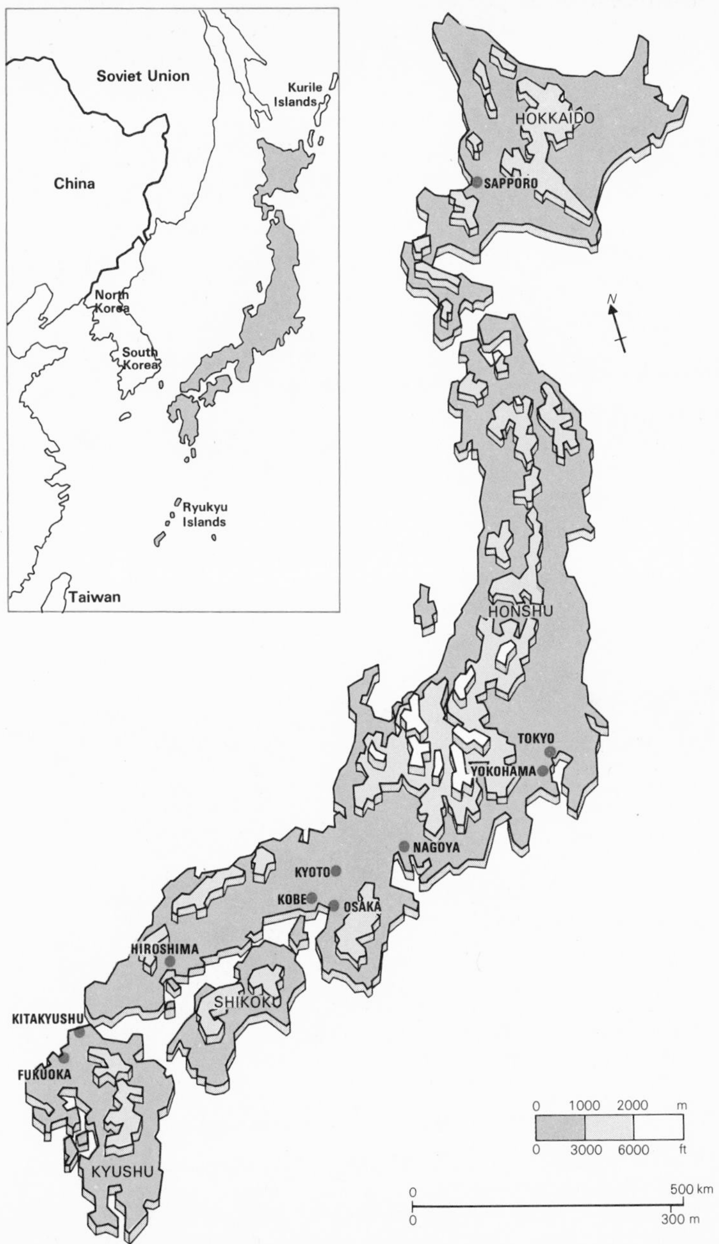
Soviet Union
Kurile Islands
China
North Korea
South Korea
Ryukyu Islands
Taiwan
HOKKAIDO
SAPPORO
N
HONSHU
TOKYO
YOKOHAMA
NAGOYA
KYOTO
KOBE
OSAKA
HIROSHIMA
SHIKOKU
KITAKYUSHU
FUKUOKA
KYUSHU
0 1000 2000 m
0 3000 6000 ft
0 500 km
0 300 m

Forestry

The proportion of land covered by forests is among the highest in the world. The variety is considerable, from soft pines to cypress, cedar and a range of oaks. Ownership is fragmented. The principal problem is access: steep gradients make felling difficult and expensive. In addition, most forests were planted postwar and have yet to mature. As a result, Japan is only 30% self-sufficient and has become the world's largest net importer of timber – mainly unprocessed roundwood.

Agriculture

Despite surprisingly high self-sufficiency (70%) in foodstuffs, agriculture poses problems and will increasingly do so. Farms are small (1.4 hectares on average) and inefficient by Western standards. The average age of farmers is over 50 and is rising, reflecting the unpopularity of farming as a livelihood and the movement of young people to the cities. Farms are often run by the women and old people, while men work in industry.

The principal output of what is essentially a market garden sector includes rice, vegetables, melons and citrus fruits. Major imports include cereals and feed grains, poultry and dairy products. Although Kyushu can produce two crops a year, even rice is now imported; domestic rice prices are kept artificially high for political reasons. Protectionist measures (citrus and beef are particularly contentious areas) are unlikely to stem the steady increase in imports, mostly from the USA.

Tastes have for some time been moving away from cereals in favour of meats, vegetables and dairy products. Domestic production has been unable to cope with rapid increases in demand or compete on price. Exports of foodstuffs are insignificant.

Fisheries

Japan is a voracious consumer of marine products, ranging from fish and seaweed to whale products. Among foodstuffs, imports of fish are second in value only to cereals; Japan has been a net importer since 1971 and the world's largest importer of fish since 1978. Imports have risen as 200-mile zones have been introduced. Seas around Japan are becoming depleted, and Japanese fleets trawl the world causing flash points off the Kuriles with Soviet coastguards and with Greenpeace in whaling grounds, though whaling is to be phased out. Fish farming has developed to provide more freshwater supplies; coastal fish ranching is one attempt to restock local waters.

Land Use (1983)

Land area (not including disputed Kurile Islands, north of Hokkaido) 377,800 km²

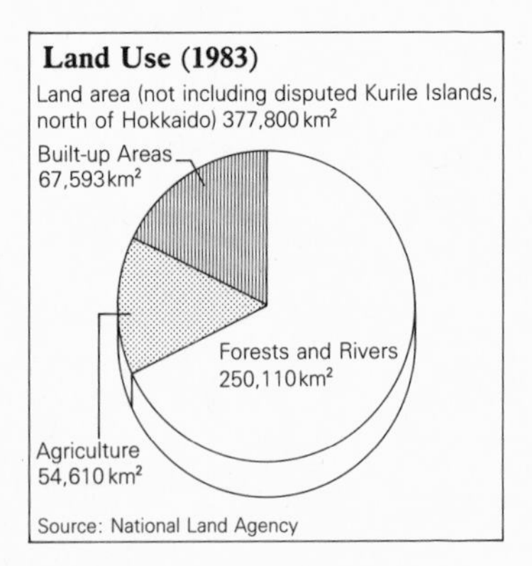

Source: National Land Agency

Land use

Rising incomes have caused an increase in housing demand. The influx of foreign businesses in urban areas has caused office rents and land values to boom. Land prices for the country as a whole rose less than 3% in 1985, but in central Tokyo they rose 53.6%. Since 1955, urban land prices nationally have risen by 4,000% (8 times the consumer prices index) and by nearly twice that in Japan's six largest cities. Land reclamation adds only marginally to the available area. Land costs remain an uncontrollable factor, especially in Tokyo and the industrial areas.

The human dimension

Japan's population is expected to reach 130m in the next century. Today, with 121m, it has the world's seventh largest population, three-quarters of whom live in cities. Overall, there are 829 people per sq mile/320 per sq km, but if uninhabitable areas are excluded more realistic figures of 3,885/1,500 emerge, making Japan the world's most crowded country. The major business centres, Tokyo and Osaka, form an urban sprawl which is home to 25m.

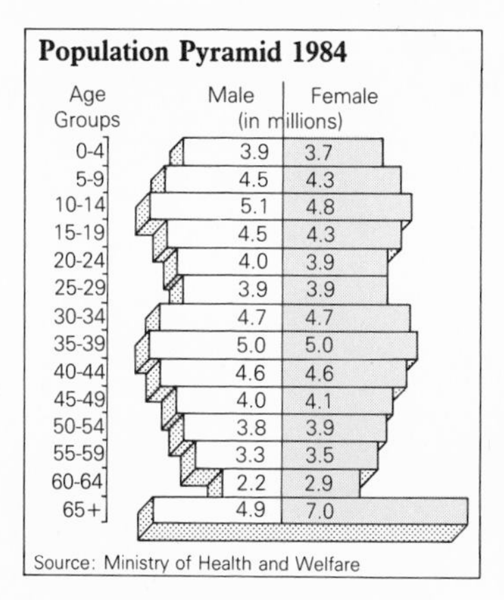

Population profile The average age is rising more rapidly than in any other industrial country. A comparatively smaller working population will, in the future, have to support a larger dependent population. One consequence is that the proportion of working women will continue to rise, particularly in the 25–43 age group, which has traditionally withdrawn from the labour force.

Trends The birth rate, 11.2 per 1,000, has fallen from 36.3 in 1870. The death rate is 5.9 per 1,000. The natural increase is just over 5 per 1,000. The rate of marriages, 6.2 per 1,000, is high for a developed country – the average age on marriage for women being 23–24 years, for men 26–29 years. The low, but rising, divorce rate is 1.38 per 1,000 population, just over a quarter of the US rate.

Immigration and emigration Neither is significant in a permanent sense. Naturalization is rare, and immigration is neither commonplace nor encouraged. Overseas postings of businessmen and their families have increased markedly since the 1970s.

The working population

The labour pool of 60m is a bigger proportion of population than in the West. In 1960 nearly 50% worked on the land or in fishing. Today only 9% do so. The fastest-growing source of employment is the service sector, which now employs 57% of the working population, compared with 70% in the USA and 66% in Britain.

The proportion and number of working women have also grown and are high by international standards. However, women are poorly paid in comparison with men, and many work for low pay in family businesses. It is still widely expected that a woman will give up work on marriage and that those who work after marriage will be content with part-time, low-paid jobs.

The skill base is very high by international standards, with 95% continuing education after compulsory schooling, compared with 40% in Britain. Half a million graduates enter the labour market each April, a high proportion of them engineers and business studies/economics graduates. Skill shortages are greatest in financial services and in foreign languages.

Unemployment has not been a problem, although there is much hidden unemployment and under-employment. In 1986 unemployment reached 2.86%, the highest official rate since 1953, when records were first kept. Declining industries have tried to maintain the size of their permanent labour forces by diversification and by offering small (or no) pay rises.

The nation's finances

Japan has a strong economy in world terms, with low inflation and continuing growth, but its public expenditure has been deficit-financed since 1975. An antiquated fiscal structure, strong popular resistance to overdue tax reforms, and the government's attempt to spend its way out of recession in the late 1970s are at the root of current problems. Strong foreign pressure to reflate the economy has been largely resisted, but increases in defence and foreign aid spending are being pushed for. At home the government faces mounting welfare demands.

Deficit financing

Between 1969 and 1980 General Account expenditure grew in double digits annually. In 1975, after the first oil shock, the government issued its first "red bonds" to spend its way out of recession. Further huge bond issues followed, and by 1986 the national debt stood at 42.3% of GNP. In the 1980s public expenditure has been cut in real terms, rising only 3% in 1986/87, with cuts in all areas except defence and foreign aid.

Inflation

Following runaway inflation in 1973/74 (24.5% consumer, 31.6% wholesale), government policy has focused on controlling inflation. Japan now has the lowest inflation among developed countries – around 2% in 1986. Mid-1980s price levels pose no threat to government or business, thanks to the fall in oil and commodity prices, low interest rates and the yen's appreciation.

Currency

The yen's exchange value has fluctuated considerably since it was floated in 1971. By international agreement the yen was effectively revalued in late 1985, rising some 30% against the US dollar by mid-1986. This was a long-overdue reflection of Japan's status as the world's third largest economy.

The system of public finance

Revenue is channelled through the General Account and the Fiscal Investment and Loan Plan (FILP). The General Account is responsible for about 70% of spending, and into this go all tax revenues and bond proceeds. FILP's revenues come from pension contributions and largely untaxed savings from the Postal Savings Bank, which has assets three times those of Citibank.

Fiscal policy The goal is to balance the budget by 1990. The government is trying to cut public expenditure, close tax loopholes and introduce tax reforms, which may include a value-added tax.

Monetary policy is based on a wish to maintain yen strength at a realistic level and to contain monetary growth at stable rates (M2 has grown 7–9% per annum since 1984). Upward pressure on interest rates is likely as deregulation proceeds.

Problems in the system Despite recent changes, the financial system lacks sophistication. There is no Treasury bill market, and a market for short-term government debt was created only in 1986. Commercial banks are loaded with government paper, and a high proportion of deposits are subject to regulated interest rates to provide cheap government funding.

Where the money comes from

Taxes account for almost 75% of General Account income, most of the rest coming from bond issues. Direct taxation provides over 73% of tax revenue, income tax contributing the largest slice, followed closely by corporation tax. Individuals are lightly taxed – rates begin at 10.5%, and few people get beyond the 30% band – while corporations pay hefty rates of 47–58%.

Among indirect taxes, liquor tax raises the most revenue, while stamp duties and gasoline, commodity, tobacco and inheritance taxes also make sizable contributions.

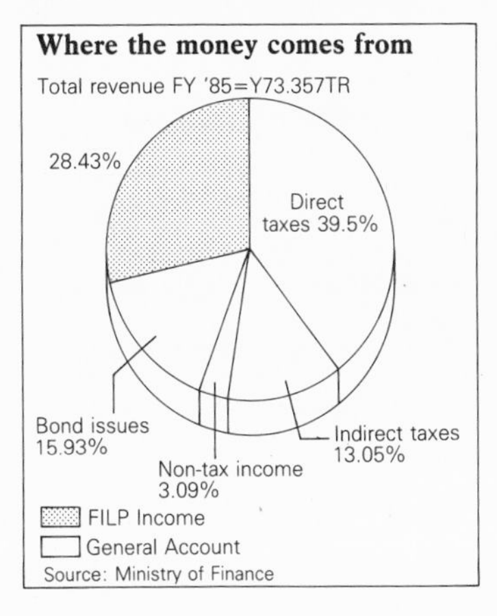

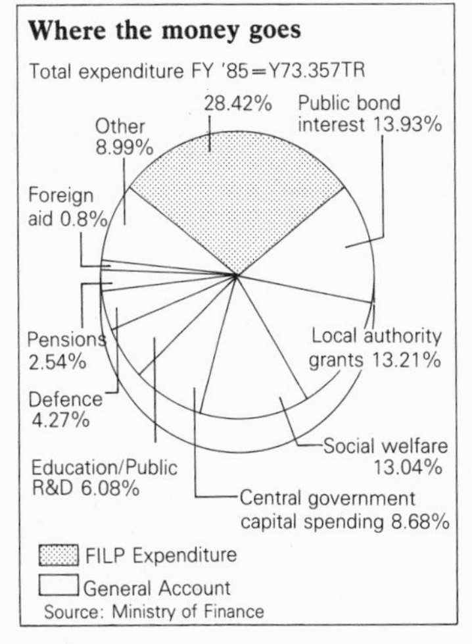

Where the money goes

Servicing the national debt accounts for almost 20% of General Account expenditure. Grants to local government, of around Y1bn, provide over a third of their income. FILP spends heavily on a deficient infrastructure (less than 60% of homes are on mains sewage), on costly public corporations and development corporations, and on state banks which fund industry.

Public corporations The biggest loss-maker is Japan National Railways, which has annual losses of $7bn, accumulated debt of over $100bn and a bankrupt pension fund.

Welfare Spending is set to become the public sector's biggest headache. Most Japanese associate public welfare with "advanced country disease"; traditionally welfare has been the responsibility of employers. Companies offer guaranteed lifetime employment and provide assistance with medical, housing, education and pension costs. Low personal tax rates are possible because of minimal provisions for the sick, the unemployed and the elderly.

Education Spending is concentrated on 5–18 schooling, since most pre-school and higher education is privately funded.

Defence The USA, which has provided a defence umbrella since 1945, wants increased spending. A war-sensitive electorate, however, is loath to see spending exceed the unwritten postwar limit of 1% of GNP, the lowest among developed nations. It exceeded 1% in 1986.

Foreign aid has been %increasing but accounts for only 0.5 of GNP, lower than in most developed countries. Much of Japan's aid is viewed as self-serving and Asia-centred.

The political debate

Despite public resistance, there is a need for tax reform to cut the huge deficit. Business wants deep cuts in the public sector and privatization. The pressure for increased spending on health, welfare, defence and foreign aid will pose problems as the government tries to balance the budget.

International trade

Japan's balance of payments, which gave it the highest surplus ever recorded ($49bn) in 1985, has become a sore point in its relations with trading partners. No aspect, from yen policy to import promotion to export restraint or financial liberalization, has been immune from scrutiny, demand for reform and threats of protectionist retaliation. There has been movement: the yen's value has soared since late 1985, tariffs and quotas are now lower on average than in other industrial nations, and a third of exports are subject to voluntary restraint.

Balance of payments

Like the yen, Japan's balance of payments has been on a roller coaster since the early 1970s. Deficits following the oil shocks have given way to seemingly in-built surpluses. Following the world recession in the early 1980s, domestic demand was flat, and exports became the vehicle of growth. The situation has been compounded by an American budget deficit which soaked up huge inflows of Japanese savings. The current account surplus is projected to reach $80bn in 1987.

Japan's Balance of Payments

($bn)	1975	1980	1985
Exports	54.70	126.70	174.00
Imports	49.70	124.60	118.00
Trade Bal.	5.03	2.13	55.99
Net Services	−5.35	−11.35	−5.17
Transfers	−0.36	−1.53	−1.65
Current A/C Balance	−0.68	−10.75	49.17
ST Cap Flows	−1.14	3.14	−0.94
LT Cap Flows	−0.27	2.32	−64.54
E & O	−0.59	−3.10	3.99
Overall Bal.	−2.68	−8.39	−12.32
Reserves	12.82	25.23	26.51

• IMF Basis. Source: Ministry of Finance

Japan's trade

Japanese goods are substantially in surplus, whereas services are in deficit (though decreasingly so). Imports of low value-added fuels, raw materials and essential foodstuffs are shaped into high value-added manufactures for export. As a proportion of GNP, exports (12.7%), and imports (10.9%) are lower than those of several other leading industrial countries. Targeted exports, though, are significant for the havoc they create abroad in selected industries and markets. Both Japan's exports and imports rank third in world terms, behind the USA and West Germany.

Main trading partners

%Exports	Country	%Imports
37.2	USA	19.9
7.1	China	5.8
4.0	South Korea	3.3
4.0	West Germany	2.3
3.7	Hong Kong	0.6
3.1	Australia	5.8
2.9	Taiwan	3.2
2.7	UK	1.4
2.6	Canada	5.0
2.2	Saudi Arabia	7.9

Source: Ministry of Finance (1985)

Major trading partners

The US and Western Europe are Japan's most important markets, accounting for nearly 60% of exports. Developing countries absorb just under a third (South Korea is most important), while the communist bloc accounts for just under 10%, with China as the main market.

More than half of Japan's imports come from developing countries; these consist largely of crude oil imports from the Arabian Gulf and Indonesia, timber from Malaysia and South Korea and Taiwanese foodstuffs. About 40% of imports come from developed countries, principally the USA, Australia and

Canada, which are major suppliers of foodstuffs, industrial raw materials and coal. The communist bloc supplied only 6.6% of imports in 1985, mainly Chinese oil and food.

Trade barriers

Liberalization since the 1970s has greatly reduced Japan's visible barriers. The major problems for foreigners seeking to export to Japan (see *Market entry*) are the strength of local competition, the unique qualities of the market and an assortment of invisible barriers.

Invisible trade

Japan still manages to earn only 70% of what it spends abroad on services. Most of this comes from net earnings on technology licences and from investment income on recycled trade surpluses. Losses from shipping are diminishing, but deficits from patent royalties and overseas travel are growing. Travelling Japanese spend four times more money overseas than do visitors to Japan.

Capital outflows Japan has been a net exporter of capital since the early 1970s. By 1986, investment outflows were running at $7bn a month. The lifting of exchange controls and gradual liberalization of finance (non-yen lending has enabled Japanese banks to become heavily involved in international syndicated lending), combined with the recent massive current account surpluses and the need to invest in overseas plant (as a hedge against protectionist threats), have made Japanese capital a significant force overseas. Net overseas assets grew by 74% in 1985.

Capital inflows have increased since the 25% ceiling on equity holdings was removed and since firms have been free to borrow abroad. Over half the external finance for the corporate sector came from overseas in 1985. Japan has become a popular choice for foreign institutions and investors. Tokyo's stock market has proved attractive and the bond market is booming.

The yen

Fluctuations in the yen have caused more problems to competitors than to Japan itself. When the yen has increased, Japan's larger firms have ridden the storm – albeit at reduced margins – because of their substantial edge in manufacturing efficiency and ability to sell on non-price factors.

Lack of internationalization The yen finances only 2% of world trade, compared with 50% for the dollar (even Japanese traders invoice 70% of exports non-yen). As a foreign exchange market, Tokyo ranks only fifth. Although government has been protective of the yen, its rise since the 1985 Plaza agreement is commensurate with Japan's status as world number three. Despite the yen being a non-petro currency and lacking reserve currency status, and despite low interest rates, the underlying power of the economy has made the yen strong.

	Top 10 exports	Top 10 imports
1.	Road vehicles	Crude petroleum
2.	Iron and steel	Natural gas
3.	Scientific instruments	Electrical machinery
4.	Telecommunication equipment	Petroleum products
5.	Consumer electronics equipment	Coal
6.	Chemicals	Non-ferrous metals
7.	Office equipment	Fish and fish products
8.	Ships	Wood and lumber
9.	Power-generating equipment	Iron ores
10.	Synthetic fabrics	Transport equipment

Sources: Ministry of International Trade and Industry, Ministry of Finance

The Industrial Scene

Industry and investment

Within a period of only 40 years, Japan has managed to drag itself from the ashes of defeat to become the second major industrial economy in the world and probably the most dynamic. During this period, a low-wage economy has been transformed into a high-technology society which is at the forefront of world industrial development.

From textiles to hi tech

Starting with fairly basic industries, Japan's industrial emphasis has progressively changed. It centred on the textile industry in the 1950s, on steel and shipbuilding in the 1960s, and on automobiles, consumer electronics and cameras in the 1970s. Diversification of the industrial structure in the 1980s has been based on high-technology industries, with semiconductors, computers and robotics particularly significant.

Dominance Japanese companies have taken a major global share of an increasing number of industries. Japan is the world's largest shipbuilder, the second largest steel producer (after the USSR), the second largest automobile producer (after the USA), the largest producer of consumer electronics and the second largest producer of electronics components. Japan has over 95% of the world market for video cassette recorders, 85% for copiers, about 70% for robots and facsimile machines, and over 60% for electroceramics.

How it was done

Between 1945 and the 1950s, when capital was in short supply, low wage rates were the key to the development of the economy. In the early years wages were only 25% of US rates. This advantage disappeared when wages doubled during the 1950s and then trebled in the 1960s.

Capital intensity High wage rates forced a move to substitute capital for labour, with the building of large-scale facilities for high-volume production, especially in steel and shipbuilding.

Targeting In the early 1970s companies in Japan were ready to expand into international markets. Due to the strong presence of Western companies in existing markets, they had either to find market niches where Western companies were weak or take on the high-volume segments where market access was easiest. By reducing product variety and applying more effective production techniques, Japanese companies entered industry after industry.

Western weakness In most of these industries, Western companies were not mentally or organizationally prepared to stand and fight. They retreated from the lower segments of the market, but the Japanese progressively took over segment after segment. By the time Western companies realized what had happened, many had almost no market left. The well-documented case of the British and US motorcycle industries is only one example out of many.

Trade friction Following the success of Japan in a number of industries, trade restrictions in the USA and, to some extent, Europe have spurred Japan to diversify into other industries. In the early days it was US restrictions on textiles. Cars became the next target, and more recently semiconductors in the USA and consumer electronics in Europe.

Unique blend The actions of MITI and other Japanese ministries in setting the direction of change since the 1950s cannot be ignored. At the same time, it has been left to individual companies to succeed in a very competitive home market. In many ways, the Japanese have evolved a unique blend of government direction and domestic competition and co-operation which has proved extremely effective in transforming their economy. The government has shown great flexibility in adapting to the pressures on the economy arising from oil crises, declining industries and growing protectionism.

Technology and research

The aggressive pursuit of technology from Europe and the USA is the other major factor responsible for the success of the Japanese economy. Japanese companies have become supreme in applying technology to develop new products, especially products that have a mass market. Combined with their mass production techniques, this gives Japan a great advantage.

R&D prominent Japan is one of the major spenders on R&D, and this area has grown rapidly. From only 1.5% in 1968, the percentage of GNP directed to R&D has now increased to over 2.8% and is targeted to reach 3.5% by 1995. Japanese companies are starting to rival comparable US companies in their R&D spending. NEC spends over 10% of sales on R&D, while Hitachi would rank among the top seven companies in the USA in terms of R&D spending.

Most R&D in Japan is centered in commercial organizations. A very low proportion of R&D – about 24% – is funded by the government. For many companies, such as Hitachi, Honda and Matsushita Electric, R&D expenditure is now greater than capital spending on plant and equipment.

Unstoppable momentum According to a recent US Defense Science Board Task Force Report: "Japan has created technological momentum that will broaden their present-day lead over the USA in some fields and will enable their long-term national commitment to technology innovation to be successful." The report goes on: "This momentum...has already carried Japan to the stage of technological equality in many fields and superiority in some, with no indication of a slowdown."

The future

Having achieved so much in so short a time, can the Japanese maintain their momentum? They face continuing and increasing protectionism, greater international competition as other countries emulate them, and workers at home who expect a better lifestyle and may be less willing to accept the ethic of hard work. Indications are that although these problems may slow the Japanese advance, social, political and economic problems in the USA and Europe are so great as to offset their impact.

Diversification Japanese firms are diversifying in their search for the high-growth markets of the future to offset declining prospects in existing markets. Toyota, for example, is devoting 30% of its research to non-automotive areas.

A yen antidote The problem of the stronger yen, which is pushing many Japanese companies to produce overseas, will spur even greater efforts at home, as companies apply automation technologies to their manufacturing as a way of maintaining their Japanese factories.

A new Japan The result of the drive into technology will be to change the Japanese economy as much in the next 30 years as in the past 30 years. Decline will affect not only chemicals, shipbuilding, steel and others that long ago started the process of contraction, but also industries such as automobiles that are still prosperous. Their decline will be more than offset by the growth of newer sectors based on modern technologies.

Shipbuilding

With the world shipbuilding industry sinking under the dual pressures of falling demand and overcapacity, exacerbated by the aggressive entry of the Koreans, the Japanese shipbuilders – for decades the leading producers in the world – are now readjusting to the new situation. Layoffs, shipyard closures and some bankruptcies have occurred.

The companies

There are over 30 shipbuilders in Japan, the seven leading ones being Mitsubishi Heavy Industries, Ishikawajima-Harima Heavy Industries, Hitachi Zosen, Mitsui Engineering and Shipbuilding, Nippon Kokan, Kawasaki Heavy Industries and Sumitomo Heavy Industries. These seven account for around 50% of employment in shipbuilding. They are desperately trying to adjust to the problems the industry is facing, and in some cases are fighting for survival. Most of the leading companies are part of major industrial groups, which makes it easier to redeploy surplus workers in subsidiaries or group affiliates.

Crisis in the industry

Demand for ships has collapsed. In the wake of the oil crises, demand for tankers – which account for just under half the world shipping fleet – was severely reduced, as was demand for bulk carriers. The bottom was reached in 1980, when worldwide production was around a third of the 1975 level. While there has since been a modest upturn, present production is still well under half the 1975 level. With around half of world production, and highly dependent on export orders, Japanese shipbuilders have been significantly affected. This has been exacerbated by the collapse of Japan's Sanko Steamship Company, the world's largest oil tanker operator, which had been ordering small bulk carriers against the tide of the industry.

The rise of Korea In the brief period from 1977 to 1983, the South Korean shipbuilding industry rose from nowhere to take almost 20% of the world market. Currently their market share is a little lower. Hyundai Heavy Industries has been at the forefront of these developments, with Daewoo Shipbuilding and Heavy Machinery, Korea Shipbuilding and Engineering and Samsung Shipbuilding and Heavy Industries also building considerable capacity. Competition from the Koreans has affected the West European shipbuilders to a much greater extent than it has the Japanese. The Japanese have, in fact, maintained their share of total world orders at between 50% and 55%. It is the price-cutting policy of the Koreans, along with the appreciation of the yen, that is having most effect on the profitability of Japanese shipbuilders.

Government action The Ministry of Transport has taken an active role in trying to minimize the industry's problems. Severe cutbacks in production capacity took place in 1980. Subsequent cutbacks under Ministry "guidelines" will mean that the industry will be operating at around 65% of capacity in 1987 (or around 40% of pre-1980 capacity).

Weathering the storm

A return to the pre-oil crisis demand levels is unlikely in the forseeable future. However, a continuation of lower oil prices and success in scrapping surplus capacity should bring about a revival of the industry's fortunes. Japanese shipbuilders, with their vigorous rationalization programmes, which include a probable further 30% reduction in employment by 1988, should be well placed to compete for orders in a slimmed-down market.

Heavy chemicals

The chemical industry in Japan is going through a period of major transformation as it struggles with problems of overcapacity and structural inadequacies. Many companies are diversifying out of heavy chemicals into specialty chemicals.

The industry

The chemical industry has played an important part in the postwar development of the Japanese economy. An extremely diverse industry, it is now the fifth largest in Japan, and its products are used in virtually all other industrial sectors.

While the origins of the modern chemical industry in Japan date back to 1914, the petrochemical and related sectors were established only in the mid-1950s when petroleum was substituted for coal as a feedstock. Petrochemicals now account for almost 50% of chemical production and supply the basic feedstock for a wide range of chemical products, notably ethylene and its derivatives. Caustic soda is the major inorganic chemical.

Major Japanese chemical companies include Mitsubishi Chemical Industries, Asahi Chemical Industry, Sumitomo Chemical, Ube Industries, Mitsui Toatsu Chemicals and Dainippon Ink & Chemicals.

Key issues

The postwar growth of the Japanese chemical industry was rapid, and prospects were good. All this was halted by the oil crises, which affected its major raw material and led to stagnant demand and an uncompetitive industry.

Size and structure Compared to the major US and European chemical companies, Japanese producers are too small and specialized to compete internationally. The largest chemical company in Japan, Mitsubishi Chemical Industries, is less than a third of the size of comparable European companies and one-sixth of the size of Du Pont. The vertical integration and financial strength of US and European chemical companies are also absent.

Forced rationalization Companies in the industry have found it almost impossible to overcome this fragmentation and adjust to a situation of overcapacity. In 1983, MITI acted. It introduced legislation to force the companies to reduce capacity, consolidate production and set up joint marketing and distribution consortia in a range of product sectors. In some cases the proposed cutbacks were almost 40% of total capacity.

In the melting pot

Feedstock costs have been reduced by lower oil prices, and this will undoubtedly benefit the industry. Nevertheless, further industry-wide rationalization is needed to overcome the small size of companies and the lack of vertical integration. A stronger yen and increasing imports of low-cost ethylene and related products from the new petrochemical-producing countries, such as Saudi Arabia and Singapore, will further undermine domestic producers.

New directions With limited growth prospects in their main sectors and profitability dependent on production cutbacks and efficiency measures, the Japanese chemical producers have started to diversify into potentially more lucrative areas. Fine and specialty chemicals – especially materials for the high technology industries – and biotechnology are the main targets.

A contracting industry Rationalization, increasing imports, and diversification into new areas have significantly reduced Japan's presence in heavy chemicals – a process that is likely to continue.

Car industry

Japan is striving to regain its leading position in world car production. Its 25% world share is only just behind the USA – Japan having bettered the USA from 1981 to 1983 – and it is more than West German and French production combined. Employing just under 10% of the Japanese work force, the car industry is Japan's largest export earner. Japan will fight to retain its dominance, despite protectionist actions from the USA and Europe, increasing competition from the South Koreans and a fall in export profits due to the strong yen.

From small beginnings

American automobiles were imported into Japan only from the latter part of the 1920s, and not until 1929 did their numbers exceed those of rickshaws. The early years were dominated by Ford Japan and General Motors Japan, which shared about 80% of the market.

Postwar protection In the early postwar years, MITI used a range of measures to protect and nurture the domestic industry, encouraging the import of foreign technology from selected producers. Initially, the taxi and hire companies provided 70% of the demand for passenger vehicles. It was only later that demand from other sectors made possible the growth of mass production.

Mass production The Japanese car industry has seen tremendous acceleration in the postwar era. A production level of a mere 32,000 vehicles in 1956 rose to almost 900,000 by 1966, 5m by 1976 and over 12m in 1985. The auto industry's share of total Japanese exports increased from only 5.5% in 1968 to almost 10% in 1973, to around 20% in the mid-1980s.

The companies

Toyota Motor and Nissan Motor are the leading automobile manufacturers in Japan, with just under 70% of the domestic market and 50% of exports between them. Nissan, however, is dropping back. From a close second position in the Japanese market in 1980, Nissan's share has fallen to about 24% against Toyota's 44%. The other major producers – Honda, Mazda and Mitsubishi – account for less than 30% of the domestic market and 37% of exports.

Domestic competition The steep rise in the value of the yen since September 1985 has sharpened competition in the domestic market as car companies seek to compensate for falling profits from exports. Following the lead of Toyota (probably the only company operating profitably in the home market), beefed-up sales forces are targetting the "sunshine industries". Companies in these industries – those that have benefited from the yen's appreciation – have recently paid out large bonuses to their employees, making them prime candidates for new cars.

Due both to the traffic congestion and the poor state of many of Japan's roads – only 54% are paved – one-third of Japanese families do not own a car. The scope for higher sales is there and meanwhile the car industry is discreetly lobbying for an increased programme of road building.

Insignificant imports Foreign car makers have had problems operating in Japan and have yet to make a significant impact. Imports, though increasing, account for only 2% of car sales. Volkswagen, BMW and Mercedes-Benz – the three most popular foreign brands – sold fewer than 40,000 vehicles in 1985.

Some foreign car firms have come in by the back door. Ford has a minority share in Mazda, as does Chrysler in Mitsubishi, and General Motors in Isuzu and Suzuki. Nissan is marketing a car produced under licence from Volkswagen, and Honda is selling a car made in collaboration with Britain's Rover Group.

Export markets

Almost 50% of Japanese car exports are to the USA. From a 9% share of the US market in 1975, Japanese cars captured over 22% by 1982. The Americans reacted in 1981, forcing the Japanese to impose "voluntary" restraints on their exports. Japanese exports are also affected by protectionism in Europe and other markets, with minimum local content requirements becoming popular.

The US market Overseas sales were extremely profitable and compensated for most companies' domestic losses. Car exporters have marked up their US prices, but not in line with the yen's appreciation, preferring to maintain market share and take lower profits.

The threat from Korea The South Korean industry is accelerating. In Canada the fastest-selling foreign import is made by Hyundai – which has links with Mitsubishi Motors, which in turn has links with Chrysler. Kia Industrial is to produce, under the Ford name, a car designed by Mazda and destined for the US market. To contain costs, Mitsubishi has moved body production of its luxury cars to one of Hyundai's plants.

The Chinese market The Japanese car makers were active in selling to the Chinese until 1985, when shortage of foreign exchange reserves caused the Chinese to close the door.

The move overseas

Most Japanese car companies are setting up overseas manufacturing projects to overcome protectionism.

Japanese as top US producers? The five largest Japanese companies are building car plants in the USA (Toyota in partnership with General Motors for one of its projects and Mitsubishi with Chrysler). Honda was the pioneer.

Planned Japanese capacity of over 1.6m cars by 1988 represents about 15% of the US market. If Japanese companies are not prepared to reduce their present export levels to the USA, this could give them as much as 30% of the market. This is not what the US car companies wanted when they forced the US government to build up a protectionist wall around them.

Bypassing EC quotas Nissan has built a plant in the UK and is developing Motor Iberica, its majority-owned Spanish subsidiary, into a major supply point for the rest of the European Community, to sidestep restrictions on imports.

The road ahead

New technology is having a major impact on the car industry, both through automation of production and through the introduction of electronic control systems in the finished car. The Japanese are at the forefront of new developments.

The Koreans again The Japanese car manufacturers believe that ultimately their greatest threat will be the Koreans – as in shipbuilding. But again as in shipbuilding, it is the Europeans that have most to lose.

Japanese automobile production 1985

	(% of total)
Toyota Motor	30
Nissan Motor	20
Mazda Motor	10
Mitsubishi Motors	9
Honda Motor	9
Suzuki Motor	6
Isuzu Motors	5
Fuji Heavy Industries	5
Daihatsu Motor	5
Others	1
Total	100

Total production = 12.192m passenger cars and trucks.

Total exports = 52% of total production.

Source: Japan Automobile Manufacturers' Association

Consumer electronics

More than any other, the Japanese can truly be said to have made this area their own. They have set standards of quality and excellence that no-one else appears able to match, and are now pioneering new products and applications that will consolidate their position. Only Philips can keep them in view, helped by protectionist measures from the EC Commission, but they are struggling.

Up to the present

Matsushita dominates consumer electronics in Japan, with sales more than double those of the other major companies – Hitachi, Sanyo Electric, Sharp, Sony and Toshiba. Exports account for 37% of Matsushita's sales but are over 60% for many companies.

The VCR revolution When Sony introduced the first half-inch tape home video recorder in 1975, few could have foreseen its potential. Fewer than 120,000 VCRs were produced that year, but by 1985 Japanese production had reached almost 30m, of which 80% were exported.

The VCRs The past decade has seen a tremendous battle between the Beta format, pioneered by Sony and supported by Toshiba, Sanyo Electric and NEC Home Electronics, and the VHS format, developed by JVC, pioneered by Matsushita (which owns 50% of JVC) and supported by Hitachi and others. Victory has gone to VHS, with Sony and its Aiwa subsidiary the only companies producing Beta format equipment, which now has less than 10% of the market.

Compact video clash Because Sony no longer has a major presence in the VCR market, it has put considerable resources behind a new 8mm compact video format, which is supported by the major camera makers, as well as by Pioneer Electronics, Sanyo Electric and others. The small size of both the tape and thereby the combined camera/recorder system, as well as its applicability to audio recording, will make it a strong competitor to JVC's compact VHS camera/recorder. Battle has begun, and it may be 10 years before a winner emerges.

Videodiscs in a spin Dominance in videodiscs, a market growing in Japan but not yet elsewhere, is again revolving around two major groups. The LaserDisk system, developed by Pioneer Electronics and supported by Sony and Hitachi, among others, is up against JVC's rival VHD (video high density) system. With 500,000 units sold in 1985, this growth market will become intense as low-priced units appear.

Tomorrow's world

Japanese production of television sets maintained its growth only through massive exports to China – now halted. Japanese manufacturers are hoping that emphasis on large-screen models and pocket-size sets with an LCD screen will overcome a saturated market until High Definition Television arrives.

Integrated TV? High Definition Television will lead to integration between high-quality audio and video systems – at least in Japan and the USA, who have agreed a common standard. The Europeans are going their own way by agreeing a separate standard to try to re-establish a major television manufacturing presence.

Sound investment After a slow start in 1982, the compact disc format has now become the saviour of the audio industry. Sales of CD players increased from just under 800,000 in 1984 to over 4m in 1985. Lower prices for the players and a wider range of available titles will fuel even faster growth.

Computers

In computers, Japanese companies are striving to repeat the international success achieved in consumer electronics, although so far with only limited results.

Hardware

Japan is the only major computer market where IBM is not dominant. It has fallen to third place. Fujitsu dominates in mainframe computers, and NEC in the personal computer market. Other major players in the mainframe market include Hitachi, Toshiba, Oki Electric and Mitsubishi Electric, with the American companies Nippon Univac, NCR Japan and Burroughs far behind.

The super Japanese To emphasize how far Japan has come in high technology, Fujitsu, Hitachi and NEC are now breaking the world dominance of Cray Research and Control Data in supercomputers, the powerful mainframe computers used for military, aerospace and other specialist applications.

Japanese pcs Use of personal computers has grown swiftly in Japan since their introduction in 1978. With a 50% share, NEC is the clear leader, ahead of more than 30 competitors. Fujitsu, IBM Japan and Sharp are struggling to catch up, but have only 30% of the market. While exports are growing, real penetration of world markets has still to happen.

Peripheral strength High product quality and competitive pricing in the peripheral sectors, such as disk drives and printers, as well as in electronic components and parts, are helping Japanese manufacturers to make significant inroads into overseas markets. Several US computer companies, notably Hewlett-Packard and Apple, have set up procurement divisions in Japan to purchase these products.

Software development

The 20–30% annual growth rates of the late 1970s and early 1980s are continuing, and the software sector now exceeds $1bn in annual sales. It is a fragmented sector, with around 1,400 companies operating.

The suppliers Software houses affiliated to the major computer manufacturers supply most systems software. They are active too in applications software, but have been joined by independent software houses selling combined hardware and software systems. Considerable subcontracting takes place. Nearly a third of applications software, though, is developed in-house by users, but there is a move towards buying in software packages.

Market preferences The Japanese prefer purpose-built software. Slowly, the US trend towards ready-made software is gaining acceptance. Off-the-peg sales are growing, due to increased use of personal computers. Applications software is notably strong in banking and robotics.

MITI's role To overcome the late start of the software industry, and the shortage of systems analysts and computer programmers, MITI organized a $100m programme to upgrade Japan's capabilities in software development.

Foreign suppliers Japanese companies are looking overseas for expertise and for computer software products. The USA and Europe are the main sources. The trading companies have exclusive distribution agreements with foreign software suppliers. It is usual for the Japanese partner to adapt the software product to the Japanese market.

Prospects Liberalization of telecommunications in Japan (see *Communications*) will have far-reaching consequences for the information services industry, with the rapid expansion of value added networks benefiting the software sector.

Automation

The Japanese dominance in robotics has been swift and complete, with more robots having been installed in Japan than in all other countries combined. As robots become increasingly linked into complete automated manufacturing systems, Japanese industry will be transformed, and the dominance of Japanese companies in many industrial sectors will be reinforced. Only the time-scales are in doubt.

Perspectives

True automation of the manufacturing sector will require the combination of several at-present disparate elements. Computer-aided design and computer-aided manufacturing (CAD/CAM) systems will make possible rapid changes in product design. Increasingly intelligent robots will translate these changes into flexible production processes, and the integration of computer and communications systems will ultimately link the elements into powerful production systems. These changes will be far-reaching, but will not happen overnight. Few truly integrated systems of this nature have been developed, and considerable obstacles have still to be overcome, particularly the need for standardized protocols for communications between electronic devices of different manufacturers.

The robot market

Japanese companies have taken a major world lead in robot production. The tremendous pressure to reduce costs in the wake of the oil crises in the mid-1970s provided the incentive. Sales are rising as the replacement phase is reached for the early installations and as diffusion into medium and small enterprises and into additional industries continues. The Japanese market is now worth well over $1bn annually, and more than 300,000 robots have been installed.

Increasing sophistication The initial strategy was to introduce robots into as many companies and as many industries as could absorb them. These very simple fixed-sequence robots, which in 1978 accounted for 70% of the total, have now given way to a high proportion of robots with much more sophisticated functions.

Penetration The automobile industry provided the early momentum for robot use, and Toyota and Nissan are among Japan's largest users, each with almost 2,000 robots. The electrical equipment industry took the lead in 1980 for the assembly of printed circuit boards. Robots are now moving into other sectors, with assembly remaining the predominant function. About 35% of all manufacturing companies in Japan use robots. On present indications, this will rise to 55% by 1990.

Intense competition Industry prospects have induced a flood of new robot manufacturers. Almost 300 companies are now involved, compared to only 120 in 1976. Whereas there are a few specialist robot manufacturers, such as Dainichi Kiko, the majority are subsidiaries of larger corporations. Taking an early lead is Matsushita Electric, with 14% of the market. Other major participants include Fanuc, Yaskawa Electric, Toshiba, Kawasaki Heavy Industries and Hitachi. With the top ten companies having barely 45% of the market, and the top 20 less than 60%, the market leaders have still to consolidate their position. Cincinnati Milacrom of the USA and ASEA of Sweden are among foreign companies that have set up Japanese factories to assemble robots.

Overseas expansion begins With 20% of production exported, many manufacturers are now setting up OEM (original equipment manufacturer) deals to penetrate the US and other major markets quickly, without having to set up overseas servicing and engineering centres. Low-cost, high-quality robots purchased from Japan are sold as part of total manufacturing systems. The most successful overseas venture is that of Fanuc, whose joint-venture with General Motors dominates the US market with a 30% share.

The future is even brighter It seems unlikely that the Japanese lead in robotics can be overcome this century by the USA or Europe. Japanese research is intensifying, and acceptance of robots by industry is higher in Japan than anywhere else. The establishment of overseas manufacturing plants by Japanese automobile manufacturers will spur further robot use.

CAD/CAM

US companies pioneered this technology in the 1950s and 1960s in the automobile, aerospace and shipbuilding industries. The US market represents a sizeable 60% of the world total. It is only since 1980 that the Japanese market has really established itself, and it is dominated by US companies and their products. Most of these US-originating systems were initially sold through Japanese agents and trading companies. Some US companies – Applicon and Intergraph, for example – are now developing a local presence. Others, such as market leader CADAM, a Lockheed subsidiary, are content to let IBM Japan, Fujitsu and other companies market their systems.

Making up for lost time Japanese companies are now entering the market at an increasing pace. They include the major computer-makers, and companies such as Seiko Epson that have developed in-house software. Some are offering specialist systems for specific applications.

Peripheral strength The US dominance in CAD/CAM peripheral devices, such as plotters and graphic displays, is being rapidly eroded by Japanese manufacturers, with their traditional strengths in this area.

Future growth assured The continual reduction in prices and increasing power of computer hardware, and especially the use of personal computers for CAD/CAM systems, will ensure rapid growth and diffusion of the market. Truly integrated CAD/CAM systems will become more prevalent, given developments in software.

Impact

These developments are important not only in the context of the market for robotics or CAD/CAM systems but also in the larger context of their impact on the Japanese industrial capability. The emphasis on automated production will enable Japanese companies to maintain, if not strengthen, the lead they have taken in a number of industries. Increasing their competitiveness will offset the effects of the stronger yen.

Acceptance of new technology There is less resistance to the introduction of new technology in Japan than in Europe or even the USA. Reduced employment in some declining sectors, such as automobiles, steel, chemicals and machinery, is being more than offset by new jobs in the growing high-technology industries. Employment will probably stabilize once robots, factory automation and CAD/CAM systems are fully introduced.

Japanese robot production

	(thousands)
1971	1.3
1981	22.1
1982	24.8
1983	30.5
1984	40.9
1985 E	52.0
1986 E	65.0

Source: Japan Industrial Robot Association (JIRA)

Communications

Computer-related information services are growing fast, in line with the rapid development of the computer industry in Japan. The advent of competing groups in telecommunications is spurring developments that will transform this sector. Links with overseas suppliers will be crucial for Japanese companies if they are to take advantage of opportunities.

Telecommunications

Japan has separate domestic and international telecommunications authorities. Kokusai Denshin Denwa (KDD) is a government monopoly handling international calls. Nippon Telegraph and Telephone Corporation (NTT) is the major domestic body. Established in 1952 as a spinoff of the old postal/telecommunications ministry, NTT was denationalized in 1985. The new, semi-privatized NTT is initially being held wholly by the government, which will release up to two-thirds of its shares for public sale by 1990.

In 1984 the Diet passed legislation deregulating the telecommunications market, opening the field to more domestic and – for the first time – foreign competitors.

Modernizing the network New information network systems are being developed. In line with the West, Japan's NTT is planning to replace all analog communications with a digital network, using optical fibre cables and communication satellites, and introducing digital switching systems and exchanges.

INS Telephone, data transmission, facsimile and video communication will be carried by the same integrated network, under a concept called Information Network System (INS).

Optical fibres The main optical fibre links have been installed with others to follow. The major wire and cable makers – Sumitomo Electric Industries, Furukawa Electric and Kujikura – hold about 80% of the market.

Competing services Challenging the still formidable NTT, a number of so-called Type 1 common carriers will be licensed to provide trunk-line services on major routes using optical fibres, microwave radio or satellite links. Competing large-scale and small-scale value added networks (VANs) are also being set up (see below).

More suppliers NTT's domestic procurement policy has long angered would-be overseas equipment suppliers. US government pressure, denationalization and deregulation have forced NTT to open the door to foreign manufacturers.

In addition to NTT's requirement for digital exchanges and switching equipment, digital private branch exchanges (PBXs) are in demand by offices. NTT's traditional suppliers – NEC Corporation, Hitachi, Fujitsu and Oki Electric – are benefiting but US and European companies are also entering the market. ITT, for instance, is supplying NTT with PBX systems worth $16m.

Non-traditional Japanese suppliers are also entering the market – notably Matsushita Communication, Sony and Sharp.

International expansion With their strong domestic base, the traditional Japanese telecommunications suppliers are attacking international markets. NEC has over 10% of the US market. This push will continue in digital exchange equipment, as well as for the newer facsimile and cellular radio sectors.

Competition for KDD Two consortia, featuring major Japanese and US corporations, are planning new telecommunications firms to compete with KDD in international communications. The Ministry of Posts and Telecommunications is backing competition but wants the consortia to merge.

Data communications

Modernization of the network, office automation and greater use of computers have led to expansion in data communications.

Large-scale VANs Under the new legislation, Type II operators can run national information networks for third parties. One of the first announced was a joint venture between NTT and IBM. Other VANs lined up include those of the Japanese computer manufacturers, while AT&T and other US telecommunications companies are also trying to enter the market.

Captain One of the first VAN services to be carried by the modernized network is the CAPTAIN system, a videotex service geared to the home user. Started with great hopes by NTT in November 1984, it has been less successful than envisaged, largely due to the high cost of equipment and limited interest from subscribers.

Small-scale VANs Many small and new firms are planning small-scale VANs geared to particular industries, but a number of heavyweight firms are also involved. Marubeni Corporation and C. Itoh, for instance, offer VANs tailored to the textile industry. Banking is a popular and competitive area and Nagoya Sogo Bank has been operating a bank-to-brokerage VAN since 1984, servicing the securities firms.

Integration The liberalization and growth of the telecommunications networks are leading to greater integration between computer and telecommunications technology. Competitive clashes between companies from these markets will speed the pace of new product development.

Computer databases

The database sector in Japan is under-developed compared with the USA and Europe. From a low base, this $650m market has been growing by about 25% a year. US databases have 16 times more users than Japanese ones, which have only 24,000 clients in total.

Foreign domination Over 110 companies provide the almost 900 databases available. US and European databases dominate and only 20% originate in Japan. Most domestic suppliers do no more than act as agents or intermediaries for foreign databases, representing most of the main ones. NEXIS, Mead Data Central's full text news retrieval service, is now available through *Nihon Keizai Shimbun*, the leading business newspaper.

Japanese supply The major Japanese databases available include the JAPIO (Japan Patent Information Online) PATOLIS database and the more extensive JICST (Japan Information Center of Science and Technology) databases on aspects of science and technology in Japan. Starting full-scale operation in 1978, JICST is now the largest Japanese database producer. *Nihon Keizai Shimbun* is another large producer. Its NEEDS database provides economic information for business.

Reluctant exporters Few of the Japanese databases – or other published Japanese business and scientific information – have been translated into English for use in international markets. Only two of the eight JICST online databases, for example, have been translated into English, and not all of the others are available to overseas clients, even in Japanese. The Japanese are less ready to export their information store than to export the products designed on the basis of this information. Equally, potential foreign users have not taken full advantage of the available Japanese databases.

Prospects Greater use of personal computers to access information sources will enable the database market to expand towards international levels, although dominance by US and European databases will continue for the present.

New materials

The key objective for many industries in Japan, in their struggle for competitive advantage, is to find new materials with higher performance characteristics. Japanese industry sees such research as a natural diversification and progression from their existing industry. Current research is in ceramics, metals, plastics and composite materials.

Overview

The applications are widespread for these new advanced materials, and they by no means comprise a distinct industry. The sectors are extremely fragmented, the companies involved in developing the new materials are numerous, and the technology in most cases is still at the development stage. The main applications will be realized in the early 1990s, with the electronics, automotive and space industries being key areas.

Foreign presence US and European companies lead in some sectors. In these, the foreign firms are using Japanese companies as sales agents or are licensing the technology to them. This enables the Japanese companies to develop their domestic capabilities for future production. Another approach by some foreign companies is to set up joint ventures to exploit the Japanese market. For example, Carborundum is collaborating with Hitachi Chemical in ceramics and Allied Corp with several Mitsui Group companies in amorphous metals.

Catching up While Japanese companies started late and are well behind the USA in basic research, they are at the forefront in applications of the technology.

Key sectors

Fine ceramics This growing market was worth over $4bn in 1985, by far the largest of the new industrial material sectors. Interest has intensified since 1981, and over 250 companies are now involved. The electrical properties of fine ceramics make them ideal as packages for integrated circuits ("chips"). Electroceramics represent 70% of present demand. The greatest prospects will be in engineering ceramics, using their insulating and structural properties. They are being used for cutting tools and other equipment for semiconductor manufacturing. Ceramic engine parts are a likely development.

Engineering plastics These date from inventions by Du Pont in 1958. High heat resistance is their significant feature. The Japanese market exceeds $1bn, and production is approaching that of the stagnant US market. The main applications are in the automotive, computer and domestic electrical appliance industries. Competition is intense, and few of the 30 companies involved in the industry are making profits. Foreign companies are prominent, but Asahi Chemical, Mitsubishi Chemical and Toray Industries are increasing their commitment. Some are ignoring the general purpose engineering plastics and developing more specialized engineering plastics.

Composite materials The most important composite material is carbon fibre: Japanese companies dominate the field with over 50% of world production. The polyacrylonitrile (PAN)-based carbon fibres were developed in Japan in 1959, and the leading companies are Toray Industries, Toho Rayon, Mitsubishi Rayon and Sumitomo Chemical. Coal pitch-based carbon fibres are being pioneered by Kureha Chemical Industry, with Dainippon Ink & Chemicals, Mitsubishi Chemical Industries and Nippon Steel entering the race.

Biotechnology

Biotechnology has the power to transform a wide range of industries. Yet the early optimism is giving way to a sober realization that significant obstacles need to be overcome before major breakthroughs are achieved. Japan aims to be there when that time comes.

Perspectives

Biotechnology is the name for three basic technologies that allow a considerable degree of control over biological systems – recombinant DNA (whereby genes from different organisms are joined to produce new features), cell fusion (the artificial joining of different types of cell into one cell) and fermentation techniques. The first two, singly or in combination, will lead to the development of new products, whereas fermentation will be critical for large-scale commercial production. Application industries include pharmaceuticals, chemicals, food, mining, pulp and paper and textiles.

The Japanese market To overcome late entry to the market, Japanese companies are aggressively pursuing licensing and joint R&D ventures with US and European companies to speed up biotechnology acquisition, and they are now up with the leaders. The existing strength of Japanese companies in mass fermentation techniques will keep Japan at the forefront of the new technology – particularly when commercialization becomes more important than product development.

In contrast to the West, where small start-up companies, formed to take advantage of the advances in biotechnology, are prominent, Japanese research is taking place in well-established companies. Major firms in diverse industries are trying to develop products through biotechnology – though many have no experience in the field.

Government backing The government is targeting this as an industry of the future, with the aim of diffusing the techniques throughout Japanese industry. But, as usual in Japan, most funding will come from industry. The Japan Key Technology Center (JKTC), a joint MITI and Ministry of Posts and Telecommunications organization, is the main channel for government funds. It is promoting research consortia, involving companies from different industries, universities and government research institutions. Protein Engineering Research Institute, a consortium led by Mitsubishi Chemical, Takeda Chemical and Toray, has been set up with a capital base of $2m (70% from JKTC), and is building a $30m research centre.

Fierce competition

Pharmaceutical companies are closest to producing products through biotechnology. Over 20 companies, for example, are racing to commercialize interferon, the anti-cancer product, with Shionogi, Sumitomo Pharmaceutical, Toray, Takeda and Yamanouchi Pharmaceutical prominent. Foreign links have been essential – Shionogi with Biogen, Sumitomo Pharmaceutical with Wellcome, and Takeda with Hoffman La Roche.

In the longer term

Starting with applications in pharmaceuticals and clinical diagnostic testing, commercialization of new developments will slowly fan out into other areas, including bulk chemicals, food, agriculture, energy and water treatment. But biotechnology is unlikely to produce major changes in these industries in the near future.

Skill shortages Inadequacies in Japan's research base in biology, and a shortage of molecular biologists, will force greater overseas collaboration in the short term.

Top ten companies

The list of the top ten Japanese companies provides a reflection of the postwar changes in the industrial structure of Japan. Companies in steel and shipbuilding are declining as their industries suffer contraction. The automotive companies improved their position, Nissan considerably. Major changes in the electronics and related industries have benefited Matsushita Electric and NEC, in particular.

Matsushita Electric Industrial

Under Konosuke Matsushita's leadership, Matsushita Electric Industrial – the nucleus of the Matsushita group – has become Japan's largest company. Success in the VCR field has made Matsushita the world's largest consumer electronics company, second only to IBM in sales of electronics products worldwide. It is undergoing a major readjustment as it shifts towards industrial and business electronics markets, and adapts to the higher yen. It is Japan's largest manufacturer of robots.

Hitachi

Katsushige Mita, president of Hitachi, recognizes that this industrial giant has to change to survive. Mass marketing has never been strong in Hitachi, a company more experienced in selling to Japan's large industrial corporations. Even in consumer electronics the company has preferred not to sell under its own name. Overdependence on mature products has contributed to a fall in sales, and more than the current reorganization of its marketing and distribution will be needed to turn the company around. Its most successful sector is information and communication systems.

Toyota Motor

A conservative company, dominant in the domestic market, Toyota was reluctant to set up overseas manufacturing but now has two projects underway in the USA and one in Canada. Car manufacture will remain its main activity, but it is keen to diversify and is reported to be considering major expansion into the electronics industry. It has taken an active part in two consortia planning international telecommunications services.

Nippon Steel

The largest Japanese company in 1975, Nippon Steel's problems reflect those of its industry. Still the largest Japanese producer of crude steel and stainless steel, its diversification plans centre on plant and civil engineering, coal-based chemicals and new industrial materials. It is centralizing production to reduce costs.

Nissan Motor

Dwarfed by Toyota in the domestic market, Nissan can hold its own overseas. Dependence on international sales has become critical, at almost 60% of total sales, and the opening of production facilities in the UK and USA will protect its position there. Its aim to expand non-automotive sales – which include space launch vehicles and boats – from under 2% to 10% of total company sales is ambitious.

Mitsubishi Heavy Industries

Japan's largest shipbuilder and heavy equipment manufacturer, Mitsubishi Heavy Industries (MHI) is a major producer of hydraulic excavators, as well as Japan's largest defence contractor. Profits have been poor and the work force has dropped almost 20% in 10 years. No great transformation seems imminent, but involvement in the aerospace industry might be beneficial longer-term.

Toshiba

Toshiba produces power plant and industrial materials, and is also an integrated electrical, electronics and household products manufacturer. Its loose organizational structure perhaps reflects its diverse activities. It is trying to become more involved with the new electronics markets at home and abroad, but its other activities are in contracting sectors.

NEC

NEC has succeeded by stressing the integration of computers and communications. Its semiconductor division – it is the world's second largest merchant chipmaker – adds to this. NEC has become the world's tenth largest producer of electronic equipment with a strong position in its markets. Heavy investment in R&D will ensure continuing dynamic growth.

Nippon Kokan

The second largest Japanese steel producer, Nippon Kokan (NKK) also has activities in shipbuilding, engineering and construction. NKK has stepped up its programme of internationalization and is diversifying into new materials. NKK bought 50% of the 7th largest US steelmaker, National Steel Corp. It also set up a joint venture with Martin Marietta Corp of the USA to manufacture aluminium and titanium alloys, and recently took over a General Electric plant in the USA to produce amorphous silicon, a semiconductor material.

Sumitomo Metal Industries

Sumitomo Metal Industries is the third largest steel producer in Japan. Rationalization and diversification into new areas are its major strategies. SMI has set up a joint plant in the USA with LTV, the USA's second largest steel producer. Diversification centres on new industrial materials, such as titanium and powder metals, coal-based chemicals and engineering services.

The next ten years

The momentum generated by NEC's unprecedented rise from 20th position to 8th in only ten years should enable it to rise to the top three within the next ten. The diversification of the steel companies into new industrial materials, coal-based chemicals and engineering is unlikely to halt their slide out of the top ten. Mitsubishi Electric, Fujitsu and Sony are the most likely new additions.

Company	Assets 1985 (US$bn)	Sales Japan (US$bn)	Sales Overseas (US$bn)	Profits (US$bn)	Employees
Matsushita Electric Industrial	21.5	13.0	7.7	1.0	133,963
Hitachi	20.2	12.9	7.6	0.9	164,951
Toyota Motor	17.2	14.3	11.7	1.6	79,901
Nippon Steel	15.4	8.2	4.3	0.2	72,081
Nissan Motor	14.5	7.6	10.6	0.3	108,500
Mitsubishi Heavy Industries	14.4	10.3	3.8	0.2	90,300
Toshiba	12.4	9.6	3.9	0.4	114,000
NEC	10.8	6.2	3.1	0.3	90,102
Nippon Kokan	10.3	3.7	2.6	0.1	36,851
Sumitomo Metal Industries	9.0	3.2	2.1	0.1	34,010

Source: Fortune International

Foreign presence

Foreign companies have experienced mixed results in the Japanese market since the war. For those that have persevered the returns have in some cases been considerable. The pace of foreign investment is increasing as companies seek to take advantage of the liberalization of the Japanese economy, notably in telecommunications and finance. Offsetting this somewhat is the retrenchment and even withdrawal by a small proportion of the foreign companies already there.

Direct investments

Foreign companies have had a long presence in the Japanese market. In 1899, Nippon Electric Co (NEC) was set up as a joint venture with Western Electric (later to become ITT), and in 1905 General Electric of the USA took majority control of the ailing Tokyo Electric Co and, in 1907, a minority share in Shibaura (later to become Toshiba).

Postwar Many of the major foreign success stories in Japan date from the postwar period, though IBM Japan, NCR and Nestlé are notable exceptions. In the early postwar years, there were no restrictions on foreign investment in Japan if companies were prepared not to repatriate profits. AMP and Coca Cola were set up in this way. Joint ventures, of which Fuji Xerox was the most successful, were allowed to repatriate profits. In the 1950s and early 1960s, few companies decided to invest in Japan due to its shaky economic position – a decision many must be regretting today.

The door closes After 1964 all direct investment needed Japanese government approval, which was difficult to obtain unless key technologies were involved. There were some exceptions, with Texas Instruments setting up a wholly-owned venture after considerable struggles with the bureaucrats.

No more excuses By 1976 virtually all regulations had been removed and foreign companies could set up wholly-owned subsidiaries or take over Japanese companies. Few have done so, and a number who had joint ventures have withdrawn or significantly reduced their presence.

Foreign penetration Almost half of all foreign direct investment in Japan is by US companies, and over 20% by European companies. More than 1,500 companies in Japan have 25% or more of their equity owned by foreigners. As a group, they represent about 2% of Japan's economic activity and just under 5% of manufacturing, a much lower proportion than in Europe or the USA. There are high penetration areas – petroleum, with almost 40% of the domestic market, rubber with over 10% and chemicals 7%. In specialized sectors there have been major successes – CPC with 84% of the dry soup market, Nestlé with over 60% of the instant coffee market, Coca Cola with 60% of carbonated beverages, Dunlop with over 50% of golf balls, Caterpillar Tractor (through Caterpillar Mitsubishi) with over 40% of bulldozers, and Braun with 30% of electric shavers.

No competition In some sectors competition from Japanese companies is non-existent. Rolls Royce in aero engines, Amersham International and Boehringer Mannheim in medical diagnostics, and Recognition Equipment Inc in data capture equipment have succeeded against competition from other Western companies. Rolls Royce have done it by bringing Japanese companies into a specially created consortium.

You don't have to be big The success of two small UK companies – Rodime with disk drives and House of Hardy with fishing gear – shows that small companies can succeed in

the Japanese market, even in the most competitive sectors.
Is it worth it? A number of the foreign firms operating in Japan through wholly-owned subsidiaries or joint ventures are successful and highly profitable, such as IBM Japan, Nestlé and Fuji Xerox. More recently, McDonald's has become Japan's largest restaurant group.
Listening post Japan's strength in high technology and in production techniques has prompted a number of companies to increase the intelligence gathering activities of their Japanese subsidiaries. Dow Chemical is looking to improve its research and product development worldwide by keeping a close watch on biotechnology and new material developments in Japan.
Into the future Financial and other service companies are stepping up their presence in Japan to take advantage of the liberalization of the financial system. High-technology companies are looking to Japan, following the liberalization of the telecommunications market. Foreign companies are also setting up manufacturing plants in the regions.

Some of the failures

Neither General Motors nor Ford tried to regain their prewar position in the Japanese automotive industry, in part because postwar government policies favoured the domestic car industry. To some extent they have come back through minority stakes in Japanese car companies.
Could not bounce back Dunlop's lack of viability as an international rubber manufacturer ended an involvement with Sumitomo Rubber Industries which stretched back to World War I. It sold its 40% share to Sumitomo, which also bought Dunlop's European tyre interests.
Failed to go it alone General Foods was unable to compete with Nestlé in the Japanese instant coffee market. It sold 50% of its Japanese subsidiary to Ajinomoto. This joint venture has prospered due to Ajinomoto's strong distribution channels and marketing abilities.
The American way Procter & Gamble increased its share in P&G Sunhome to 75% and took over management control in 1975, later boosting its share to 100%. It tried to introduce American management methods, including bypassing the traditional distribution channels. This failed and P&G has still to find the right recipe in Japan.

How to make it work

It is necessary to have clear aims in the Japanese market, but not to expect quick results. Overambitious plans can soon lead the performance of a subsidiary to diverge from expectations at head office. Changing top management every two years – a characteristic of the less successful US companies – will only make matters worse. Commitment, patience and a long-term strategy are the keys to success, along with management training for this specialized market and reasonable fluency in the language.
Not Japan alone A Japanese venture should be considered as part of a total world strategy. It can provide useful product additions, as Xerox (with Fuji-Xerox) and Philips (with Marantz) have found to their benefit. Equally, companies like Apple Computers use Japan for locally sourced components, and yet others value their subsidiaries as listening posts.
Taste is everything Different consumer habits or distribution practices have proved difficult to overcome. The food industry is a case in point, although Coca Cola, McDonald's and Nestlé show local tastes can be changed with spectacular results.
Local talent It is essential if a venture is to be a success to hire talented local managers (not just those fluent in English). This can be difficult for foreigners, especially in the high-technology sectors where shortages exist.

The Political Scene

The government of the nation

The present-day Japanese political system owes much to the changes made by the Americans during their postwar Occupation and the subsequent modifications made by the Japanese themselves.

The American model

The USA revamped the extremely centralized and bureaucratic Japanese political structure which had entered World War II. A new constitution, a reduced role for the Emperor, a considerable decentralization of government and a major programme of social, political and economic reforms were introduced to demilitarize and democratize Japan.

Japanese changes Since the Occupation forces left in 1952, the Japanese have continually modified the American reforms. Nearly 40 years of conservative rule have been largely responsible for a growing re-centralization of economic and political power. The main elements in the power structure are the Liberal Democratic Party, the bureaucrats of the major ministries and the large industrial companies (see *The reins of power*).

A new constitution

Three principles form the corner stone of the 1947 constitution: a shift of sovereign power to the people, with the Emperor the symbol of the state; a declaration of pacifism and renunciation of war; and a respect for human rights.

Checks and balances The constitution attempted to divide and balance the powers of the legislature, the executive and the judiciary. The Diet (parliament) makes the laws, while executive power resides in a Cabinet nominally responsible to the Diet and forming the pinnacle of Japan's government institutions. Judicial power is vested in a Supreme Court and a number of lower courts.

The legislature

The House of Representatives and the House of Councillors, both of them elected bodies, are the two constituents of the Diet. The Americans favoured a single-house legislature, but the Japanese insisted on a second house.

House of Representatives Members face an election whenever the prime minister dissolves the house. This must be done at least every four years and in practice happens every 2–3 years. Standing committees, corresponding approximately to the Cabinet ministries, have become the most important method of operation.

House of Councillors This house was set up to provide a check on the House of Representatives. With few actual powers and dominated by the ruling LDP, the House of Councillors is something of an anachronism, tending to rubber-stamp decisions. The term of office is six years, with half the house running for election every three years.

Elections

The 512 members of the House of Representatives are elected from 130 multi-seat constituencies, with three to five members from each constituency. Each voter has one vote. Elections to the 252-seat House of Councillors follow a mixed system; 100 candidates are elected from national constituencies, with the remaining 152 elected from 47 local multi-seat constituencies.

Gerrymandering The electoral boundaries are heavily weighted in favour of the rural districts. Because the ruling LDP has its power base in the rural constituencies, a redrawing of the boundaries is unlikely, despite court rulings declaring some results of the 1983 elections unconstitutional.

The executive and judiciary

Prime minister As the leader of the majority party, the prime minister is in control of the Diet, at least in principle. He is also leader of the Cabinet, responsible for the appointment of ministers, and can influence the judiciary through the appointment of judges. He is the supreme centre of power under the constitution, though in practice he is limited by the exigencies of party politics.

Cabinet The parliamentary cabinet system is the basis of the executive arm of the government. Most of the 20 or so ministers are members of the House of Representatives, and all have to be civilians. Apart from a few top jobs, ministries are regularly re-allocated to senior party members, most of whom will serve at least one stint.

Supreme Court Set up to guard the constitutional rights of citizens against the excesses of government, the Supreme Court has not had the desired impact. Justices are appointed by the prime minister, and 40 years of conservative consensus have ensured the Supreme Court's unassertive character. Much of its time has been spent solving disputes concerning the constitutional status of the military, but it has avoided making political decisions.

Local government

Japan's local government is organized in a two-tier system, with the 47 federal prefectures mediating between central government and the city, town and village assemblies.

Coping with development Local administrations have had to cope with the effects of Japan's rapid industrial development, which has produced a dramatic shift of population to the cities. Central government, however, has provided the funding for many of the necessary public works and major projects. During the Tanaka premiership in the early 1970s these large-scale projects were used to consolidate the power of the ruling faction of the LDP in the regions, but specific support for the regions is now much reduced.

Political issues

Electoral reform Efforts to reform the electoral system and prevent clashes between members of the same party in multi-seat constituencies have so far failed. The desire of many – especially the opposition parties – to eliminate the imbalance between the rural and urban constituencies also remains unfulfilled; Prime Minister Nakasone introduced a bill for the reform of constituencies, following the adverse court rulings in 1983, but dropped it for lack of support from his own party.

Campaign funds Enormous sums – $1–4m – are spent in trying to win a seat in an election. This encourages corruption and factionalism; candidates needing cash are recruited by party factions. The ties of money are strong, and attempts at reform have been unsuccessful.

Defence The anti-military consensus in Japan is under pressure from the USA, which feels that Japan should contribute more to its own defence. Voluntary restraints keep spending low, but the issue is at the forefront of political debate.

Finance The significant upward revaluation of the yen in the mid-1980s has had a mildly depressive effect on the economy. There is conflict between those who wish to reflate the economy and more conservative elements wishing to cut the government budget deficit.

Internationalism For a major economic power, Japan has limited interest in international affairs; domestic issues are paramount with the electorate. Nakasone, however, has been a great deal more active on the world stage than his predecessors.

Party politics

Japan's political parties are all relatively recent creations, the results of mergers and breakaways. The main interest centres on the factional infighting of the Liberal Democratic Party, which has been in power since its formation. Opposition is weak and divided, but there is the possibility of a coalition of the less radical opposition parties, which could be influential in the years to come. The LDP rarely uses its majority to force through unpopular legislation. Here, as elsewhere in Japanese life, consensus is of the essence, and opposition parties can wield power by boycotting, or threatening to boycott, Diet proceedings; a suitable compromise is usually arranged.

Liberal Democratic Party

A merger of the Japan Democratic Party with the Liberal Party in 1955 led to the formation of the LDP, which is particularly strong in the over-weighted rural constituencies. Its politics are broadly conservative.

Factionalism From the first, the LDP has been a collection of competing factions based on key political personalities. The factions have changed over the years but remain a central element, influencing the election of the party president (i.e. the prime minister), the appointment of ministers and party officials, and the selection of candidates in national elections. This factionalism encourages nepotism and corruption. On the plus side it lends the party a chameleon quality, enabling it to change its stance and leaders to adapt to shifts in the mood of the electorate.

The factions There are five main factions. The two largest, the Tanaka and Suzuki factions, are known as the mainstream factions. The others are named for Nakasone, Fukuda and Komoto. The factions are not ideologically based; rather they depend on ties of loyalty, marriage and cash. They are the money-brokers, collecting cash from party supporters and disbursing it to candidates.

Nakasone – winner yet loser It is ironic that having led the LDP to a landslide victory in 1986, Nakasone found his position weakened by the resurgence of the Tanaka faction, which won sufficient seats to make it by far the largest. With ill-health removing Mr Tanaka from politics, Noboru Takeshita is the *de facto* head of the Tanaka faction. Now secretary-general of the party, the traditional route to the premiership, he is in line to be the next prime minister. Other possible contenders are Shintaro Abe, the former Foreign Affairs Minister, and Minister of Finance Kiichi Miyazawa. Under LDP rules, Nakasone will probably have to step down in 1987, though he will still have a role to play as leader of his faction and a power broker within the party.

The Japan Socialist Party

The JSP was born of a merger of many diverse elements. It was the majority party in 1947 and led the subsequent coalition government which was brought down by dissenters within the JSP's own ranks. Since 1947 it has been going downhill in electoral terms, though remaining the largest of the opposition parties. It is progressively losing support in the large cities and having increasingly to rely on support from the small town and country constituencies.

Union party The trade unions have a strong control over the JSP. The Sohyo union group, the largest in Japan, contributes 75% of party funds.

Policies Although traditionally a Marxist-Leninist party, erstwhile leader Masashi Ishibashi attempted to move the JSP towards the middle ground. It remains committed to "unarmed neutrality" and would scrap Japan's defence forces.

New leader Despite Mr Ishibashi's policy changes, the JSP was trounced at the 1986 election, losing 25% of its seats. His successor, Miss Takako Doi, is the first woman party leader in Japan. She is committed to a continuance of Mr Ishibashi's more moderate policies, though she will probably find the unions and her own left-wingers resistant to change.

Komeito

Also known as the Clean Government Party, the Komeito grew out of the Soka Gakkai, a group linked to the Shoshu Buddhist sect. Since its formation in 1964, the Komeito has established itself as the second largest opposition party and would be a key element of any opposition coalition. Its highly disciplined organization prevents the factionalism apparent in the other political parties.

Turning its back on Buddha The Komeito has publicly distanced itself from the Soka Gakkai during the last 15 years, though strong links remain. The Komeito began as an anti-corruption party with leftish leanings, but has shifted ground to the middle of the road. It supports small businesses and is concerned with local improvements, especially in the inner city areas where its main strength lies.

Japan Communist Party

Efficiently organized at the grass-roots level and soundly financed, the Japan Communist Party is the most extreme of all parties, with a Marxist-Leninist philosophy and links with the Soviet Union. For many years its existence was turbulent, marked by mass arrests and subsequently a purging of its leadership by the American Occupation forces, as well as by internal divisions. The JCP reached its zenith in 1972 when it was the second largest opposition party. The prospects for political influence are small, except for the nuisance value of its strong rump in the Diet. Opposition parties have kept their distance, due both to a strong ideological distaste and to a belief that future election prospects would be damaged by any connection or cooperation.

Democratic Socialist Party

Formed in a right-wing breakaway from the Japan Socialist Party in 1960, the DSP soon gained, and kept, the backing of the Domei, the second-largest union group. Despite this, the party has never made much of an impact.

United Social Democratic Party

The smallest of the opposition parties to have made any impact at all, the USDP was formed as recently as 1978, through defections of moderates within the JSP. The subsequent right-ward shift of the JSP has left the USDP isolated, and its role will continue to diminish.

Future possibilities

A coalition of the JSP, the Democratic Socialists and the Komeito – a possibility striven for by the parties concerned for over 10 years – represents the only alternative to a continuation of LDP rule, and then only if the LDP makes a major mistake. It is difficult to see what form this mistake might take.

State of the parties
Results of July 1986 elections

	Representatives	Councillors
LDP	310	144
JSP	86	41
Komeito	57	25
JCP	27	16
DSP	26	12
USDP	4	1
Others	2	12
Total	512	251
(vacant)	-	1

The reins of power

Power in Japan is highly centralized, a coalition between the LDP, the ministry bureaucrats and "big business" (see *Power in business*). Business provides considerable funds to the LDP, although its power is not as great as might be expected, due to the demands of the many sectional interests on which the LDP is electorally dependent.

The prime minister's power

The power vested in the prime minister by the Constitution is tempered by the political realities of the LDP. In his appointment of ministers, for example, he is restricted by the need to please all the factional interests. The same restraints apply to any attempts to force unpopular legislation through the Diet. The biennial elections for party leader prevent any individual from building a power base.

The power of ministers

Ministers derive their power from their position in the party rather than from their ministry. Most serve only for a year, and even those who last longer rarely stamp their authority on the ministry. The prime minister rotates available ministerial posts in order to balance factional elements within the government, and to reward loyalty and repay political debts.

A few charismatic leaders, like Tanaka, are able to tie the interests of their various ministries to their own political ambitions, but most ministers take advantage of their positions only to repay favours in their constituencies. Agriculture and Construction are among the most prized "pork barrel" ministries.

The power of the ministries

While the prime minister appoints the ministers and parliamentary vice-ministers, the ministries make appointments below this level. The ministers' and prime minister's power in setting policy is thus severely restricted. The Agriculture and Education Ministries are most closely controlled by the LDP, while the Ministry of Finance and MITI are the most independent – and powerful.

Centres of power Postwar constitutional reforms have done little to break the power of the civil service. The bureaucrats are largely responsible for drafting legislation, controlling budgets and setting policies.

Ministry power struggles

The main struggles for political power in Japan are those within and between the ministries.

Internal factions Within the ministries, each year's intake from Tokyo University forms a faction that struggles to achieve the positions of section chief and, ultimately, administrative vice-minister (the senior civil servant). The personnel chief may use his position to improve the chances of contemporaries by moving promising members of other classes into unpromising positions.

Culling the old Promotion up to section chief is based on a strict system of seniority. In some ministries only one member of the same entering class can become vice-minister, all the others being asked to resign. This early retirement, coupled with low pension provisions, leaves bureaucrats free and willing to enter industry or commerce (see *Government and business*), as well as public corporations or politics.

Brother against brother Struggles between the individual ministries can be severe as they attempt to extend their responsibilities. Even ostensibly independent agencies, such as the Economic Planning Agency and the Science and Technology Agency, are battlegrounds where the ministries fight to control certain key appointments. Many of the main claims have already been staked out, but changes in the industrial and economic structure are opening up new avenues for rivalry.

Key ministries

Ministry of Finance Employing 76,000, this is the most powerful of the ministries, with a key role in the function of government, and is run by an enormously influential clique of arch-conservatives. Its most important role is the preparation and implementation of the national budget. Negotiations with other ministries and with the Cabinet and LDP members concerning the precise allocations may lead to some changes to accommodate special interests. Control of the budget gives the Ministry of Finance considerable influence over other ministries.

Dedicated to a policy of fiscal austerity, and exercising direct control of interest rates and the financial and banking systems, it plays the dominant role in deciding the extent of liberalization of the financial sector.

Ministry of International Trade and Industry MITI's financial structure gives it a greater independence from the Ministry of Finance than that of any other ministry. Despite receiving only a small part of the budget, it has been instrumental in setting the direction of Japan's postwar economic development. In this, its control of a number of key public corporations, such as the Export-Import Bank and the Japan Development Bank, were crucial, as was its control of the foreign exchange budget in the 1960s. More recently it has concentrated on the reorganization of dying industries. Its power has waned slightly as the private sector has placed less reliance on help from government.

Ministry of Foreign Affairs This is not as important in Japan as in most industrialized countries, reflecting Japan's concentration on domestic affairs. It has a low budget and a small staff.

Bureaucrats in government

The ministries' hold over government has been assisted by the number of their members who have entered politics. As many as one-third of LDP Diet members at a time have been former career bureaucrats, and many of the postwar prime ministers have been ex-ministry officials.

Paradoxically, in recent years this trend has tended to weaken the hold of the bureaucracy over the legislature. Ex-bureaucrats in the Diet have made it more competent and confident about legislation. Instead of bills being drafted by the ministries, debated by the Diet and passed by the committees, more are being initiated by the politicians themselves on behalf of the interest groups they represent. Additionally, the policy affairs councils of the LDP are growing more confident in altering bills drafted by the civil service before they come up for debate.

Into the future

The liberalization of the economy and the growth of powerful independent industrial corporations have weakened the control of the ministries, especially in the case of MITI. The authoritarian style of government in Japan has moderated, reflecting the changed circumstances of the country itself. Less respect is accorded the civil service now than formerly, and the politicians' argument that their public accountability justifies their taking on more responsiblity is gaining strength.

Considerable power is still retained by the ministries, although pressures on them have increased from all sides. The prime minister and the Cabinet have improved their own position in the decision-making process but must still share power with the bureaucracy.

International alignments

Alignment with the USA was thrust upon Japan by the realities of defeat and occupation. More recently this policy has been fuelled by a desire to match the world's major economic power. While relations with China have improved since its split with the USSR, those with the Soviet Union remain distant. Perhaps Japan's largest international problem is its success in Western markets, which leads to friction with the USA and the EC.

The United States

With US help Japan rebuilt its economy after the war and was accepted back into the international community. The USA is Japan's largest trade partner, and it provides vital defence cover. However, traditional US industries have suffered from Japanese competition, and trade imbalances in Japan's favour have led the Americans to apply pressure on Japan to open up her home markets. Anti-Japanese feeling sometimes runs high in the States, but the strategic value of US bases in Japan militates against a permanent rift.

The Soviet Union

No peace treaty has been signed following World War II, but the two countries maintain diplomatic relations. These can be rather strained due to the USSR's postwar occupation of the Kurile Islands. Siberian raw materials and Japanese technology seem made for each other, but it is difficult to see the USSR giving up its bases on the Kuriles. A more enlightened Soviet leadership could change the nature of Asian politics and make Japan less dependent on the USA.

China

Japan's long-time adversary, China, is now its second largest trade partner; a formal peace and friendship treaty was signed in 1978. China's response to growing imbalances in trade – unilateral cancellation of contracts – has caused some friction. A more long-term threat to friendly relations with Japan lies in the existence of a pro-Soviet element in China.

ASEAN

Japan has endeavoured to take the lead in the Pacific Basin, although a formal concept has yet to evolve. A third of Japan's foreign aid goes to the six nations in ASEAN, to which it also lends diplomatic and technological support. However, Japan's tendency to discriminate against manufactured exports in favour of ASEAN's raw materials causes some resentment.

Europe

With no strategic links between Japan and Europe, relations centre around trade, which has proved a constant source of tension. Japan has come to terms with individual countries, in some cases voluntarily restricting its exports; with the EC as a whole, however, growing trade imbalances have led to conflicts in GATT. Nothing less than Japan setting and meeting an increased import target is likely to satisfy the Community, but frictions are eased by Japanese manufacturing investment in the EC.

International acceptance

Japan has progressively re-entered the international community through its membership of the IMF, GATT, the UN and the OECD. Within the UN, it has not taken the leading role its economic status would suggest, and although it participates fully in the international economic community – it is the second largest shareholder in the World Bank – its continual trade surpluses have put it at odds with fellow members of GATT.

National security

Japan's national security is highly dependent on US assistance. The defence forces, restricted by low government spending levels, would not be sufficient to repulse any serious military attack on Japan.

Constitutional constraints

The postwar Constitution explicitly stated that Japan would "forever renounce war as a sovereign right of the nation and the threat or use of force as a means of settling international disputes." In addition, Japan, with its unique experience of nuclear warfare, adopted in 1967 its three non-nuclear principles, stating that it would never produce, possess, or allow to be introduced any nuclear weapons.

Defence

Japan's Self Defence Forces were created from the Police Reserve Force in 1954. Since then the LDP has continued a policy of limited non-nuclear defence under the US nuclear umbrella. Currently the Self Defence Forces have 155,000 personnel in the Ground Force and 44,000 each in the Air and Maritime forces. There are also 55,000 US servicemen, stationed at two naval bases, two air bases and at Okinawa's marine base.

Civilian control The Self Defence Forces are administered by the Defence Agency (not by a ministry – an indication of their lesser status), which is composed of civilians. The three services are run individually and take orders only from the Cabinet.

Self-imposed limits Pacifism runs deep in Japan, and despite US pressure the LDP had (until 1986) kept spending within a limit of 1% of GNP. With Japan's GNP being so high this still amounts to a substantial sum – the tenth largest military budget in the world. Defence spending restrictions and a ban on the export of weapons have prevented the emergence of a defence industry. The USA acquires much of Japan's defence-linked technology under the security treaty, making Japan an R&D annex to the US military-industrial complex.

Intelligence services

In the early postwar years Japan relied heavily on US intelligence to counter Soviet, and later Chinese and North Korean, infiltration and subversion. However, a country with no offensive military forces and no defence ministry cannot be thought of as having any secrets; and it is not illegal for foreign nationals to collect military information in Japan, unless it relates to US equipment.

There are several agencies with their own independent intelligence services – the Ministry of Justice, the Defence Agency and the Police Agency, among others – but no secret service as such. The uncovering of a Soviet spy ring in 1980 led to the leader, a naval officer, being charged with the theft of official papers and receiving the maximum possible sentence – one year in jail.

The police

Japan has an exceptionally low crime rate. The police force is very efficient and fairly large, with one officer to every 30 households. Each prefecture runs its own force, and all are coordinated by the Police Agency.

There are around 35,000 far-left activists in Japan. 1986 saw renewed activity by the Chukakuha (Core faction), who made token rocket attacks on the Tokyo Economic Summit. Narita Airport, the site of riots in the early 1970s, is to be expanded, and a resurgence of trouble is expected. However, the crack national anti-riot police rarely let any situation get out of control, and the security at Narita makes it one of the world's safest airports.

The Business Scene

Government and business

Government and business are closely allied in Japan. The postwar dominance of the government in aiding and directing industrial recovery and development with subsidy, regulation, market protection and binding advice (known as administrative guidance) is beginning to give way to a more liberal and equitable situation. As the economy has prospered, larger companies have been able to seize the initiative.

Elected politicians

By ensuring an atmosphere in which business could prosper, the LDP has kept itself in power. Money talks in Japanese politics, and business has provided the funds that support the LDP. Not only does the leadership strive to support business as a whole, but individual members of the Diet repay those companies who have supported them by speaking up for industrial interests and pressure groups, especially those based in their home constituencies.

Support from Keidanren and Keizai Doyukai (see *Power in business*) for impending legislation is important. Where there is opposition from the business community – especially where established business interests are threatened – Keidanren has been vociferous in its criticisms and has been heeded.

The public sector The government is progressively privatizing a number of state corporations. In April 1985 Japan Salt and Tobacco and Nippon Telephone and Telegraph were privatized, after strong US pressure on Japan to liberalize markets. Privatization Japanese-style is a slow process, with the government taking up the whole of the share issue and releasing it onto the market in stages.

More controversial is the plan to regionalize, then privatize, the loss-making Japan National Railways. The public sector industries are the last bastions of union militancy, and, economics aside, the dismantling of the public railway monopoly will help the LDP politically and has much popular support.

The civil service

State control over the economy has been exercised largely through the ministries, particularly MITI and the Ministry of Finance. Administrative guidance has been backed up by financial controls and subsidies, and sometimes by direct action. Prices of key goods are the subject of guidance: for example, in the 1970s, after the first oil shock, direct price controls were imposed to mitigate inflation. Influence, rather than direct action, remains the preferred method. In recent years the success of the economy has made state control more difficult; major companies can go against state guidelines.

Negative assistance Besides receiving direct help from MITI and the Ministry of Finance, Japan's industry has been helped by other ministries' erection of obstacles to foreign products. Foremost among these has been the Ministry of Health and Welfare, which is responsible for setting testing standards for all imported foods, drugs and chemicals. Its refusal to accept foreign test results, insisting on replication in Japan and setting of standards different from those pertaining worldwide, allowed local industry to get established.

Monopoly legislation Based on US anti-trust laws, this was introduced in the Anti-Monopoly Act of 1947, amended in 1953 and toughened in 1977. The Act is enforced by the Fair Trade Commission (FTC), which, like other Japanese government departments, has quasi-judicial and quasi-legislative powers. Its administrative guidance must be adhered to.

There is no strong anti-monopoly tradition in Japan; indeed MITI encouraged co-operation and mergers to strengthen the world trading position of Japanese companies. The 1977 amendment, though, permits the FTC to break up companies with more than a 50% share of a market, or two companies with more than a 75% share. This tough line is seldom taken, since any break-up has to be made with the co-operation of MITI.

The FTC is also empowered to outlaw mergers that seek to restrain competition or to threaten national security, public order and safety, or the running of the economy. Although there are still areas where cartels are possible, even encouraged, heavy fines can be imposed on companies guilty of parallel pricing.

Bureaucrats in business

Amakudari, or "descent from heaven", describes the practice of bureaucrats from government ministries taking up senior management positions in private industry on their retirement. The considerable licensing and approval authority of the ministries is one reason why companies are prepared to accept and even embrace this practice. Contracts and awards are often made to those companies with ex-bureaucrats on the board.

Contacts In Japan many of the top politicians, bureaucrats and senior executives are graduates of Tokyo University. Informal meetings with classmates add another dimension to communications between business and government.

Aid and subsidies

The era when the government disbursed large sums of money through MITI for the promotion of industry in general and exports in particular is now over. JETRO, the arm of MITI concerned with external trade, is now principally concerned with the promotion of imports (see *Market entry*). Current government aid to industry, in the form of long-term low interest loans and the reduction or deferral of taxation, as well as direct subsidy, is limited to specific industries and certain areas.

Legislation drafted by MITI seeks to create hi-tech industrial centres in rural areas, by providing sites, discretionary funding and other incentives, especially for priority industries such as those related to energy conservation, pollution control and biotechnology. Tax exemption is granted on real estate sales to any firm moving from central Tokyo.

Long-term low interest loans are available from the Japan Development Bank; again, rural developments are favoured, as are urban renewal, hi-tech industries and energy projects.

Local government The prefectures have joined forces with MITI's Industrial Location Guidance Division to promote decentralization by sponsoring tours for foreign companies and media. More than half of Japan's 47 prefectures offer packages of subsidies to foreign firms setting up factories or offices (see *Other sources of finance*).

Unravelling the bureaucracy

The bureaucracy is labyrinthine, but Japanese officials are at least approachable. Foreign companies wanting background on their own fields will find that English-language publications such as the *MITI Handbook* and *Organization of the Government of Japan* provide, in most cases, the basic information for identifying the contact point. These publications and others are available from Japanese embassies and offices of JETRO worldwide. Advice can also be sought through your embassy, a chamber of commerce or a consultancy.

Power in business

Power in the postwar Japanese business community is concentrated in four main organizations: the Keidanren, Keizai Doyukai, Nikkeiren and Nissho. Representing the business community's interests, they put pressure on the LDP, on government ministries and on labour. They are also influential in trade discussions with other countries.

The zaikai

The power brokers of the Japanese financial and business world are known collectively as the *zaikai* (*zai* meaning "money" and *kai* meaning "world"). Its members are the top management of the major industrial and financial corporations.

The prewar *zaibatsu* – Mitsubishi, Mitsui, Sumitomo and others – were disbanded during the US Occupation (though they have since re-emerged in rather different form). A generation of younger executives was thus pushed to the top. With a long period in power they have established themselves as influential business leaders. Only recently has a generational change in leadership taken place.

Power and influence The *zaikai*'s power is based on generous funds, personal connections between themselves and with politicians and bureaucrats, and organizational muscle. The four main business organizations – Keidanren, Keizai Doyukai, Nikkeiren and Nissho – exert enormous influence on the government's policy decisions. Part of their role is to encourage politicians to guard the capitalist system. To this end they channel hefty donations through Keidanren to political parties, mainly the ruling Liberal Democratic Party.

Overseas diplomacy As part of the establishment, *zaikai* leaders have regular breakfast meetings with LDP leaders, sit on government councils and meet visiting world leaders. A network of committees and conferences keeps them in touch with overseas business leaders, especially the Americans. In addition, government-instigated missions travel abroad, particularly to solve instances of trade friction.

Keidanren

The Federation of Economic Organizations (Keidanren) is the most powerful of the business organizations and acts as the headquarters of the business community. Its members are the major trade associations as well as prominent companies in virtually all fields of industry and commerce. Its organizational strength revolves around 48 standing committees, which address specific problems, and a full-time secretariat of 170 people.

Objectives Keidanren's role, first, is that of a pressure group representing the business community's interests. Second, it undertakes private-level diplomacy to resolve international problems in conjunction with similar business organizations overseas. And third, it acts as the business community's public relations office, to inform both the Japanese public and overseas opinion.

Its PR arm – the Keizai Koho Center – organizes seminars, sponsors TV programmes, conducts surveys, advertises in the press, organizes speakers at international conferences and publishes numerous magazines and booklets in both Japanese and English.

Policies Easing trade friction with other countries is a major concern. On the home front Keidanren is lobbying for cuts in government expenditure, simplified formalities for obtaining government approval, cuts in corporation taxes, privatization and flexible implementation of anti-monopoly policy.

New leaders Yoshihiro Inayama, honorary chairman of Nippon Steel, was 82 when he stepped down in May 1986 as chairman of Keidanren after his third two-year term. Eishiro Saito, chairman of Nippon Steel, took his place at the age of 74. Gaishi Hiraiwa, chairman of Tokyo Electric Power, is to succeed Saito in 1988, when he will be only 73. Age and seniority are considered great assets in Japanese business.

Keizai Doyukai

The Japan Committee for Economic Development (Keizai Doyukai) was formed in 1946. Its two distinguishing features are, first, that its members are individuals rather than corporations and, second, that it is a policy-oriented organization. Its 1,000-plus members are mainly managing directors, chairmen or presidents of big corporations. A number of them are also officials of Keidanren.
Objectives It acts as a forum for *individual* views on the economy and on management philosophy, addressing itself to medium- and long-term structural problems. It has long-standing ties with overseas economic organizations and regularly dispatches study missions abroad. Since its members are individuals, Keizai Doyukai sometimes submits proposals and reports that conflict with the majority of the business community and the government.
Policies Keizai Doyukai believes strongly in the free enterprise system, advocates liberalization of trade and capital in Japan, and is much concerned with lessening international trade friction.
A new engine The present chairman is Takashi Ishihara, also chairman of Nissan Motor. His main task is to revitalize a once progressive but ageing organization.

Nikkeiren

The Japan Federation of Employers' Associations (Nikkeiren) represents employers' interests in the fields of labour and wage negotiations. It was set up in 1948 to counteract the growing strength of the union movement. Through prefectural and trade associations it represents over 30,000 companies which employ around 30% of the work force. Its president is Bunpei Otsuki, chairman of Mitsubishi Mining and Cement.
Objectives With the more peaceful labour situation in Japan since the 1960s, Nikkeiren has softened its stance towards labour. It now aims to improve management-labour relations through social education of employers, corporate training of workers and publicity for employers' policies.
Advisory role Nikkeiren is campaigning to keep average wage increases in line with productivity improvements. It does not negotiate directly with workers but issues guidelines on wages and conditions which, set alongside union recommendations, are influential in the annual round of wage negotiations.

Nissho

The Japan Chamber of Commerce and Industry (Nissho) is a federation of 481 local chambers of commerce and industry. Established in 1878, it is the oldest and biggest business organization with 11,000 staff and branches overseas.
Objectives Nissho not only represents its chambers but acts on behalf of the small- and medium-size business sector, notably by lobbying against the projected large-scale indirect taxation and changes to inheritance tax. It is strengthening ties with the foreign business community through liaison with overseas chambers in Japan. Recent overseas missions include one to China, which has set up a body to promote joint ventures and technical cooperation. Nissho also actively liaises with the USA, and its president, Noboru Gotoh, is influential in the Pacific Basin Economic Council.

The business framework

Since World War II the successful business executive has emerged as the modern Japanese hero. Today's parents groom their sons almost from birth for the long, hard struggle through the corporate ranks. The stars who inspire the ambitious are men like Akio Morita, the co-founder of Sony, and Honda Soichiro or Matsushita Konosuke, whose trading names are known around the globe. They have forged their business success in the modern world, outside the framework of the prewar industrial families.

The Western executive approaching the Japanese market is faced with daunting paradoxes. High-profile, traditional corporate structures intimidate with their behind-the-scenes deals, yet there is a profusion of non-corporate enterprises competing in a more familiar fashion. Great stress seems to be laid on non-aggressive business conduct, yet competition is patently ferocious.

Company size

The high-profile empires are the exception. Most of Japan's 6m businesses are small, though a large proportion of them are linked directly or indirectly to the corporate sector. Some 30% of Japanese workers are engaged in long-term employment in the highly productive, high-technology industries. The other 70% have a far lower degree of security as employees of smaller, less efficient operations offering few of the financial and social benefits of the well-known corporations. About 75% of businesses have fewer than 100 employees, whereas the 10 largest each employ more than 40,000 workers.

Corporate attitudes

Japanese attitudes towards takeovers differ radically from those in the West, where the large fish gobble up the small fish as fast as they can, and with impunity. Among Japanese companies, the hostile takeover is considered immoral. It is fiercely resisted on the rare occasions when it does occur. The government also acts against unwanted takeovers. In 1981 the Ministry of International Trade and Industry assisted Katakura, the country's major silk manufacturer, to avoid the acquisitive advances of Newpis Ltd of Hong Kong.

The same moral imperatives that restrain takeovers also inhibit Japanese companies from headhunting one another's key employees. These attitudes are part of the traditional values which still regard the company as a human community rather than a mere legal entity or set of assets. Private companies have public service ethics. ***Competition*** can be fierce – but a sense of balance and restraint should not be lost. Opponents are not to be destroyed, and litigation is avoided except as a last resort (see *The law*). "Face" is an intrinsic factor in business success. Bankruptcy involves a heavy loss of face and is avoided at all costs among major companies. There is nevertheless a high bankruptcy rate among small businesses.

Company ownership

The structure of company ownership is much more internal than in the West, with finance coming predominantly from borrowing and reinvestment of profits. Shares are allotted to employees rather than floated on the market. Some 80% of quoted firms prefer to generate share capital in this way, so that in a real sense the company is run by and belongs to its members. For example, in what the president of the zip manufacturer YKK calls the "cycle of goodness", the firm's employees deposit 10% of their wages in return for shares. Dividends are low, averaging $1\frac{1}{2}$% over the last 10 years.

Large individual shareholdings within a company are rare. Even in family corporations like Matsushita and Honda, the founding fathers hold less than 5%, and only one in 30 companies has a shareholder with more than 10% of the equity.

AGM business is a speedy formality, and some companies still hire *sokaiya*, heavies with nominal shareholdings, whose job is to shout down the queries of troublesome shareholders at the annual meeting.

Japan's "dual economy"

A salient feature of Japan's economy is the interdependence of the highly visible corporate sector and the less publicly visible small businesses which service them: the so-called "dual-economy". The Japanese categorize businesses according to differences not only in size of capitalization and work force, but also in their terms and conditions of employment, the source of their finance, and their public standing.

Large corporations About a quarter of the labour force works for the *dai kigyo*. These are the 1% of businesses employing more than 500 workers. (See *The Japanese at work* and *Corporate hierarchies* for aspects of the corporate psyche.)

Medium and small firms Known as the *chu-sho kigyo*, these companies are the ones in which probably the greatest initiatives and risks are taken. Future Sonys or Hondas begin here. The grouping includes entrepreneurial operations designed to exploit gaps in the market not yet filled by the big corporations, such as unmanned business offices.

Often with fewer than 100 employees, *chu-sho kigyo* provide the contractors and subcontractors so essential to the efficiency of the majors. Unlike the corporations, these smaller firms are usually non-unionized.

In the automobile industry the major manufacturers depend on the small business sector to manufacture and supply parts for the highly successful "just in time" (JIT) delivery system, thereby saving warehouse costs and over-stocking problems, as well as reducing the payroll. Space is at a premium in Japan. Firms such as Nissan have even exported the JIT system to their overseas operations.

Japanese cars contain about 70% bought-in parts, compared to 50% in the US industry. Quality control is achieved by close co-operation between manufacturer and parts supplier. Some majors have strong equity positions in their key suppliers, and some firms, such as Toyota, even share research facilities with suppliers. Staff visit one another's plants, and there are monthly joint meetings.

Although small and medium-sized businesses provide the cutting edge in high technology, their existence is precarious. Bankruptcy rates are highest and credit notes longest as their size diminishes.

Family enterprises The smallest businesses of all, making up 80% of the total, are the *rei-sai kigyo*, or family enterprises. These are often registered as public companies, though they may have fewer than 10 employees. Family firms dominate retail distribution.

Corporate networks

Cartels are an integral aspect of business in Japan. They are well established and usually legitimate, since neither the government nor the business community accepts the idea of free competition as understood in the USA and Europe (see *Government and business*). Japanese traditions call for a high degree of collusion and collective action, often under the state's leadership.

The automobile and steel industries serve as classic examples of market bypassing. They make periodic agreements dividing up steel demand between a limited number of steel producers in negotiated proportions, at pre-agreed prices. Outsiders have no chance to tender.

The sogo shosa Negotiations are carried on under the auspices of the *sogo shosha*, the major trading companies which between them handle more than half of all Japanese trade, internal and external (see *Market entry* and *Distribution*). The largest of these are Mitsubishi, Mitsui, Marubeni, C. Itoh and Sumitomo.

Industrial groups These are the descendants of the prewar *zaibatsu* groupings (see *Power in business*). The present-day groups, known as *keiretsu gaisha*, are generally based around a trading company and a major bank and have associated companies in a wide range of industries.

Each major company holds equity in several of the others, both directly and through others in the group, although the individual percentages are small, often on the order of 3–5%. Traditionally, the banking member has exerted considerable influence as the major source of finance for most of the group's members, but this situation is gradually changing as bonds replace bank finance.

The relationships among the members of a group are often flexible enough to allow alliances between members of different groups, particularly on large-scale deals and overseas business. However, the inertia and set trading patterns of the powerful groups can prove inefficient because they prevent competition and make it difficult for newcomers to break into a market that is carved up among vested interests.

Company types

Public limited liability company (*kabushiki kaisha* or kk). This is the most popular form of incorporation among Japanese and foreign firms. Seven promoters put up a minimum Y350,000 and form a board of at least three directors and a statutory auditor.

Private limited companies (*yugen gaisha*) are generally very small family businesses. They have a maximum of 50 company members, each with limited liability, and require only one director. Minimum capital is Y100,000. Foreign firms rarely opt for this form because of its small business image.

Partnership companies may have either limited (*goshi gaisha*) or unlimited liability (*gomei gaisha*). Neither form is widely used by foreign businesses. There is no partnership law and few relevant provisions in the Civil Code.

Sole proprietorships (*hitori kaisha*) are uncommon, but are found among small retail outlets. They have high tax rates and a "small" image.

Self-employment (*jiei gyosha*) is very common, especially among professionals, and is an option for foreigners in service industries, though not usually for those in professions, due to legal restrictions.

Establishing a Japanese presence

The process of establishing a presence in Japan entails careful study. Companies planning to set up in Japan should seek expert advice from international accountancy and consultancy firms.

Foreign exchange controls and legal barriers to direct investment from overseas are no longer problems, but the prospective entrant needs to choose the correct business "face". Manufacturing products in Japan, or marketing services there, is best carried out through joint venture companies or wholly owned subsidiaries.

A liaison office is not much more than a local base and mail drop. It is a useful, and tax-free, presence but needs to be registered. The temporary nature of the enterprise makes local recruitment difficult, and swift upgrading is recommended.

Branch office (*shiten*) is a step up, but still regarded as temporary. The registration fee is Y90,000, and the legal costs Y400–750,000. Bank and securities companies require Ministry of Finance licences. Expect close scrutiny by the tax authorities.
Joint ventures are popular, as this eases problems of language, bureaucracy, and market complexity. Pioneered by leading multinationals like Xerox and Union Carbide, joint ventures are increasingly used by smaller firms in commercial and consumer services. Problems include the difficulty of convincing Japanese staff that they have a prosperous future and the tendency of the Japanese partner to wish to control a venture.
The wholly owned subsidiary (*genchi hojin*) was the form chosen by Coca Cola and IBM. Among foreign firms, IBM Japan was the preferred choice recently for job hunters from prestige universities. Costs are considerable, and time lags from investment to profit are long. With all-Japanese staff and Japanese business methods, *genchi hojin* can be attractive employers for the growing numbers of Japanese educated abroad, who may find it hard to fit into a major Japanese company.

Checking out possible partners

Investigating a potential partner can be difficult, especially since much of the published material is available only in Japanese.
Embassy commercial departments in Tokyo not only have good, current information on many Japanese companies but can put you in touch with clients who have dealt with the companies and with the relevant trade associations.
Overseas chambers of commerce in Tokyo are also a good source of similar information and contacts.
Private investigators (*koshinsho*) and "***research offices***" (*chosa jimusho*) will go beyond public information – as they do when investigating possible marriage partners.
City banks will provide substantial amounts of key information about companies they are linked with through the *keiretsu gaisha* system if they scent new business from you.
Company directories are a good source of publicly available information, since companies are legally required to disclose detailed information on their finances (see *Business media*).

Legal considerations

Incorporation normally takes one month from the completion of all paperwork, which is entirely in Japanese. Articles of association for public companies need to conform to a highly standardized format to pass official scrutiny. Incorporation of a public company will cost Y1–2m in legal fees and Y150,000 or 0.7% of paid-in capital for registration.

Japanese firms have no company secretaries or treasurers, but statutory auditors instead. Large companies must have two, as well as independent auditors.

Financial considerations

Although accounting principles are broadly similar to American ones, tax returns must effectively be prepared by Japanese accountants. Dealing with tax officials is an arcane art beyond the skills of all but local tax specialists.

Tax authorities are strict about accepting deductions for bad debts; depreciation rates are much slower (an office building depreciates over 60 years). There is no allowance for capital gains; gains from the sale of property can be taxed at 65–70%.

The tax burden on corporations, which can exceed 60% of income, is one of the highest in the world; and although tax reform is on the cards, cuts are not a certainty. Allowances for business entertainment decline according to the capital size of a company (zero above Y50m), which is ironic considering the enormous cost of business entertainment.

Employment

Many Westerners regard Japan as having exemplary labour relations. Although true in general, it has not always been so, nor is it always the case today. Employers are having to contend with protectionist threats, the strengthening currency, increased international competition and rising labour costs, which have led to enforced production overseas, a slow-down in growth, increasing mechanization, redundancies and plant closures. Employees are under pressure from these market forces, and also face greater competition as a result of the 1950s baby boom and the rising number of working women. Employment practices that evolved in the postwar era of skilled labour shortages and high growth are being modified, and even the cherished principle of lifetime employment within one company is being gradually whittled away.

Employment figures

Japan's exceptionally low unemployment rate – at a peak 2.9% in spring 1986 – is the combined result of company recruitment for life, a high proportion of self-employed or family workers (18% of the work force) and an increasing tendency for firms to engage temporary employees who can be shed as circumstances change. The underemployment created in some instances by lifetime recruitment can no longer be sustained in more hostile economic times. Unemployment is highest among the young (7.1% of 15–19s) and older workers (4.4% of over-60s).

About 57% of Japan's 60m workers are engaged in service industries, 34% in manufacturing and only 9% in farming, fishing and forestry.

Recruitment

Teamwork is the traditional keystone of Japan's system of lifetime employment. Personnel departments are ultimately more interested in character than in individual skills or hard-won academic qualifications – although there is a slow drift to more Western attitudes.

"Virgin" workers, who expect to be engaged for life, sit a company examination and attend interviews during the autumn recruitment drive, for vacancies becoming available in the following spring. Major companies have long practised *aota-gai* ("buying up the harvest before the season"), luring students into employment agreements well before graduation. Graduate recruitment fell in 1986, though more female graduates were taken on in response to equal employment opportunities legislation.

Temporary workers have none of the privileges of lifetime staff and can be released at any time.

Post-retirement applicants A third, increasingly important group are those workers over 55 who have been retired and who still wish to work, sometimes part-time, sometimes in a different field.

Agency recruitment is rarely used by large companies when seeking long-term staff, and speculative applications are uncommon. Personal recommendation is important for an applicant.

Employment legislation

The Labour Standards Law, Trade Union Law, Labour Relations Adjustment Law and Equal Employment Opportunites Law govern Japanese employment practices formally. Custom and convention determine attitudes and practice. In the matter of redundancies, for example, employers go to extraordinary lengths to avoid lay-offs, and when all else fails will attempt, often

Pointers for prospective employers

Working for a foreign firm has until recently been regarded as mildly unpatriotic and risky. The higher salaries, faster promotion and greater responsibilities offered by foreign firms are not always enough to overcome the fear of being fired or left without a job if the company pulls out of Japan. Working for a foreign firm may spoil a worker's chances of getting a later job with a Japanese company. The Japanese are also used to the discrimination exercised by Japanese companies overseas against "locally employed staff", and may assume the worst unless reassured.

Although "headhunting" is rare, and changing firms in mid-career can cost the Japanese considerable loss of lifetime earnings, a growing number of foreign firms are attracting specialists with a track record. This trend will develop as Japan's growing recruitment-services industry matures. In the current economic climate, major corporations are now seeking to place prematurely retired top executives – lifetime employees – with other companies. Foreign firms can also draw on the experience and invaluable contacts of retiring civil servants.

Students returning to Japan after being educated overseas – most of them women – have fewer inhibitions about working for a foreign company. Many have excellent language and cross-cultural skills.

Foreign employers should take Japanese recruits back to home base for training. It enables them to understand better what the company is trying to do in Japan.

successfully, to place their work force *en masse* with another company or an affiliate. Sackings are rare, though increasing in line with other Western employment practices.

New employees are designated as either *permanent* or *temporary*. Permanent workers normally serve a 2–6 month probation, following which they are entitled by law to expect lifetime employment unless their contract stipulates a specified period or they breach contract. Temporary staff have short-term contracts, which if renewed regularly could imply a lifetime obligation. Provided it is not contrary to the terms of an individual contract, dismissal with 30 days' notice or pay in lieu is legal; conventionally, however, it is regarded as unethical.

Foreign companies taking on staff should seek expert advice, for a poorly handled personnel matter can damage a firm's reputation out of all proportion.

Unions

Some 12.5m of Japan's 43m dependent employees belong to nearly 35,000 unions throughout Japan. Overall, numbers are about what they were when unions were helped back to their feet by postwar reforms. But the unions' inability to win substantial pay increases has brought the level of unionization down from 35% in 1975 to below 30% – and it is still falling. It is lower than in Western Europe, somewhat higher than in the United States.

Enterprise unions More than 90% of union members belong to enterprise, or company, unions. Each plant has its own union association which negotiates locally on some issues and combines with associations in the company's other plants to represent the work force nationally. There are a few Western-style unions, such as the teachers' union (*Nikkyso*) and the Japan Seaman's Union, but they are rare.

Union attitudes are remarkably cooperative by Western standards, reflecting both the failure of direct action immediately after the war and the unions' subsequent ability to negotiate settlements higher than the the level of inflation in the years of high growth and full employment. Brief stoppages (often for no more than a few hours) are little more than a symbolic flexing of industrial muscle. Union representatives at company level are often well-paid managers within the company. They negotiate with company representatives who may once have been active union members. The emphasis is on negotiation, not confrontation. The focus is on pay and conditions rather than on individual grievances.

Wage bargaining, known as *shunto* or the "spring wages offensive", takes place in April (private sector) and May (public sector). This is preceded by four months of public posturing by pundits, academics and leaders of employers' federations which moves both sides towards norms for pay and bonuses. In the private sector, 2.2m mainly blue-collar workers bargain through *Domei*, the Japan Confederation of Labour. The 4.5m white-collar and more militant public-sector workers belong to *Sohyo*, the General Council of Trade Unions.

Disputes Japan loses fewer days in disputes than other major industrialized countries, with the exception of West Germany. Disputes are settled by collective bargaining or, failing that, by a professional mediator who is appointed from local or national labour relations commissions established by law.

Labour costs

These have risen rapidly in postwar Japan, linked closely with increases in national product. Annual increases of up to 15% were common before the first oil shock, but they fell to single figures in the 1980s. Direct earnings vary by as much as a third between the small and big business sectors; effective earnings in terms of benefits vary even more. In big businesses, labour costs for the permanently employed are particularly high. Average Japanese incomes overtook those of the Americans in 1986.

Remuneration packages include three elements in addition to basic pay – bonuses, allowances and fringe benefits – which can double annual earnings. For the permanently employed, most of these benefits are linked to seniority rather than performance, but Western job evaluation techniques are starting to be used.

Low starting pay is a frequent cause of complaint. School-leavers entering at 18–19 start at Y1.5–2m a year; graduates start at Y2–2.5m. Apart from sales-oriented employment, most Japanese take a long-term view, regarding monthly income as an instalment of lifetime income. An employee's starting wage is based on his job classification, age, education, experience and sex; women are paid 50–75% of male rates for the same work. All employees receive gradual increases until their early 30s, when the likelihood of remaining for life with the company, combined with increased family commitments, produces a substantial boost in male pay levels. Pay levels peak for most men between 47 and 50, with an average private-sector wage of Y5m. This declines until retirement and will, on average, reach only Y3.5m in secondary employment afterwards.

Wage discrimination affects temporary workers, employees of small businesses and, most of all, women. Nearly one fifth of females earn only Y1m a year; only 10% earn more than Y4.5m, the average for a male section chief in his mid-30s.

Bonuses are paid in cash twice a year, in June and December. Although introduced as an incentive, they are now regarded as an entitlement. Effectively they are a means of deferring higher basic pay. They are on average 2–4 times the worker's basic monthly wage. They are linked to seniority and are substantially higher in large firms and the financial sector, where they may be twice the basic pay.

Allowances paid on top of the basic wage are significant in boosting effective income by up to 20–30%. They are a vital element in the seniority wages system. Some relate to personal circumstances: housing, commuting costs, marriage, family and educational commitments. Others are related to work: payment in lieu of direct remuneration for overtime, unsocial hours and posts of responsibility; for more senior managers, there are lavish budgets for entertainment of clients and junior colleagues. Many allowances are not taxed, which is an incentive to pay more, given the high rates of corporate taxation.

Fringe benefits paid in kind are the preserve of larger firms, which can afford low-cost housing for new recruits, sports and recreational facilities, subsidized holidays at company resorts, cheap loans, and, most important, private medical insurance.

Executive salaries Even the most senior managers rarely earn more than six or seven times the salary of those just beginning their careers. Presidents of small and medium companies earn Y10–15m, directors of larger companies up to Y20m. The biggest payers are finance, banking and insurance companies, followed by the *sogo shosa* and the manufacturing industries. Senior civil service jobs offer more prestige than cash – top earnings being Y10–15m. The highest earners of all are doctors, who receive significant payments (quite legally) from the pharmaceutical companies.

Large companies run a pool of cars and drivers: higher management have regular but not exclusive use of company cars. Few employees have cars as part of their payment package.

Personal taxes

Personal tax levels are the lowest among advanced countries, though big earners pay more than Westerners, with the exception of Scandinavians.

Tax bites (1985)

Annual income	Marital status	Income tax
Y3m	Single	8.7%
	2 Children	2.6%
Y5m	S	13.0%
	2C	7.9%
Y7m	S	17.4%
	2C	12.7%
Y10m	S	22.9%
	2C	18.9%
Y20m	S	38.1%
	2C	35.0%
Y50m	S	57.2%
	2C	55.7%

Source: Ministry of Finance

Japanese pay two types of direct taxes (on worldwide income): national income tax and local inhabitants' tax. Foreign residents staying for less than five years pay only income tax and only on income earned in and/or remitted to Japan from abroad. Few Japanese file tax returns; for incomes under Y15m, companies do the work.

Tax rates for individuals range from 10.5% climbing to 70%. Average incomes fall into the 12–21% bands. Local inhabitants' tax rates range from 4.5–17%, with the average taxpayer falling into the 8–12% bands. Deposits of up to Y3m in post office accounts, government and trust bonds and up to Y5m in employee savings plans are tax-free. Capital gains on stocks, bonds and debentures are, with qualifications, tax-exempt. In addition, remuneration packages that include housing, life insurance and low-cost loans (provided the employee pays up to 3%) are not treated as taxable income.

Tax evasion Annual random checks by tax officials always uncover vast tax evasion by companies and individuals across the spectrum.

Financial institutions

A highly rigid financial system is evolving into a fast-moving and internationally competitive one. Japanese banking is emerging as a strong force in the international financial community, and the Tokyo Stock Exchange has taken its place as part of a 24-hour global trading network. As Japanese banks and securities houses aim for a major presence abroad, yet another Western industry is under threat.

Isolation

Japanese companies' access to capital in the postwar years was rigidly controlled by the Ministry of Finance. The Ministry and the central bank, the Bank of Japan, set limits on how much money the banks could lend in each quarter. Japan was, in effect, a closed society financially, isolated from international sources of capital.

Opening the economy Inward investment was eased in the late 1970s, but foreign exchange controls were not abolished until 1980, and significant liberalization began only in 1984. This included a lifting of the interest ceiling on large deposits, easing of restrictions on the issue of short-term certificates of deposit, partial liberalization of the Euroyen market and concessions to foreign securities houses, which allowed some to operate on the Tokyo Stock Exchange.

Pressures within the system

Savings The Japanese have an exceptionally high savings rate, at 16–20% of disposable income. This is the highest rate in the industrial world (over two and a half times the US level) and is due to the high cost of housing, the need to prepare for retirement, an inadequate system of social security, and the practice of paying lump sum bonuses.

Tax-free postal savings, at 20% of the total, are the largest area of personal savings, the tax concessions helping to keep interest rates low. This system is controlled by the Ministry of Finance and is an important source of funds for the public sector.

Article 65 of the Japanese Securities and Exchange Law, based on the US Glass-Steagall Act, maintains a strict separation between banks and securities dealers. This has been breached by some foreign banks, which can own up to 50% of a securities house; Japanese banks are restricted to a 5% share.

Foreign exchange dealings remain in the hands of the banks, hampering the securities houses in currency swap dealings. Both banks and securities houses see Article 65 as a restraint on potential profits, but others see it as preventing the build-up of financial oligopolies.

Government influence Until the early 1970s the government did not run a deficit and kept interest rates artificially low. Long-term government borrowing was minimal and financial institutions were protected. The oil shock of 1973 and subsequent deficit spending changed this. The process continued through overseas pressure for access to Japanese financial markets, an increasingly international outlook from Japanese industry and finance, and a surplus of funds within Japan seeking new investment opportunities.

Interest rates After the 1979 oil crisis the Bank of Japan used interest rates, rather than credit ceilings, to control the money supply and inflation. Deposit rates in banking and postal savings systems are tied to the Bank of Japan's discount rate by administrative fiat. The May 1984 agreement with the US Treasury continued pressure to remove controls on deposit interest rates, but these remain the government's most effective means of intervention.

The banks

Japanese banks are strictly divided according to their functions and permitted methods of raising funds. They have played an active role in the industrial development of modern Japan, both in the provision of finance and in their shareholdings in the major companies. Japanese banks are now the largest holders of foreign banking assets in the world.

Types of bank

Long-term credit banks The three long-term credit banks were set up in 1952, in the face of an underdeveloped capital market, to provide inexpensive long-term funding for Japanese industry. They were given the right to raise money through the issue of five-year debentures. Although they can offer short-term loans, they are barred from soliciting funds from small depositors. With Japanese industry now mature, and likely to seek long-term funding by bond issues, the *raison d'être* for these banks has almost gone. Their know-how and expertise, however, has stood them in good stead, especially in their underwriting of Eurobond issues.

The Industrial Bank of Japan, which has retained its right to underwrite public sector bonds, is the largest, with total fund volume of around $100bn; the Long Term Credit Bank has a fund volume of over $85bn and the Nippon Credit Bank just over $50bn.

City banks The 13 city banks are commercial banks, with 2,730 branches and half the total assets of all Japanese banks. They operate in the retail end of the market. Deregulation has squeezed their profits. Fixed low interest rates for deposits cannot attract all the individual and company business they would wish, and they have to make up the shortfall in the money markets at higher rates. At the same time, loan income has fallen because of high corporate liquidity and the trend towards raising money on the securities market.

In Japan city banks have turned covetous eyes on the lucrative securities market, and as a sop the government allowed them, in 1984, to become secondary dealers in government bonds. They have also sought new markets overseas, where they are in the vanguard of Japanese banking expansion.

Japanese city banks are among the strongest financial institutions in the world. Five of the leading six banks worldwide in 1985 were Japanese, and Dai-ichi Kangyo overtook Citicorp as the world's most asset-rich bank in 1986. This reflects the way the dynamism of the Japanese economy has been translated into the prosperity of its financial institutions.

City banks' assets 1985

	$bn
Dai-ichi Kangyo	166
Fuji Bank	146
Sumitomo Bank	141
Mitsubishi Bank	135
Sanwa Bank	130
Tokai Bank	94
Mitsui Bank	92
Bank of Tokyo	82
Taiyo Kobe Bank	78
Kyowa Bank	50

Source: Fortune International

Regional banks The 64 regional banks, with average assets of $7bn, have their headquarters in the major prefectural towns and cities. They have no separate legal status from city banks, to whom they are important suppliers of funds. They take short-term deposits, mainly from individuals, and finance local industry. Regional banks are responsible for 40% of local government finance and also provide fiscal services, disbursing subsidies and handling pensions. Some banks are involved in international expansion, particularly the largest, the Bank of Yokohama.

Trust banks The eight trust banks have total assets of $315bn; the largest of them, Mitsubushi Trust and Banking, accounts for $80bn. They undertake a wide range of asset management activities. Most importantly, they share with insurance companies a legal monopoly on the running of private pension funds, a huge growth area, worth $100bn a year. The trust banks also take part in regular lending and in real estate broking. They are funded by deposits, savings and the money markets. High asset management fees made them staid and complacent, and in 1985 the government allowed in five American and four European banks to act as trust banks. They are unlikely to make heavy inroads into this conservative sector, and in the meantime the Japanese hope to acquire from them the knowledge and technology to become expert asset managers.

Foreign banks In keeping with the new opportunities in the Japanese market, foreign financial groups have set up or extended their Japanese presence. More than 80 foreign banks are operating, with around 3% of the total market. A quarter of these are American, but the largest in terms of fund volume are French. Banque Nationale de Paris and Société Générale both exceed Citicorp, the largest US bank. These three are in a class of their own: in 1985 they held funds in Japan in excess of $6.5bn. Some way back are Crédit Lyonnais, Chase Manhattan and Bank of America.

Foreign banks are seeking footholds in corporate finance and fund management rather than retail banking; their special interest is in securities, the richest financial market in Japan. To bypass Article 65, foreign banks have taken advantage of an anomalous law which allows them to own up to 50% of a securities firm. Those without a banking licence in Japan could apply for a securities licence; UK merchant bankers S G Warburg followed this route. Citicorp, through its takeover of Vickers da Costa, now operates in Japan as a commercial bank, trust bank and securities dealer.

Japanese banks' envy is tempered by the reciprocity this gives them in foreign markets and by the thought that this may be the beginning of the end for Article 65.

Offshore banking The Japanese offshore banking market, open to all foreign exchange banks in Japan, began trading in December 1986. The main immediate benefit was to the regional banks, which can operate on an equal footing with the city banks for international syndication and bond issues. Despite gloomy predictions and, initially at least, no gold or securities being traded, the new banking market took off with a flourish.

Choosing a bank

Japanese banks have enormous amounts of cheap money at their disposal, and the desire to build long-term relationships with their clients makes them very competitive. They can usually offer cheaper loans than the local branches of the foreign banks, which they dwarf; and, of course, they fully understand the intricacies of the Japanese financial system. The banks often fulfil the advisory function that is the province of accountants in other countries.

Investment capital The long-term credit banks offer competitive rates for the financing of investment in Japan. It is also worthwhile consulting the regional banks in the area in which investment is planned, especially if your company is small or medium-sized. The regional banks are also the experts on local government grants and subsidies. If money is to be raised by a stock flotation, one of the Big Four securities companies should be approached (see *The markets*).

The markets

Financial deregulation has initially favoured the securities markets, and the top securities houses are at the forefront of Japanese finance. Bond markets are underdeveloped compared to the frenetic equity markets, but Japanese companies are very active in overseas bond markets.

Securities market

Strict separation between commercial banking and the securities business assisted four securities houses to become dominant in both broking and underwriting.

The houses The Big Four – Nomura Securities, Daiwa Securities, Nikko Securities and Yamaichi Securities – together account for 44% of equity-trading and 80% of bond-trading in Japan. Nomura is twice the size of the others, with shareholders' funds of well over $4bn and a market capitalization of over $35bn. Daiwa's strength is in its links with institutional investors. Nikko is strong in bonds, while Yamaichi's specialities are corporate finance, mergers and acquisitions.

In April 1985 security houses were allowed into lending, using local government bonds as collateral. At the same time they were freed to deal in certificates of deposit, foreign CDs and commercial paper.

Foreign entrants After pressure from overseas governments, several foreign brokers have been admitted to the Tokyo Stock Exchange; these include Goldman Sachs, Merrill Lynch and Morgan Stanley from the USA, Jardine Fleming of Hong Kong, and Vickers da Costa and S G Warburg from the UK.

The Japanese abroad The major securities houses have intensified their own overseas challenge. Nomura is well established in the USA and is active in the UK following deregulation in October 1986, while Daiwa is participating in the US trust business. Massive profits in their home markets mean that the Big Four can be very competitive in overseas money markets, such as the $400bn Eurobond market, risking losses to build market share.

Barred from setting up banking operations at home, the Big Four are setting them up overseas as part of their long-term strategy to become comprehensive global financial institutions. Nomura was the first to be granted a banking licence in the UK, and set up Nomura International Finance.

The stock market

The Tokyo Stock Exchange (TSE) is the second largest in the world in terms of total equity, nearly half the size of Wall Street. It is extremely active, however, with turnover rivalling that of New York.

Institutional stockholding Since the war, banks, life insurance companies and major non-financial companies have built up interlocking shareholdings. Japanese companies tend to hold on to shares long-term for capital appreciation and as a sign of the cooperative relationships between companies. This institutionalizes the market and minimizes takeovers.

At one time companies owned more than 60% of shares and accounted for just 10% of turnover. Since any stock must have a minimum annual turnover in order to be listed, companies simply swap portfolios, and many shares never come onto the open market. Individual shareholders are reasserting themselves but do not yet account for more than a quarter of total holdings.

Gains before dividends Trading on the Tokyo Stock Exchange is concerned with the making of tax-free capital gains rather than earning dividends. Yields can be lower than 1%. It is a gamblers' market, where the prices of shares bear only a passing resemblance to the economic fundamentals of a company.

Making a profit in capital gains involves moving in and out of shares quickly, and this explains the recent increase in turnover from 400m shares per day to over 2bn on some days in 1986. Ramping is endemic in the market. With such dedicated chasing, the market can get overheated, and collapses do happen. Such is the basic strength of the economy, however, that the market tends to bounce back.

Small shareholders One-sixth of the population have shareholdings, with an average portfolio size of Y5m. The current popularity of playing the market is largely the responsibility of the Big Four, whose 80,000 salesmen run hundreds of branch offices and sell door-to-door.

Commissions under fire Foreign brokers have had only a small impact on the Tokyo Stock Exchange. They are, however, inducing large Japanese life insurance houses to purchase Japanese equities in London or New York at negotiated commissions, thereby undercutting Tokyo's fixed rates (0.25–1.25%). This could put pressure on the TSE members to reduce their commissions, and the pressure will increase as the international 24-hour market develops, based on the golden triangle of Wall Street, London and Tokyo. Best estimates suggest a freeing of commissions sometime between 1988 and 1990.

Foreigners get listings In 1984 Sears Roebuck was the only foreign company with a listing on the TSE. Since then listings have proliferated. The companies involved are a diverse group, including Walt Disney Productions, Cable and Wireless and Compañía Telefónica Nacional de España. About one-third are banks.

A secure future? When Article 65 goes, the securities houses will face their biggest threat. The banks will move in, though whether via merger, acquisition, or head-on competition remains to be seen. It is widely rumoured that the Big Four have each set up mergers with major city banks should this happen.

Bond markets

Companies and successive Japanese governments have become major issuers on bond markets that were once dominated by the long-term credit banks. A medium-term government bond market was not introduced until 1980. The value of foreign bonds bought by Japanese investors rose from $12.5bn in 1983 to $53.5bn in 1985.

Samurai, sushi and shogun Strong growth has been seen in samurai and sushi bonds. The former are issued by foreign companies in yen on the Tokyo market, whereas the latter are issued by Japanese companies in dollars. Less popular are shogun bonds – dollar bonds issued by overseas companies on the Japanese market.

Yen Eurobonds Since 1984, foreign and Japanese companies have issued yen denomination bonds on the Euromarkets. Japanese securities houses dominate these issues with cut-price rates.

Commodities

Markets exist in a wide range of commodities. Tokyo's Commodity Exchange is the largest of 16, resulting from the 1984 merger of the Gold, Rubber and Textile Exchanges.

The future of futures Commodity futures have been slow to develop, due to lack of support from producers, importers and distributors. The bond futures market, introduced in 1985, got off to a chaotic start, due to a system limiting price movements in bond futures at a time when spot markets were moving rapidly. The plans are to develop these activities. By 1988, commodity options could be a reality. Trading in stock futures is planned from April 1987 on the large Osaka Securities Exchange.

Other sources of finance

Until fairly recently, there were few alternative sources of finance available to the overseas businessman in Japan. Recently this position has eased, as Japan has come to welcome foreign business.

Setting up a factory

Companies considering building a factory in Japan have a range of tax and financial incentives available that stand comparison with those of other industrial nations.

Labour subsidies In areas where employment prospects are poor, an employment promotion subsidy, averaging around $150 per person per month, is available for the first year. If employees are transferred, moving expenses are also subsidized.

Relocation subsidies Incoming companies and those already in Japan might consider moving to a designated industry induction area in order to obtain an industrial relocation promotion subsidy.

Cheap public money Low-cost loans for companies locating in the regions, or for ecologically beneficial factory improvements, are available from the government-run Japan Development Bank and Hokkaido-Tohoku Development Finance Public Corporation.

Tax reductions A number of tax incentives are available under various Regional Development Laws. At their best, these give incentives for relocation of business assets, special depreciation and reduction of local taxes – specifically reduction of enterprise tax, fixed asset tax, real property acquisition tax and special land-holding tax.

Technopolises Many of the prefectural and municipal authorities have schemes to attract industry. Most significant are the localities chosen by MITI as sites for the so-called Technopolis programme. By the 1990s, 19 high-technology towns, combining factories, universities and living quarters, will have been built.

Alternative finance

Venture capital is still fairly new in Japan. Efforts by MITI and others to establish a venture capital market on the US model are being hindered by the conservatism of the financial community; venture capital is unlikely to become a major force in Japan.

Government research programmes R&D funding is usually available only to Japanese companies. A few opportunities do exist, especially if the field of research is demonstrably of use to Japan. Foreign companies, however, may not wish to share the fruits of their research efforts with Japanese companies or agencies.

Some useful contacts

MITI Industrial Location Guidance Division, 1-3-1 Kasumigaseki, Chiyoda-ku, Tokyo ☎ (03) 501 0645.

Bank of Japan Exchange Control and Foreign Investment Division, 2-1-1 Nihonbashi-Hongokucho, Chuo-ku, Tokyo ☎ (03) 279 1111.

Center for Inducement of Industry to Rural Areas Senkoku Choson Kaikau, 1-11-35 Nagoda-cho, Chiyoda-ku, Tokyo ☎ (03) 580 1668.

Hokkaido-Tohoku Development Finance Public Corporation Koko Building, 1-9-3 Otemachi, Chiyoda-ku, Tokyo ☎ (03) 270 1651.

Japan Development Bank Planning Department Bureau for Regional Development, 1-9-1 Otemachi, Chiyoda-ku, Tokyo ☎ (03) 270 3211.

Japan Industrial Location Center 1-4-2 Toranomon, Minato-ku, Tokyo ☎ (03) 502 2361/2366.

Japan Regional Development Corporation Sales Promotion Division, Toranomon Mitsui Building, 3-8-1 Kasumigaseki, Chiyoda-ku, Tokyo ☎ (03) 501 5211.

Insurance

The changing structure of the market is transforming the static Japanese industry and bringing the insurance companies closer to the mainstream of the modern financial world.

Life insurance

Over 300m life insurance contracts are in force, an average of 2.5 policies per person with a per capita value of Y6.76m. Both per capita figures are the highest in the world. The total sum insured is more than Y800,000bn, equal to two-thirds of the US market and placing Japan firmly in second place.

The companies There are 23 life insurance companies with total assets of $250bn. Nippon Life Insurance dominates with about 25% of the market. Just over half its size are Dai-ichi Mutual and Sumitomo, followed some way behind by Meiji Mutual and Asahi Mutual.

Forces of change After more than 20 years of steady growth, the market is approaching saturation, with over 90% of Japanese families now having life insurance policies. This, coupled with the rapidly ageing population and financial deregulation, is forcing insurers to introduce new services and to improve their traditionally weak asset management. The main life insurance companies are setting up investment advisory businesses as a new source of profit.

Investment portfolios are moving away from a dependence on loans, which dropped to 43% of assets in 1985, although overseas loans are expanding. The share of securities is going up, with the fastest growth in government bonds and overseas securities. There is a legal ceiling of 10% of assets in foreign securities, and there is a strong lobby for this to be removed. Outside its ambit are sushi bonds (see *The markets*), which are popular among life insurance companies.

Annuity insurance Life insurance is a major form of saving, accounting for 18% of personal savings. Annuity insurance, benefiting from the inadequacies of the public pension scheme, is the leading form of life insurance. These schemes include sickness benefits. Some companies now offer regular three-yearly interest payments on lump-sum old age policies or, at a higher risk, profit participation by policyholders.

Non-life insurance

Japan is a low-risk society, and non-life insurance premiums are correspondingly low. As a result, the 23 casualty and liability companies have assets of just $60bn, a quarter of those held by the life companies. The largest non-life companies are Tokyo Marine and Fire, Yasuda Fire and Marine, Taisho Marine and Fire, Sumitomo Marine and Fire and Dai-Tokyo Fire and Marine.

Liquid assets The non-life insurers traditionally sell only one-year policies. They are excluded from managing pension funds – a strong profit centre for the life companies – and their assets tend to be concentrated in short-term investments providing high liquidity but at a level of risk most Western insurance companies would consider inadvisable.

Higher yields More professional asset management is the order of the day in the non-life companies. Annuity-type policies, combining conventional insurance cover with a strong savings element, were devised in the 1980s. These higher-yielding policies provide a refund at maturity, and now account for over one-third of the sector's total assets.

The earthquake risk A major earthquake is expected any year now, and this – especially if it directly affected Tokyo – would have a devastating effect on the insurers. The last big earthquake was in 1923 – the next one is due around 1990.

The law

The Western executive has to be aware of Japanese law and should take expert advice, but it is ultimately much more important to be familiar with Japanese attitudes to the law. The legal niceties will be taken care of but the success of an enterprise will depend on the will to cooperate and the ability to be flexible about legal detail, as opposed to the desire to gain ground.

The Japanese approach

All Japanese law is framed in written codes introduced in the 19th century. But this "dry" framework of law sits awkwardly on Japanese shoulders and the tendency is to take a more comfortable "wet" approach which enables legal relationships to be varied as circumstances change and which avoids conflict. Furthermore, except in new fields of law, the Japanese do not base legal decisions on precedents, preferring to treat each case as a new one, to be decided on its merits.

The courts

The American occupation of Japan resulted in the Constitution of 1947 which placed a Supreme Court at the apex of a pyramidal judiciary. A Chief Justice designated by the Cabinet and appointed by the Emperor presides. The Cabinet also appoints the other 14 Justices of the Supreme Court, which in its turn nominates the list from which are chosen the lower court judges. All judges are appointed on ten-year engagements, and they can be removed prematurely from office only by public impeachment.

Beneath the Supreme Court are eight High Courts, and the district courts, one for each of the 46 prefectures except Hokkaido, which has four. The bottom layer of the pyramid consists of a large number of family courts, specializing in domestic and juvenile cases, and summary courts that handle certain claims of less than Y900,000.

Litigation

Wherever possible, disputes are settled without recourse to the courts. This is because a lawsuit results in a decision which can be construed as penalizing one or other of the parties involved. The penalized party loses face, and so does the other party for causing the penalty to be enacted. No-one escapes the dishonour.

With only 150 lawsuits per 100,000 people each year, Japan is far less litigious than the USA or the UK. The British bring over three times as many cases and the Americans ten times as many.

Procedure and style There are 2,800 judges in the country. They operate with a lack of courtroom fireworks which owes something to the fact that there are no juries, the jury system having been abandoned after World War II. Details of cases are often thrashed out in chambers, specifically to avoid courtroom surprises. There are no class action suits but a representative party may be appointed for cases involving numerous parties, such as pollution litigation.

Mediation Many cases are subject to forms of mediation, which may replace or complement court proceedings. Arbitration (*chusai*) is an alternative to litigation. However, conciliation (*chotei*) is a preliminary part of litigation, and compromise (*wakai*) may take place either prior to or during litigation. Mediation may take place in or out of court and can be handled by quasi-legal professionals skilled in fields such as contracts, patents or tax law. Their findings are often legally enforceable.

The profession

Prospective Japanese lawyers must either be graduates or must pass a preliminary examination before taking the bar examination. This demanding examination requires mastery of 1,000 civil code laws and a great deal of archaic specialist legal terminology. Of those that sit the bar examination 2% pass and enter the Legal Training and Research Institute of the Supreme Court for a two-year professional training course. Most complete this, and some 80% choose to become attorneys (*bengoshi*), the others opting to become assistant judges or prosecutors.

Status The social status of lawyers is high, because they are seen as protectors of the vulnerable, and because their book learning is considerable. Their financial rewards are high and are equivalent to those of doctors.

Numbers There are comparatively few lawyers, due to the prohibitively difficult qualification demands, and the low level of Japanese litigation. With some 13,000 lawyers in private practice, Japan has approximately one for every 9,000 people. In the USA there is at least one attorney for every 400 citizens.

Working practices The qualified lawyer wishing to work as an attorney is most likely to be self-employed, either working as an individual, or joining a law associate practice with other self-employed lawyers. Only about ten attorneys have permission from their local bar association to work as in-house counsel but many attorneys serve as outside counsel to corporate clients. Corporate legal departments are rare, and usually staffed by unqualified graduates.

A large amount of the spadework carried out by qualified lawyers in the West, is undertaken in Japan by some 90,000 legal workers who have not passed through final training, although they may have law degrees.

Specialization Within the law associate practices, individual lawyers may specialize in certain legal sectors such as labour or criminal law. Patent law, in particular, is usually dealt with in specialist practices, as is international business law, but to a lesser degree.

Complaints The profession is regulated by the Japan Federation of Bar Associations (*Nichibenren*) and by local bar associations which consider (free of charge) complaints from clients on such matters as negligent advice.

Costs Litigation in Japan is both extremely expensive and extremely time consuming. A judgement may be reached within a year but an appeal would extend the process to three or four years and exceptionally up to ten years. Bringing a civil damage suit requires payment of a court fee, and the losing party must usually bear additional court costs; each party must pay its own lawyer's fees. In domestic litigation lawyers usually charge on a lump sum or contingency basis but in commercial cases an hourly fee (Y10,000–40,000) is common. Fees for leading Japanese law firms in Tokyo are midway between top London and New York rates.

Contracts

One of the greatest problems for the Western businessman approaching Japan is the status of the business contract. Where the Westerner's final goal in negotiations is often the watertight contract, the Japanese businessman places little confidence in contracts as guarantees of business relationships, preferring to see how cooperative ventures develop. The Japanese contract is deliberately vague, and often no longer than a single page. Large companies, like Sony, like to boast of the millions of dollars' worth of business they have carried out in the past without any written contracts at all.

Flexibility Though more common these days, contracts are still not viewed as a serious restriction on freedom of action. Flexible terms are preferable to what could, in changing circumstances, become punitive formulae. In this situation the Japanese will renegotiate rather than feel tied. This cuts both ways, of course, and once ties have been forged you can claim the same sort of room to manoeuvre.

Softly, softly... The contract is unavoidable in the modern business context, but Westerners need to understand the Japanese position if collaboration is to be successful. Insistence on watertight terms couched in obscure legal jargon will deter potential partners.

Jurisdiction International financial contracts are traditionally negotiated under English or New York law. With commercial contracts it generally depends who initiates them: a joint venture or licensing agreement initiated by a foreign firm will usually fall under the law of their country or state. If you are dealing with a Japanese firm that has no international assets it is wise to negotiate under Japanese law as there are no reciprocal enforcement treaties between Japan and other countries. However, a contract can provide for both a choice of law and a choice of jurisdiction. Also, it may be possible to obtain a guarantee under your own law from the Japanese firm's bank or an associated company.

Aspects of business law

Statutes covering business are comprehensive, and Japanese courts have a reputation for integrity and for enforcing individual rights. See *Government and business* for details of the Fair Trade Commission and anti-monopoly legislation; see *Employment* for relevant labour law.

Industrial property rights Japanese law specifically protects four kinds of industrial property rights: patent, utility model, design and trademark.

Patents are granted for new and highly developed industrial inventions which have not had any public airing in Japan, or written publicity in Japan or abroad. Uniqueness and technical sophistication are stressed in patent requirements.

Utility models are defined as "technical ideas by which a law of nature is utilized" and may relate to design or construction methods. They are easier to register than patents, and unsuccessful patent applications can be adapted to utility model applications within three months of the patent application failure.

Design applications seek registration of "the shape, pattern or colour or combination thereof of an article" and are only successful where the design is new and unpublished worldwide.

Trademark restrictions are long and complex, and set out in the Trademark Law. Trademarks and trade names should be registered as early as possible, by the exporter rather than his Japanese agent, who would technically retain control otherwise.

Registration of all categories of industrial property should be carried out through a specialist Japanese patent attorney. All documentation is in Japanese.

Consumer laws Western businessmen hoping to operate within Japan need to be aware of the rigorous legal standards now applicable through consumer protection and anti-pollution laws.

The Consumer Products Safety Law of 1973 covers safety standards, inspection requirements, product recall, registration of manufacturers and the approval of model specification. It also provides for compensation to be paid to consumers injured by defective goods. Legislation on these matters is constantly being updated, and judgements on compensation can be extremely harsh against erring companies.

Confidentiality is a problem during business negotiations, as protection against disclosure is vague and limited, and at an early stage Japanese negotiators expect to discuss far more detailed technical and cost information than would be common in the West. There is provision for non-disclosure in agreements with employees, though it is not unknown for '*sokaiya*' extortionists to infiltrate companies in order to gain information which they can then threaten to reveal unless payment is made.

Using a lawyer

For any matter under Japanese jurisdiction it is obligatory to use a lawyer qualified at the Japanese bar. With the exception of a few Americans, who set up before restrictions on foreigners were imposed in 1955, this will be a Japanese lawyer. Some 500 Japanese lawyers have studied and practised abroad, many in the USA, and several are members of the English bar.

Under new legislation scheduled to come into force on April 1 1987 (it is dependent on US reciprocation), foreign law firms will be opening offices in Japan. They will, however, be restricted to advising on their own national law or, with permission, the law of other overseas countries, but not that of Japan. The international firms, many of which will be associates or partners of Japanese law firms, will have liaison lawyers able to brief Japanese lawyers and work in conjunction with them on translating paperwork. The regularly updated, 8-volume *Doing Business in Japan*, published by Matthew Bender, is a legal reference work for the executive, with translations of relevant laws and an informative commentary, but should be used with care.

In business negotiations the use of a Japanese lawyer will reassure prospective partners, where the introduction of Western legal advisers might be seen as a poor indication of future cooperation.

Selecting a lawyer Those expecting to use legal services in Japan should consult international law firms and their own bar association before departure. These will be able to make recommendations, but consult your embassy and chamber of commerce in Japan who will be more familiar with the relative competence and alacrity of individual Japanese law firms. Having short-listed firms, visit each to gain a first impression.

The language barrier is a major impediment to consistently high quality legal advice. For foreign companies the best sort of Japanese law firm is one that is in partnership with an international law firm or one that employs foreign legal assistants who are relatively fluent in Japanese. These assistants often act as go-betweens and may actually conduct the bulk of a foreign client's business. However, the relationship requires tact, and foreign clients should show deference to their Japanese lawyers in personal conferences and should address correspondence to them with a copy to the assistant.

Local offices of *Nichibenren* will also recommend law firms. Contact: *Nichibenren* 1-1-1 Kasumigaseki, Chiyoda-ku, Tokyo 100 ☎ (03) 580-9841.

Patent attorneys

These are Tokyo firms experienced in handling foreign business.

Asamura Patent Office Room 331 New Otemachi Building, 2-1 Otemachi 2-chome, Chiyoda-ku, Tokyo ☎ (03) 211 3651.

Nakamura, Yamamoto, Takeda and Partners Shin Tokyo Building, 3-1 Marunouchi 3-chome, Chiyoda-ku, Tokyo ☎ (03) 211 8741/5.

Sugimura International Patent and Trademark Agency Bureau 7th Floor, Kazan Building, 2-4 Kasumigaseki, Chiyoda-ku, Tokyo ☎ (03) 581 2241.

Tokyo Aoyama Law Office 4th Floor, Room 410 Aoyama Building, 2-3 Kita Aoyama 1-chome, Minato-ku, Tokyo ☎ (03) 403 5281. Partners: Baker & McKenzie.

(See also *Top law firms.*)

Top law firms

These are firms experienced in handling foreign business, arranged alphabetically by cities. Japanese law firms are not permitted to have branch offices and it is therefore necessary to deal with a different firm in each city.

Minoru-Shimizu Ueno Building, 9-15 Daimyo 2-chome, Chuo-ku, Fukuoka ☎ (092) 741 2951.

Kunio Kono 4-30 Kamihatchobori, Hiroshima-shi, Hiroshima ☎ (082) 221 3766.

John J. Gentilellia Jarvis Building, 75 Kiyomachi, Chuo-ku, Kobe ☎ (078) 331 7810/2911.

Akira Kobayashi Room 206 Sky Mansion, 561-4 Komano-cho, Nakamichi-sagaru, Marutamachi-dori, Kamigyo-ku, Kyoto ☎ (075) 256 0715.

Idokawa Hayashi Law Office 8th Floor, Keihan Yodabashi Building, 3-6 Kitahama, Higashi-ku, Osaka ☎ (06) 203 7112.

Adachi, Henderson, Miyatake and Fujita 10th Floor, Time Life Building, 3-6 Otemachi 2-chome, Chiyoda-ku, Tokyo ☎ (03) 270 7461 (member of English bar).

Anderson, Mori and Rabinowitz 6th Floor, AIU Building, 1-3 Marunouchi 1-chome, Chiyoda-ku, Tokyo ☎ (03) 214 1371.

Braun Moriya, Hoashi and Kubota Room 911 Iino Building, 1-1 Uchisaiwai-cho 2-chome, Chiyoda-ku, Tokyo ☎ (03) 504 0251 (member of English bar).

Nakagawa Godo Law Office, 6th Floor, Akasaka Nakagawa Building, 11-3 Akasaka 3-chome, Minato-ku, Tokyo ☎ (03) 589 2921. Associates: Clifford-Turner.

Tokyo Aoyama Law Office 4th Floor, Room 410 Aoyama Building, 2-3 Kita Aoyama 1-chome, Minato-ku, Tokyo ☎ (03) 403 5281. Partners: Baker & McKenzie. Note: This firm is also a leader in the field of Japanese industrial property rights.

Top audit corporations

The following list gives the largest internationally affiliated companies, ranked by number of partners.

Showa Ota Hibiya Kokusai Building, 2-2-3 Uchisaiwai-cho, Chiyoda-ku, Tokyo 100. Regional offices: Fukuoka, Hokoriku, Kansai, Nagoya, Naha, Niigata, Sapporo, Sendai. 169 partners. Affiliates: Ernst & Whinney International.

Chuo Audit Corporation Kasumigaseki Building 32F, 2-5 Kasumigaseki 3-chome, Chiyoda-ku, Tokyo 100. Regional offices: Fukuoka, Hiroshima, Kyoto, Nagoya, Osaka, Yokohama. Over 150 partners. Affiliates: Coopers & Lybrand International.

Tohmatsu, Awoki & Sanwa Toranomon-Kotohira-Kaikan, 2-8 Toranomon 1-chome, Minato-ku, Tokyo 105. Regional offices: Fukuoka, Hiroshima, Kobe, Kyoto, Nagoya, Naha, Osaka, Sapporo, Sendai, Takamatsu. 141 partners. Affiliates: Touche Ross International.

Asahi Shinwa Nihon Jisho Daiichi Building, 13-5, 1-chome, Kudankita, Chiyoda-ku, Tokyo 102. Regional offices: Hiroshima, Kanazawa, Kobe, Kyoto, Nagoya, Oita, Osaka, Sapporo, Sendai, Takasaki, Tokuyama, Wakayama, Yonago. 133 partners. Affiliates: Arthur Young International, Grant Thornton International, Binder, Dijker Otte.

Century Audit Corporation Asahi Building, 3-12-2 Nihonbashi, Chuo-ku, Tokyo 103. Regional offices: Chiba, Fukuoka, Kobe, Kyoto, Matsue, Nagoya, Osaka, Sapporo, Sendai. 118 partners. Affiliates: Peat Marwick International, Moore Stephens.

Shinko Audit Corporation Shin-Aoyama Building Twin-West, 20th Floor, 1-1 Minami-Aoyama 1-chome, Minato-ku, Tokyo 107. Regional offices: Kumamoto, Nagoya, Osaka, Yokohama. 69 partners. Affiliates: Price Waterhouse International.

Accountants

Accountancy as a profession is still in its infancy in Japan. Though attitudes are changing, it is still regarded as something of a Western obsession. The country's position as the world's largest net creditor and the home of many multinationals has required the adoption of Western standards but the profession has yet to mature to self-sufficiency.

Beginnings

In 1948 the Ministry of Finance established the Japanese Institute of Certified Public Accountants (JICPA) on the American model. JICPA was made responsible for issuing guidelines on acceptable accounting practices. Auditing began in the 1950s, though at a low technical level. Certified Public Accountants (CPAs) worked on an individual basis until 1966 when the law was changed to permit the formation of audit corporations (*kansa hojin*), the Japanese equivalent of the Western accounting partnership.

Company framework

International accountancy firms established themselves in Japan in the 1960s, as emergent Japanese industry sought overseas finance. The new domestic audit corporations sought affiliation with these major accounting groups. Few audit corporations have developed their internal capacity to meet international reporting requirements; most perform domestic audits while their international affiliates maintain essentially separate offices for international business. A continuing wave of mergers is creating larger audit corporations, some affiliated with two or three international accountancy firms.

The profession

To qualify as a CPA a candidate must pass a series of three examinations, followed by three years in an audit corporation or with an individual CPA. Standards are rigorous, with pass rates as low as 10–20%. There are currently some 8,000–9,000 qualified CPAs in Japan.

Regulation The government is the major influence on financial reporting. The Commercial Code, operated by the Ministry of Justice, covers all Japanese companies. The Code places stress on the protection of creditors, putting more emphasis on balance sheet strength than on measurement of income. The Securities and Exchange laws, operated by the Ministry of Finance, apply only to the 2,800 or so publicly traded companies. An advisory body, the Business Accounting Deliberation Council (BADC), prepares a set of accounting and auditing principles for all publicly traded companies.

Status Accountancy is a low-status profession in Japan compared with the West and it is rare for the financial managers of Japanese companies to be members of JICPA.

Activities are generally restricted to auditing, bookkeeping and taxation work. Insolvency is the prerogative of the legal profession. Bankers traditionally fill the management consultancy role, though the international accountancy firms are trying to raise their profile as consultants in Japan.

Audits

Business in Japan tends to be debt-financed rather than equity-financed, so the auditor's usual role of protector of the shareholders' interests is not so important.

The statutory examiner The Commercial Code requires that the financial statements of all companies must be reported on by a statutory examiner (*kansayaku*). His brief is to audit the performance of the directors rather than the financial condition of the company. In larger companies the *kansayaku* has to be, or be assisted by, a CPA. Only in the publicly traded companies is there a legal requirement for an audit by an independent CPA or audit corporation.

A different approach While Western multinationals see auditing as a central management tool and employ one firm worldwide, Japanese multinationals tend to leave the choice of accountants for their overseas operations in the hands of local management.

Audit standards are not so rigorous as in the West, and audits are often done very quickly. The quality of auditing in Japan has recently been brought into focus by the collapse of large companies such as Sanko Shipping and Ozawa Trading. It is unheard of for an audit corporation to be sued on the collapse of one of its clients.

Fraud Large-scale fraud is rare and embezzlement is often handled in-house. To save company face, offenders may be pensioned off or moved to another job rather than fired or prosecuted.

Company reports

Company reports of the major companies are usually available in English and Japanese versions. The English versions are drawn up in formats that will be familiar to most Westerners.

Tax laws There is a tendency for accounts to be kept in line with Japan's complex tax laws, sometimes at the expense of giving a true picture of the underlying commercial realities. For example, the tax laws permit only a certain percentage of outstanding debts to be written off as bad debts in each year. The auditor, rather than examining the possibility of each debt being paid, will simply record the permitted percentage. The same principle applies to depreciation of assets, amortization, and profit from instalment sales. In recent years a shift has begun towards reporting based on commercial actualities rather than the maximization of tax benefits.

The almighty tax inspector

Company bookkeepers are trained in-house and have very high standards of efficiency. The critical test of their efficiency is not, however, the twice-yearly audit – most Japanese companies work on a financial year beginning on the first of April – but the enormously thorough tax inspections every two or three years. There is a large tax bureaucracy in Japan and it descends in force for an inspection, which may last for weeks and even months. The tax inspectors have a fixed budget of extra tax to find, and they will stay until they find it. Company bookkeepers will leave errors for them to find.

Using audit corporations

The largest audit corporations (for addresses see page 67) all have international affiliates, staffed by expatriate accountants familiar with the Japanese business scene. Some will be Japanese speakers.

Services for the visitor Audit corporations or their international affiliates can provide the visiting executive with valuable introductions and advice. Local branches of international accountancy firms can usefully be consulted before you set out for Japan. When in Japan, Japanese or expatriate staff may join you at meetings to help with discussions, give advice and interpret the mood of the meeting.

Setting up in Japan An accountant is indispensable. Apart from offering advice on legal matters and taxation, they can help find offices and are essential for dealing with Japanese red tape. International affiliates will provide a Western audit as a management tool.

Fees Statutory audits are carried out for a fixed fee based on a percentage of assets. Fees for other services are high to cover the cost of maintaining the necessary expatriate staff.

Advertising

The larger Japanese advertising agencies wield considerable power in a highly concentrated industry. The top ones are aiming to take a strong hold over the new media to maintain their dominance. Extremely conservative and domestically oriented, Japanese agencies have belatedly arranged tie-ups with Western agencies to wrest back some of the overseas business that Japanese companies have been placing abroad. Public relations is not traditionally allied to advertising in Japan and is relatively under developed, but it is likely to grow.

The advertising agencies

The Japanese advertising scene is dominated by Dentsu Inc, which is majority-owned by the Kyodo News Service. With 1985 sales of $5.5bn (over a quarter of total Japanese advertising expenditure), it continues to strengthen its position. Its supremacy in the domestic market – the second largest market after the USA – makes it the world's largest ad agency in terms of billing.

Why Dentsu? Dentsu was one of the first agencies to recognize the importance of television. It arranged finance for these new television ventures, in some cases taking a share of the stations concerned and even supplying staff to manage them. This gave Dentsu access to large blocks of prime TV advertising time, forcing the large Japanese companies to use Dentsu. As television grew in importance, so did Dentsu.

Number two The next largest agency, Hakuhodo, is only just over a third of Dentsu's size, with 1985 sales of over $2bn, representing 11% of total Japanese advertising expenditure.

The rest Apart from these two, Japanese advertising agencies are minnows. The combined market share of numbers three to ten in the market is still only two-thirds that of Dentsu. The remaining agencies handle 43% of the market, a share that is continuing to decline as the larger agencies go from strength to strength.

Development of an industry

Modern advertising in Japan dates from the introduction of commercial radio in 1951 and commercial television in 1953.

Radio's decline From a high point of attracting over 17% of total advertising revenue in 1956, radio has steadily lost ground to television as an advertising medium. The opening of new FM stations is providing some opportunities, especially for reaching young audiences in the cities, but radio can never regain its previous importance.

TV's rise Television's impact was immediate, and by 1959 it was the second largest advertising medium; it achieved first place in 1975. There are now more than 100 VHF and UHF commercial stations operating. The major national commercial networks are Nihon TV (NTV), Tokyo Broadcasting Service (TBS), Fuji TV and Asahi TV.

The main outlets Total advertising expenditure in Japan is now over $20bn. Television takes a sizeable 35%. Newspapers are second with under 30%; direct mail and outdoor advertising have 22%, with magazines and radio a long way behind.

The clients

Advertising in Japan is very much a seller's market. Faced with a few agencies controlling advertising space, Japanese companies usually find themselves using the same agencies that their competitors use. The large agencies ostensibly protect clients' interests by placing competing accounts in separate divisions.

Major sectors With the market for

many highly advertised consumer durables now saturated, other sectors are receiving a larger share of advertising revenue. In terms of total advertising expenditure, food and beverages still take the largest share with just under 20%, but this is declining. Other major sectors include services and amusements with 10%, wholesale and department stores with 7%, and automobiles and motorcycles with around 6.5%. Advertising by foreign companies in Japan is also increasing.

Costs For one of the 15-second commercial slots on television a company will have to pay over $3,500. Given the size of the audience, this is considerably cheaper than the almost $70,000 for a full page or $11,500 for 13 column centimetres in the *Nihon Keizai Shimbun.*

Style

Japanese advertising takes a much softer approach than the hard sell of many American and European advertisements. This is beginning to change as consumers – especially the young – become more cynical about traditional Japanese advertising.

American influences American lifestyles and characters are entering Japanese advertisements – as in the representation of a young California lifestyle in some of Suntory's advertisements. Animations based on films such as *Rocky* or on Walt Disney characters are popular. Dai-ichi Mutual Life, for example, is using Disney characters for selling insurance products.

Comparative advertising has also crossed the Pacific. Despite complaints by foreign importers, the Fair Trade Commission has ruled comparative advertising to be perfectly legal.

Sponsorship Sport and cultural sponsorship are increasing in importance. Mazda, for example, sponsored 55 top track and field athletes in 1986; Toyota is a major sponsor of tennis, and Nissan of Japanese baseball. Toshiba has donated almost $500,000 to the Victoria and Albert Museum in London towards a new gallery to display its Japanese collection.

The female touch In a male-oriented industry, Dentsu has taken the unusual step of setting up a female-staffed subsidiary, Dentsu Eye, to handle female-oriented advertising for cosmetics and similar products.

New directions

Sluggish growth in conventional advertising expenditure is inducing agencies to look for new fields.

Direct marketing This was slow to develop in Japan but is catching on, with the advertising agencies taking a prominent role, often through links with US direct marketing firms. Dentsu and Dai-ichi Kikaku both have such tie-ups.

Cable To maintain their control over advertising space in the new media, both Dentsu and Hakuhodo have established cable networks. They are also involved in the supply of programming to these new networks. However, cable TV is developing only slowly and is not yet widespread.

Expansion overseas Japanese ad agencies rely almost exclusively on their domestic markets. With the rapid internationalization of Japanese business, this has been a major opportunity lost – Japanese companies place more than $1.5bn of advertising overseas each year.

Some of the Japanese agencies are now trying to capture this overseas Japanese business through tie-ups, especially with US firms. Dentsu has formed a number of joint ventures with Young & Rubicam, while Hakuhodo has ties with the Interpublic Group companies – a joint venture with McCann-Erickson Worldwide and links with SSC&B Lintas Worldwide. These arrangements also assist the US partners to enter the Japanese market, albeit in a small way.

Market entry

In the initial postwar period of industrial expansion, the Japanese economy was heavily protected by exchange controls, import quotas and high tariffs. Would-be exporters found it one of the toughest markets in the world to crack. In the last few years, many of these formalized barriers to trade have been removed as the Japanese have responded to pressure from their major trading partners to reduce Japan's huge visible trade surplus; the Japanese take the protectionist threat to their own exports very seriously. Since the G5 Plaza agreement in 1985 the value of the yen against the dollar has soared, improving the terms of trade by more than 30% – although this is somewhat offset by a very low level of inflation in Japan and a marked consumer preference for home-produced goods. The new, advantageous terms of trade and the liberalization of controls on imports make exporting to Japan less difficult than it has been, but some barriers, cultural and economic, remain.

Barriers and openings

No fewer than seven packages of measures aimed at promoting imports have been introduced in Japan since 1981. These have reduced average industrial tariffs to below Western levels and overhauled testing and certification standards that worked against imports. The most recent package, a three-year action programme introduced in 1985, was typical. It reduced or abolished numerous tariffs, increased acceptance of foreign test data to replace time-consuming and costly testing in Japan, relaxed importation standards and certification procedures, and introduced further low-cost financing of imports.

Direct foreign investment began to be liberalized in the early 1970s. Exchange controls were removed in 1980, the same year that foreign firms were finally allowed to use the JIS (Japan Industrial Standard) mark on their products. Further financial liberalization, initiated in 1984, is proceeding slowly but surely to expose the soft underbelly of the economy, its vast potential for financial services.

Import quotas have largely disappeared. Those that remain are concentrated in the politically sensitive agricultural sector – the ruling LDP is heavily dependent on the farming vote. Beef, citrus fruits and juices are among the products affected. Not all quota levels are published.

The average tariff is just over 3%, and Japan is committed to achieving zero duties on industrial imports. A small number of industries are still protected by high tariffs. Among these are leather footwear (as much as 60%), confectionery and biscuits. Some products designated as luxuries attract a commodity tax of 5–30%.

Technical standards and certification procedures are in many instances unique to Japan, and have formed a barrier to trade in the past. Generally accepted international standards do not necessarily apply; foreign laboratory data and quality certificates are not always accepted. The time and money involved in setting up a Japanese test may prove prohibitive. Rather than maintain a list of banned products, the Japanese policy is one of "positive listing"; only those items listed are allowed in. Finding out why a product is not listed can be difficult, and altering the situation more difficult still.

Japanese government tenders may carry qualification conditions and deadlines that effectively exclude the foreign bidder.

Customs procedures can be over-elaborate, time-consuming and tedious. Variations in interpretation of the customs regulations can be found at different ports.

The Office of Trade Ombudsman investigates complaints of discrimination against imported products in favour of domestic ones. It can claim reasonable success in the clearing up of misunderstandings, but has yet to totally convince Western businessmen of its effectiveness. Cases may also be submitted to your Trade/Commerce Department at home, your embassy in Japan, or to any JETRO office.

Invisible barriers Despite liberalization of trade and the government-sponsored import promotions, some features of the Japanese economy still militate against the exporter. The days of protectionism have left Japanese consumers with an underdeveloped appetite for imported manufactures. The Japanese consumer manufacturing sector is highly efficient and competitive; a premium is placed on design innovation and rapid product development. This leads to a short product life and requires the exporter to be more in touch with Japanese markets than might be necessary elsewhere. The Japanese distribution system (see *Distribution*) is complex; it inflates retail prices and tends to confine foreign goods to the major big-city outlets.

The way in

Japan is a special market. It is not for novices – successful experience in other export markets is a must if simple mistakes are to be avoided. It is important for the would-be exporter to adapt his approach to suit a unique trading environment and to take the time necessary to develop a successful business relationship with the Japanese. Preplanning is of the essence.

Research is vital. You need to establish market potential and the best means of market entry. Check whether product modifications have to be made to meet exacting Japanese technical standards and increasingly individualized tastes. Market research should locate the best channels for distribution, and care should be taken to select the best segment in a market where positioning and image are all-important.

A niche market Mass marketing is not really an option. Japanese consumers are most particular about what they buy. Buying is not just about design, quality and price, but about lifestyle. Japan is a niche market where imported products fill gaps rather than set trends. For all their efficiency, the Japanese are not leaders in everything. They have weaknesses, for example in technology. But they are quick to recognize these and to put considerable resources into catching up. If you think you are ahead of the game, watch out for the competition.

Filling that gap Once the exporter has identified a gap in the market, he must be sure that he is able to commit adequate time and resources to the gradual building-up of market share. The whole approach should be geared to becoming established in the market and then staying there. Diligence and persistence are qualities much admired in Japan and will gain you respect.

Food for thought The Japanese often genuinely believe that their products are superior, and frequently they may be right. Justified or not, the most commonly voiced complaints by Japanese consumers about imported goods are: that prices are too high compared with domestic products; that the goods are not adapted to local tastes in their marketing, packaging and contents; that there is insufficient after-sales service; that instructions in Japanese are inadequate, or lacking completely; and that the goods are inadequately stocked.

Entry options There are many ways to get a foothold in the Japanese market apart from direct export to a retail, wholesale or industrial customer. Sales can be made through a Japanese general trading company or a specialist importer. Goods can be shipped in bulk for packaging and/or assembly in Japan, or manufactured there under licence – in this case you should make sure that your industrial property rights are fully protected. Other possibilities are joint ventures or the setting up of a representative office (see *The business framework*) to establish a "face" in the market. Expatriate staff should be committed to the market long-term, receive language training and have full support and commitment from their home office.

Two fundamentals should be borne in mind when dealing with the Japanese: the importance of personal relationships and the extended time-scale in which business is conducted. The Japanese are interested in the person with whom they are dealing. They will judge his company and his product by the way he conducts himself. An open and co-operative nature will count for more than a slick sales presentation. An aggressive and impatient manner will not win friends. The building of relationships contributes to the length of time it takes for things to happen. The Japanese will want to be convinced of your long-term commitment to the relationship before becoming involved; they cannot be hurried.

Japan is perhaps the most competitive market in the world and one of the most affluent. It requires wholehearted commitment and considerable patience. Potential exporters should be sufficiently financially secure to carry the burden of non-profit involvement for some years rather than months.

Getting to know the market

Complex and daunting though the market may be, copious advice, information and assistance are available from various sources. At home, government Trade, Industry and Commerce Departments will have Japan desks. Some capital cities have Japan Associations, formed by businessmen who deal regularly with Japan – they are a good source of contacts. In Japan, your embassy's official commercial section or trade centre will be a source of information, as will Japanese and overseas chambers of commerce.

JETRO, the Japan External Trade Organization, now concentrates heavily on the promotion of imports into Japan, due to pressure from overseas. It has 30 offices in Japan and 76 overseas and can provide advice, market information and other forms of assistance. It also maintains specialist libraries and data banks and is the source of an unquenchable optimism about the market. JETRO head office is at 2-2-5 Toranomon 2-chome, Minato-ku, Tokyo 107.

General trading companies There are 13 such companies, known as *sogo shosha*. The nine largest handle about half of Japan's total trade. They dominate commodity and capital goods imports into Japan, and are particularly interested in high-volume, high-value trade. All offer market intelligence based on worldwide local office networks.

Specialized traders, (*senmon shosha*) who number 8,000, are smaller than the *sogo shosha*, and specialize in particular product areas; they, too, have deep market knowledge in their fields.

Nissho, the Japanese Chamber of Commerce and Industry, represents 1.2m businessmen in Japan and has overseas representation and ties with local chambers of commerce.

Japanese embassies, though principally concerned with trade policy, sometimes have attached to them officials from *Keidanren*, an employers' organization which represents more than 1,000 Japanese industrial associations (see *Power in business*).

Distribution

Japan's distribution system is notorious for its complexity and, by Western standards, inefficiency. Despite some recent streamlining it is likely to remain so for the forseeable future.

Coping with the system

The distribution set-up is a multi-stage one with up to three levels of wholesaling to service the small stores that predominate in Japanese retailing. Dealing directly with the distribution network is nearly impossible for the prospective exporter because of the importance of inside knowledge and personal connections. The key to success is a good agent.

He may not be the wholesaler or distributor himself but will handle importation and will set up marketing and distribution. He will aim to build up sales over a long period to establish and maintain a satisfactory market share. To do this he will need support and the exporter must be prepared to make regular visits to the market, changes to the product and/or its packaging or presentation and contributions to advertising and other expenses.

Retail outlets Department stores are the major force in the distribution of top quality products, accounting for an estimated 50% of all sales of imported consumer goods. However, they are in a position to pick and choose and to drop less successful products at will and, with relatively few branches, they may not produce sufficient volume business in the long run. Your best policy may be to deal with them through a wider ranging agent.

Chains of speciality shops may provide the best route. However, while it is sometimes possible to service a department store adequately, it is effectively impossible to do the same for numerous speciality stores, and you may need to warehouse in Japan. Once again, a local agent may be the answer.

Industrial goods The distribution chain for industrial and capital goods is likely to be shorter but the technical support required becomes a major consideration. Ensure that your agent has the technical ability to do the best job.

The agents The major importers who will act as agents are the huge general trading companies (*sogo shosha*), such as Mitsubishi and Mitsui, who handle an enormous range of products and have offices worldwide. Below them are numerous smaller trading companies and specialist importers. Both have representatives in major centres abroad, and may well have the right strengths and connections for your product.

Choosing the right agent may take a year or more of thorough research, correspondence and discussions at home before meeting a few potential agents in Japan to ascertain exactly where their distribution channels lead. At the start it is worth getting both a broad overview and recommendations from organizations such as JETRO, the Japanese Chamber of Commerce and Industry, international banks and relevant government departments. Your embassy in Tokyo can give specific advice on the Japanese market, and institute inquiries to identify suitable agents or distributors. Dodwell Marketing Consultants' *Retail Distribution in Japan* is an invaluable guide to the retail network.

Talk to a range of agents from the giants down to the small specialist. In order to maintain confidence it is often unwise to negotiate with several agents simultaneously – news can travel fast. Changing agents in Japan can be extremely difficult, so it is essential to make the right appointment the first time.

Business awareness

Business in Japan is as much about building human relationships as negotiating contracts. Many Westerners find dealing with the Japanese a unique and difficult experience because, despite government efforts at internationalization, Japan remains an insular society, psychologically open to new techniques but sociologically closed.

The main difficulty that outsiders from both the West and East face is the very fact that they are outsiders, or *gaijin.* The trick of succeeding in business is not to become an insider – that is an impossibility – but to prove you are a reliable person. The Japanese are intensely loyal to existing suppliers – because they know and trust them – and, as a newcomer, your first step must be to build an atmosphere of trust and friendliness. Personal rapport is the *sine qua non.*

The Japanese at work

The Japanese are generally regarded as workaholics. There is an element of truth in this. Workers put in on average 2,110 hours per year, about 500 more than their West German counterparts and about 200 hours more than US workers.

But do they actually work harder? In a sense they do: their commitment to the company is greater. In the corporate sector, particularly, the job comes first, ahead of family, holidays and other commitments. On the other hand, they generally work less hard during the course of the day – notably in offices – and their productivity, by Western standards, is lower. Manufacturing productivity still lags behind the West in many areas and has only recently overtaken the USA in certain industries, largely due to high investment in new technology.

The working week The norm is still a five-and-a-half-day week, though the trend, particularly among large firms, is towards a five-day week. In small businesses managers may get a two-day weekend (a "thinking holiday") once a month. Japan's labour law sets 48 hours a week as the upper limit without overtime pay.

Business hours Office hours are 9 to 5 or 5.30. Factories start at 8 and work an 8½ hour shift. Shift-working is less common than in the West.

Punctuality The importance of this is emphasized by time clocks or sign-in books for all staff in offices, factories and shops. The Japanese are good time-keepers. Senior staff often turn up early.

Setting the mood The day often begins with limbering-up exercises (*taiso*) for everyone from the chairman down. This may be followed by a section leader's pep talk.

The office day The desire for consensus means that much of the day is taken up with "desk conferences". People consult frequently with both senior and junior colleagues. The open-plan nature of the offices – senior executives usually sit with juniors – contributes to this cross-flow of ideas. Executives tend to spend less time on administration than in the West.

Lunch breaks are staggered from 12 to 2. Everyone takes a brisk 30min break in the staff canteen or at one's desk or at nearby restaurants. Lunchtime drinking is frowned upon and Western-style business lunches are rare (see *Business meetings*).

Going home Factory and shop workers and many who are not in lifetime employment leave on the dot, contributing to the frenzied rush hour between 5 and 6. Lifetime employees – *salarymen* – often work on, but few executives take work home, even at weekends. Increasingly, some executives are prepared to risk future promotion for more home life, and will leave work promptly.

After hours Though most Tokyo workers have a long journey home – 90min is the norm – few senior executives or junior *salarymen* rush straight home. They rush instead for the bars where much serious drinking and informal businesss discussion takes place. Top executives mingle readily with juniors. No ambitious *salaryman* turns down an invitation. It is an extension of the working day in which discussion is franker, though off-the-record and best not referred to the next day. Visiting businessmen are expected to take part and it is an ideal opportunity for cementing relationships. This blending of business and pleasure is aided by substantial tax-free entertainment allowances. There is a second rush hour at 11.30pm as businessmen stagger for last trains or wait in line for taxis.

Weekends are spent at home, though a visitor may be invited for a round of golf or to a baseball game or Sumo on the Saturday. Sunday is a day of rest with the family. Visitors are unlikely to be invited home (see *Invitations, hospitality and gifts*) and it is unwise to phone Japanese contacts at home, either at weekends or in the evenings.

Holidays Manual and shop workers and those in small companies get only a few days' leave plus 13 days of public holidays. New Year and May's Golden Week are the major public holidays. Many Japanese – particularly executives – take only 60% of their holiday entitlement and few executives take more than 10 days. Company holidays – three days away with family and/or colleagues – are common in larger companies.

The salaryman's work ethic

To succeed in a Japanese company a *salaryman* must combine sensitivity, tact, flexibility and, above all, enthusiastic commitment.

One of the group The old adage "the nail which sticks up gets hammered down" neatly sums up corporate thinking. The work group rather than the individual is the key unit. Authority is more diffuse and control over budgets, resources and decision-making more collective than in the West. Individual talent is more highly prized in small, newly established firms, but the corporate world still values those skilled at working harmoniously with others.

Other awareness Japanese culture emphasizes "other awareness" before self-concern. One consequence is that the company time-my time distinction has been deliberately and shrewdly blurred by management. An evening spent with clients, or playing mahjong with a senior, or drinking with colleagues is all part of a day's work.

Commitment Japanese come of age at 20, but a more significant rite of passage occurs when entering full-time employment (generally at 22 in the corporate sector) for the first time. One then becomes a *shakaijin* (a member of society) and is expected to put responsibilities and obligations before personal wishes and individual rights. Some *shakaijin* pack away their bluejeans – a potent libertine symbol – as a demonstration of their commitment. Commitment is more generally expressed through correct dress, punctuality and flexibility, and by taking holiday cues from senior management.

Flexibility Apart from areas where technical skills are essential, Japanese corporations recruit generalists for career posts. Career employees are the elite and, as generalists, must demonstrate flexibility – about what they do and where they may be asked to do it. Companies are increasingly training workers for possible future foreign postings.

Corporate hierarchies

Hierarchy is fundamental to Japanese thinking. Industries are ranked in terms of status, prospects and performance, as are the companies that make them up, and these rankings are widely known. Corporations have higher status than medium-sized and small companies. Within a firm, seniority is important, and older staff normally have higher rank.

Understanding rank

Kaicho	Chairman
Shacho	President
Fuku shacho	Vice president
Senmu torishimariyaku	Managing director
Jomu torishimariyaku	Senior executive director
Torishimariyaku	Executive director
Kansayaku	Statutory examiner
Sodanyaku/Sanyo	Non-exec director
Bucho	Dept manager
Bucho dairi	Deputy dept manager
Bucho hosa	Assistant dept manager
Kacho	Section manager
Kakaricho	Supervisor
Hancho	Foreman

Visitors may come across other titles, for companies often create them to satisfy an executive's ego. The chairman (often a past-president) is the company figurehead and the president is the chief executive. Large corporations have many vice presidents and managing directors. The statutory examiner protects shareholders' interests (see *Accountants*). *Sodanyaku* are often retired senior executives.

Titles denote status in relation to other ranks, rather than a specific job. The Japanese like to deal with those of equivalent status: a *bucho* in the medium-sized sector would expect to deal with a *kacho*, or his deputy, in the corporate sector. ***Middle management*** are the key players. Ranging from section manager to department manager, they have wide experience and usually 15 to 20 years' service. They have access to most company data and are the contact point with other firms. As in-house specialists, they work in such areas as market research and product development analysis, rarely using outside consultants.

Managers must ensure that their team feels part of decision-making, and they work hard to motivate subordinates. They look after staff welfare both in and out of the office.

When approaching a company, avoid going over the heads of middle management. These are the people who implement decisions. You will meet top management when a decision has percolated upwards – timing is all.

Decision-making

Top management initiates decisions on matters of strategy but many other decisions are formulated in the lower ranks, through a long process known as *nemawashi* – consensus-building.

Nemawashi occurs formally at meetings between managers and informally in discussions with junior colleagues. The details of a plan are ironed out in verbal agreements before it is drafted.

The draft, or *ringi-sho* – a decision-requesting circular – is passed to each manager involved for approval and comments. A final draft is submitted to directors. Once the plan is sanctioned, instant action is required by the staff, who are already aware of what it entails.

Ringi-sho are used widely in large corporations, sometimes to rubber-stamp decisions already taken. Decisions can, however, be made without *ringi-sho* at management meetings. In small and medium-sized companies *ringi-sho* are often not used.

Women in business

Although changing slowly under the influence of Western ideas, sexual role stereotypes remain strong in Japan and women in management are rare. Although younger Japanese men – those in the post-war generation – accept that *foreign* women do business, older men may need convincing.

Women in the work force

Japanese women make up 40% of the total work force, but only 6% of the managers and officials. Of these, most are in small businesses and are concentrated in a handful of industries – design, PR, fashion, cosmetics and advertising. In the large trading companies and banks women in upper and middle-management are almost unheard of. These companies, though they may take on female graduates, neglect their business training as it is assumed – and often required – that they will leave on marriage or at least on the birth of their first child. The long hours of the *salaryman* are seen as incompatible with the roles of wife and mother. Women running their own small businesses are typically single or divorced. Equal opportunity legislation was passed in April 1986, but it is too soon for its effects to be noticeable.

The overseas businesswoman

A polite respect will be afforded the visiting businesswoman as a matter of course. However, in the masculine world of Japanese big business, the Western businesswoman must prove she is at least the equal of the men. As with visiting male executives she must be fully briefed and professional in presentation and manner, taking particular care to dress in a conservative business-like style. In addition, she must emphasize her business qualifications and show she has the full backing of her company. If her company is not well known, gaining business respect may be a struggle. Persistence will pay off.

Male and female colleagues in the same delegation should emphasize the working arrangement when setting up a visit, or they may find the man scheduled for meetings while the woman is set for a round of sightseeing.

Chivalry towards women is a foreign concept to the Japanese, where the custom is for men to take precedence. Men will grab seats on public transport and go through doors first. Westernized Japanese do try to adapt, holding doors open and helping women into their coats. Their efforts may be unwelcome but should not be spurned. Be prepared to give way when jammed in a doorway.

Socializing Most Japanese men are not accustomed to socializing on an equal footing with female colleagues. However, a foreign businesswoman can become "one of the boys" fairly easily, providing her business credentials are established at the outset, and so long as she takes care not to flaunt her femininity. The key to acceptance is to join in. Be prepared to answer personal questions: if single, why not married; if married, who is looking after the home. These questions may be among the first you are asked, and a ready supply of stock answers is useful, the lighter the better.

Drinking Some Japanese might be ill-at-ease inviting visiting businesswomen to the essentially male environment of the drinking clubs. It is in the informal atmosphere of the clubs that many business relationships are cemented, however, so if you are keen to join your hosts make this clear to them. It is inadvisable to drink anything stronger than your hosts, as this may cause them loss of face. *Shochu* is a fashionable drink among women.

Business meetings

Meetings, formal and informal, are the essence of Japanese business. Western businessmen, especially first-time visitors, can be taken aback by the amount of detailed information they are expected to have at their fingertips and by the time taken to come to a decision. Meetings are not about decisions and conclusions; their purpose is the exchange of plans and information and the building of relationships. The key to successful negotiation is planning and preparation at home, and flexibility and patience in dealing with the Japanese face-to-face.

Planning and preparation

Information Japanese in middle management are experienced generalists, exceptionally well briefed about their company and the markets in which it operates. They will expect the same from visitors. Be prepared to answer searching questions about your company's size, finances, affiliations, work force, plant, production, markets, competition and strategy. Be especially sure of production capacity and delivery dates. It is best to talk about concrete facts rather than vague future plans, as asking for a reaction to an idea can leave your audience nonplussed.

You should be armed not only with information on the companies you are dealing with and their competitors but with details of relevant design standards and tariffs.

Materials The Japanese are happier with the concrete and visual than the abstract and spoken. Company reports and corporate brochures detailing the history, standing and aims of the company are much appreciated, as are reference lists of international customers. Material written in English is acceptable, while brochures printed in Japanese are a large plus. English materials with a summary insert in Japanese are a happy compromise. It is best to have Japanese translations and printing done in Japan, as those done elsewhere can be embarrassingly inept.

Visual aids Photographs, videotapes and short audio-visual presentations are welcome. Be sure to check with your agents that compatible VCRs, projectors and so on are available at the companies to be visited.

Business cards (*meishi*) are indispensable in establishing the credentials of you and your company. It is best to arrange with a Japanese representative to have a supply printed and ready for your arrival. JAL and other airlines also provide this service. Your *meishi* should carry your name, company and precise title on one side, and a correct Japanese translation on the other. Any additional information that helps to define your status – qualifications, membership of professional bodies, and so forth – can be added to the Western side. Take advice from Japanese friends and colleagues on the layout of the other side. *Meishi* are of a standard size (90mm x 55mm) and should be impressive without being ostentatious.

Arranging meetings Introductions through a go-between are helpful in setting up initial meetings. This may be an individual or government agency. In either case, try to keep a flexible programme. Unless you insist, your agent will totally fill your agenda from 9.00am until 6.00pm or later. The Japanese are very accommodating to the Western visitor, and will make every effort to set up follow-up meetings at short notice if required. Those who suffer from jet-lag should arrange enough time to recover.

The meeting

Getting there The big cities are notoriously difficult to get around, and the taxi drivers rarely know the way. Your hotel will provide a map and directions in Japanese for the driver if required. Always allow plenty of travelling time; the Japanese value punctuality, often arriving up to 30 minutes early at meetings.

The venue Japanese offices are open-plan. Only rarely will a Japanese meet an outsider at his desk. Meetings generally take place either in a separate conference room or mini-lounge among the desks.

The people Even if your appointment is with one person, the meeting will not be one-to-one. Depending on your status, and the topics to be covered, as many as a dozen might turn up. It is wise, if possible, to take along at least one other person. This will ease the strain. You will be greeted by your contact in the company, who will introduce his colleagues by their family name, in order of seniority. The suffix "-san" added to a name implies respect. To refer to Moto as Mister Moto is fine, but Moto-san is better. As "-san" is an honorific, you should never use it for yourself; say "I am Brown," not "I am Brown-san." You may be greeted with a bow or a proferred hand. Take your cue from this, and return the gesture, remembering to bow from the hips and to use only light pressure in the handshake.

Exchanging cards is an important formality on first meeting. This initial ritual exchange of information, establishing relative status, helps get the relationship off to a good start. Visitors go first; after the bow or handshake proffer your card smoothly, holding it so that it can be read immediately. Showing the English side shows respect for your opposite number's linguistic ability. Courteously study the card you receive in exchange. This is a gesture of respect and enables you to fix name and rank in your mind. Repeat the surname – the first name on the card – to ensure you have the correct pronunciation and ask for a translation of titles if none is offered.

Lay the cards in front of you in seating order for reference. The Japanese are very formal in business situations and will almost always be known by their family names; you, in turn, will be addressed by yours. You should not use forenames or suggest they use yours.

Present your card only to those to whom you are introduced at meetings. At future meetings present your card only to people you have not met. Only when your own status changes through promotion, should you pass out a new card to those you have already met.

Treat cards with great respect. Don't bend them or shove them unceremoniously into a pocket. Other people's cards should not be passed on without their permission.

Seats are allocated according to status. Generally, the most senior Japanese sits furthest from the door and the most junior nearest. Wait until you are given a seat before sitting down. The Japanese team will sit together on one side of the table and the visitors will be placed opposite; this is customary rather than confrontational.

The working language is almost always Japanese. Be sure to check this. As your host may have no command of spoken English and you probably have none of Japanese, your relative linguistic abilities are best clarified in advance. The Japanese company will then usually take responsibility for providing interpreters. Do not be surprised if a man who can entertain you in English prefers to do business through an interpreter. Even if the meeting is in English, it is a good idea to have a well-briefed Japanese speaker with you.

Professional interpreters are usually best avoided at the first meeting. To use one may be construed as trying too hard, and as showing disrespect for your host's command of English. If language does prove a problem it is better to struggle through good-humouredly, to make it fun, and even to try a few phrases of Japanese. Your hosts will be helpful and positive and try to make the best of the situation.

If a series of meetings with the same people presents a difficulty, consider hiring a professional interpreter for subsequent meetings (see *Language* for details). The meeting will still be conducted in Japanese. If you are being interpreted, give them time – remember it can take around three times as long to say something in Japanese as it does in English – and be prepared to repeat yourself. Talk in short "thought blocks", not rambling sentences or discontinuous phrases.

Informal conversation begins the meeting, setting the tone. Be prepared to chat about the weather, your impressions of Japan, your family, sport, anything but business. Let your hosts initiate this conversation.

Who speaks? Everyone at the meeting will have their say, but not all of them will necesarily have it at the meeting. The senior personnel are the main channels of communication and the juniors defer to them. Although there is no formal chairman of the meeting, those wishing to speak will need to catch the eye of the senior Japanese. He himself may speak little, preferring to listen and to judge. The Japanese are likely to break off and talk among themselves in Japanese. No discourtesy is intended, but without an interpreter present you may be missing vital information on how the meeting is going.

Speaking in meetings You should keep to short sentences and clear concepts; slang, jargon and buzz-words should be avoided. Jokes and facetiousness do not readily translate into Japanese and tend to be misunderstood. Interrupting is considered rude, as is directness in disagreement and correction. If you feel that one of your hosts has not understood, or is drifting from the point, do not leap in to correct him but wait patiently until he has finished before beginning "Yes, but..."

Preface a divergent point of view with "Perhaps" or "Maybe" or "I wonder if..." or "It may seem from your point of view." Do not say "No". "Let me think it over" or "I'm not sure" are usually understood as meaning "No". The Japanese do not say "No"; instead rejection is implied by a lukewarm tone of agreement.

When talking technicalities, beware bland answers of "Hai, hai" (I am listening, I hear you, I understand). This may indicate that you are *not* understood, and your hosts are merely being polite. Take a different approach, ask the same questions in a different way to check. Sketching on a pad or a blackboard is an invaluable aid to any presentation, as it is a universal language; be prepared to improvise to get your point across. Long speeches are best avoided lest they be interpreted as trying too hard.

A printed list of your main points can be circulated at the meeting. Japanese read English far better than they understand the spoken word.

Silence is no embarrassment to the Japanese. Indeed, they savour moments of silence in a meeting to reflect on what has been said and the atmosphere in which it has been said. Do not fill in these "awkward" pauses.

The right attitude Business meetings can seem both baffling and agonizingly slow. This is par for the course and is no reflection on you or your proposals. The Japanese are a very patient people and it is important to approach meetings in this spirit. It is essential to let matters take their course; and useless to force the pace. It is permissible, though, to show a degree of keenness. After all, your hosts are also eager to do business. Above all, however, avoid getting excited or showing strong emotion.

Strategy Little or no hard business will be done at the first meeting. The visitor's main aim should be to establish himself as the sort of person that the Japanese like to do business with: reliable, flexible, interesting and interested. Answer questions about your business as fully as you can. There is no loss of face in not knowing the answer to more off-beat questions; promise to find the answer as soon as possible, and do so. Avoid the hard sell as it is always counter-productive, but take the opportunity to outline firm future plans. Remember the Japanese are more concerned with quality than price; show that you are ready to adjust prices and product specifications to suit their markets. Show an interest in the people and in their company and its products.

Taking the hint Politeness is so deeply engrained in the Japanese character that even if they are totally uninterested in your product they will not say so. Signs of lack of interest include evasiveness, monosyllabic answers and a tendency to stop asking questions. On the other hand, you may realize that they are not the right customers for your product. In neither case should the meeting come to an abrupt end. See it through and maintain a polite interest.

Success in dealing with the Japanese is more to do with the negotiator than the product. Be sensitive to the mood of the meeting, gauge what is expected of you, and avoid making extravagant promises.

The end of the meeting is usually timetabled but it can often overrun. If your hosts show no signs of stopping, the meeting will continue. If there are long silences and a lack of questions the meeting is winding down. The proceedings end when your hosts initiate a round of courteous thank-yous and hopes to meet again. If the next appointment is not fixed, now is a good time to do it. Gather up the *meishi* you have been given and keep them for future reference – it is a good idea to invest, as do the Japanese, in a custom-made holder. *After* the meeting make notes on each card – for example, vegetarian, non-smoker – and you will build up an invaluable data-bank on the most important aspect of Japanese business: people.

Minutes are not kept and circulated by the Japanese. This leaves room for discussion, with nothing cut and dried, and is appreciated by the Japanese. It is often a good idea, though, to circulate a note of the points covered as an early-warning system in case of misunderstandings.

Other venues can be suggested for subsequent meetings. Meetings at your hotel are fine, with the proviso that they do not take place in your room, as this might embarrass the Japanese. Also, an invitation to a hotel might suggest an offer of hospitality.

Business lunches are getting-to-know-you affairs, not used for hard discussions. The visitor should not suggest a lunchtime meeting unless he knows the Japanese well. There is little lunchtime drinking, and meals start at 12.00 or 12.30, and rarely take longer than an hour. If you are in a meeting that is scheduled to end at lunchtime, your hosts may invite you to lunch. This is a courtesy, and not an invitation to continue the business of the meeting.

Decisions should never be expected at first meetings. Perhaps a trial order might be made at a second meeting. Although the Japanese are adjusting to Western time-scales, you should be prepared for a wait of two years or more before beginning business in earnest, and up to five years before a firm business relationship is established. During this time you should maintain constant communications with the Japanese and make at least one visit a year to Japan; two or three visits might be needed in the first 18 months.

Dressing for business

Western executives visiting Japan need to be more aware of their dress and physical appearance than they might be at home. People are judged by appearances much more in Japan than in the West, and your hosts' evaluation of you for the vital "right attitude" will include a careful, though unobtrusive scrutiny of your clothing and grooming.

The ubiquitous suit

Uniformity within the group is prized by the Japanese. Factory workers all wear company overalls or smocks, and even office workers may wear a uniform. At Sony, for example, everyone, up to and including the chairman, dons a Sony jacket for the working day. A more widespread convention is the ubiquitous dark business suit (*sebiro* or "Savile Row"), worn with a crisp, white shirt, sober tie and black shoes.

Expensive Western tailoring is appreciated by the Japanese. Visiting businessmen should wear conservative colours and styling, avoiding flagrant checked suits or shirts that might appear too casual. Take all the clothing you need with you, for it can be difficult to find the right size in Japan (especially in footwear). Slip-on shoes are most convenient.

Smart clothing is essential. The Japanese do not wear or appreciate "old but comfortable" clothing. Adapt your wardrobe to the level of company hierarchy you will be dealing with. Most Japanese businessmen aged over 40 are not fashion conscious, and they dress like American politicians or British City businessmen. Younger Japanese businessmen are still conservative, but will be more aware of fashion.

Japan's weather in summer is hot, humid and hard on clothing. To appear in battle-fatigued garb at a business appointment would be disastrous, so take advantage of hotel facilities such as two-hour suit renovating services. The Japanese carry umbrellas rather than raincoats, and it is wise to do the same. The summer visitor should pack enough shirts for at least two changes a day, plenty of underwear and socks, and at least two suits. The Japanese are obsessive about personal cleanliness and tidiness. Short, well-groomed hair, frequent showers, and a constant supply of clean clothing, preferably with a high cotton content, are all good investments.

Western women have to be careful not to overwhelm their hosts. Make-up, jewellery and perfume should all be used sparingly. Avoid high heels if they make you tower over your hosts. Women are seldom found at executive level, so business dress should be restrained, to reduce the "threat". Trousers should not be worn. Accessories can be upmarket; fashionable Japanese women spend a lot on items like Louis Vuitton handbags and Yves Saint Laurent shoes. Styles associated with teenagers, such as dresses and tights in pink or red, or with *femmes fatales*, such as split skirts or plunging necklines, should be avoided. Dark colours – traditionally worn by women over 40 – may give a woman the desired mature image. Shaggy or way-out hairstyles are not appreciated.

High fashion is increasingly important among the young and affluent, and those doing business with highly image-conscious sectors might well find their opposite numbers decked out in the creations of Japanese designers with international reputations, like Mitsuhiro Matsuda or Rei Kawakubo. In general, however, the visiting business traveller should only step outside convention on the golf course, where chic wear will be the latest thing from the golf pro's shop – casual, elegant, and probably very expensive.

Invitations, hospitality and gifts

The Japanese are the world's most assiduous business hosts, and unless you make arrangements to the contrary, you are likely to be entertained every evening, often at short notice. This is is partly because the Japanese are naturally hospitable and wish to shield a foreign visitor from any difficulties in coping with their culture. On a less altruistic level, they enjoy the prestige attached to entertaining visiting Westerners and the opportunity to demonstrate the size of their expense account. But it is mainly because the Japanese prefer to do business with people that they not only know, but also like; and the relationship is deepened by after-hours contact, where conference-room defences and formalities can be dropped.

Being entertained

Breakfast meetings are unusual, except among US residents, and lunches are normally brief, abstemious affairs. Most business entertaining takes place after office hours – which usually means from about 7pm.

A typical evening may begin at your hotel, or in a small bar directly after work, then move on to a restaurant. Thereafter, if it is not too late, you will go on to a hostess bar before being delivered back to your hotel in a taxi, by someone often a great deal more inebriated than you (the Japanese have a notoriously low alcohol threshold). (See *Planning and reference* for more information on bars, restaurants and types of cuisine.)

Some bars that cater for expense-account drinkers charge astronomical prices. But if you are taken to any bar, it will be as a non-paying guest and your hosts will order all the drinks. The usual drinks are beer (*biru*), sake (*o-sake*) or whisky and water (*mizuwari*).

Dinner Rather than select your own meal – in many cases this will be impossible since the menu will be solely in Japanese – it is tactful and in keeping with the harmony of the evening to allow your host to order on your behalf. Seldom will a Japanese person be so inconsiderate as to have you presented with anything too difficult. Perceptions differ, of course, and your host may be surprised if you balk at the idea of eating live prawns.

The best advice is to abandon preconceptions and be adventurous, following your host's suggestions and expressing delight at the different dishes. Those with dietary preferences or allergies should make these clear to their hosts *before* any invitation is accepted. (See *Manners and conversation* for meal etiquette.)

Hostess bars The most common venue for business entertaining is a hostess bar, presided over by Mama-San, a Japanese woman of indeterminate age but indisputable authority, and served by hostesses whose fundamental role is to boost male egos, giggling prettily and flirting mildly at an hourly rate. The Japanese like to eat while drinking, so rice biscuits and other snacks will be served up periodically.

You may be entertained by your usual contact on his own, but more often he will be accompanied by an interpreter or one or more close colleagues.

The conversation veers between small talk and general business discussion and should be seen as an opportunity to forge links of friendship. However, business matters may be discussed in some detail, without too much prejudice on either side, since binding offers and agreements are left to daytime meetings.

Other entertainment

As you get to know your contact better, you can venture forth to enjoy some of the rich variety of entertainment on offer. You may like to use the opportunity to watch some Sumo wrestling; grapple with the formalities of Noh traditional theatre; or even indulge in the unique pleasures of a *karaoke* ("empty orchestra") bar, where you must take your turn singing along to a backing tape of a popular song. There is an innocence to these quaintly Japanese pastimes that makes them easier to enjoy than you might expect.

Whether you will be invited to explore further or whether you need to make the suggestion yourself depends on the individual you are dealing with and the length of time you are spending there. It is best to allow a couple of evenings of traditional wining and dining to pass before broaching the topic, but most business hosts will welcome the opportunity to take you off the beaten track.

If an invitation is issued for a weekend, it may include one of any number of sporting events. It is a signal honour to be invited to play golf, and it demonstrates the importance of your host if he is in a position to issue such an invitation.

Less innocent recreation is available but is unlikely to be offered. You can ask, but this may cause embarrassment and you should judge the situation carefully.

An invitation home

On rare occasions, or if a relationship has progressed well beyond normal courtesies, you may be invited for an evening meal at a Japanese person's home.

You should ascertain who is the lady of the house (often your host's mother or mother-in-law) and arrive with a gift for her. A small present from home would be most appreciated, but a box of chocolates or a bunch of flowers is quite appropriate.

All but the most senior and highly-paid executives will be found to live in surprisingly humble and usually overcrowded circumstances.

Remove your shoes at the door. Except in *tatami* (straw mat) rooms, you will be lent a pair of slippers for indoor use. The living room will be sparsely furnished, and you will join the family sitting cross-legged around a low central table. Most hosts will be able to offer you a folding back-rest to ease the discomfort of this position.

As at business meetings, conversation will seem stilted and slow-moving, unless you have already adjusted to the pace. The usual exchange of toasts will typically be followed by a leisurely meal of sushi, perhaps preceded by an informal tea ceremony, and proceedings will be brought to a close at about 11 with coffee or yet more green tea.

As elsewhere, you will be guided through the necessary formalities, and allowances will be made for your gaffes. Expect to be charmed by the simplicity of it, but remember that it is a great honour to be invited home, and you should show that you appreciate this.

Returning hospitality

The tireless generosity of the Japanese can become embarrassing, since circumstances often make it very difficult to reciprocate.

The standard recourse is to arrange a dinner for your Japanese colleagues. But instead of inviting just the one or two senior personnel who have been working on the deal, it can make – if at all appropriate – a favourable impression to ask up to, say, half a dozen others who have been associated with the work. The Japanese may well protest that this is not permitted; that allowing a foreign guest to pick up a bill is virtually a sackable offence; don't take them literally. Do not attempt to invite the wives: although some Westerners have succeeded in scoring points for this unwarranted courtesy – quaint and eccentric in the eyes of the Japanese – it is just as likely to cause embarrassment. Do not invite anyone outside the immediate circle of acquaintance in the company.

Choose an evening towards the end of the visit and inform everyone verbally, with ample notice, of the invitation; there is no need to issue formal invitations.

It is inappropriate to build an evening around an event such as a baseball game or theatre – and logistically difficult. Anyway, the Japanese are used to thinking of a business dinner as a semi-ceremonial occasion whose purpose is to cement a relationship. It is sound practice to repay hospitality at a restaurant with non-Japanese cooking where you can remain in charge.

After the meal it is good form to acquiesce in the Japanifying of the evening by agreeing to adjourn for *nijikai* – the second round. This will typically be in a neighbourhood bar, perhaps followed by a hostess bar, where once again it will be your turn to be entertained at their expense.

Gifts

The giving and receiving of gifts is an important element in the development of good will in Japanese business relationships.

Receiving Gifts will be produced not in the conference room, but after hours, either to mark the successful conclusion of a phase of the business, or more likely towards the end of your visit. The gift should not be opened in front of your host (unless you are asked to do so), but you should express suitable thanks, with further thanks at a later date. If the present is a company tie or cuff links, wearing it at the next meeting will be much appreciated.

Giving Westerners are excused the strict formalities that govern the value and timing of reciprocal gifts, and it is the spirit of the giving that counts.

It is important to bring in your full allocation of duty-free Scotch whisky, which is very expensive in Japan. These three bottles are ideal gifts for important contacts, to be handed over on or soon after your first meeting. Name brands generally carry more weight than lesser-known single malts.

Once you have exhausted your limited supply, the matter becomes more difficult. Your opposite number is likely to have the latest model of every imaginable consumer durable, so calculators and electronic executive games are out.

A stock of company gifts is a good idea – especially good quality, name-branded Western goods, which carry a status out of proportion to their cost at home. Swiss Army knives, Dunhill or Zippo lighters, English leather wallets, silk ties, and almost anything with a Harrods, Nieman Marcus or similarly well-known label will make a good impression.

The wrapping of the gift is very important. Anything purchased in Japan will be wrapped at the store for you, and many hotels offer a wrapping service for things you may have brought with you. Proffer a gift with style, rather than slipping it unceremoniously across the table, and avoid praising the value of your gift.

The timing of the gift-giving is dependent on circumstances and can usually be managed as a direct response to any gift you may receive. However, if this might be awkward, it is as acceptable to send a gift by post after your return home.

Gift or bribe? The Japanese are conventionally more generous than Westerners, and a gift of surprisingly high value is considered quite normal. Provided it can reasonably be interpreted as a gift to ease the progress of a major deal, the question of bribery should not arise.

Cash handouts are to be avoided. The best advice is to stick to gifts that are relatively inexpensive but foreign-made.

The business media

An extremely wide range of English-language material is available for the business traveller to Japan, some of it extremely valuable. The offerings in other languages are much more limited.

Japanese-language media

The dailies Selling almost 70m copies, Japan's daily press has the largest circulation per head of population in the world. Sales of the morning editions of the three leading nationals, *Yomiuri Shimbun* with around 9m, *Asahi Shimbun* with around 8m and *Mainichi Shimbun* with 4.5m are only exceeded by the Soviet Union's *Pravda* and *Izvestia*. Evening editions of the same papers sell about half as many. The big three quality newspapers like to think of themselves as liberal in outlook.

The leading business paper is *Nihon Keizai Shimbun*, with a total morning and evening circulation of over 3.5m. It is extremely influential and more widely read than any other business publication.

English-language media

The dailies The daily morning newspapers available in English are the *Japan Times* (the most widely read), the *Mainichi Daily News* and the *Daily Yomiuri*. With circulations of less than 50,000 these are very much oriented to the foreign business community and visiting executives. They provide little more than English summaries of the main domestic and international news from the Japanese-language press. In the evening, there is the *Asahi Evening News*.

The businessman's weekly The *Japan Economic Journal* is published weekly by Nihon Keizai Shimbun. Based on their influential daily Japanese newspaper, its coverage of economic and business developments is comprehensive, and its 30,000 circulation belies its importance among Western businessmen interested in Japan.

Monthlies The best of these is *Tokyo Business Today* (formerly the *Oriental Economist* – no relation to London's *The Economist*). The *Journal of Japanese Trade and Industry* (a bimonthly) often has good articles, as does *Diamond's Economic Journal Industria. Business Japan* has a distinctly political flavour, although its industry content is often good.

Directories Company directories include the invaluable twice-yearly *Japan Company Handbook* and its accompanying *Second Section Firms*, Nihon Keizai Shimbun's *Japanese Companies Consolidated Data*, and the *Japan Business Directory* from the Diamond Lead Company. The *Japan Economic Almanac* (formerly the *Industrial Review of Japan*) from Nihon Keizai Shimbun is an excellent review of Japanese industry. An alternative is the Oriental Economist's *Japan Economic Yearbook. Electronic Buyers' Guide* and *Japan Electronics Almanac* from Dempa Publications are essential reading for those in these industries.

Some others Several banks publish regular monthly reports, notably Long-Term Credit Bank, Industrial Bank of Japan and Fuji Bank. Their less frequent but more detailed in-depth reports on topics such as Japan's high-technology industries are perhaps more interesting. The *Keidanren Review on Japanese Economy* is worthwhile, as are the authoritative and free English language publications from the Keizai Koho Center (see *Power in business*).

Cable TV Japan Cable Television (JCTV) runs an English-language station, available in leading hotels and modern apartments. No TV station broadcasts regularly in English, though there are bilingual English/Japanese newscasts on the main TV channels.

Cultural Awareness

A historical perspective

A major effect of Japan's defeat in the Pacific War was to sever it from its lengthy and often illustrious history. This was the first occasion on which Japan had been conquered, and it continues to reel from the shock. Much that is mysterious about modern Japan may be clarified by a nodding acquaintance with the nation's history.

The China impact: c600–800

Japan entered the mainstream of world history in the late 6th century when official support for Buddhism and the sophisticated Chinese culture that followed in its wake produced radical changes.

An emperor is made The title emperor was applied for the first time to the leader of the dominant Yamato clan, and the myth-makers invented the genealogy of the Emperor's descent from the Sun goddess (the present Emperor Hirohito is number 124). Chinese political institutions and land reforms were also imported.

Culture China's influence went beyond attempts to unite the state under the figurehead of the newly-fashioned imperial house. From China, too, came writing, literature and the visual arts. These the Japanese assimilated, assessed, remodelled – and, in many cases, rejected; for they were not mere imitators. Located at Nara for most of the 8th century, the imperial capital was moved at the end of the century to Heian (now Kyoto).

Heian period: c800–1200

The period of foreign influence was followed by an era of reappraisal and an assertion of things Japanese.

Politics and culture Politically, the Heian period saw emperors manipulated by nobles of the Fujiwara family. Although the imperial family was never to regain the political power it had enjoyed in Nara, it would not be destroyed. For successive regimes imperial sanction became the mark of legitimate rule.

Culturally, the Heian period was one of superb aesthetic refinement which left an enduring stamp on Japanese artistic ideals. The *kana* scripts were devised; poetry and prose – no longer in Chinese – flourished, and the world's first and Japan's best-loved novel, *Tale of Genji*, was written. But while the refined, humane courtiers composed poetry, the neglected provinces became increasingly ungovernable. The Taira and Minamoto, two warrior families of noble descent, were commissioned to quell provincial unrest. A string of military successes brought them onto the national stage. Formerly servants of the court, they became its masters.

Kamakura period: c1200–1300

Military government and martial values characterize the Kamakura period and all periods until 1868.

The shoguns The Minamoto, the first of Japan's shoguns, established headquarters at present-day Kamakura, far from the debilitating influence of Kyoto. But the shoguns, like the emperors who remained in Kyoto, soon became puppets of counsellors who ruled in their name. It is clear that the modern Japanese aversion to individual responsibility and decision-making has a very long history. Culturally, Kamakura was coloured by the less-refined taste of warriors, as reflected in stirring war epics like the *Tale of the Heike*.

Invasion At the end of the 13th century, the stability of Kamakura Japan was rocked by two massive invasion attempts. The failure of these attempts to conquer Japan can be attributed less to the fierce fighting of the Japanese than to *kamikaze*, or "divine winds", which on both occasions destroyed the Mongol fleet. In the short term, victory over the Mongols was pyrrhic. The cost of maintaining armies on the alert until the death of Kublai Khan bankrupted the Kamakura regime. In the long term, these victories persuaded the Japanese that Japan was divine and undefeatable, a conviction that survived intact until Japan's surrender in 1945.

Muromachi period: c1300–1600

The Kamakura regime was overthrown by samurai of the Ashikaga family who set up headquarters in the Muromachi sector of Kyoto. The grip of the Ashikaga shoguns on the nation was never strong, and incessant warfare scarred their rule.

Zen culture A renewed interest in trade with China characterizes this anarchic period. Foreign trade led to economic growth and enabled towns such as Osaka to expand. Once again, Kyoto saw the flowering of a dazzling culture. This time, however, it was centred on the court of the Shogun and not that of the Emperor. Ashikaga culture was a mixture of Chinese influence, traditional Japanese taste, and warrior asceticism. The period saw the refinement and development of many of modern Japan's aesthetic pursuits – the tea ceremony, flower-arranging, gardening, ink-painting, calligraphy and the Noh theatre. All bear the mark of Zen Buddhism.

Unification Not until the end of the 16th century did a warrior powerful enough to topple the Ashikaga emerge from the anarchy of provincial warfare. The man was Oda Nobunaga. If Nobunaga quarried the stones for Japan's later unification, his brilliant successor, Hideyoshi, shaped them. Hideyoshi is remembered, too, for his disastrous invasion of Korea in 1592. This left a legacy of bitterness that survives today in Korean-Japanese relations. It was his successor, Tokugawa Ieyasu, who set the stones of unification in place.

Edo period: c1600–1867

Ieyasu was appointed Shogun in 1603. He made the small fishing village of Edo (modern Tokyo) his headquarters. From here the Tokugawa guaranteed Japan's peace for over 200 years.

Christianity Europeans had arrived and begun trading in Japan in the mid-16th century. But soon European missionary success was seen as a threat to the state unity that European muskets had helped achieve. Christianity was all but eradicated in the early 17th century and all foreigners, except the Dutch and the Chinese, were expelled.

State and society The isolationist Tokugawa regime was a police state, which bound the regional lords to Edo, both by a hostage system and by the enforcement of crippling financial contributions. Oaths of loyalty to the shogun also bound them. This loyalty was rationalized by Confucian ethics, which emphasized a man's duties to his lord and the supreme importance of harmony within society. The ethics of modern Japan are deeply rooted in the Confucian ideals inculcated during the Edo period. Tokugawa society was strictly hierarchical: the samurai, idle now in peacetime, occupied the top rung. Beneath them were the peasants. The despised money-handling merchants were at the bottom. Social harmony depended on there being no social mobility, but the reality was different.

Edo culture Most that is memorable in Edo culture was inspired by the rise of the merchant class: the Kabuki and puppet theatres, haiku poetry, and the woodblock prints of Hiroshige and Utamaro. The trading houses of Mitsui, Mitsubishi and Sumitomo all sprang up in the expanding and changing economy of the Edo period.

Stability threatened The real power of the money-lender merchants was painfully evident to the samurai class, who were increasingly in their debt. By the end of the Tokugawa period, the samurai and their government were impoverished. But pressures were not solely financial. Ideologically, there was a dangerous new questioning of the imperial family's right to rule, and curiosity about the outside world (always a Japanese trait) was fanned by information seeping in via Dutch traders in Nagasaki. Alone, these pressures were not sufficient to bring down the Tokugawa. In combination with the new 19th-century threat from the West, they were.

Collapse The American Commodore Perry prised open Japan in 1854, but the beleaguered Tokugawa were caught between those who favoured isolation and those who thought the Tokugawa stood in the path of modernization. A brief civil war ensued, and control of the court was seized by enemies of the Tokugawa.

The modern period

In the Meiji Restoration, Edo was renamed Tokyo and became the seat of the Emperor Meiji.

Meiji rule The Meiji government's aims were twofold: spiritual unity of the nation under imperial rule and "pure Shinto", and political, economic and military modernization. It was to prove a poisonous mixture. Westernization was forced on Japan, and the Prussian-inspired Meiji Constitution was promulgated in 1889. With the state guiding industrial growth, as it does today, Japan became a powerful constitutional monarchy.

Termination in the 1890s of unequal trade treaties with the West was followed by Japan's defeat of China in 1895, and then the astonishing victory over Russia in 1905. Annexation of Formosa, parts of Russia and then Korea followed. In less than 50 years Japan had developed from a feudal state to a respected and feared world power. Culturally, it produced novelists of world stature, such as Natsume Soseki, who combined Western realism with Heian sensibility.

Militarism Japan's support of the Allies in World War I brought her rich material rewards. But success on the world stage convinced many Japanese that they were divinely called to lead the rest of Asia to greater prosperity. The depression of the early 1930s and the perennial problems of scarce resources and over-population were at the root of Japan's expansionist ideals. In 1931 it invaded Manchuria, and the military came to dominate policy-making. The attack on Pearl Harbor in 1941 was the natural consequence.

Defeat and Occupation In 1945 the Pacific war was ended by the atom bomb, with Japan conquered and occupied for the first time in its history. The Allied Occupation, under General MacArthur, gave Japan a "peace constitution" which forbade it to make war and banned state involvement with Shinto. It also guaranteed freedoms of speech and religion and universal suffrage.

Postwar prosperity The Liberal Democrats, in power since 1955, have given Japan political stability. This and the government's close involvement in industry have ensured Japan's continued material prosperity. The spiritual void, in the painful postwar years, is perhaps best seen in the novels of Mishima Yukio.

Future challenges Postwar Japan has shown that affluence is not the exclusive property of the West. Democracy and freedom can thrive in Asia, and Westernization does not necessarily entail the loss of traditional values. However, over-population and lack of natural resources continue to cause concern. Japan's greatest challenge, though, is to overcome its historical sense of isolation – and, hence, uniqueness – and to play a full part in the international community.

Important events in Japanese history

660 BC Legendary Jimmu Tenno founds the present imperial dynasty.
AD 300 *Yamato* period begins.
mid-6thC Buddhism introduced.
710-94 *Nara* period; Chinese influence strong.
794-1185 *Heian* period; imperial capital established at Heian (Kyoto).
1192-1333 *Kamakura* period; Yoritomo becomes first Shogun.
1227 Zen introduced to Japan.
1274&1281 First Mongol expedition, Second Mongol expedition.
1333-1573 *Muromachi* period.
1338 Ashikaga Takauji is appointed Shogun.
1397 The Golden Pavilion is built.
1404 Japan's trade with China is officially inaugurated.
1467 A century of civil war begins.
1542-3 Portuguese (first Europeans) reach islands of southern Kyushu.
1549 Francis Xavier, first Christian missionary, lands at Kagoshima.
1573 The Ashikaga are overthrown by Oda Nobunaga.
1582 Nobunaga is assassinated.
1590 Hideyoshi unifies much of Japan.
1600 Will Adams, first Englishman, arrives in Japan.
1603-1867 *Edo* period. Tokugawa Ieyasu is appointed Shogun.
1609 Dutch establish a trading "factory" at Hirado.
1612-38 Christians throughout Japan persecuted.
1639-1854 Japan sealed off to all trade except with Dutch and Chinese.
1853 Commodore Perry's US fleet sails into Tokyo Bay.
1854-5 Reluctant trading treaties with USA, Britain, Netherlands, Russia.
1868-1912 *Meiji* period; Japan's modernization begins. Edo renamed Tokyo.
1871 Samurai class abolished in *Meiji* Reforms.
1871-3 French-style education system and Gregorian calendar adopted.
1889 First constitution establishes national Diet; first general election.
1894-5 Japan victorious in first Sino-Japanese War; Taiwan occupied.
1902 Alliance with Britain; Japan fights alongside Allies in World War I.
1904-5 Russo-Japanese War; Asia's first modern defeat of European power.
1910 Korea annexed as a colony.
1912 Death of *Meiji* emperor; *Taisho* period (1912-1926).
1923 Great Kanto earthquake levels Tokyo; 100,000+ killed.
1926 *Showa* period begins (under Emperor Hirohito).
1931 Manchuria invaded.
1937 Marco Polo Bridge Incident begins second Sino-Japanese War.
1940 Tripartite Treaty with Germany and Italy signed.
1941 Pearl Harbor attacked on Dec 7th; Japan enters World War II.
1945 Atomic bombs dropped on Hiroshima and Nagasaki. Unconditional surrender to Allies on Sept 2nd; Emperor renounces divine descent.
1945-52 Japan occupied. Reform Constitution promulgated in 1947.
1951 Peace Treaty ending Occupation; first Security Treaty with US.
1954 Liberal Democratic Party formed; postwar domination begins.
1956 Japan joins the United Nations.
1964 Tokyo Olympics signal international reacceptance; *Shinkansen* starts.
1969 Japanese economy overtakes Western Europe's.
1973 First oil crisis; high growth era ends.
1976 Prime Minister Tanaka indicted in Lockheed bribes scandal.
1978-9 Second oil crisis.
1980 Foreign exchange controls lifted.
1983 Deregulation and liberalization of financial system begun.

Beliefs, attitudes and lifestyles

The Japanese are a strictly ordered people who, by and large, cling to traditional values that are rigid enough to impose harmony and foster a way of working in groups and, paradoxically, flexible enough to adjust to modern influences. Individuality is not encouraged, yet the individual founders of major industries are much admired.

Tradition and modernity coexist in the major religions – Shinto and Buddhism – which, along with Confucian ethics, retain a strong hold on the Japanese consciousness and which, instead of clashing with the new materialism in Japan, contrive to lend it an air of spirituality.

Insularity

Japan opened its borders over 100 years ago, but it remains in many ways a sealed society. Outside Tokyo and other major cities, where Westerners nowadays pass almost unnoticed, even a Japanese-speaking visitor will feel very foreign indeed.

The face the Japanese show to foreigners, however, could hardly be kinder. You will find that passers-by will even shed their usual reticence to offer help and advice to a bemused Westerner.

But a Westerner can no more join this closed society than he can avoid looking conspicuously different. The very word for foreigner – *gaijin* – translates as "outside person". The Japanese view themselves as superior, not only to Westerners but also to other Asians.

The heirs to a hierarchy

A strictly defined pecking order is an important part of Japanese social as well as business life; and an almost unquestioning obedience to authority is an important element in their ability to work in teams and to make decisions as a committee. Juniors automatically respect and obey their seniors in business, as youngers do their elders in the larger context (though less so than in the past).

The group mentality The roots of Japanese conformity are pragmatic. Many years of severe overcrowding have taught them to avoid open conflict at almost any cost.

The Japanese enjoy doing things in groups. Thus it is rare to see individuals jogging in the park but common to see large groups taking their exercise *en masse*. You will see many examples of this in business and in social activities.

Prized qualities are those attained and proven within the group: a good reputation, integrity, loyalty and trustworthiness. The strategy of "divide and conquer", even on a small business scale, is not successful.

Life in the herd can seem oppressive to Western eyes, but the Japanese are predominantly a good-humoured people – remarkably so, considering the stresses of the hyper-competitive business world.

An aesthetic society

Much of Japan's cultural heritage may have been borrowed, but it has been assimilated and refined to a high degree of elegant simplicity.

This refinement pervades many aspects of Japanese life: its fine art; its simple houses and spartan furnishings; and, of course, the spare and polished ritual of the tea ceremony.

Traditional theatre flourishes in various forms, including the highly-stylized Noh theatre, bunraku puppet theatre, and Kabuki.

Paradoxically, the characteristic Japanese good taste vanishes in relation to Western objects. For example, some hotel lobbies are painfully gaudy, and the Japanese have an inexplicable fondness for plastic flowers and other kitsch.

Japanese TV is often bizarre. Respectably dressed presenters front programmes that are frequently erotic, violent or even pornographic. On game shows, for instance, participants go through rituals of humiliating self-abasement. Similar violence – also frequently pornographic – is evident in the comics widely read by businessmen on trains.

Traditional good taste reasserts itself in Japanese fashion, which vies with that of Paris, Milan and New York in its combination of striking colours and bold but simple themes.

Religion

Although commonly denied by the Japanese, religious conviction is an integral part of their life, and is approached in a matter-of-fact manner. To Westerners, Japanese religions seem inordinately flexible and multi-faceted. It is common, for example, to follow both the Shinto and Buddhist faiths, each one serving a different area of spiritual life.

More remarkable still is the way the old religions fit into modern life, just as Shinto temples take their place comfortably among modern skyscrapers.

Shinto, "The Way of the Gods", is the predominant religion but is not one of particular piety or reverence. The main concern of Shinto is to obtain the approval of the gods for projects ranging from a birth or marriage to a sporting endeavour; from a journey to a new business enterprise. It is quite common for a new business venture to be blessed either by a visit to a nearby shrine, or by a visiting Shinto priest.

Buddhism Whereas Shinto takes care of daily life, Buddhism takes care of death. It is normal custom to be married Shinto but buried Buddhist; and most Japanese families have their own domestic Buddhist shrine dedicated to the ancestral spirits.

Other religions The spiritual tolerance of Japan allows other religions to take their place with no great clashes. These range from Christianity (a growing force) and Judaism to the many sects of Buddhism, including the main Zen sects of Soto and Rinzai.

Present-day society

The real conflict in modern Japan is between its traditional lifestyle and the fast-food culture imported from the USA. In Tokyo, especially, the younger generation has embraced Western fads and fashions with great enthusiasm. To the bulk of society this is a worrying phenomenon.

The new attitudes are expressed in an erosion of the extended family and in freer sexuality among the young. Perhaps in future these aberrations will be absorbed, as others have been in the past, in the same way that highly competitive commercialism coexists with a spirit of respect for others – just one of many paradoxes that the Japanese take in their stride.

The growing middle class Class divisions are closely related to material success, but are not as pronounced as in some parts of the Western world, with the majority of the population fitting happily into a homogeneous middle/working class.

Subdivisions within this group are defined by the status of a person's job, and by his income. A white-collar worker is higher up the pecking order than a blue-collar labourer; but in the modern industries the distinction between clerk and assembly-line worker is no longer so clear-cut.

There is, nevertheless, a powerful elite, largely composed of the wealthy heads of industry. The Emperor and imperial family are still revered, but more popular idols include film and pop stars, Sumo wrestlers and top golfers.

Standards of living are high in terms of material possessions, from cars to hi-fi systems, but low in terms of living space. Apartments are very small – a couple with children may live in one large room with a kitchenette and bathroom.

The family

The pressures of work mean that the male breadwinner is usually absent six days a week, often from early in the morning until late at night.

As a result, domestic life, in this ostensibly male-dominated society, is basically maternalistic; and although a Japanese woman is subservient to her husband's wishes, she rules in his absence, controlling all major family matters, including the finances. It is usual for him to hand over to her the whole of his wage packet, receiving an allowance for his expenses.

Thus a Japanese child's life takes place in a calm and well-ordered environment. Typically, he will live with his parents and one or the other pair of grandparents.

Love and marriage Marriages often result from introductions arranged by families, for it can otherwise be difficult to meet a suitable partner. The resulting marriage is usually a love match, however, and the practice of formally arranging a marriage is dying out.

Unless the wife is one of the new breed of career women, she will be consigned to the family home, to take second place to her mother or mother-in-law.

Premarital sex is probably not much more common than it was in the past, but it is more openly accepted.

Beyond the family

Pubic hair is erased from Western men's magazines, but pornography in Japan is alive and well, to an extent not commonly seen in the West.

Prostitution is illegal, but there is, nevertheless, a flourishing sex trade which thrives on the custom of middle and upper management and is priced accordingly.

In the larger cities there are bars where bizarrely under-dressed waitresses serve drinks, "soapland" parlours offering erotic massage, and "love hotels", which have fantasy rooms catering to young couples, adulterers and prostitutes alike with legendary discretion. Homosexuality is tolerated, and there is an active gay scene in Tokyo.

Geishas There are still many geisha girls – who are not prostitutes, although some may fill the role of expensive mistress. Regular geisha entertainment is very expensive, perfectly innocent and somewhat like a formalized children's party. Westerners, who may be invited as a special treat, tend to find it boring.

Leisure

As a nation of workaholics, the Japanese take their leisure seldom and generally in large groups.

Weekday evenings are usually a time for working men to enjoy themselves, drinking with their fellows in the cities or, more rarely, taking their families out, sometimes to the theatre, more often to a meal.

Sundays are family days, when the breadwinner takes his wife and children on an outing. This may be simply a walk in the park or a trip to another branch of the family, or to the recently opened Disneyland near Tokyo. The Japanese are voracious sightseers, both at home and abroad, and flock to popular tourist sites on holidays and at weekends.

Under company patronage, a Japanese *salaryman* can even play golf, a game that is a Japanese obsession, yet is limited as a rule to those wealthy enough to afford the exorbitant club membership and green fees. Many keen Japanese golfers seldom if ever play anywhere except in a multistorey driving range.

Tradition rules

The Japanese may be shy with foreigners, but they have few inhibitions when in their own groups. Their long, highly cultured, independent history has fitted them well to adapt to and cope with the strains of modern living. In spite of the many changes in their society, it is still the traditional values that really matter in Japan.

Education

The child crouched over his desk in the examination hall wears a white headband inscribed with the message "sure victory in exam". Exams are at the heart of Japanese education, which is highly competitive from the earliest age. Pressures on children are intense, and there is growing demand for changes in both the style of education and the syllabus.

The importance of education

The Japanese are dedicated to their children's education. About 10% of Japan's GNP is spent on private and state education, and parents, particularly mothers, devote themselves to facilitating and overseeing intensive routines of extra study to give their offspring the edge in the series of qualifying exams that culminate in university or college entry at the age of 18. Mothers will attend school when children are ill so that they can take notes to be written up and learned by the invalid. To avoid disrupting the children's schooling, families sometimes split up when the father is posted elsewhere in Japan or overseas. This feverish competition for academic success has as its goal a secure job in a high-status industry or profession.

The education system

The Japanese state school structure is based on the US model. The system is styled "6-3-3-4", with six years at elementary school, for 6- to 12-year-olds; three years at junior high, up to the age of 15, when compulsory education ceases; three years at senior high, which is completed by over 90% of all pupils; and a four-year university degree course. Over 35% of Japanese students go to university, although not all courses last four years; there are many two-year junior colleges, especially for girls.

Schools

Japanese schooling is motivated by Confucian ideals of unceasing learning and punctuated by frequent exams. Great stress is placed on learning by rote, and progress is usually at the pace of the slowest, with streaming almost nonexistent because of the problems of "face" implicit in such categorizing. Mixed-sex and mixed-ability classes of up to 50 pupils are not unusual. Children work a 5½-day week, with a total of 240 school days per year (most Western children put in about 200 days).

Rigorous exams are taken in the top grade of each level of school to determine which candidates attend the most favoured establishments.

Early schooling Prestigious private universities have their own feeder systems, for which ferocious competition starts at a tender age. Ambitious parents start the process earlier than the state system, sending their children to private nursery schools at the age of three. The most sought-after nursery schools have entrance exams.

Modern business requirements have invaded even the preschool sector, and some nursery schools introduce their tiny charges to computers.

Nursery and elementary schooling is dominated by the learning of the 96 *kana* (phonetic symbols) and the almost 2,000 *kanji* (Chinese characters) necessary for general reading. As a result, the country's literacy rate is close to 100%.

High school In addition to Japanese and Chinese literature, the curriculum includes linear algebra, inorganic chemistry, mechanical and electronic physics, statistics, and calculus. English instruction, which begins at 12, is geared to passing exams rather than to communicating.

Private tuition With the competition for success so intense, there has arisen a large private educational sector. *Juku*, or private crammers, cater particularly for 12- to 15-year-olds seeking coveted places in the best senior high schools. Urged on by their *kyoiku mama* ("education mothers"), some youngsters get up as early as 4.30am, travel to the crammer, put in an hour's work, go to their state school and complete a normal day, then return to the crammer for another session, getting home as late as 11pm in some cases. Weekend time, too, may be sacrificed to the cramming of work already covered by the formal syllabus. As the time for university entrance approaches, the pressures intensify even further.

Technical colleges have not been a great success. They teach trades and practical subjects, but most 15-year-olds opt for senior high schools, because employers prefer to teach their own trades.

University entrance In the February of their senior year, high school students take the university entrance exams. Around 38% pass first time; those who fail go on in most cases to do a further year or two at a crammer before re-taking the exams. Every candidate takes the common entrance exam, consisting of multiple-choice questions in seven subjects. This is followed by exam papers for the specific university. A good memory is the main factor in success; there are no interviews for university places.

Universities Only a quarter of Japan's 460 universities are public – either national or municipal. The remainder are private institutions, only the best of which can compete with the leading public universities. At the top of the pyramid is the state-run Tokyo University, whose prestigious law faculty has provided all but one Finance Minister. Most top people in government or business are graduates of the national universities in Tokyo or Kyoto, or the private Tokyo universities, Keio and Waseda.

Starting a career Once at university, most students are past the ordeal of exams. Acceptance at a top university is virtually all that's required for a high-status job. A good degree is unimportant, since major companies, using recent graduates as talent scouts, compete for students from the elite universities, recruiting them well before graduation. (See also *Employment*.) It is here that Japan's old-boy network (*gakubatsu*) starts.

Postgraduate courses at universities are dominated by engineering (50%) and medical or technical subjects. An increasing number of Japanese are doing postgraduate studies overseas.

In-house training by major corporations is substantial. Vocational courses can be taken in a variety of subjects with a view to switching direction, or just improving general knowledge of the industry. Where technical changes have affected jobs, state subsidies encourage retraining within the company.

The educational debate

A recent British government report commented that "the purpose of Japanese education is clear cut. It provides what the dominant voices in industry and commerce want, in the national interest, and generally does so to their satisfaction."

However, many Japanese fear that the emphasis on rote learning has sacrificed education to mere ability to pass exams. Teenage suicides and a growing trend of classroom violence are blamed on postwar Occupation education policies which eradicated *shushin*, the moral education that was the essence of traditional schooling, with its emphasis on loyalty, filial piety and nationalism.

What is clear is that education will become the subject of increasing political debate, not least because policy makers fear that the system is stunting originality and creative thought. What is good for the multinationals now may not, in the long run, be good for the nation.

Language

The Japanese language seemed so complex to a 16th-century Jesuit that he dubbed it "the Devil's tongue". Modern spoken Japanese, however, is as easy to get by in as most European languages. Pronunciation is easy, not impossibly tonal like Chinese, a language to which Japanese is *not* structurally related. The grammar is manageable, though sentence structure differs fundamentally from English and other European languages. There are, however, two devilish areas: the written word and respectful forms of speech.

The written word

Japanese may be written in three directions (left to right or right to left horizontally, and right to left, reading down vertically) and in four scripts.

Hiragana A phonetic system whose 46 symbols represent the 46 sounds of Japanese. It is used principally for writing prepositions and assorted verb endings.

Katakana Another phonetic system with 46 symbols. It is used principally for imported words and is standard in telegrams and in much advertising.

Kanji Pictograms of Chinese origin, representing nuggets of meaning. In, for example, "I am learning Japanese," "I", "learn" and "Japanese" will be in *kanji*, while "am ...ing" and particles modifying the subject and object will be in *hiragana*.

The sound of *kanji* can be transcribed in *hiragana* (and often is, when the writer forgets a *kanji*); but Japanese is not easily read without *kanji*, since homonyms abound (the word *sei*, for example, has 12 meanings). Some 2,000 *kanji* are required for daily use (professionals will use perhaps twice this number) and countless compounds also exist.

Romaji Romanized Japanese. It is used in advertising and for Anglicized place names.

The language of respect

The special style of speech used to show respect to social superiors and strangers is in a state of disarray. It can be so complex that the Japanese regularly misuse it. There are, for example, at least nine different words for "I", the appropriate one depending on the relative status of the speaker and listener. For foreigners, an appropriate facial expression is a good substitute for the correct form of words.

Borrowed words

The number of words adopted from other languages is staggering. Formerly Japanese borrowed from the Chinese both the *kanji* and their pronunciation, but English is now the major source. Some 25,000 English words, such as *takushi* (taxi) and *esukareta* (escalator), are in daily use. Most, however, are rendered unrecognizable to the Westerner by unpliable Japanese lips or by the phonetic system (neither of which can distinguish "b" from "v", "l" from "r" and "s" from "th"). Words are also dramatically changed by the Japanese passion for truncation, which produces such variants as *terebi* (television), *suto* (from *sutoraiki*, strike) and *depato* (department store).

Getting by without Japanese

For most of your stay you will probably be chaperoned by an English-speaking company man (very few Japanese, incidentally, speak any other foreign language). Coping alone in Japan without the language is not impossible, since the Japanese are always helpful. Your main problem will be locating places, since most signs and place names are in *kanji*, *hiragana* and *katakana*.

However, English translations are increasingly found in Tokyo, Osaka and Kobe, and on highways, subways and JNR stations. Also, despite an ability to read and correspond in English, most Japanese do not speak it. If in difficulties, approach a young person, who is more likely to be conversant with English, or write your question clearly. The Japanese are touched when foreigners try to speak their language, and mastery of a few everyday phrases will enhance your standing.

Interpreters

Rather than go it alone, you may wish to employ an interpreter (but see *Business meetings*). Interpreters can be contacted through your agent or embassy, or through major hotels, travel bureaus and specialist agencies (listed in *City by city*). Standard rates for student and pro respectively are around Y20,000 and Y75,000 daily, plus expenses.

Your interpreter will probably be a woman. Brief her fully in advance. At the meeting, seat her where she can hear easily. Speak slowly and clearly and allow adequate pauses between sentences. Write out large numbers and check frequently that she has understood. Don't overwork your interpreter or interrupt when she is listening, and avoid arcane terms and questions phrased in the negative. For example, the reply to "Don't you smoke?" will be "Yes (you're right, I don't smoke)", rather than "No", as in English.

If short requests take a long time to translate, it is either because your interpreter is using the appropriate (lengthy) forms of respect or because she is explaining cultural differences.

In understanding your interpreter, a glance at your Japanese colleague's face may reveal more than he cares to put into words – especially when it comes to a refusal.

Japanese phrases

The English phrases here have Japanese translations in *romaji* (Romanized Japanese) and a guide to pronunciation in brackets. In phrases with ... insert the appropriate name or word, or a word or phrase from this list.

Basic courtesies

Yes, please	*O-negai shimasu* (oh-nehguy shemass)
No, thank you	*Kekko desu* (kek-kaw dess)
Excuse me/sorry	*Sumimasen* (suememahsen)
Please do! Come in!	
Here you are	*Hai dozo* (high dawzo)
After you!	*O-saki ni dozo* (oh-sahkey nee dawzo)
Thank you	*Arigato gozaimasu* (arigahtaw gozighmass)
It's my/It was a pleasure	*Do itashimashite* (daw eetahshemahshtay)

Greetings and farewells

Good morning, Mr, Mrs, Miss	*...san, o-hayo gozaimasu* (san, oh-highyoh gozighmass)
Good evening, ...	*...san, konban wa* (konban wah)
Hello, ...	*...san, konnichi wa* (kon-nichee wah)
I am pleased to meet you	*Hajimemashite* (hahjemaymahshtay)
How are you?	*O-genki desu ka* (oh-genkey dess kah)
Very well, thank you	*O-kage sama de* (oh-kahgay sahmah day)
My name is John/Jane Smith	*John/Jane Smith to moshimasu* (toh mawshemass)
This is my business card	*Watakushi no meishi desu ga* (wahtahkshe no mayshe dessoo gah)

I look forward to doing business with you	*Yoroshiku o-negai shimasu* (yoroshekoo oh-nehguy shemass)
Shall we go for a drink/meal?	*Nomi/Shokuji ni ikimasho ka* (nohmee/shokoojee nee ikimahshaw kah)
Thank you for...	*...arigato gozaimasu* (arigahtaw gozighmass)
Today	*Kyo wa* (kyaw wah)
Last night	*Yube wa* (youbeh wah)
The other day	*Senjitsu* (senjitsoo)
Please accept this (gift)	*Kore o dozo* (kawray oh dawzoh)
That's very kind of you	*Domo arigato gozaimasu* (dawmow arigahtaw gozighmass)
Please give my regards to...	*...ni yoroshiku* (...nee yoroshekoo)
Excuse me, I must leave	*Shitsurei itashimasu* (shitsueray eetashimass)
Goodbye	*Sayonara* (sahyohnahrah)
Goodnight	*O-yasumi nasai* (oh-yahsueme nahsigh)
See you tomorrow	*Ashita mata* (ahshtah mahtah)
Thank you for taking care of me/us	*O-sewa ni narimashita* (o-sehwah nee narimashtah)
Let's meet again	*Mata o-ai shimasho* (mahtah oh-eyeshemahshaw)

Eating or drinking out

...please!	*...kudasai* (koodasigh)
How about...?	*...ikaga desu ka* (eekahgah dess kah)
This	*Kore* (kawreh)
A light breakfast	*Moningu* (mawningoo)
Coffee	*Kohi* (kawhe)
Tea (English-type)	*Kocha* (kawchah)
Juice	*Jusu* (joosoo)
Beer	*Biru* (beeroo)
Scotch	*Sukotchi* (skotchee)
Whisky with water and ice	*Mizuwari* (meezoowahree)
Rice wine	*O-sake* (oh-sahkeh)
Cigarettes	*Tabako* (tahbahkoh)
Menu	*Menyu* (menyou)
Another one	*Mo hitotsu* (maw hetotsu)
A little more	*Mo sukoshi* (maw skoshee)
The bill	*O-kanjo* (oh-kanjaw)
What is this?	*Kore wa nan desu ka* (kawray wah nan dess kah)
That looks delicious	*Oishiso desu ne* (oisheesaw dess nay)
It tastes delicious	*Oishii desu* (oishee-ee dess)
That was delicious	*Oishikatta desu* (oisheekat-tah dess)
Cheers!	*Kanpai* (kanpigh)
Bon appétit!	*Itadakimasu* (eetahdahkeymass)
Thank you for the meal	*Go-chisosama deshita* (gocheesawsama deshtah)
Where is the toilet?	*O-tearai wa dochira desu ka* (oh-tayarigh wah docheerah dess kah)

Small talk

Do you speak English?	*Eigo ga dekimasu ka* (aygo gah dekeemass kah)
I speak only a little Japanese	*Nihongo wa sukoshi shika dekimasen* (neehongo wah skoshee shkah dekeemahsen)
Japanese is very difficult	*Nihongo wa totemo muzukashii desu* (neehongo wah totehmow moozookashee-ee dess)

How do you say...in Japanese?	*...wa Nihongo de nan to iimasu ka* (wah neehongo day nan toh ee-eemass kah)
What does...mean?	*...wa do iu imi desu ka* (wah daw you eemee dess kah)
Are you married?	*Kekkon shite imasu ka* (kek-kon shtay eemass kah)
I'm married	*Watashi wa kekkon shite imasu* (wahtahshe wah kek-kon shtay eemass)
I'm single	*Dokushin desu* (dokooshin dess)
Have you any children?	*Kodomo wa imasu ka* (kodomow wah eemass kah)
You're very good (eg at English or golf)	*O-jozu desu ne* (oh-jawzoo dess nay)
Not really	*Chigaimasu* (cheeguyeemass)
What lovely weather!	*Ii o-tenki desu ne* (ee-ee oh-tenkey dess nay)
It's hot, isn't it	*Atsui desu ne* (atsooee dess nay)
It's cold, isn't it	*Samui desu ne* (samooee dess nay)
Do you understand?	*Wakarimasu ka* (wakahreemass ka)
Yes, I do (understand)	*Hai, wakarimasu* (high, wakahreemass)
No, I don't (understand)	*Ie, wakarimasen* (ee-eh, wakahreemasen)
Yes, that's right	*Hai, so desu* (high saw dess)

Asking directions

Excuse me, where is the...?	*Sumimasen, ...wa doko desu ka* (suememahsen, ...wah dohkoh dess kah)
Excuse me, is there a... near here?	*Sumimasen, kono chikaku ni...arimasu* (suememahsen, kohnoh chikahkoo nee...ahreemass kah)
Taxi rank	*Takushi noriba* (takshee noreebah)
Station	*Eki* (ehkey)
Subway station	*Chikatetsu* (chickahtetsoo)
Hotel/Japanese-style hotel	*Hoteru* (hohtehroo)/*Ryokan* (ryohkan)
Pharmacy	*Yakkyoku* (yak-kyohkoo)
Post office	*Yubinkyoku* (youbinkyohkoo)
Police box	*Koban* (kawban)
Public toilet	*O-tearai* (oh-tayarigh)
Public telephone	*Koshu denwa* (kawshoo denwah)
Travel agent	*Kotsukosha* (kawtsoo kawshah)
I'd like to make an international call	*Kokusai denwa o-negai shitai n'desu ga* (koksigh denwah oh-nehguy shtay'n dess gah)

Taxis and trains

To...please	*...made o-negai shimasu* (...mahdeh oh-nehguy shemass)
The airport	*Kuko* (kookaw)
Please let me/us off here	*Koko de oroshite kudasai* (koko deh oroshteh koodasigh)
How much is it?	*Ikura desu ka* (eekoorah dess kah)
A single/return to..., please	*...made katamichi/o-fuku o-negai shimasu* (...mahday kahtahmitchee/awfookoo oh-nehguy shemass)
First class	*Guriin ken* (green ken)
What time does it depart?	*Nanpunhatsu desu ka* (nanpoonhatsoo dess kah)

Manners and conversation

Etiquette is the indispensable lubricant in a society as hierarchical, and as crowded, as Japan's. Although the foreign visitor is not expected to be conversant with all the traditional courtesies, a willingness to learn is important. The essence of etiquette lies in the preservation of surface harmony. Humility, reserve, patience and tolerance are all qualities that contribute to this. Effusive apologies (for even minor errors) and effusive thanks (for even minor favours) also oil the wheels. Displays of anger, disappointment or frustration serve only to disrupt the surface harmony – often to the Westerner's disadvantage – and should be avoided.

Conversation

Be sensitive to status, and always address the most senior of your hosts, who may not be the best English-speaker. Listen rather than lecture, and when you speak, do so with modesty and reserve. Silent pauses in conversation are not feared but savoured in Japan. It is not Japanese practice to use first names, and it is best not to do so even if invited to, except in the most informal situations.

Clarity and tact Get into the habit of speaking carefully and clearly (but not patronizingly so), at least until you have gauged the English-speaking ability of your host. It is often wise to ask the same question twice, in a different way, to ensure understanding, but avoid constant (and especially ever-louder) repetition of questions and statements. This may require you to pretend that your host has understood when you have good reason to believe otherwise, but it saves face and maintains the harmony. Informal notes confirming the points discussed can be exchanged after any meeting (most businessmen are able to correspond without difficulty in English, though not in other European languages).

Yes? "Yes" (*Hai, hai*) very rarely means "Yes, I agree." It means "Yes, I'm listening," or "I see." The written word is always the surest indication of an affirmative answer.

No? "No" (*Ie*) is considered too blunt to be used often. Vaguer expressions such as "Maybe" or "Let's think about it" are most common. You, also, should use these less direct terms. A Japanese businessman will, for example, often appear to go along with what you say, especially if you pursue a point with vigour, even when he disagrees. His purpose is to maintain harmony. Try to take an indirect approach yourself until mutual trust has been established. Take care to conceal frustration and anger at the length of time it takes to make decisions. This is the way business works in Japan.

Sensitive subjects No topics are taboo. The political scene, sex and religion are less sensitive subjects in Japan than in many Western societies. The following, however, *are* sensitive: the role of MITI in Japanese industry, dumping, the Japanese work ethic, housing conditions, militarism and the War, attitudes towards – and the status of – women, and the treatment of the Korean and *B'rakumin* (outcast) minorities. The Koreans, for example, are discriminated against in Japan, especially when it comes to marriage. People of Korean ancestry are usually careful to hide the fact.

It is a common Western gaffe to suppose that the Japanese worship their ancestors; they do not, but they do honour their memory.

Opening gambits Topics of endless interest include the family (family snaps always make useful conversation openings), the weather, sport (baseball, golf and Sumo are avidly followed) and, above all, your impressions of Japan. Some familiarity with Japan's culture, its history (with the exception of World War II) and places of historical interest creates a very favourable impression.

Small talk Serious business negotiations will often begin with less serious conversation. Let your hosts initiate these informal exchanges and decide what topics are appropriate to the situation. This is the first step in building a business relationship.

Intimate questions Foreign visitors should be careful not to take umbrage at the intimate nature of certain questions on age ("How old are you?"), money ("How much do you earn?") and marital status ("Why are you not married?").

Humour Despite the stereotype of the Japanese as a race both serious and single-minded in its devotion to work, they have a great sense of fun. Although jokes as such are not told in Japan, the Japanese are certainly able to appreciate the funny side of things. Men laugh openly in Japan, but etiquette requires women to cover their mouths when they laugh. Raucous laughter should be confined to drinking establishments.

Body language

Harmony may be disturbed by transmitting inappropriate non-verbal signals or by failing to interpret signals received.

The bow As a Westerner, you may often be welcomed by a handshake, but the bow is the accepted form of greeting and farewell. If greeted with a bow, try to return the depth and intensity of the host's bow. The arms should be kept fairly straight with palms flat against the thighs. The eyes are lowered, as well as the upper body. Often you may be greeted with a compromise combination of a slight bow and handshake. The weak, almost reluctant, handshake of many Japanese should not be mistaken for weakness of character.

Physical contact Public displays of affection for the opposite sex, such as kissing, hugging and holding hands, are both rare and generally frowned upon. Male displays of camaraderie, such as back-slapping, vigorous handshakes and arm-touching, should also be avoided.

Personal space The Japanese tend to require more personal space than Westerners, so when conversing take a position a little farther from your host than normal.

Eye contact should not be insisted on, as it often is in the West. It may be considered impolite and an infringement on personal space. A demure, downward look is not a sign of weakness or dishonesty.

The smile expresses pleasure, joy and affection, but it may also conceal embarrassment, frustration and discontent. The ubiquitous smile may be less a sign of affirmation or approval than of self-control.

Western ways

Because Western non-verbal language differs from that of the Japanese, there is much that may confuse. The Westerner should remember not to exaggerate emotions or those gestures that accompany them.

Shrugging The Japanese do not shrug their shoulders or understand what may be meant by it.

Winking While younger men may wink at women, the "affectionate wink" between friends will not be understood and is best avoided.

Pointing Avoid pointing, since it is thought too direct. The Japanese use the whole hand, palm up, in a horizontal, wavy motion in the general direction of the object, place or person being referred to.

Beckoning The Japanese beckon with the motion that in the West suggests "Go away." It is exactly the opposite of the Western beckoning action, with the fingers pointing down from the extended hand.

Nose blowing Handkerchiefs are used for wiping the fingers and the brow but almost never the nose. Paper tissues are used instead. The Western use of handkerchiefs for nose-blowing is considered extremely unhygienic. The Japanese will sniff, snort and spit with relish, but loud nose-blowing will certainly cause offence.

Dress Both men and women should avoid loud colours and flashy styles. For women, skirts and dresses are acceptable but trousers are generally best not worn in a business context. Classic restraint is preferable to glamour.

Japanese behaviour

Foreign visitors will need to adjust their expectations of what is acceptable social behaviour.

Chivalry has yet to reach Japan. Businesswomen should not expect seats to be offered or doors to be opened, since men precede women in everything. Likewise, the foreign businessman should not insist on Japanese women accepting chivalry. It may cause embarrassment, especially among the older generation. Indeed, the modern Japanese seem increasingly to place youth before age. It is not unusual for a frail old lady to be deprived of a seat by a healthy young child.

Pushing and shoving Although strict codes of etiquette govern behaviour within any identifiable group, in the outside world anarchy sometimes reigns. Pushing and shoving in crowds, particularly in the subway, and reluctance to form orderly queues are both commonplace. Try to suppress any annoyance.

Excuse me "Excuse me, I'd like to get past" is often expressed non-verbally, by a combination of a bow and a karate-chop movement of the hand, repeated several times over.

Urination Urinating and spitting in public do not always cause the offence they do in some Western nations.

Women beware Japan is one of the safest places in the world, but this applies primarily to men. On crowded and late-night trains it is not uncommon for women (including foreign women) to be harassed. Harassment can take the form of staring and attempts at touching. Curiously, Japanese society seems to turn a blind eye to such male harassment (perhaps because Japanese women are reluctant to make a scene). Most offensive approaches can be stopped instantly with shrieks of anger.

Mealtime etiquette

To order steak when your hosts suggest raw fish disturbs the harmony; to refuse to try a dish may offend. The rule is to conform. In all things follow your host, who will take pleasure in teaching you. Let him decide the menu. He will say *itadakimasu* ("bon appétit") before beginning the meal, and you should reply *itadakimasu.* Remember to say *go-chisosama deshita* ("Thank you") at the end of the meal or to express effusive thanks in your own language.

Chopsticks Take your cue from the host and remove the wooden sticks from the paper sleeve, splitting them if necessary. Mastery of chopsticks is guaranteed to impress your hosts. Those less dextrous should practise in private or enter into the fun of being shown in public. Alternatively, ask for a fork. Never point chopsticks at anyone, never leave them crossed and never stick them vertically in the rice bowl. Align them neatly on the china chopstick rest.

Bowls Follow your host, who will first take the lid off his rice bowl and place it to the left. Next he will remove the lid of the soup bowl and place it to the right. The rice and soup bowls can both be held in the hand while eating. When drinking soup it is not impolite to slurp a little. Use both hands when holding out a bowl to have it refilled.

Alcohol Women traditionally pour for men and inferiors for superiors. Having had wine or beer poured for you, take the bottle and offer to pour in return. The host may offer you the cup from which he has drunk, carefully wiping it first. If this honour is extended to you, accept the cup graciously and raise it with both hands to be filled. If you are teetotal or just dislike sake, it is sufficient to bring the filled cup to your lips without drinking. An ability to consume vast quantities of alcohol is much admired, but when you have had your fill, do not leave the glass or cup standing empty or it will be refilled.

Toasts It is common practice to propose toasts, usually at the beginning of a meal. Etiquette is the opposite of that in the West, however, and the person being toasted should always drink the toast along with those who have proposed it.

Smoking The Japanese tend to smoke more than Westerners, and the conference room and drinking establishments can be very smoky places. Some Japanese smoke during meals. If you are a nonsmoker, do not be offended if your permission is not requested. If you are a smoker do not be offended if a cigarette is not offered to you. Cigarettes are considered very personal things.

The bill It is not necessary to offer to pay or split the bill in any establishment. To insist may offend. A return invitation to a Western-style restaurant or bar is the best way of repaying hospitality.

Living Japanese-style

Special care is called for when visiting a Japanese home (a rare honour) or a Japanese-style inn, or *ryokan.*

Shoes Remember to take your shoes off before entering a Japanese house or inn (slip-on shoes save time). Turn them around to face the door so that they will be easy to put on when leaving. You will then shuffle to the main room in "corridor slippers", provided at the entrance. Remove the slippers before entering a matted room (clean socks save embarrassment!). Use the corridor slippers again to take you to the toilet, where you must change into toilet slippers. Do not forget to remove your toilet slippers on leaving the toilet.

The toilet Toilets are usually squat-style, sometimes with no lock on the door. Knock on the door, and if it is engaged you will hear a counter-knock.

Bathing The Japanese bathe for relaxation as well as cleanliness. You will find Japanese-style baths in some hotels, in all inns, in the still-popular public baths and in all households. Although the bath may be private, one is expected to use it in the prescribed manner; ignorance of bathing etiquette is unforgivable. First remove your clothes in the antechamber and place them in the basket provided. You will be given a hand towel to take into the bathroom. Squat on a stool and, with the bowl provided, scoop water from the tub and pour it over you. Using the hand towel and soap, wash your body thoroughly before rinsing off with water scooped from the bath. Only now can you step into the bath. You may take your well-rinsed hand towel in with you. Often the water is extremely hot. Add a little cold water from the tap if you wish. To avoid getting scorched, it is best to slip into the tub gently and keep still once in.

Never get into the bath without cleaning yourself first; don't use soap in the bath and don't pull out the plug. Others will be using the bath after you. After relaxing in the bath, climb out and wring your hand towel dry. With this you are expected to dry yourself. There may be a cotton kimono provided in the antechamber. If there is, slip it on over your underwear, wrapping the left side over the right (only corpses have their kimonos wrapped right over left!) and tying it with a sash. Baths are to be enjoyed, so don't hurry excessively or you may offend your host.

City by City

Introduction

To the travelling executive, Japan can appear to be one immense city. The urban sprawl begins with Tokyo, which merges imperceptibly into Kawasaki and Yokohama – enormous cities in their own right – to form one of the biggest conurbations in the world. This megacity spreads westward along the Pacific coast, in an industrial belt that runs through Nagoya, Osaka and Hiroshima to the far tip of Honshu and, almost without interruption, on across the water to Kita-Kyushu, Fukuoka and beyond.

The cities within this 550-mile urban landscape are those that the business traveller is most likely to visit, for it is here that Japan's main commercial and industrial centres are concentrated. The ten cities selected for this guide all have a population of 1 million or more, and all but one – Sapporo, a refreshingly provincial, northern city – fall within the southern urban area.

The endless urban wilderness may leave the business traveller wondering what has happened to the mysterious Orient. It is, of course, still there, hidden just beneath the surface. Even in a cosmopolitan centre such as Tokyo, the plastic cherry blossoms lining the street or the bowing elevator girls remind you with a jolt that this is Japan.

Japan's intercity transport system is excellent. The Bullet Train links every major city except Sapporo, and that omission will be remedied in the near future. It takes, for example, just seven hours from Tokyo to Fukuoka. The major cities are also linked by efficient airlines. Internal flights are only marginally more expensive than the Bullet Train and, frequently, a return journey is cheaper by air than by train.

Finding your way around the cities is likely to be your major problem. Japan's address system is notoriously difficult to understand. An address may appear in English as, for example, 4-14-3 Ginza or 14-3 Ginza 4-chome, which are in fact the same; "chome" means district and the other numbers refer to blocks. However, the address of a place often seems to bear little relationship to its location. The easiest course is to take with you the name and address of your destination in Japanese (and phone number, in case of crisis) and let the taxi driver worry about finding it. Be patient; he, too, may have little idea where it is, but he will consult a policeman or call for directions. If you travel by subway (thus avoiding the traffic jams) telephone ahead to get exact directions, including the number of the subway exit and the appearance of the building.

Your difficulties will be eased by the helpfulness of the Japanese people. Japan may appear to be a land of cities, but what other country has cities where people look at you askance if you check a restaurant bill? The streets are safe, public transport runs exactly on time, public phones invariably work and the people are scrupulously honest.

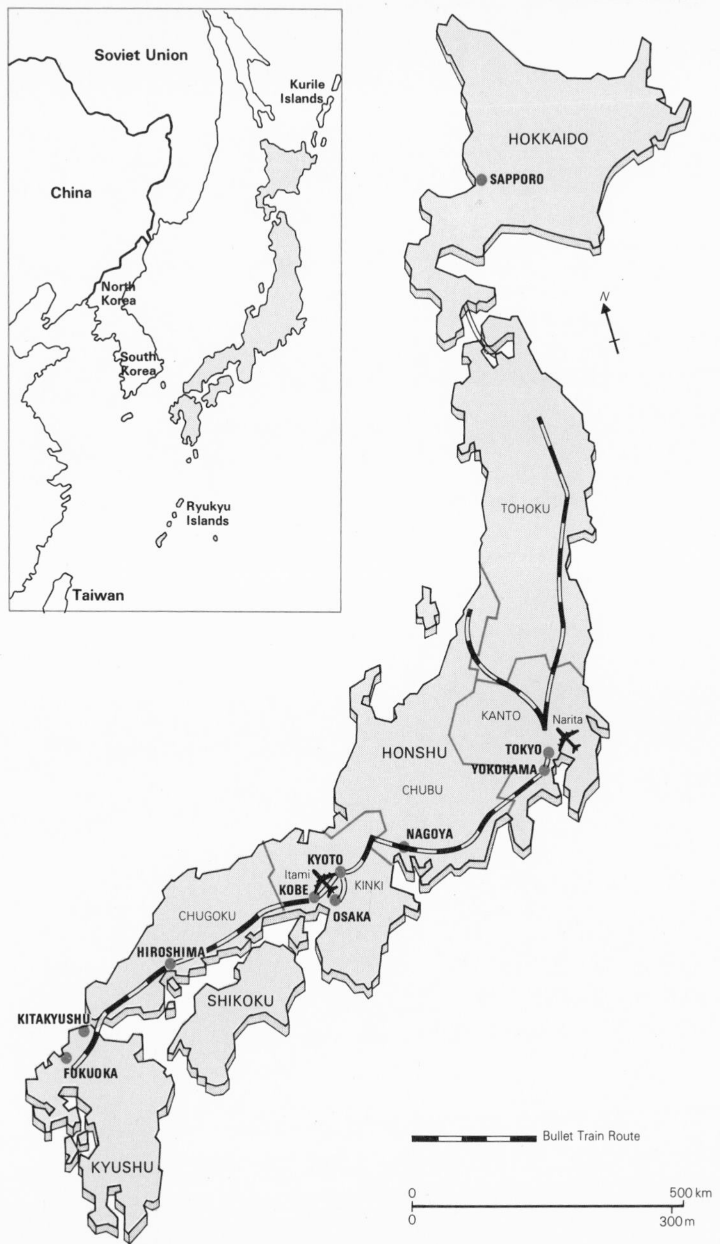
Soviet Union
Kurile Islands
China
North Korea
South Korea
Ryukyu Islands
Taiwan
HOKKAIDO
SAPPORO
N
TOHOKU
KANTO
Narita
HONSHU
TOKYO
YOKOHAMA
CHUBU
NAGOYA
KYOTO
Itami
KOBE
KINKI
OSAKA
CHUGOKU
HIROSHIMA
SHIKOKU
KITAKYUSHU
FUKUOKA
KYUSHU
Bullet Train Route
0
500 km
0
300 m

TOKYO

Area code ☏ 03

The second largest city in the world with a population of nearly 13m, Tokyo sprawls over more than 800 square miles/2,000 sq km. Government, industry and commerce, including most major companies and the stock market, are based here; and it is also the centre for sports, education and the arts. At the hub of the city are the commercial areas, with the residential areas lying on the periphery. Heavy and light industries, located in the coastal area, include electrical appliances, electronics, optical products, precision engineering, textiles, printing and publishing.

When shogun Tokugawa Ieyasu took the minor castle town of Edo as his capital in 1590, it marked a major transition in Japan's development, from a country dominated by the decadent Kyoto aristocracy to a modern commercial state. During the 250 year rule of the Tokugawas, Edo grew into the largest city in the world (in 1700 the population reached 1m). To service the enormous population of *daimyo* and samurai warlords, forced to spend part of each year there under surveillance, Tokugawa brought merchants and artisans to the city, and set about the reclamation of the eastern marshes (the present Tsukiji, Shimbashi and Nihonbashi) for their use. Theoretically one of the lowest classes in the rigid Tokugawa hierarchy, the merchants actually became more and more prosperous, and the impoverished samurai had to come to them for money.

In 1868, Emperor Meiji abolished the shogunate and moved his court from Kyoto to Edo, renaming it Tokyo (Eastern Capital). The city began a period of rapid modernization to bring it into line with the West. The *daimyo* left, and the merchants, now able to move freely, settled in the hilly areas in the western part of the city.

Tokyo continues to grow and change. The main area of expansion at present is around Shinjuku and out into the western suburbs where there is still empty land for building. In 1990 the metropolitan government will move from Marunouchi to Shinjuku, where a new City Hall, designed by Kenzo Tange, is under construction. There are plans for the Bullet Train to stop there and for a high speed underground road link between Shinjuku and Marunouchi. In central Tokyo, between Akasaka and Roppongi, the Ark Hills complex has recently been completed; this houses the offices of many foreign companies as well as providing cultural facilities such as a concert hall and a broadcasting channel.

Arriving

The building of a new international airport at Narita has been the source of much well-publicized controversy. As far as the business traveller is concerned, its most controversial aspect is its distance – 40 miles/66km – from Tokyo. The much-mourned previous international airport, Haneda, a mere 15min from town, now handles mainly domestic flights. There is a limousine bus connecting the two airports, which takes about 2hrs.

Narita Airport

Completed in 1978, Narita is a small but highly efficient modern airport, designed to ensure the smoothest possible passage for the traveller. Immigration procedures are extremely rapid, signs are in English as well as Japanese and even the porters are friendly and helpful. The only complaint is the time it takes to get to Tokyo. A wide range of good-quality restaurants, coffee shops and bars, most of them closing at 8pm; VIP lounges for first class passengers; plenty of useful shops, including a branch of Mitsukoshi and shops selling electronic goods, woodblock prints and kimonos; several banks, open from 7.30am to 11pm. JAL Cargo Services ☎ (0476) 32 3350. Airport information ☎ (0476) 32 2800.
Nearby hotels *Narita Prince* 560 Tokko, Narita ☎ (0476) 33 1111 TX 3762147. *Holiday Inn* 320-1 Tokko, Narita ☎ (0476) 32 1234 TX 3762133. *Narita Airport Resthouse* PO Box 126, New Tokyo International Airport, Narita ☎ (0476) 32 1212 TX 3762154.
City link The easiest way to cover the 40 miles/66km into Tokyo is to be met, or to dig deep into your wallet for the taxi fare. Failing that, the comfortable limousine bus is a good alternative. The journey by road takes 60–75min; allow an extra 30min in rush hours.
Bus There are buses direct to 30 major hotels, departing every few minutes between 6am and 10pm. Alternatively, take the bus to Tokyo City Air Terminal, where you change to another bus for the 10min ride to Tokyo Station.
Train The Keisei Skyliner is fast, reliable and cheap. Comfortable, air-conditioned trains depart every 30min between 8am and 10pm, with a journey time of exactly 1hr. However, Keisei Narita Station is a bus ride from the airport and you will need to take a taxi or subway from the Tokyo terminal, Keisei Ueno, to your hotel. There are also stopping trains on the Keisei and JNR lines, which take slightly longer.
Taxi and limousine There are always plenty of taxis. A chauffeur-driven limousine can be arranged at the limousine bus counter.
Car rental Major firms have offices at Narita.

Haneda Airport

Most domestic flights use Haneda, and there are connections with every major city. Facilities are somewhat more basic than at Narita, and you will have to walk across the tarmac to your plane. Several restaurants, coffee shops and bars on landside, all closing at 8.30pm; a few shops with a limited range of goods – mainly local foods, tea and cakes; bank closes at 4.30pm.
Nearby hotels *Haneda Tokyu*, 8-6 Haneda Kuko 2-chome, Ota-ku ☎ 747 0311 TX 2466560.
City link *Monorail* is the best way to get into Tokyo. Trains depart for Hamamatsucho on the Yamanote line, every 6–7min between 6.40am and 11pm. The journey takes 16min. There are no porters or trolleys available at the station.
Bus The limousine bus departs every 40min and stops at the main hotels in Shinjuku. There are also buses to Narita and Yokohama.
Taxi It takes about 45min to get to Tokyo Station by taxi.

Railway stations

Bullet Trains heading west from Tokyo run from Tokyo Station; those heading northeast depart from Ueno Station.
Tokyo Station Built in 1914, Tokyo Station is vast and labyrinthine, with north, central and south exits connected by a passageway. The Marunouchi subway line is at the north exit of the station, and the south exit connects with Daimaru department store and a large underground shopping arcade. The Bullet Train tracks are at one side. When you surrender your Bullet Train ticket, retain the remaining

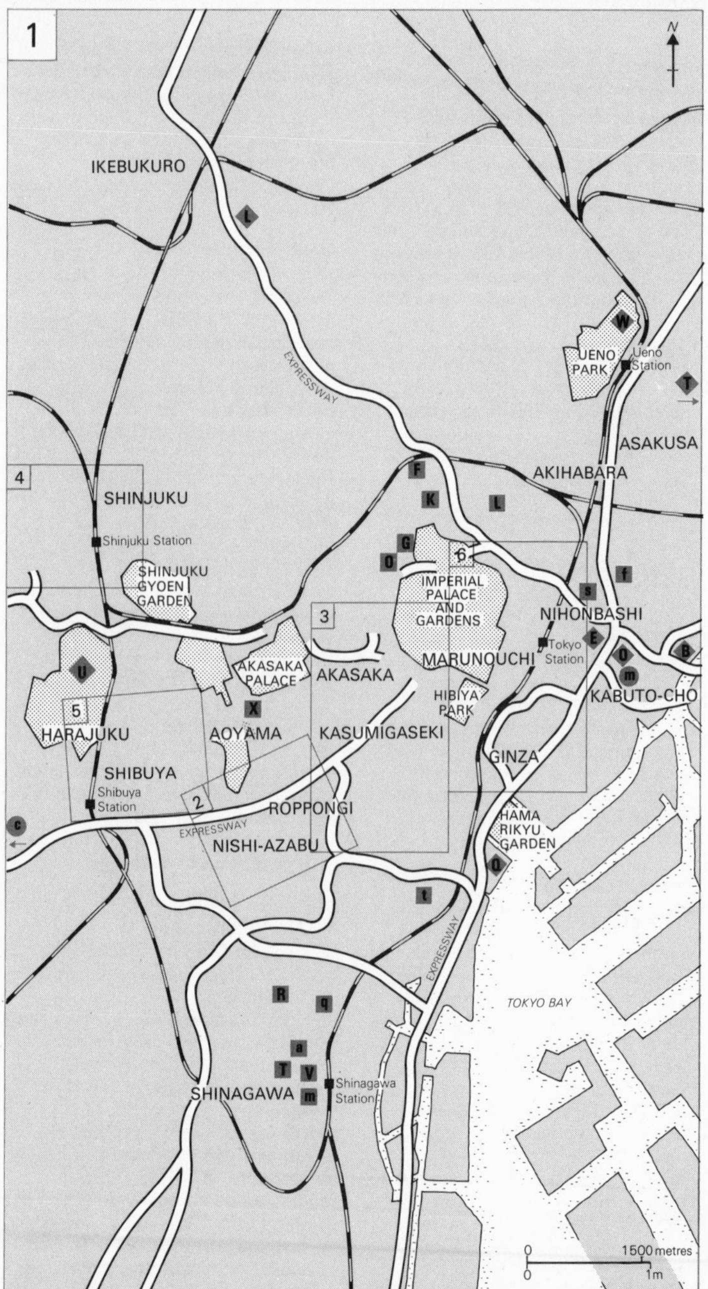
1
N
IKEBUKURO
EXPRESSWAY
UENO PARK
Ueno Station
ASAKUSA
AKIHABARA
4
SHINJUKU
Shinjuku Station
SHINJUKU GYOEN GARDEN
6
IMPERIAL PALACE AND GARDENS
NIHONBASHI
3
Tokyo Station
MARUNOUCHI
AKASAKA PALACE
AKASAKA
KABUTO-CHO
HIBIYA PARK
5
HARAJUKU
AOYAMA
KASUMIGASEKI
GINZA
SHIBUYA
Shibuya Station
2
ROPPONGI
HAMA RIKYU GARDEN
EXPRESSWAY
NISHI-AZABU
EXPRESSWAY
TOKYO BAY
SHINAGAWA
Shinagawa Station
0
1500 metres
0
1m

	HOTELS	MAP No.
A	Akasaka Prince	3
B	Akasaka Tokyu	3
C	ANA	3
D	Capitol Tokyo	3
E	Century Hyatt	4
F	Edmont	1
G	Fairmont	1
H	Ginza Daiichi	6
I	Ginza Marunouchi	6
J	Ginza Tokyu	6
K	Grand Palace	1
L	Hilltop	1
M	Hilton	4
N	Imperial	6
O	Kayu Kaikan	1
P	Keio Plaza	4
Q	Marunouchi	6
R	Miyako	1
S	New Otani	3
T	New Takanawa Prince	1
U	Okura	3
V	Pacific Meridien	1
W	Palace	6
X	President	1
Y	Roppongi Prince	3
Z	Shiba Park	3
a	Takanawa Prince	1
b	Tokyo Prince	3
c	Yaesu Fujiya	6
d	Atagoyama Tokyo Inn	3
e	Atamiso	6
f	Gimmond	1
g	Ginza Daiei	6
h	Ginza International	6
i	Ginza Nikko	6
j	Kokusai Kanko	6
k	Mitsui Urban	6
l	Shimbashi Daiichi	6
m	Shinagawa Prince	1
n	Shinjuku Prince	4
o	Shinjuku Washington	4
p	Sunroute Tokyo	4
q	Takanawa	1
r	Tobu	5
s	Tokyo City	1
t	Tokyo Grand	1
u	Tokyo Station	6

	RESTAURANTS	
A	Al Porto	2
B	Bistro Lotus	2
C	Borsalino	2
D	Brasserie Bernard	2
E	Brasserie Pantagruel	3
F	Capitolino	2
G	Chez Hiramatsu	2
H	Chez Inno	6
I	Crescent	3
J	Daini's Table	5
K	Ile de France	2
	Imari (Hotel M)	4
M	I Piselli	2
N	Isolde	2
O	Joel	5
	Keyaki Grill (Hotel D)	3
	La Belle Epoque (Hotel U)	3
R	La Granata	3
S	La Rochelle	5
T	La Terre	3
	La Tour d'Argent (Hotel S)	3
U	L'Ecrin	6
V	Le Garcon	2
	Les Saisons (Hotel N)	6
W	Le Vert	6
X	Lohmeyer's	6
Y	L'Orangerie de Paris	5
	Maxim's de Paris (Building K)	6
Z	Metropole	2
a	Mireille	2
b	Moti	3
c	Pachon	Off map
d	Petit Point	2
e	Queen Alice	2
f	Red Lobster	2
g	Sabatini Aoyama	5
	Sabatini de Firenze (Building K	6
	Sonne (Hotel e)	6
i	Spago	2
	Star Hill (Hotel D)	3
	Tokhalin (Hotel U)	3
k	Edogin	6
l	Hassan	2
m	Inagiku	1
n	Inakaya	3
o	Isehiro	6
p	Kushinobo	3
q	Kyubei	6
r	Mon Cher Ton Ton	2
	Nadaman (Hotel S)	3
s	Nambantei	2
	Seryna (Restaurant r)	2
u	Sushi Bar Sai	5
v	Tempura Tenichi	6
	Tempura Yamanoue (Hotel L)	1
x	Tenkuni	6
y	Yamanochaya	3
z	Zakuro	3

	BUILDINGS AND SIGHTS	
A	Central Post Office	6
B	City Air Terminal	1
C	Immigration Office	6
	Japan Chamber of Commerce (Building N)	6
D	Japan National Tourist Organisation	6
E	Japan Travel Bureau	1
F	JETRO	3
G	MITI	3
H	Mitsukoshi Department Store	6
I	National Diet	3
J	Seibu/Hanku Department Store	6
K	Sony Building	6
L	Sunshine City Convention Centre	1
M	Takashima Department Store	6
N	Tokyo Chamber of Commerce	6
O	Tokyo Stock Exchange	1
P	Tokyo Tower	3
Q	Tokyo Trade Centre	1
R	Tourist Information Centre	6
S	Yoyogi National Stadium	5
T	Asakusa Kannon Temple	1
U	Meiji Shrine	1
V	Riccar Art Museum	6
W	Tokyo National Museum	1
X	Tokyo National Museum of Modern Art	6

■ Main line station

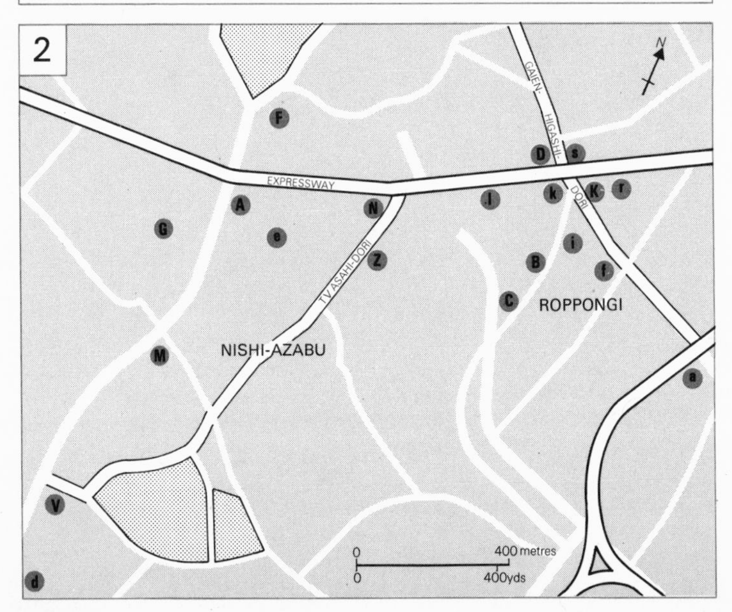

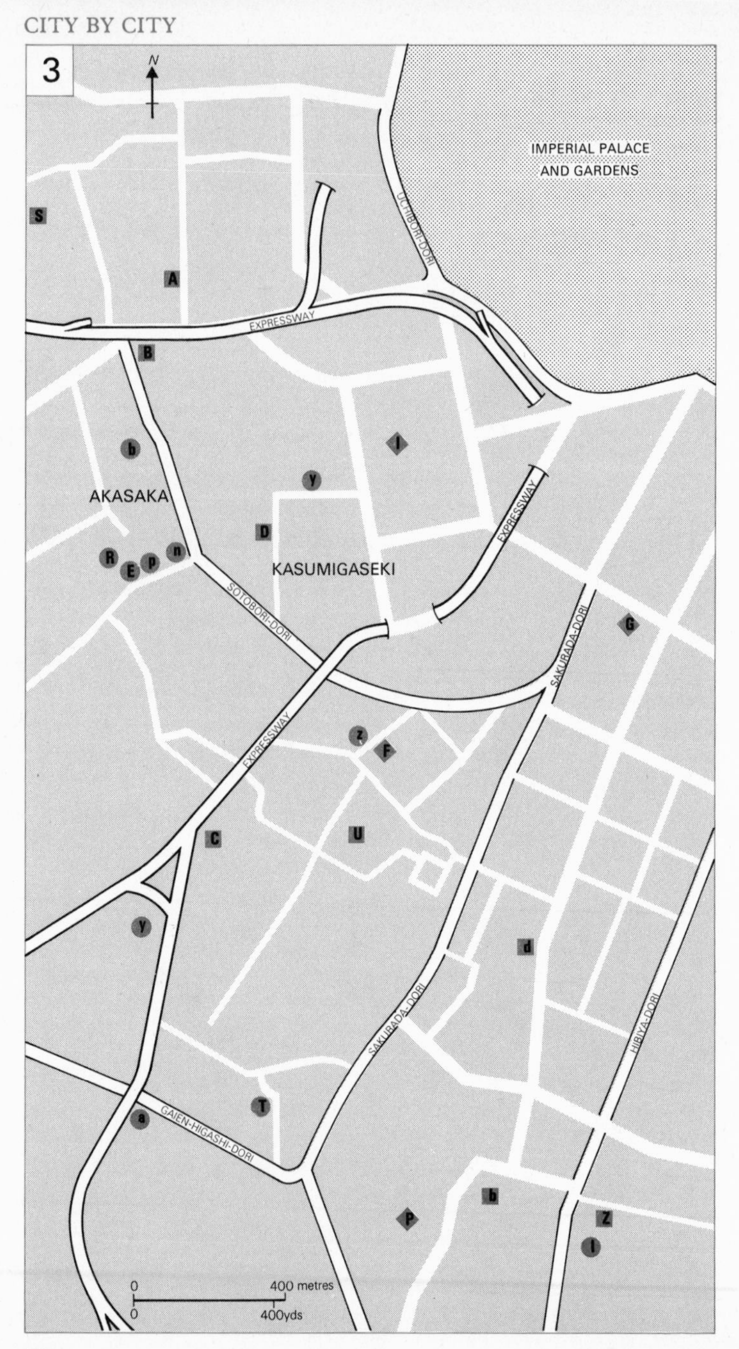
3
N
IMPERIAL PALACE
AND GARDENS
UCHIBORI-DORI
EXPRESSWAY
S
A
B
b
y
AKASAKA
D
KASUMIGASEKI
R
E
p
n
SOTOBORI-DORI
EXPRESSWAY
SAKURADA-DORI
G
EXPRESSWAY
z
F
U
C
y
d
SAKURADA-DORI
HIBIYA-DORI
T
a
GAIEN-HIGASHI-DORI
b
P
Z
0
400 metres
0
400yds

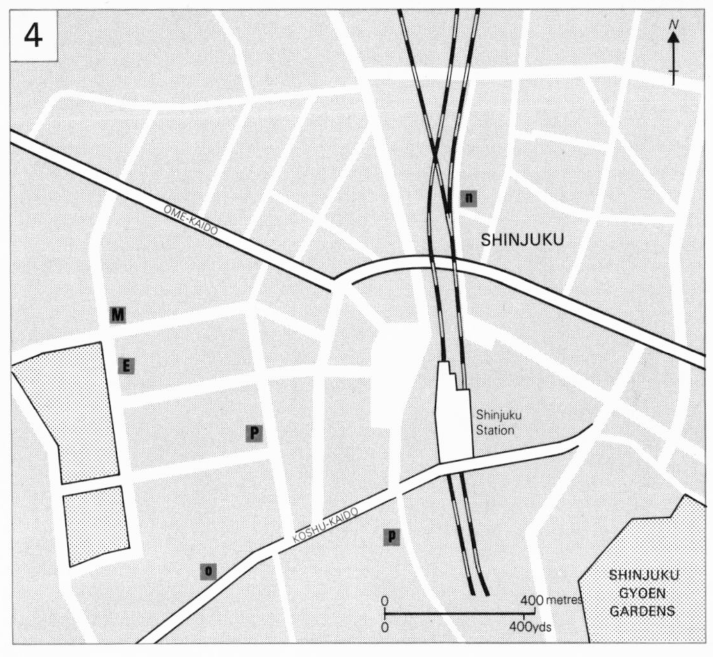

MAP 3

■ HOTELS
- **A** Akasaka Prince
- **B** Akasaka Tokyu
- **C** ANA
- **D** Capitol Tokyo
- **S** New Otani
- **U** Okura
- **Y** Roppongi Prince
- **Z** Shiba Park
- **b** Tokyo Prince
- **d** Atagoyama Tokyo Inn

● RESTAURANTS
- **E** Brasserie Pantagruel
- **I** Crescent
- **P** Keyaki Grill
- **Q** La Belle Epoque
- **R** La Granata
- **T** La Terre
- La Tour d'Argent (Hotel S)
- **b** Moti
- **j** Star Hill
- Tokhalin (Hotel V)
- **n** Inakaya
- **p** Kushinobo
- Nadaman (Hotel S)
- **y** Yamanochaya
- **z** Zakuro

◆ BUILDINGS AND SIGHTS
- **F** JETRO
- **G** MITI
- **I** National Diet
- **P** Tokyo Tower

MAP 4

■ HOTELS
- **E** Century Hyatt
- **M** Hilton
- **P** Keio Plaza
- **n** Shinjuku Prince
- **o** Shinjuku Washington
- **p** Sunroute Tokyo

● RESTAURANTS
- **L** Imari

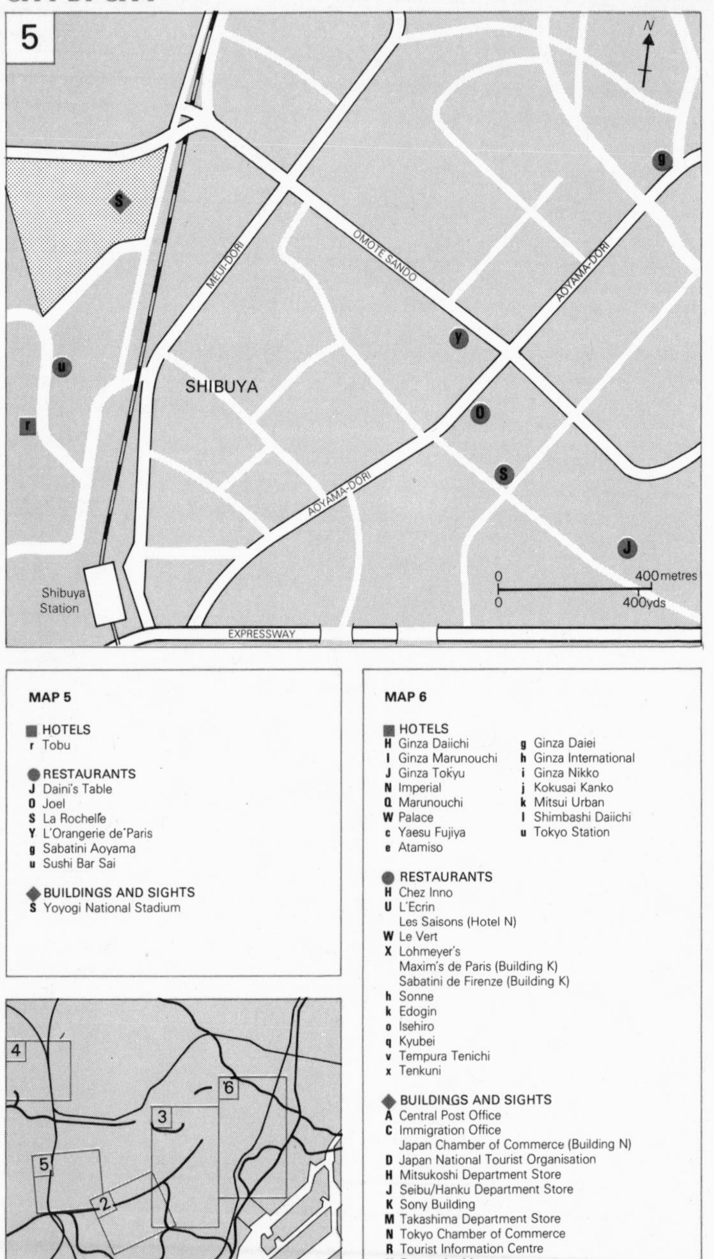
5
N
SHIBUYA
MEIJI-DORI
OMOTE SANDO
AOYAMA-DORI
AOYAMA-DORI
EXPRESSWAY
Shibuya Station
0 400 metres
0 400yds
MAP 5
HOTELS
r Tobu
RESTAURANTS
J Daini's Table
O Joel
S La Rochelle
Y L'Orangerie de Paris
g Sabatini Aoyama
u Sushi Bar Sai
BUILDINGS AND SIGHTS
S Yoyogi National Stadium
MAP 6
HOTELS
H Ginza Daiichi
I Ginza Marunouchi
J Ginza Tokyu
N Imperial
Q Marunouchi
W Palace
c Yaesu Fujiya
e Atamiso
g Ginza Daiei
h Ginza International
i Ginza Nikko
j Kokusai Kanko
k Mitsui Urban
l Shimbashi Daiichi
u Tokyo Station
RESTAURANTS
H Chez Inno
U L'Ecrin
Les Saisons (Hotel N)
W Le Vert
X Lohmeyer's
Maxim's de Paris (Building K)
Sabatini de Firenze (Building K)
h Sonne
k Edogin
o Isehiro
q Kyubei
v Tempura Tenichi
x Tenkuni
BUILDINGS AND SIGHTS
A Central Post Office
C Immigration Office
Japan Chamber of Commerce (Building N)
D Japan National Tourist Organisation
H Mitsukoshi Department Store
J Seibu/Hanku Department Store
K Sony Building
M Takashima Department Store
N Tokyo Chamber of Commerce
R Tourist Information Centre
V Roccar Art Museum
X Tokyo National Museum of Modern Art
4
6
3
5
2

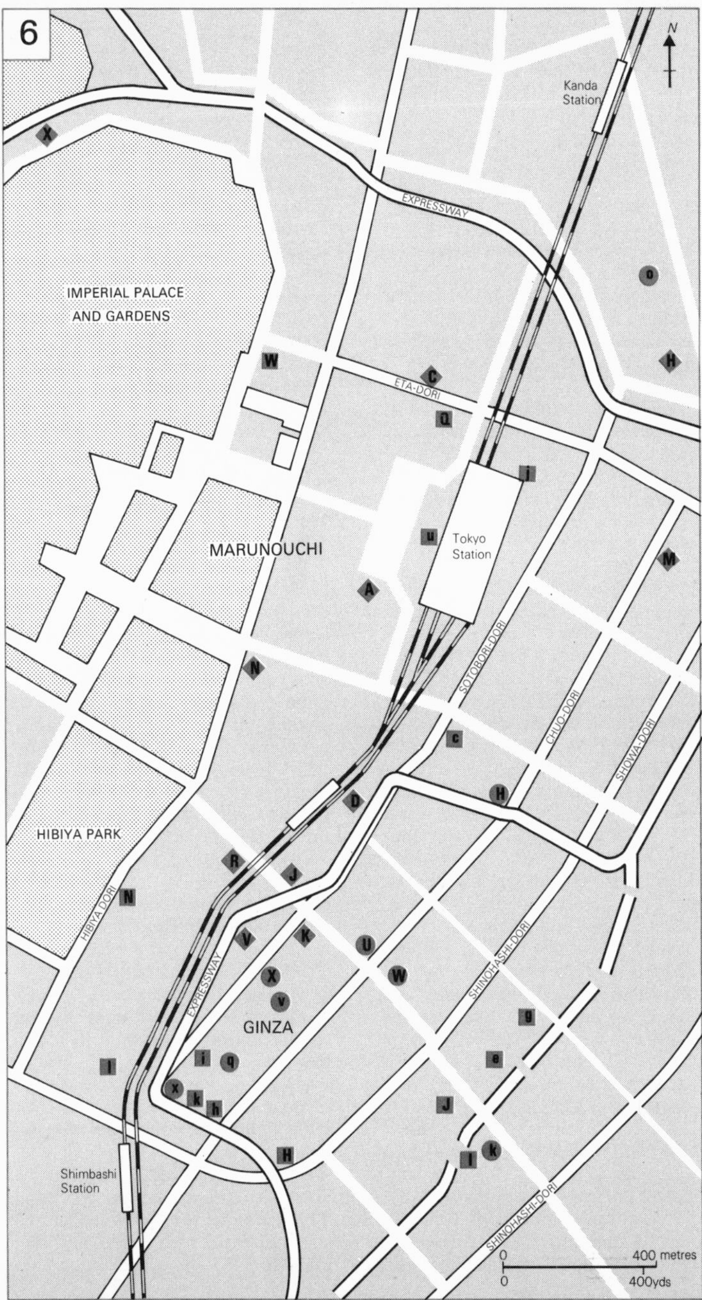
6
N
Kanda Station
EXPRESSWAY
IMPERIAL PALACE AND GARDENS
ETA-DORI
MARUNOUCHI
Tokyo Station
SOTOBORI-DORI
CHUO-DORI
SHOWA-DORI
HIBIYA PARK
HIBIYA DORI
EXPRESSWAY
SHINOHASHI-DORI
GINZA
Shimbashi Station
SHINOHASHI-DORI
0 400 metres
0 400yds

ticket, which enables you to transfer to other JNR lines and get off at any JNR station in Tokyo. Inquiries ☎ 212 4441/4456.

Getting around

Tokyo's streets were first laid out in irregular zigzags to confuse the enemy, and it is still notoriously difficult to find your way around. Taxi drivers will know hotels and major landmarks but otherwise will be as baffled as you are. The Japanese usually draw maps for each other. The best procedure is to consult your hotel concierge or to phone your destination and find out the nearest subway or train station and the direction from there. Tokyo policemen in small neighbourhood police boxes are helpful and usually speak some English. As a last resort, telephone the TIC's Travel Phone ☎ 502 1461. A map of Tokyo including subway and train routes is essential; the TIC issues several good ones, and maps are available at hotels. Travel in Tokyo during the rush hours (7.30–9.30am and 5–7pm) by any mode of transport is to be avoided if at all possible.

Subway Tokyo's subways are clean, safe and the quickest, most efficient way to get around, although some of the lines are more convenient than others. With the aid of a map, the system is easy to use. The major lines, each a different colour, are operated by Teito Rapid Transit Authority. The Chiyoda line (green) is particularly useful, linking Shibuya and the western suburbs with Otemachi, in the business area, in a matter of minutes. You can transfer easily and conveniently between the Chiyoda, Ginza (orange), Hibiya (grey) and Marunouchi (red) lines. Connections are more difficult on the Hanzomon (purple), Tozai (pale blue) and Yurakucho (yellow) lines. There are also three Toei lines run by Tokyo Metropolitan subways. Subway trains run every 2–3min from 5am to midnight, more frequently in rush hour and less frequently in early morning and late evening.

Subway stations are marked by a dark blue circular symbol. Buy your ticket from a machine, some of which will change a Y1,000 note. If in doubt, buy the cheapest ticket and pay the difference at the Fare Adjustment Office at your destination. Platforms are signposted in English, with the terminal, the preceding station and the next one all indicated. Subway system maps in stations are in Japanese only, with a blank red square to indicate where you are. At large subway stations there are maps of the many exits, again only in Japanese; the company you are visiting should tell you the letter and number of the exit.

Train The JNR trains are all colour-coded. The most useful are the Yamanote line (green) which circles the city, with 29 stops, including Tokyo, Ueno, Shinjuku, Shibuya, Shinagawa and Hamamatsu-cho, and the Chuo line (orange) which cuts across, linking Tokyo Station with Shinjuku and the western suburbs. The yellow Sobu line follows the same line across Tokyo as the Chuo, stopping at every station. The train is somewhat more difficult to use than the subway, since most signs are in Japanese only. Beware of boarding an express, which will speed you out to the western suburbs without stopping. Some of Tokyo's stations are vast, extremely crowded and very confusing; Shinjuku, probably the largest station in the world, is notorious.

Taxis Taxis are clean and taxi drivers generally courteous. Unfortunately, almost none of them speak English, and even if they did, they would still not know the way. It is always worthwhile having the name and address of your destination in Japanese; ask your hotel concierge to write it for you. Tokyo's streets are full of taxis – simply flag one down. A red light means "for hire". There are taxi ranks at hotels, stations, department stores and on main streets such as the Ginza.

Beware of the passenger door, which opens and closes automatically. Tipping is not customary. Although subways and trains are faster than taxis for daytime travel, taxis are the only form of transport late at night, when public transport closes down. After 11pm you may need to hold up two or three fingers (to show that you will pay two or three times the fare) to get a taxi to stop.
Walking It is possible, interesting and, apart from a few streets around Shinjuku, completely safe to walk around Tokyo; but distances are enormous.
Bus Even for those who speak Japanese, the buses are fairly confusing and to be avoided.
Car rental The roads are crowded, the traffic system is complicated and road signs are in Japanese only. The main car rental chains have branches in the city, but driving will only add to the difficulties of coping with Tokyo's boisterous complexity.

Area by area

Tokyo grew up around Edo Castle, gradually expanding into a huge metropolis. The Imperial Palace is still the heart of the city; in its shadow is Marunouchi, the main business and administrative district. However, central Tokyo has reached its limits. The development of a New Metropolitan Centre in west Shinjuku began in 1971, and by 1986 there were 11 skyscrapers there and a total of 460 offices, including most of Japan's high-tech and computer companies – whose laboratories and factories are based in satellite industrial parks still farther out to the west. In 1981 plans were mooted to move the city government to Shinjuku. In spite of much opposition in Marunouchi, the move will take place in 1990.
Marunouchi Marunouchi is the business centre of Tokyo and business heart of the nation. Strategically located around Tokyo Station, to the south east of the Imperial Palace, it extends north to Otemachi and south to Nihonbashi. It is an area of trim office blocks, their height limited by earthquake regulations, and neat tree-lined avenues, full of hurrying businessmen by day and completely deserted at night. Here you will find the headquarters of most major Japanese companies, including trading and financial firms and insurance companies, and the offices of international corporations, banks and airlines. Until 1990 the metropolitan government offices are located here.
Nihonbashi The first of the merchant areas to be reclaimed from the sea, Nihonbashi is an important mercantile and commercial district. Banks, including the Bank of Japan, and national government offices are concentrated here, as is the main branch of Mitsukoshi, Japan's most prestigious department store.
Kabutocho Japan's premier financial district is on the other side of Nihonbashi. It houses the Tokyo Stock Exchange.
Ginza The Ginza is Japan's most famous shopping district, full of expensive shops, famous department stores and restaurants, as well as art galleries, theatres and cinemas. The San-Ai Building, at the main Ginza crossing, stands on one of the most expensive pieces of land in the world. On Sundays the main street is closed to traffic and crowded with pedestrians. At night Ginza dons a sybaritic aspect and is revealed as the home of some of Japan's most expensive hostess clubs, the scene of lavish expense account entertaining by Japanese executives.
Kasumigaseki Kasumigaseki is the country's administrative centre, full of government offices, ministries and agencies. Here you will find the National Diet and the prime minister's official residence.
Akasaka This is an area of high-class entertainment of all varieties. The small, exclusive *ryotei*, where politicians and company directors dine to the accompaniment of geisha

entertainment, are concentrated here, and Akasaka's cabarets, nightclubs, discos, bars and restaurants are among the smartest in town. Dominating the bustling side streets is the TBS television headquarters, and up the hill are two of Tokyo's best hotels, the New Otani and the Akasaka Prince.

Roppongi At night Roppongi's neon-lit main street is packed with pleasure-seekers. You can eat, drink and dance in its restaurants and discos until morning. The crowds here are younger and more international than in Akasaka. Just off the main street are expensive residential districts and embassies. To the south is Shiba with its large and pleasant park. Towards Akasaka, near the prestigious Okura Hotel, is the new Ark Hills development, a centre for foreign companies, such as the Bank of America and IBM. There are also cultural facilities such as a concert hall and broadcasting channel, and a subway station is planned.

Nishi Azabu Nishi Azabu is host to some of Tokyo's most stylish and fashionable bars and restaurants. Just down the road is Hiroo, where many of the resident foreign executives live.

Aoyama Aoyama, between Shibuya and Akasaka, is full of sophisticated and expensive boutiques, antique shops and restaurants. Much of it is residential, and there are several embassies here.

Shibuya The young people's end of town, Shibuya is the haunt of trendy young Japanese, including college students, and is becoming more and more of a fashion centre. The denizens of nearby Harajuku are even younger and considerably more outrageous.

Shinjuku Shinjuku, boasting one of the world's largest and most confusing stations, is Tokyo's liveliest area. The main streets are full of department stores and boutiques. Kabukicho, up by the station, a maze of tiny streets bright with neon, is Tokyo's amusement centre and a place to explore Japan's phenomenal range of pleasures of the flesh – strip shows, "pink" cabaret, "soapland" massage parlours, no-pants coffee shops and more besides. In parts of Kabukicho it is sensible to be a little wary at night. You may bump into not only the executives you did business with in the morning, but also the *yakuza*, the Japanese Mafia. In west Shinjuku, on the other side of the station, is the New Metropolitan Centre with its skyscrapers (theoretically earthquake-proof). High-tech and computer companies such as Computervision and Canon are based here. The New Sumitomo, a high-tech business centre with Japan's biggest concentration of computer hardware and software companies, opened here in 1984.

Shinagawa There is not much in Shinagawa besides hotels, but it is a particularly pleasant and green district with plenty of space and trees. Along the coast lies the Keihin industrial belt, full of factories and warehouses.

Other areas Akihabara is Tokyo's electronics district. Ueno is where the national museums are located. Ikebukoro is a student area and a major shopping district.

The suburbs

Most of Tokyo's residential areas are outside the city centre in the suburbs, and many people commute from as far as Saitama and Chiba. The western suburbs, out from Shibuya and Shinjuku, are the fashionable ones. Setagaya, sprawling out west of Shibuya, and Mejiro, on the Yamanote line, are traditionally the places where old families and the very rich live, whereas Denenchofu and Minami Azabu are for those who are both well-off and stylish. The up-and-coming areas are west of Shinjuku, in the direction of the developing industrial zones. Quiet residential areas such as Kichijoji and Kokubunji are rapidly becoming boom towns, with land prices rocketing.

Hotels

Tokyo's hotels rank with the best in the world, from the grand old hotels like the Okura, still the top as far as prestige is concerned, to ultra-modern international-style hotels such as the stunningly designed Akasaka Prince. In spite of the city's reputation for high prices, Tokyo's hotels are no more expensive than those of other major capital cities. You will find many moderately priced hotels conveniently located for the business centres and even – appropriate to Tokyo as electronic leader of the world – futuristic high-tech hotels.

Akasaka Prince ¥¥¥¥¥

1-2 Kioi-cho, Chiyoda-ku 102 ☎ 234 1111 ⓉⓍ 2324028 • 637 rooms, 124 suites, 7 restaurants, 2 bars, 3 coffee shops/tea lounges

The décor is stunning in this very modern and fashionable hotel, designed by Kenzo Tange. The rooms, the largest in Tokyo, are completely white and very stylish, with huge windows and vistas over the city. In spite of its glamorous style, the Akasaka Prince is notably business-oriented, with a well-equipped Executive Service Centre run by two efficient young women, and spacious executive suites on four floors; it is possible to reserve an entire floor complete with meeting rooms. 24hr room service, concierge and travel desk, limousine bus to airport • swimming pool • business service centre with extensive facilities, 25 meeting rooms (capacity 15–1,000).

Akasaka Tokyu ¥¥¥¥

14-3 Nagata-cho 2-chome, Chiyoda-ku 100 ☎ 580 2311 ⓉⓍ 2224310 • 564 rooms, 2 suites, 1 restaurant, 2 bars, 2 coffee shops/tea lounges

Hidden behind a long arcade of fashionable shops and directly opposite Akasaka Mitsuke Station, the Tokyu is better known as the "Pyjama Hotel" because of its striped exterior. It is not in the same class as the other Akasaka hotels. The rooms are acceptable, but basically one stays here for the location and the price. Sauna, steam bath • secretarial services, 4 meeting rooms (capacity 28–240).

ANA ¥¥¥¥

12-33 Akasaka 1-chome, Minato-ku 107 ☎ 505 1111 ⓉⓍ 2424625 • 867 rooms, 33 suites, 5 restaurants, 3 bars, 2 coffee shops

The recently opened ANA is part of the brand new Ark Hills development. An American-designed luxury hotel, it features an enormous lobby overflowing with greenery, a waterfall and a stream, and attractive bedrooms (all with mini-bar) each with a view of Mount Fuji, Tokyo Bay or the Imperial Palace. There is an executive floor, and the business centre is run by American-born Mr Takazawa. For enthusiasts of the game *Go*, there is a salon devoted to it on the top floor. Concierge and travel desk, shopping arcade • outdoor pool, sauna, massage (men only) • business service centre with extensive facilities, 35 meeting rooms (capacity 10–870).

Capitol Tokyu ¥¥¥¥¥

10-3 Nagata-cho 2-chome, Chiyoda-ku 100 ☎ 581 4511 ⓉⓍ 2223605 • 461 rooms, 18 suites, 4 restaurants, 1 bar, 3 coffee shops

Some people still consider the Capitol Tokyu, the old Hilton, to be the best hotel in Tokyo, and certainly it is among the top hotels, although foreigners rate it more highly than Japanese. The décor is quiet and classic with many Japanese touches, a huge flower arrangement in the lobby, and spacious bedrooms, all with mini-bar. A business service centre and executive floor are being planned. The Keyaki Grill (see *Restaurants*) is well used by foreign executives and diplomats, and Star Hill (see *Restaurants*) is one of Tokyo's best Chinese restaurants. 24hr room service, express check-out, concierge, theatre bookings and travel information, arcade of shops including hairdresser, chemist and bookshop, bus to airport • swimming pool • secretarial services, 9 meeting rooms (capacity 30–1,000).

Century Hyatt ¥¥¥¥¥
2-7-2 Nishi-Shinjuku, Shinjuku-ku 160 ☎ 349 0111 TX J29411 • 780 rooms, 20 suites, 6 restaurants, 5 bars, 1 coffee shop
Located among the Shinjuku skyscrapers, the Century Hyatt is particularly popular with American business travellers. The executive floor, the Regency Club, offers a private lounge, conference facilities and a helpful concierge. There is a rooftop pool with spectacular views, and a popular discotheque, the Samba Club. On the negative side, there have been reports of bad service; and some might find the seven-storey atrium lobby with its enormous chandeliers somewhat over the top. 24hr room service, express check-out, concierge • indoor pool • secretarial services, 23 meeting rooms, audio-visual equipment available.

Edmont ¥¥¥
10-8 Iidabashi 3-chome, Chiyoda-ku 102 ☎ 237 1111 TX 2320510 • JNR/Seiyo • 450 rooms, 2 restaurants, 2 bars, 2 coffee shops/tea lounges
The Edmont, opened in 1985, is Seibu's first venture into hotel-building, and as with their department stores, the concept has been carefully developed. The customer being wooed is the travelling executive: each bedroom is equipped like a mini-office, with a large desk on which a fax machine or word processor can be installed on request; and there is a seminar room with audio-visual equipment. Members of the Edmont Club can use a private lounge with secretarial services. Unfortunately, the hotel is somewhat off the beaten track, at Iidabashi. 4 meeting rooms.

Fairmont ¥¥
2-1-17 Kudan Minami, Chiyoda-ku 102 ☎ 262 1151 TX 2322883 • 240 rooms, 2 restaurants, 1 bar, 1 coffee shop
Many European businessmen name the Fairmont as their favourite low-budget hotel. It has a pleasant air of comfortable restraint and is set in a quiet backwater surrounded by avenues of cherry trees beside the Imperial Palace moat. The twin and double rooms are much more spacious than the singles. Swimming pool • 2 meeting rooms.

Ginza Daiichi ¥¥
13-1 Ginza 8-chome, Chuo-ku 104 ☎ 542 5311 TX 2523714 • 800 rooms, 1 suite, 4 restaurants, 1 bar, 1 coffee shop
The Ginza Daiichi is a large mid-range hotel, very popular with Japanese tourists and business travellers. The rooms, recently refurbished, are spacious and good value. The Daiichi is within walking distance of Shimbashi Station and near the nightlife areas of Ginza. International calls via hotel switchboard, express check-out, travel desk, shops, hairdresser, pharmacy • sauna • 8 meeting rooms (capacity 8–100).

Ginza Marunouchi ¥¥
1-12 Tsukiji 4-chome, Chuo-ku 104 ☎ 543 5431 TX 2522214 • 114 rooms, 1 restaurant, 1 bar, 1 coffee shop
A branch of the popular Marunouchi Hotel, the smaller Ginza Marunouchi is on the Tsukiji side of Higashi Ginza. Rooms are small but comfortable. No room service, express check-out.

Ginza Tokyu ¥¥¥
15-9 Ginza 5-chome, Chuo-ku 104 ☎ 541 2411 TX 2522601 • 444 rooms, 3 suites, 4 restaurants, 1 bar, 2 coffee shops

European and American business travellers make up nearly half the clientele of this exceptionally popular moderately priced hotel in Higashi Ginza, which is within walking distance of Marunouchi. The rooms are soundproofed and efficiently furnished, with a good-sized desk. Service is brisk, efficient and friendly. Travel desk, shops • sauna, massage • 10 meeting rooms (capacity 12–400).

Grand Palace ¥¥¥
1-1 Iidabashi 1-chome, Chiyoda-ku 102 ☏ 264 1111 TX 2322981 • Friendship, affil. Palace Hotel • 500 rooms, 7 restaurants, 2 bars
Pleasantly located close to Kitanomaru Park and the Imperial Palace, and right above Kudanshita subway station, only two stops from Marunouchi, the Grand Palace is a tranquil hotel, popular with visiting foreign executives. The friendly staff aim to make the hotel like a home for the business traveller, and there are plans to install an executive floor. The recently refurbished twin rooms are considerably more spacious than the singles. Travel desk, arcade of shops, hairdresser • jogging in Kitanomaru Park • secretarial services, 24 meeting rooms.

Hilltop ¥¥¥
1-1 Surugadai, Kanda, Chiyoda-ku 101 ☏ 293 2311 TX 2226712 • 74 rooms, 1 suite, 4 restaurants, 2 bars, 1 coffee shop
A long-time favourite of writers and artists, the Hilltop is a faintly eccentric, lovely old hotel. The 1930s atmosphere has been lovingly preserved, from the ceramic borders along the corridors to the velvet curtains, tasselled lampshades and heavy wooden furniture in the bedrooms. In keeping with the plan of the founder, a wealthy philanthropist, health-giving negative ions are circulated around the rooms. The Tempura Yamanone restaurant (see *Restaurants*) is outstanding. There is also a more down-to-earth business annexe. 1 large meeting room.

Hilton ¥¥¥¥¥
6-2 Nishi-Shinjuku 6-chome, Shinjuku-ku 160 ☏ 344 5111 TX 2324515 • 788 rooms, 53 suites, 4 restaurants, 2 bars
The curving new Hilton opened in 1984 among the skyscrapers in the developing business area west of Shinjuku Station. It offers all the standard Hilton facilities, and foreign executives, particularly Americans, make up a large proportion of the guests. The bedrooms, all with mini-bar and in-house movies, are attractively furnished with Japanese touches including paper *shoji* windows and Nishijin silk framed on the walls. The executive suites, on three floors, have a private lounge and check-in counter and a helpful concierge. The Imari Restaurant (see *Restaurants*) is popular for business dining. 24hr room service, express check-out, concierge and travel desk, shopping arcade, pharmacy, hairdresser, hotel bus to Shinjuku Station, Narita and Haneda • fitness centre with sauna, gymnasium, massage room, swimming pool, tennis courts • business service centre with extensive facilities, 11 meeting rooms (capacity 10–1,300).

Imperial ¥¥¥¥¥
1-1 Uchisaiwai-cho 1-chome, Chiyoda-ku 100 ☏ 504 1111 TX 2222346 • 1,048 rooms, 88 suites, 12 restaurants, 3 bars, 1 coffee shop
Founded in 1890, the Imperial is Japan's oldest Western-style hotel. For prestige it is second only to the Okura, and for quality many would now give it top place. The style is solid and traditional, from the imposing lobby to the impeccably furnished bedrooms with views over the Imperial Palace and Tokyo Bay; the rooms in the new Tower block are particularly popular. The Executive Service Lounge is the best in town, and the Old Imperial Bar (see *Bars*) is one of Tokyo's most popular meeting places. The Imperial

also boasts Tokyo's only non-smoking coffee shop. Les Saisons (see *Restaurants*) is a favourite for business lunches. The Imperial is conveniently located close to Ginza and within walking distance of the major trading companies. 24hr room service, concierge, theatre and travel bookings, 2 shopping arcades, beauty salon, post office, medical and dental clinics • indoor pool, sauna, massage, jogging • business service centre with extensive facilities, 27 meeting rooms, including vast Fuji room with 6-channel translation facilities.

Kayu Kaikan ¥¥
8-1 Sanban-cho, Chiyoda-ku 102 ☎ 230 1111 TX 2323318 • Okura • 116 rooms, 11 suites, 2 restaurants, 1 bar, 1 coffee shop
The Kayu Kaikan is a rare find, in spite of its rather inconvenient location, near Hanzomon. Owned by the Ministry of Foreign Affairs and managed by the Hotel Okura, it offers exceptionally spacious (if somewhat spartan) rooms and fine cuisine prepared by Okura chefs, along with a serene, peaceful atmosphere, all at budget prices. Service is pruned to a minimum. The airline crews of visiting dignitaries are often housed here. Hotel guests have access to the Executive Service Salon at the Okura. Japanese television only. No room service, international calls via hotel switchboard • 5 meeting rooms.

Keio Plaza ¥¥¥¥¥
2-1 Nishi-Shinjuku 2-chome, Shinjuku-ku 160 ☎ 344 0111 TX J26874 • Intercontinental • 1,485 rooms, 23 suites, 17 restaurants, 8 bars, 2 coffee shops/tea lounges
The first skyscraper in Shinjuku and Japan's tallest hotel, the Keio Plaza opened in 1971. The rooms on the upper floors have views across Tokyo to Mount Fuji and have to be reserved well in advance. The Keio Plaza has all the features of a de luxe international-style hotel. The rooms are spacious, with a separate dressing area and in-house movies, and there is an executive floor and a business service centre. The vast convention complex is geared to cater for meetings and conferences, large or small. Concierge, travel desk, theatre bookings, arcade of shops, hairdresser, medical and dental clinics, overseas and domestic courier service, florist, pharmacy, hotel bus to airport • outdoor pool, men's sauna, jogging, concessionary rates at Do Sports Plaza and Sakuragaoka Country Golf Club • business service centre with extensive facilities, 30 meeting rooms (capacity up to 3,000).

Marunouchi ¥¥¥
6-3 Marunouchi 1-chome, Chiyoda-ku 100 ☎ 215 2151 TX 2224655 • 208 rooms, 2 suites, 4 restaurants, 2 bars, 1 coffee shop
In a prime location, between banks and offices around the corner from Tokyo Station, the Marunouchi is a solid, well-established hotel, designed to suit the needs of the travelling executive. The lobby and bedrooms are appropriately sober in décor, and service is brisk and efficient. Foreign executives make up a large percentage of the clientele. Concierge, shuttle bus to airport • 8 meeting rooms (capacity 10–180).

Miyako ¥¥¥
1-50 Shirogane-dai 1-chome, Minato-ku 108 ☎ 447 3111 TX 2423111 • 475 rooms, 25 suites, 6 restaurants, 1 bar, 2 coffee shops
In an exclusive residential district and built around a beautiful Japanese garden, the Miyako has an air of quiet distinction. Service is impeccable, and the tastefully decorated bedrooms, many overlooking the garden, are exceptionally spacious. The location is at present rather inconvenient, although a new subway station, Seishoko-mae, will open near by in 1988. Concierge, arcade of shops,

free hotel bus to railway stations and Ginza • health club with sauna, pool, gym; jogging • business service centre with limited facilities, 15 meeting rooms (capacity 20–800).

New Otani ¥¥¥¥¥
4-1 Kioi-cho, Chiyoda-ku 102
☎ 265 1111 TX J24719 • Sheraton • 2,057 rooms and suites, 23 restaurants, 5 bars, 5 coffee shops/tea lounges
An immense hotel, the largest in Asia and fourth largest in the world, the New Otani lacks the prestige of the Okura or the Imperial, but is still the choice of many Japanese and foreign executives. It is a mini-city, with more than 100 shops selling luxury goods and many excellent restaurants, including the spectacular Tour d'Argent (see *Restaurants*), and Nadaman (see *Restaurants*), where Prime Minister Nakasone entertains. There is also Japan's first (and only) women-only floor, a non-smoking floor and facilities for the disabled. Some of the rooms (all with mini-bar) in the older main block are rather small; foreign executives usually prefer the spacious rooms in the new Tower Block, overlooking the beautiful 10thC Japanese garden. There are two executive floors in the Tower Block and an executive lounge. Concierge, theatre bookings, travel desks, free shuttle bus to Aoyama, Azabu and Ginza • New Otani Golden Spa health club, outdoor pool, jogging • secretarial services, 48 meeting rooms.

New Takanawa Prince ¥¥¥¥
13-1 Takanawa 3-chome, Minato-ku 108 ☎ 442 1111 TX 2427418 • 968 bedrooms, 32 suites, 6 restaurants, 1 bar, 1 coffee shop
Separated from the older Takagawa Prince by a large and beautiful Japanese garden with winding paths, a lake and a tea house, the New Takanawa was designed by Togo Murano, and in typical Prince fashion incorporates many innovative features. Not only can you open the windows (unusual for Tokyo), but each of the enormous and attractive rooms has its own private balcony overlooking the garden. The Executive Floor includes a large and well-equipped business service centre, a variety of meeting rooms and a lounge. Guests have access to the sports facilities at the nearby Shinagawa Prince Hotel. 24hr room service, concierge, travel desk, shops, hairdresser, shuttle bus to airport • swimming pool, jogging • business service centre with extensive facilities, 13 meeting rooms (capacity 4–5,000).

Okura ¥¥¥¥¥
10-4 Toranomon 2-chome, Minato-ku 105 ☎ 582 0111 TX J22790 • 831 rooms, 79 suites, 6 restaurants, 4 bars, 2 coffee shops
Set in a Japanese garden with a carp-filled pond and a waterfall topped with a shrine, the Okura is designed and furnished with restrained elegance. The emphasis is on service, and the Okura is geared particularly towards fulfilling the foreign executive's every need. The Executive Service Centre is considered by many to be the best in the city, and the bedrooms, all with mini-bar, are large enough to work in. Tokhalin (see *Restaurants*) is generally agreed to be the best Chinese restaurant in Tokyo, and La Belle Epoque (see *Restaurants*) is popular for business entertaining. The many luxury shops include branches of Takashimaya, Mikimoto and Hanae Mori. Even the sauna and massage are famous, and the pool and gym are excellent. Complimentary entrance to the Okura Art Museum in the grounds. Concierge, theatre bookings, travel arrangements, arcade of shops • health club with indoor and outdoor pools, sauna, gymnasium, platform tennis, jogging course • business service centre with extensive facilities, 36 meeting rooms (capacity up to 3,000).

Pacific Meridien ¥¥¥¥
13-3 Takanawa 3-chome, Minato-ku 108 ☏ 445 6711 ⓉⓍ J22861 • 954 rooms, 41 suites, 5 restaurants, 3 bars, 2 coffee shops
Set in a Japanese garden which once belonged to the Imperial family, the Pacific Meridien is an enormous luxury hotel a minute's walk from Shinagawa Station. The rooms are spacious and well designed, overlooking the city and Tokyo Bay. Rooms on two upper floors are currently being upgraded to form executive suites. There are special rates for Pacific Club International members. The luxury shops include a branch of Takashimaya. Of all the Shinagawa hotels, the Pacific is the most popular with foreign executives. Concierge, arcade of shops, hairdresser, pharmacy, shuttle bus to airport • pool, steam bath, men's sauna, jogging • secretarial services, 19 meeting rooms (capacity 15–3,000).

Palace ¥¥¥¥
1-1 Marunouchi 1-chome, Chiyoda-ku 108 ☏ 211 5211 ⓉⓍ 2222580 • 404 rooms, 7 restaurants, 2 bars, 1 coffee shop
The Palace is the choice of many visiting foreign executives and is recommended by resident Westerners. Superbly situated opposite the Imperial Palace, on the edge of the Marunouchi business district, it is set well back from the road, behind an attractive plaza. The style is low-key and sober. The bedrooms are a good size and all soundproofed. Concierge, arcade of shops, hairdresser, airline offices • secretarial services, 19 meeting rooms (capacity 10–2,500).

President ¥¥
2-3 Minami Aoyama 2-chome, Minato-ku 107 ☏ 497 0111 ⓉⓍ 25575 • 212 rooms, 2 restaurants, 1 coffee shop
Located in fashionable Omotesando, the President sports a marble staircase, grand piano and life-size ceramic Dalmatian in its lobby. The rooms are small but pleasantly furnished. Limited hotel parking • 1 meeting room (capacity 150).

Roppongi Prince ¥¥¥¥
2-7 Roppongi 3-chome, Minato-ku 106 ☏ 587 1111 ⓉⓍ 2427231 • 221 rooms, 5 restaurants, 2 bars, 1 coffee shop
The Roppongi Prince was designed by noted architect Kurokawa, clearly in playful mood. Both physically and conceptually built around the central pool, it has a starkly minimalist décor, with waterproof silver sofas in the black-and-white bedrooms and Escher optical illusions incorporated into the stairwell and the bar. The hotel is located very close to the Ark Hills complex. 24hr room service • heated outdoor pool • 3 meeting rooms.

Shiba Park ¥¥
1-5-10 Shiba Koen, Minato-ku 105 ☏ 433 4141 ⓉⓍ 2422917 • 384 rooms, 16 suites, 3 restaurants, 1 bar, 2 coffee shops
This unpretentious, economical hotel is linked to the Imperial and has a reputation for excellent service. English-speakers are plentiful, and many of the guests hail from New Zealand, as does one of the staff. The popular bar, Fifteen's, is hung with rugby club shields. The hotel features a popular Chinese restaurant, the Peking. 18 meeting rooms (capacity up to 300).

Takanawa Prince ¥¥¥¥
13-1 Takanawa 3-chome, Minato-ku 108 ☏ 447 1111 ⓉⓍ 2323232 • 384 rooms, 34 suites, 6 restaurants, 3 bars, 2 coffee shops
Linked to the New Takanawa Prince by a large landscaped Japanese garden, the Takanawa Prince was built in 1970 and has recently been renovated. The décor is businesslike, solid and unfussy, and the rooms are spacious with windows opening onto the garden. It is popular with business travellers. 24hr room service, concierge, travel desk, shops,

hairdresser, shuttle bus to airport • 2 swimming pools • business service centre with extensive facilities (in New Takanawa Prince), 29 meeting rooms (capacity 4–950).

Tokyo Prince Hotel ¥¥¥¥¥
3-1 Shiba Koen 3-chome, Minato-ku 105 ☏ 432 1111 ⊠ 2422488 • 484 rooms, 7 restaurants, 3 bars, 1 coffee shop
While the top executives stay at the Okura, younger Japanese businessmen choose the Tokyo Prince; politicians and financiers often hold receptions and meetings here. Situated in the middle of parkland, it has a European ambience and décor with a comfortably antique flavour. The Beaux Séjours is popular for business lunches. 24hr room service, concierge, theatre booking, shopping arcade, direct bus to Narita • swimming pool, jogging, gymnasium planned, golf driving range and bowling alley nearby • business service centre with limited facilities, 26 meeting rooms (capacity 20–3,000).

Yaesu Fujiya ¥¥
9-1 Yaesu 2-chome, Chuo-ku 104 ☏ 273 2111 ⊠ 2223801 • 373 rooms, 4 suites, 3 restaurants, 1 bar, 1 coffee shop
The Yaesu Fujiya is a branch of the hundred-year-old Fujiya Hotel in Hakone and has a particularly appealing atmosphere reminiscent of a resort hotel, although catering mainly for business travellers. The staff are friendly and the rooms pleasant. The hotel is within walking distance of Ginza, Marunouchi and Tokyo Station. Japanese television only. International calls via hotel switchboard, concierge • 2 meeting rooms (capacity 130–380).

OTHER HOTELS

Atagoyama Tokyu Inn (¥¥) *1-6-6 Atago, Minato-ku 105 ☏ 431 0109 ⊠ 2425179.* Near the Shimbashi and Toranomon areas.

Atamiso (¥) *4-14-3 Ginza, Chuo-ku 104 ☏ 541 3621 ⊠ 2524557.* Formerly a *ryokan*, now Swiss-owned, with a good Swiss restaurant, the Sonne (see *Restaurants*). Very small rooms.

Gimmond (¥) *1-6 Odenma-cho, Nihonbashi, Chuo-ku 104 ☏ 666 4111 ⊠ 2522317.* Popular with Japanese businessmen, comfortable rooms and a central location.

Ginza Daiei (¥) *12-2 Ginza 3-chome, Chuo-ku 104 ☏ 541 2681 ⊠ 2523877.* Friendly, English-speaking staff; small rooms.

Ginza International (¥¥) *7-13 Ginza 8-chome, Chuo-ku 104 ☏ 574 9843.* In the main Ginza entertainment area, near Shimbashi Station. The rooms are surprisingly spacious for the price.

Ginza Nikko (¥¥) *4-21 Ginza 8-chome, Chuo-ku 104 ☏ 571 4911 ⊠ 2522812 • JAL.* Popular with Japanese businessmen. Rooms are reasonably spacious, though a little airless.

Kokusai Kanko (¥¥) *8-3 Marunouchi 1-chome, Chiyoda-ku 100 ☏ 215 3281.* Next to Tokyo Station.

Mitsui Urban (¥¥) *6-15 Ginza 8-chome, Chuo-ku 104 ☏ 572 4131 ⊠ 2522949.* A superior business hotel near Shimbashi Station.

Shimbashi Daiichi (¥¥) *1-2-6 Shimbashi, Minato-ku 108 ☏ 501 4411 ⊠ 2222233.* Near the Shimbashi Station. Quiet but cramped rooms.

Shinagawa Prince (¥¥) *10-30 Takanawa 4-chome, Minato-ku 108 ☏ 440 1111 ⊠ 2425178.* Popular business hotel at Shinagawa Station.

Shinjuku Prince (¥¥¥) *30-1 Kabuki-cho 1-chome, Shinjuku-ku 160 ☏ 205 1111 ⊠ 2324733.* A member of the highly reputable Prince chain, beside Shinjuku Station, in the lively Kabuki-cho area.

Shinjuku Washington (¥) *2-9 Nishi-Shinjuku 3-chome, Shinjuku-ku 160 ☏ 343 3111 ⊠ 2322101.* Reasonable-size rooms, equipped with space-age gadgets.

Sunroute (¥¥) *2-3-1 Yoyogi, Shibuya-ku 151 ☏ 375 3211 ⊠ 2322288.* Close to Shinjuku Station.

Takanawa (¥) *1-17 Takanawa 2-chome, Minato-ku 108* ☏ *443 9251* TX *2422553.* A bit faded, but rooms are spacious for the price.
Tobu (¥¥) *3-1 Udagawa-cho, Shibuya-ku 151* ☏ *476 0111* TX *2425585.* A better-than-average business hotel.
Tokyo City (¥) *1-9 Nihonbashi Hon-cho, Chuo-ku 104* ☏ *270 7671.* In the Nihonbashi business area, near Mitsukoshi department store.
Tokyo Grand (¥¥) *2-5-3 Shiba, Minato-ku 105* ☏ *454 0311* TX *2423147.* A small hotel located in the headquarters of the Soto Buddhist sect; vegetarian dinners and Zen meditation.
Tokyo Station (¥¥) *1-9-1 Marunouchi, Chiyoda-ku 100* ☏ *231 2511* TX *2313513.* At Tokyo Station.

Clubs

The *Tokyo Club* (Kasumigaseki) ☏ 580 0781 is the most prestigious club in Japan and has reciprocal arrangements with Britain's Oxford and Cambridge clubs. It is an excellent place to entertain Japanese colleagues. Among the resident Western community the *American Club* ☏ 583 8381 is most used; it has a reciprocal arangement with the Hong Kong American Club. The *Foreign Correspondents' Club* (Yurakucho) ☏ 211 3161 is a popular gathering place, particularly at lunchtime, and many resident Western executives are members. Guest membership is available on the introduction of a member. There are bars, a library and a workroom with telex and fax.

Restaurants

In Tokyo the business traveller is spoilt for choice. For entertaining, top foreign executives use the grand French restaurants in the Okura and New Otani hotels or in the Ginza, while their Japanese counterparts – if the expense account will run to it – choose among the exclusive *ryotei* in Akasaka. Young Western businessmen on a tighter budget gravitate to Roppongi, while those who want to impress with their grasp of the local scene follow the fashionable Japanese to Aoyama and Nishi Azabu. Although in other Japanese cities there are few really excellent Western-style restaurants, in Tokyo the most exciting and popular cuisine is a fusion of Western and Japanese: non-Japanese dishes – usually French, but also Italian or Chinese – prepared *kaiseki*-style, light and mild in flavour.

NON-JAPANESE

Al Porto ¥¥
24-9 Nishi-Azabu 3-chome, Minato-ku ☏ *403 2916 • closed Mon • AE DC V*
Al Porto is currently highly fashionable. The stylish and well-heeled clientele includes young Western executives with plenty of savoir-faire, who bring their Japanese clients here. The dining room is tiny and like a Victorian parlour, with engravings on the walls, rows of porcelain figures and heavy draperies. Owner/chef Kataoka serves superb Italian cuisine, *kaiseki* style.

Bistro Lotus ¥¥¥
B1 JBP Bldg, 8-17 Roppongi 6-chome, Minato-ku ☏ *403 7666 • closed Sun • AE DC MC V • reservations essential*
Hidden away down a back street in Roppongi is Bistro Lotus – no mere bistro but one of Tokyo's most distinguished French restaurants, with a clientele to match. The rich and famous who have dined here range from royalty and diplomats to rock stars. Chef Takao Zemba serves an innovative and elegant *nouvelle cuisine*, and the wine list is outstanding.

Borsalino ¥¥¥
8-21 Roppongi 6-chome, Minato-ku
☏ *401 7751* • *closed Sun L, Mon*
• AE DC MC V
Borsalino is a haunt of the smart set, both Japanese and Western. The fashionably minimalist interior, all white walls, black seating and silver wall lights, tends to distract one from the excellent cuisine. The chef cooks light Italian food in the *nouvelle* idiom, using imported Italian ingredients. The wines are all Italian.

Brasserie Bernard ¥¥
7F Kajimaya Bldg, 7-14-3 Roppongi, Minato-ku ☏ *405 7877* • AE DC MC V
Brasserie Bernard serves classic French cuisine at prices that are reasonable for Tokyo. The setting is rustic French, with low ceilings, wooden beams and shelves of wine (all French). The clientele, almost entirely Western, comes here as much for the lively atmosphere as for the food. Brasserie Bernard has proved so popular that owner/chef Bernard Anquetil has opened two more branches, in Ginza and Kobe.

Brasserie Pantagruel ¥¥
B1 TBS Kaikan Bldg, 3-3-5 Akasaka, Minato-ku ☏ *582 5891* • AE DC MC V
Pantagruel offers good French *nouvelle cuisine* at reasonable prices in a relaxed environment. At lunchtime the bistro-style restaurant is a popular gathering spot for local Akasaka businessmen and media folk, but is quieter in the evening. There is a well-stocked bar, and the barman claims to be able to prepare any cocktail you care to name.

Capitolino ¥¥
1-11-13 Nishi-Azabu, Minato-ku
☏ *479 5696* • *closed Sun* • AE DC MC V
Capitolino is a modest little restaurant, rather like an Italian *trattoria.* The menu of the day is scrawled up on a blackboard by the door, and Italian peasant crockery hangs around the whitewashed walls. In spite of its unpretentious air it is always packed out, for Chef Yoshikawa is considered among those in the know to be one of Japan's foremost experts on Italian cooking; his meat dishes are particularly famous. The clientele includes diplomats, business people and members of the local Italian community.

Chez Hiramatsu ¥¥¥
B1 Udagawa Palace, 4-3-10 Nishi-Azabu, Minato-ku ☏ *498 3364*
• *closed Mon* • AE DC MC V
• *reservations essential*
This fashionable tiny basement room in Nishi-Azabu is stylishly decorated in whites and greys. Hiramatsu, one of the new generation of owner/chefs, serves classic French cuisine to a cosmopolitan clientele.

Chez Inno ¥¥¥¥
3-2-11 Kyobashi, Chuo-ku
☏ *274 2020* • *closed Sun L* • AE DC V
At the Tokyo Station end of Ginza, half hidden among offices, is a discreet marble doorway with "Chez Inno" carved into the lintel. It leads to a small restaurant which has one of the highest reputations in Tokyo. Chef Innoue Noboru spent seven years in France and cooks the lightest and most superb *nouvelle cuisine* imaginable. The décor, like the cuisine, is understated but classy, making this a particularly impressive place to entertain business clients. Set price menu available.

Crescent ¥¥¥¥
Crescent House, 1-8-20 Shiba Park, Minato-ku ☏ *436 3211-4* • *closed Sun during Jul and Aug* • AE DC MC V
• *reservations essential*
Crescent House looms incongruously among the office blocks south of Shiba Park. Inside the mock-Victorian mansion you dine at an ornately carved wooden table, among grandfather clocks, gas lamps and brocade draperies with enormous tassels. The excellent French cuisine matches the stately atmosphere of the surroundings. Crescent has immense

style and is an impressive place to take a Japanese colleague. There are also seven private rooms for entertaining small groups.

Daini's Table ¥¥
6-3-14 Minami-Aoyama, Minato-ku ☏ *407 0363* • *reservations essential*
Daini's clientele is as stylish as its décor. The cuisine is *nouvelle* Chinese, *kaiseki*-style, tiny portions of many different Shanghai dishes, served on black and red lacquerware. The severely minimalist interior, with curving walls and rows of spotlights, is set off by a large lacquered screen at one end of the room. There are *dim sum* (assorted snacks) after 10pm at the bar.

Ile de France ¥¥¥
Com Roppongi Bldg, 3-11-5 Roppongi, Minato-ku ☏ *404 0384* • *closed Dec 31–Jan 3* • AE DC MC V
André Pachon came to Japan from Carcassonne in 1972. He now has two fine restaurants, Pachon (see below) and Ile de France, in Roppongi. His cooking is uncompromisingly French, and the selection of cheeses is said to be the best in Tokyo. The restaurant is decorated in rustic French style, with copper pans hanging on the whitewashed walls. The faithful clientele, largely foreign executives, often drop in for a working lunch.

Imari ¥¥¥¥
2F Tokyo Hilton International, 6-2 Nishi-Shinjuku 6-chome, Shinjuku-ku ☏ *344 5111* • AE DC MC V
The restaurant houses many antique Japanese objets d'art and a magnificent collection of Imari porcelain. Chef Siegfried Jaeger's cuisine is classic French, but he reveals his Austrian origins in his famous cakes and pastries. The wine list is extensive and the service impeccable. Diplomats and executives are among the clientele, and Imari is popular for high-level business entertaining.

I Piselli ¥¥¥
1F Nikko Palace, 5-2-40 Minami-Azabu, Minato-ku ☏ *442 9771* • *closed Sun* • AE DC MC V
I Piselli, owned by the Bigi fashion group, has a starkly minimalist interior, with three white walls and one black, square white tables and black chairs. The cuisine is Italian regional with a Japanese slant; the fish is particularly good. As befits a restaurant whose bar (see *Bars*) is the most fashionable in Tokyo, the wine list is enormous and good value. Professionals and business people make up the clientele.

Isolde ¥¥¥¥
2F Hokushin Bldg, 3-2-1 Nishi-Azabu ☏ *478 1055* • *closed Dec 31* • AE DC MC V • *reservations essential*
One of Tokyo's grand old French restaurants, Isolde offers impeccable service in an elegant Belle Epoque setting. The cuisine is *nouvelle*, reliably good and not too adventurous, and tableware and wine are imported from France. The clientele includes Japanese executives and diplomats from the nearby embassies. Less expensive set meals are available.

Joel ¥¥¥¥
2F Kyodo Bldg, 5-6-24 Minami-Aoyama, Minato-ku ☏ *400 7149* • AE DC V • *reservations essential*
Joel Bruant was sent to Japan in 1972 by his mentor, Paul Bocuse, and continues to ravish the palates of gourmets of all nationalities in his small restaurant in Omotesando. Both the cuisine and the décor are classic French of the highest quality. Many businessmen, both Japanese and Western, pay their clients the compliment of entertaining them here.

Keyaki Grill ¥¥¥¥¥
B1 Capitol Tokyu Hotel, 10-3 Nagata-cho 2-chome, Chiyoda-ku ☏ *581 4511 ext 567* • AE CB DC MC V • *reservations essential*
Under Austrian chef Karl

Hoermann, the distinguished Keyaki Grill continues to maintain its reputation as one of Japan's finest hotel restaurants. The standard of cooking is uniformly high, the wine list superior and service incomparable. The clientele, largely businessmen, many of them Western, make full use of the quiet and dignified Keyaki for business entertaining.

La Belle Epoque ¥¥¥¥¥
12F Hotel Okura, 2-10-4 Toranomon, Minato-ku ☎ 505 6073 • AE CB DC MC V • reservations essential
La Belle Epoque, at the top of the Hotel Okura, is stunningly baroque in flavour, with a rich Art Nouveau décor of purples, golds and wrought iron lamps. Partitions of stained glass between tables give a degree of privacy. The clientele is cosmopolitan and has included President Reagan and the Prince and Princess of Wales. The chef, Philippe Mouchel, studied with Paul Bocuse, and cooks a lighter version of traditional French cuisine.

La Granata ¥¥
B1 TBS Kaikan Bldg, 3-3-5 Akasaka, Minato-ku ☎ 582 3241/3 • AE DC MC V
The interior of this popular and fashionable restaurant is like an Italian farmhouse, with heavy wooden beams, plaster walls and a huge brick hearth for grilling the home-made sausages. In the evening local Italians mingle with the Akasaka media people, and Western businessmen bring their Japanese colleagues here to dine. The cuisine is Roman, and the wines, imported direct from Italy, unusually inexpensive.

La Rochelle ¥¥¥
B1 Aoyama Ohara Bldg, 5-7-17 Minami-Aoyama, Minato-ku ☎ 400 8220 • closed Sun • AE DC V
La Rochelle, with its pink walls and antique dressers, feels like a provincial French restaurant. Though small, it is seldom crowded, for it is one of Tokyo's better-kept secrets. Here Hiroyuki Saito, trained as a *kaiseki* chef, wields his magic knife. His hors d'oeuvres, each a minuscule work of art, are legendary among discriminating diners.

La Terre ¥¥
1-9-20 Azabu-dai, Minato-ku ☎ 583 9682 • closed Sun and hols • AE DC MC V
A tiny, friendly restaurant hidden away at the top of a flight of steps near the Okura, La Terre, with its pink check tablecloths and red chairs, has a very French atmosphere. Customers include diplomats from nearby embassies, local businessmen and resident Westerners. In the spring you can eat outside under the cherry blossoms.

La Tour d'Argent ¥¥¥¥¥
2F Hotel New Otani, 4-1 Kioi-cho, Chiyoda-ku ☎ 239-3111 • AE CB DC MC V • reservations essential • no smoking
Duck is the dish to eat in this extremely expensive branch of the three-star Paris Tour d'Argent which opened in 1985. The setting is truly palatial. You step through the marble-lined reception area hung with portraits of 16thC French dignitaries into a vast, high-ceilinged dining room with massive chandeliers, spun gold draperies and dark blue china printed with the Tour d'Argent motif. The duck is flown over from Paris and each diner receives a "duck number", a centuries-long tradition. This is dining on the highest level, and both the setting and the cuisine will be regarded as a great compliment by your Japanese guests.

L'Ecrin ¥¥¥¥
B1 Mikimoto Bldg, 4-5-5 Ginza, Chuo-ku ☎ 561 9706 • closed Sun and hols • AE CB DC V • reservations essential
A top-class Ginza restaurant, L'Ecrin has the reputation of being one of Tokyo's finest. The Paris-

trained chef, a member of the Académie Culinaire, prepares classic French cuisine of the old school, and the wine list is outstanding. The discreet service and aristocratic atmosphere, with its plush red carpets and elegant Art Nouveau décor, make it an obvious choice for business entertaining. At lunchtime you will find many top Japanese executives here.

Le Garçon ¥¥
2F Comt. Hiroo, 5-16-6 Minami-Azabu, Minato-ku ☏ *473 3040*
• *closed Sun D, Mon* • AE DC V
A new restaurant, Le Garçon features the cuisine of the legendary Joel Bruant (see *Joel*) in a relaxed, informal setting.

Les Saisons ¥¥¥
Imperial Hotel, 1-1 Uchisaiwaicho 1-chome, Chiyoda-ku ☏ *504 1111*
• AE DC MC V
The dècor, with a central veranda, white cane chairs and potted palms, is southern French in mood, light and sunny. Chef Fukuzawa Kunio cooks a light cuisine to match, in the French idiom. A popular venue for business lunches.

Le Vert ¥¥¥
Sanwa Bldg, 4-6-1 Ginza ☏ *535 3232*
• *closed Dec 31-Jan 3* • AE CB DC MC V
Le Vert, one of the earliest restaurants to serve *kaiseki*-style *nouvelle cuisine*, is now a Ginza institution, rather than a haunt of the smart set. In a discreetly elegant setting of cool moss greens and pale pinks, company directors discuss business over seafood dishes, exquisitely prepared and presented by chef Yabuki Minoru. There is a moderately-priced lunch menu and a teppanyaki restaurant downstairs, popular with Japanese businessmen.

Lohmeyer's ¥¥
5-3-14 Ginza, Chuo-ku ☏ *571 1142*
• AE DC MC V
August Lohmeyer, from Westphalia, started producing ham and sausages in Japan in 1921, and when they proved popular, opened a German restaurant. Lohmeyer's is still crowded with businessmen from the local Ginza companies and is popular with Westerners. *Eisbein*, pickled pig's knuckles, is the speciality.

L'Orangerie de Paris ¥¥¥
5F Hanae Mori Bldg, 3-6-1 Kita-Aoyama, Minato-ku ☏ *407 7461*
• *closed Sun L* • AE DC V
L'Orangerie, in trendy Harajuku, serves elegant French cuisine, and an excellent buffet style Sunday brunch.

Maxim's de Paris ¥¥¥¥¥
B3 Sony Bldg, 5-3-1 Ginza, Chuo-ku ☏ *572 3621* • *closed Sun* • AE DC MC V • *reservations essential*
An 80% scale replica of the Paris original, Maxim's is undoubtedly one of Japan's top French restaurants. The cuisine, though expensive, is well worth it, the setting is magnificent, and the wine list the finest in the city. The cosmopolitan clientele encompasses diplomats, visiting executives and connoisseurs of the famous cakes. There is a private room appropriate for large-scale business entertaining.

Metropole ¥¥¥
TV Asahi-dori, 6-4-5 Roppongi, Minato-ku ☏ *405 4400* • *closed hols*
• AE DC MC V
The Metropole is a Chinese restaurant, its décor a cross between a Victorian theatre and an English club. At the front is a well-stocked bar, popular with executives working locally, with an 18thC library on the balcony overhead. The restaurant itself is like a stage, with red velvet curtains and a backdrop, changed regularly. Tables are big and widely spaced, and the customers, who are mainly young and professional, include plenty of Westerners. The Japanese chef cooks authentic Shanghai cuisine.

Mireille ¥¥
3-1-6 Azabudai, Minato-ku
☏ *586 9050 • closed Sun and national hols • AE DC MC V*
European businessmen are prominent among customers at the wooden tables in Mireille's whitewashed basement room. Both décor and cuisine are authentically Provençal, and the chef is well known for his subtle use of herbs, garlic and fresh local ingredients.

Moti ¥
2F Akasaka Floral Plaza, 3-8-8 Akasaka, Minato-ku ☏ *584 3760/582 3620 • AE DC V*
Generally reckoned to serve the best value and most authentic Indian food in Tokyo, the Moti, in Akasaka, is popular among diplomatic and business circles and with Westerners, both visiting and resident. The 13 chefs are all from North India and include specialists in tandoori and curry. The Moti is a convivial place to dine alone or with colleagues, but probably somewhat too noisy and cramped for a working lunch.

Pachon ¥¥¥¥
29-18 Sarugaku-cho, Shibuya-ku
☏ *476 5025 • AE DC MC V*
André Pachon's second restaurant (see *Ile de France*) is in fashionable Daikanyama. Pride of place goes to the huge stone fireplace, with iron grill and bellows, where M Pachon's nightly roast includes sides of beef, pheasant, marinated duck and fresh local fish. The clientele is cosmopolitan, and there is a private room for business entertaining. In summer you can dine outside on the veranda.

Petit Point ¥¥¥
TGK Bldg, 4-2-48 Minami-Azabu, Minato-ku ☏ *440 3667 • closed Mon • AE DC MC V*
Petit Point, named after the chef's mentor, the great Fernand Point, is considered one of the best of the new-wave French restaurants. Owner/chef Kitaoka, a long-time resident of Paris, cooks authentic French cuisine with Japanese flair; his ten-course *Plaisirs de Table* is particularly celebrated. The tastefully decorated interior is European in flavour, with dried flowers, Toulouse-Lautrec prints, Victorian brass curios and fringed lace curtains. The clientele ranges from executives to artists, with a large proportion of Westerners.

Queen Alice ¥¥
3-17-34 Nishi-Azabu, Minato-ku
☏ *405 9039 • closed Mon • AE DC • reservations essential*
Queen Alice is the creation of young owner/chef Yutaka Ishinabe. He has turned the dining room of his house in Nishi-Azabu into a conservatory, full of trailing vines and huge potted palms. On fine days you can dine outside. Japanese professionals and well-informed Westerners book well in advance to savour Chef Ishinabe's cuisine, a marvellous fusion of French *nouvelle* and *kaiseki*.

Red Lobster ¥¥
Forum Bldg, 5-16-4 Roppongi, Minato-ku ☏ *582 6677 • AE DC MC V*
Red Lobster features, as the name suggests, lobster, imported from Boston. The dining room is like a boat, with curved windows, ropes and nets, and the atmosphere is comfortable and relaxed. Red Lobster is popular with the young professionals, both Japanese and Western, who haunt Roppongi.

Sabatini Aoyama ¥¥¥¥
B1 Suncrest Bldg, 2-13-5 Kita-Aoyama, Minato-ku ☏ *402 3812 • closed Jan 1-3 • AE DC MC V*
A re-creation of the Rome Sabatini, Sabatini Aoyama occupies a vast vaulted cellar, with heavy wooden beams, candelabra and a stone chimney with charcoal barbecue. The cuisine is classic Roman, with much fresh seafood. The clientele, generally affluent, professional and cosmopolitan, either love or loathe the strolling musicians who serenade them with guitars.

Sabatini di Firenze ¥¥¥
7F Sony Bldg, 3-1 Ginza 5-chome, Chuo-ku ☏ *573 0013/4* • AE DC MC V
The setting is magnificent in this branch of the Florence Sabatini, with marble floors, carved beams and panelling, huge bouquets of fresh flowers and heavy flowered draperies. At lunchtime the restaurant is crowded with businessmen. Dinner is more leisurely. The food is, needless to say, excellent, with Tuscan specialities, and the wines, all Italian, are surprisingly inexpensive.

Sonne ¥¥
2F Hotel Atamiso, 4-14-3 Ginza, Chuo-ku ☏ *541 3621* • AE DC MC V
The Swiss-owned Atamiso Hotel (see *Other Hotels*) houses Tokyo's best Swiss restaurant. Visiting Swiss entertain here, enjoying authentic fondue, *raclette* and *roesti.* The room is small and atmospheric, cluttered with cuckoo clocks and alpenhorns, but tables are well-spaced and suitable for a working lunch.

Spago ¥¥¥
5-7-8 Roppongi, Minato-ku ☏ *423 4025* • AE DC V
A branch of the Los Angeles Spago, this outpost of the United States is the inspiration of American chef Wolfgang Puck. Spago serves California cuisine, a mix of many culinary traditions, with *nouvelle* influence notably strong. Of the clientele, Westerners, mainly groups of businessmen, outnumber Japanese. The décor, like the food, is stylish, with a multicoloured mural splashed across one wall and a huge spotlit bar where the chefs cook.

Star Hill ¥¥¥
B1 Capitol Tokyu Hotel, 10-3 Nagata-cho 2-chome, Chiyoda-ku ☏ *581 4511 ext 577* • AE CB DC MC V
Star Hill has an air of restrained opulence, with a red and gold décor. The cuisine is predominantly Cantonese, although the menu includes dishes from Shanghai and Peking. During the week the restaurant is the scene of much business entertaining, and reservations are essential for the private rooms. There is a good-value all-you-can-eat buffet at weekends.

Tohkalin ¥¥¥
6F Hotel Okura, 2-10-4 Toranomon, Minato-ku ☏ *505 6068* • AE CB DC MC V
Long rated Tokyo's best Chinese restaurant, Tohkalin is the haunt of Sumo wrestlers, media men and sundry entertainers. It is also the first choice of many businessmen, both Japanese and Western, for a working lunch or dinner (there are nine private rooms set aside for the purpose). The cuisine is mainly Cantonese and the surroundings tastefully opulent in the Chinese fashion, with red carpets and delicate gold screens. Excellent wine list.

JAPANESE

Edogin ¥
4-5-1 Tsukiji, Chuo-ku ☏ *543 4406* • *closed Sun* • AE DC MC V
Edogin is a famous old sushi shop, a Tokyo institution, occupying almost a whole street on the way to Tsukiji fish market. The friendly staff, sporting Wellington boots and white caps, serve up superbly fresh sushi straight from the market. The sushi is not only tasty but also enormous; the staff boast that they serve the biggest pieces of fish in town. Go to Edogin on a night off for an excellent and economical meal and a glimpse of old Japan.

Hassan ¥¥
B1 Denki Bldg, 6-1-20 Roppongi, Minato-ku ☏ *403 8333* • *closed Dec 31–Jan 3* • AE DC MC V
Hassan is a tranquil oasis in the midst of noisy Roppongi, a classic Japanese restaurant with *tatami* rooms, sliding paper doors and a bamboo grove. The kimono-clad waitresses serve a set price meal of *shabu shabu*, as much as you can eat, and an excellent value and tasty *kaiseki.* Hassan is a popular choice

among Japanese executives entertaining Western guests, but it is also welcoming to Westerners who venture in on their own.

Inagiku ¥¥¥¥
2-9-8 Nihonbashi Kayabacho, Chuo-ku ☏ *669 5501* • *closed Sun* • AE DC MC V
Inagiku is one of Japan's most famous and high-class tempura restaurants, patronized by the rich and famous and recommended by the top hotels. The rooms and service are immaculate. Your fellow diners are likely to include managing directors with their foreign guests or high-powered foreign executives from nearby Nihonbashi.

Inakaya ¥¥
3-12-7 Akasaka, Minato-ku ☏ *586 3054* • *closed Dec 31–Jan 4* • AE DC MC V
Among the glossy shops on the small streets around the TBS Building in Akasaka is a battered old wooden house with an enormous waterwheel, two storeys high, in front. Inakaya, a venerable establishment, is full of shouting and merriment. Customers sit around the hearth on which the chefs grill meats, seafoods and vegetables, which they pass across on wooden paddles. Among the clientele are entertainers, Akasaka media folk and foreign visitors, brought by Japanese friends or colleagues to enjoy the lively atmosphere and Japanese country cooking.

Isehiro ¥¥
1-5-4 Kyobashi, Chuo-ku ☏ *281 5864* • *closed Sun* • DC V
Down a small back alley just behind the business area of Nihonbashi is a little restaurant which has been serving *yakitori* since 1922. At lunchtime local businessmen, including many Westerners, crowd in to savour the skewers of finest Shamo chicken, grilled over charcoal and served at budget prices. In the evening the tiny upstairs rooms are reserved for business entertaining.

Kushinobo ¥
3-10-17 Akasaka, Minato-ku ☏ *586 7390* • AE
Kushinobo serves *kushi-age*, tiny portions of fish, meat and vegetables in apparently endless variety, strung on to skewers and crisply deep-fried in batter. The atmosphere is lively and friendly and Westerners are welcome. An interesting place for a culinary adventure on a night off.

Kyubei ¥¥¥
8-5-23 Ginza, Chuo-ku ☏ *571 6523* • *closed Sun and hols* • AE DC MC V
Ginza businessmen literally rub shoulders in this tiny, intimate sushi shop; the two floors together hold a total of 20. Kyubei is quite unlike the usual noisy neighbourhood sushi shop. The staff are well aware of its status as possibly Tokyo's best, and the quality of the sushi more than justifies the steep prices. There are branches of Kyubei in the Okura, the New Otani and the Keio Plaza.

Mon Cher Ton Ton ¥¥¥
3-12-2 Roppongi, Minato-ku ☏ *402 1055* • *closed Dec 31–Jan 3* • AE DC MC V
Part of the Seryna complex (see below), Mon Cher Ton Ton is a sophisticated teppanyaki restaurant. In its cavernous basement room customers sit around gleaming steel-topped tables on which four chefs fry up finest Kobe beef and seafoods. There are small tables grouped around the edges of the room, and side rooms specifically for business entertaining, which makes up a large part of the custom.

Nadaman ¥¥¥¥
Hotel New Otani, 4 Kioi-cho, Chiyoda-ku ☏ *265 7591* • AE DC MC V
Nadaman, modestly located in a small but exquisite Japanese house in the garden of the New Otani, is one of Japan's most exclusive *ryotei*, and one of Prime Minister Nakasone's favourites – the 1986 Summit leaders were entertained here. If you are fortunate enough to be invited,

regard it as a supreme compliment. Fellow diners will be from the top strata of Japanese society. You can savour Nadaman's famous Kansai-style *kaiseki* cuisine in a more relaxed atmosphere in a branch on the sixth floor of the New Otani, overlooking the spectacular garden. At lunchtime there is a good value mini-*kaiseki*. There are also branches of Nadaman in the Imperial Hotel and in Osaka, Nadaman's birthplace, at the Royal and the Tokyu.

Nambantei ¥
4-5-6 Roppongi, Minato-ku
☏ 402 0606 • AE DC
Nambantei means "the inn of the Southern barbarians", and it was they – that is, the Portuguese – who introduced *yakitori* to Japan. Customers sit around open charcoal grills where the young chefs in dark blue *happi* coats grill not only skewers of chicken but many different types of meat and vegetables, seasoned with spices or marinaded and served with rich sauces. Nambantei is a popular and lively restaurant, and there are branches throughout Japan, in the United States and in England.

Seryna ¥¥¥¥
3-12-2 Roppongi, Minato-ku
☏ 403 6211 • closed Dec 31–Jan 3 • AE DC MC V
Seryna, a venerable institution with a good solid reputation and a lot of prestige, is one of the first choices for Japanese executives entertaining their Western counterparts (and vice versa). It occupies a large three-floor building in the heart of Roppongi, lavishly decorated in Japanese style, with rock gardens on each floor, stone lanterns and waterfalls. The food is classic Japanese, *shabu shabu* and *sukiyaki*, prepared to a reliable standard. It is not the place for a culinary adventure, but one can be sure of a meal of the highest quality.

Sushi Bar Sai ¥¥
2F Rambling Core Andos Bldg, 1-7-5 Jinnan, Shibuya-ku ☏ 496 6333 • AE DC MC V
Sushi Bar Sai serves sushi in the modern idiom, California-style, using *tofu* and meat as well as the more traditional ingredients. The sushi is served *nouvelle cuisine*-style, in the exact centre of fine Arita and Kiyomizu dishes, and the décor is fashionable high-tech. Sushi Bar Sai is much patronized by young businessmen, both Japanese and Western, who appreciate the carefully selected wine list; it is probably the only sushi bar in Tokyo to serve wine.

Tempura Tenichi ¥¥¥
Namiki-dori, 6-6-5 Ginza, Chuo-ku
☏ 571 1949 • closed Jan 1–3 • AE DC MC V
Tempura Tenichi was founded by the present owner's father in 1930, and has been one of the best and most popular tempura restaurants in Tokyo ever since. Young Japanese businessmen flock here for lunch, and there are plenty of Western guests. In addition to sake, French wines, carefully selected to go with tempura, are served; and a Chagall hangs beside a Japanese flower arrangement. The upstairs rooms are reserved for the most distinguished customers, top politicians and company directors, who entertain their guests with tempura *kaiseki*. There are another nine branches in Tokyo, and several throughout the country.

Tempura Yamanoue ¥¥
1F Hilltop Hotel, 1-1 Kanda Suruga-dai, Chiyoda-ku ☏ 293 2311, ext 229 • AE DC MC V
A quiet, homely restaurant in the Hilltop Hotel, Tempura Yamanoue has an excellent reputation. Like the hotel, the restaurant is charmingly dated, with enormous old Japanese chests and woven bamboo ceilings. You sit at the counter and watch tempura being cooked. In spite of its modest air, Tempura Yamanoue is quite a famous place for business

entertaining, and there are two small *tatami* rooms at the back for this purpose.

Tenkuni ¥¥
8-9-11 Ginza, Chuo-ku ☏ 571 1092 • closed Dec 31–Jan 1 • AE DC MC V • reservations essential for groups
A tempura shop with a hundred-year history, Tenkuni occupies three floors of a large building near Shimbashi Station. Down in the basement Japanese businessmen and their Western colleagues sit along the polished wooden counter as the chef prepares tempura using the finest fish and vegetables and pure sesame oil. The ground floor has tables and chairs, and the top floor consists of *tatami* rooms, used for business entertaining; *kaiseki* is also served.

Yama-no-chaya ¥¥¥
2-10-6 Nagata-cho, Chiyoda-ku ☏ 581 0585 • reservations essential
Squeezed in between the Capitol Tokyu and Hie Shrine, just behind the Diet, this little Japanese house is reached via a thatched gate and some stone steps leading through a garden full of bamboos and the song of birds and frogs. The house was built in 1923, and here Madame Endo, the present owner's grandmother, used to entertain. In 1950 they began serving eel; and their eel is legendary. If you are lucky, your Japanese colleagues may bring you here; it is a popular place for business entertaining. Otherwise you will have to book well in advance for one of the four small rooms.

Zakuro ¥¥¥
1-7 Kyobashi, Chuo-ku ☏ 563 5031 • closed Dec 31–Jan 3 • AE DC MC V • reservations essential for dinner
Zakuro, Tokyo's first *shabu shabu* restaurant, opened in 1955. It is built like a Japanese farmhouse, with big beams and whitewashed walls hung with Munakata prints, and fine handcrafted pottery, including some of Hamada's. Foreign visitors mingle with Japanese entertainers in the lively dining rooms, whereas knowledgeable executives hire one of the quieter private *tatami* rooms for business entertainment. Service is reckoned to be among the best in Japan. There are several other branches of this high-quality chain in Tokyo, including Ginza (Sanwa Ginko Bldg, Ginza ☏ 535 4421) and Akasaka (TBS Bldg, Akasaka ☏ 582 6841).

Bars

In Tokyo there are three main areas for those all-important after-hours drinking sessions. Ginza's elite and astronomically expensive hostess clubs are for executives, mainly Japanese, on maximum expense accounts. Here, your professional status and credentials are rated by which bar you patronize, and you are likely to be rubbing shoulders with politicians, industry magnates and entertainers. Only the top Western executives are taken to these clubs; it is unlikely that you would be allowed to enter on your own. Akasaka, too, has high-class geisha and hostess bars, less expensive than Ginza, but still far from cheap. For a relaxed evening, you can join the international set in Roppongi, which has a huge concentration of bars and discos, or slip down to one of the stylish and fashionable bars in Nishi Azabu. Shinjuku is for very late night drinking, in an environment that is relaxed, to say the least. The standard pattern is drinks in a hotel bar before dinner and a hostess bar afterwards; your Japanese colleagues will take you to their favourite. Most bars stay open until 1 or 2am; some are open later.

Charleston Club
3-8-1 Roppongi
Ignore the sign on the door that says "Members only"; it is not intended for you. Located behind the Berni Inn, the Charleston is a small friendly bar packed with Westerners, with an enormous drinks menu; it is also a comfortable place for a single woman.

Club Morena
3-7-16 Roppongi • AE DC
There are English-speaking hostesses to tend to the needs of tired male executives in this popular Roppongi hostess bar. Club Morena is particularly well known among Westerners and not ruinously expensive.

Ex
B1 Junikagetsu Bldg, 1-18-7 Jinnan, Shibuya-ku • AE DC V
Celebrated for its stunning interior, this vast sleek cellar bar is patronized by the Shibuya fashionable. There is inexpensive food and an extensive wine list as well as cocktails.

Ex
1F Roppongi Maisonette, 7-7-6 Roppongi, Minato-ku
This Ex is the gathering place for local Germans, Germanophile Japanese and all lovers of sausages, wurst and German beer.

Henry Africa's
2F Hanatsubaki Bldg, Roppongi
A long-time favourite of Tokyo's resident Westerners, Henry Africa's is tropical in décor, and is also equipped with pinball machines. Mexican snacks, spirits and "tropical cocktails" are on offer.

I Piselli
1F Nikko Palace, 5-2-40 Minami-Azabu, Minato-ku
I Piselli in Hiroo, currently one of *the* places to go, is packed out nightly. The bar features a variety of classy drinks, including Wild Turkey and I.W. Harper 12-year-old bourbon, and food is available from the restaurant of the same name next door (see *Restaurants*).

Le Club
B1 Plaza Kay, 5-1-1 Minami-Azabu
Undoubtedly the most stylish bar in Tokyo, Le Club is the creation of alternative ikebana master Koichi Saito, intimate of fashion luminaries, rock musicians and artists. Elegant young barmen clad in black, with hair oiled back, serve an extensive, carefully selected range of high-class drinks, much appreciated by the international clientele. The setting is austerely elegant, with a spotlight picking out the master's flower arrangement on the shiny black bar.

Maggie's Revenge
Takano Bldg, 3-8-12 Roppongi
Tucked away behind the Berni Inn, Maggie's is a popular meeting place for resident Westerners and a pleasant place for a single woman. As well as the standard spirits and cocktails, it serves Australian beer.

Old Imperial Bar
Imperial Hotel, 1-1 Uchisaiwaicho 1-chome, Chiyoda-ku • *all major credit cards*
The Old Imperial, affectionately known as the Frank Lloyd Wright Bar, is the usual gathering place for Western executives and for many Japanese also. You will need to reserve a table (☎ 504 1111). The bar is an exact reconstruction of the original, designed by Wright, in the old Imperial Hotel: full of leather, dark wood and old-fashioned quality.

Orchid Bar
5F Hotel Okura, 2-10-4 Toranomon, Minato-ku • *all major credit cards*
Among Western executives the Orchid Bar ranks in popularity with the Old Imperial, and at lunchtime it is always packed. Spacious, with an elegant atmosphere and plenty of prestige, it is a good place to invite your Japanese colleagues.

Radio Bar
B1 Villa Gloria, 2-31-7 Jingumae, Shibuya-ku • *all major credit cards*
The waiters in black tuxedos and wing collars serve precision-made cocktails in this tiny, sophisticated bar. There is a vast range of drinks, and the décor – natural wood walls inlaid with iron and tiny Tiffany lamps along the bar – is suitably classy.

Entertainment

Tokyo is the nation's centre for entertainment, as for everything else, and a sizeable proportion is in English, or accessible to the western visitor. The traditional arts such as Kabuki continue to flourish here, and western artists of all varieties, from ballet companies and orchestras to rock stars, are frequent visitors. At the far end of the spectrum, you may be lucky enough to catch a performance of one of Tokyo's very lively, and frequently outrageous, avant garde theatre groups. *Tokyo Journal*'s pull-out, *City Scope*, or *The Magazine's* listing *Around Japan* will keep you up to date with what's on. There are also several free English language publications such as *Tour Companion* and *Tokyo Weekender*, available in hotels. Make reservations through your hotel or at Play Guide ticket agencies in main stations and the ground floor or basement of department stores. Your Japanese colleagues will be able to help you locate entertainment of a rather less sophisticated variety. If left to your own devices, make your way to Kabuki-cho's Sakura-dori, in (of course) Shinjuku.

Theatre Tokyo is the home of Kabuki. For maximum enjoyment of these spectacular dramas, bone up beforehand with *The Kabuki Handbook*, which gives detailed descriptions of the highly complicated plots. The actors to see are the immensely popular Tamasaburo, the celebrated player of female roles, and his consort, Takao, who appear at the *Kabuki Theatre*, 4-12 Ginza. This is the place to see the best, classic Kabuki. Performances, usually three or four plays, start at 11am and 4.30pm and last up to 5 hours. Cheap tickets to watch a single play are available on the day, and there are English language programmes and earphone guides. The programme changes once a month. The innovative and energetic Ennosuke and his troupe usually perform at the *Shimbashi Embujo*, 6-8-12 Ginza, or the *National Theatre*, 4-1 Hayabusacho, Chiyoda-ku, which also shows modern Japanese dramas.

Each school of Noh has its own theatre in Tokyo. The Kanze, the oldest and most popular school, is based at *Kanze Nohgakudo*, 1-16-4 Shoto, Shibuya-ku. The other main schools are the Hosho, at *Hosho Nohgakudo*, 1-5-9 Hongo, Bunkyo-ku, and Kita, at *Kita Nohgakudo*, 4-6-9 Kami Osaki, Shinagawa-ku. The *National Noh Theatre*, 4-18-1 Sendagaya, Shibuya-ku, opened in 1983.

Ballet The world's great ballet companies frequently visit Tokyo, and the Matsuyama Ballet Company performs ballets choreographed and directed by, and sometimes featuring, Rudolf Nureyev.

Cinema There are plenty of foreign movies in Tokyo, most of which are original language with Japanese subtitles. Japanese films by internationally famous directors like Kurosawa are shown with English subtitles at one or two cinemas. The most popular foreign movies show all over town and play for months, but there are many small cinemas, listed in the local press, which show revivals and serious films.

Music Japan's musical luminaries range from internationally acclaimed composer Toru Takemitsu to synthesizer magicians Ryuichi Sakamoto and Kitaro, and with luck you will be able to see one of these play. The choice of music in Tokyo is immense. There are some excellent local orchestras such as the NHK Symphony (considered the best), Tokyo Philharmonic and Yomiuri Symphony, as well as visiting international orchestras. Several international rock bands have made their name in Japan, and regularly perform here, together with Japanese rock artists. There are also concerts of traditional Japanese music, including the immensely popular *enka*, sung with a throb in the voice, as well as the more familiar classical

koto and shamizen music. Concert tickets rapidly sell out, and should be bought as far in advance as possible.
Nightclubs Much of Tokyo's entertainment finishes early. Films, plays and concerts end by 9pm and most restaurants have closed by 10pm. For late night entertainment, Roppongi is the place to go; you will also find pockets of activity in Akasaka and Shibuya, and of course Shinjuku never sleeps. Tokyo's sophisticated cabarets are for the affluent or those on liberal expense accounts. Among the best are the *New Latin Quarter*, 2-13-8 Nagatacho, Chiyoda-ku, an elegant cabaret and hostess bar, *Crazy Horse*, 3-18-12 Roppongi, which features dancing and foreign entertainers, and *The Crystal Room*, a theatre-restaurant in the New Otani Hotel. Japanese colleagues might entertain you at *Furusato*, in Shibuya, where you watch traditional Japanese dances and dine on traditional fare. In high-tech style, fashionable *Ink Stick*, B1 Casa Grande Miwa Bldg, 7-5-11 Roppongi, has live music on Friday and Saturday nights, while *Mint Bar*, across the hall, is a chic mint green cocktail bar with a large video screen.

Less sophisticated, and packed with Western businessmen, is the *Cavern Club*, 3F Roppongi Hosho Bldg, 7-14-1 Roppongi, which features Beatles' lookalikes (Japanese) in Cuban-heeled boots. *Red Shoes*, B1 Azabu Palace Bldg, 2-25-18 Nishi-Azabu, used to be *the* place to go, and is still very popular; it is a small club with videos and a good jukebox. The young international set crowds into *Hot Co-rocket*, B1 Daini Omasa Bldg, 5-18-2 Roppongi, to dance to reggae played by an English band; there is Brazilian music on Sundays.

Of Tokyo's many discos, the two in which to be seen are the glamorous *Lexington Queen*, B1 Daisan Goto Bldg, 3-13-14 Roppongi, where the visiting rock stars go, and the *Neo Japanesque*, B2 Roppongi Forum Bldg, 5-16-5 Roppongi, small and sophisticated. *Mugen*, 3-8-17 Akasaka, was the place to go in the sixties and still has psychedelic paintings on the walls; it is a good place for black music.

Shopping

Japan is like an enormous production line, continually producing new goods of higher and higher quality; and Tokyo is the nation's shop window. There are, however, certain goods that it is better not to buy in Japan: canny shoppers buy their antiques and pearls in Hong Kong. Prices are not low, particularly for imported goods, but the range and quality available is unbeatable. The main shopping areas are Ginza (for luxury goods), Shibuya and Shinjuku. Apart from Ginza, the best places for top-quality goods are the arcades in the Imperial, Okura and New Otani hotels. The best news for foreign shoppers is the Foreign Customers' Liaison Office on the fifth floor of the enormous new Seibu department store in Yurakucho. The staff, all foreign, guarantee to search out any product not in stock. They also have clothes in foreigners' sizes (that is, large), run a catering service and even organize jaunts to the country.
Department stores Tokyo is the home of Japan's oldest and most prestigious department stores, *Mitsukoshi* and *Takashimaya*, both in Nihonbashi. The most vigorous of the newer stores is *Seibu*, whose newly-opened Yurakucho branch, dwarfing the neighbouring *Hankyu*, is the largest in Tokyo. At the centre of Ginza, opposite the two old standbys *Matsuya* and *Matsuzakaya*, is *Wako*, a store selling high-class luxury fashions. Outside Ginza, *Isetan*, in Shinjuku, is worth looking at; Shibuya seems to be a battle-ground between the two rivals, *Seibu* and *Tokyu*, each of which has mammoth stores.
Arcades There are some arcades designed specifically for foreign

tourists, full of shops selling tax-free goods from cameras to kimonos: *International Arcade*, 1-7-23 Uchisaiwaicho, Chiyoda-ku ☏ 591 2764; *Japan Tax-free Centre*, 5-8-6 Toranomon, Minato-ku ☏ 432 4341; *Sukiyabashi Shopping Centre*, 5-1 Ginza ☏ 571 8027/8.

Multi-purpose stores *Axis*, 5-17-1 Roppongi, is a complex of stores selling high-quality up-to-the-minute merchandise with design as a theme. Issey Miyake's former fabric designer has a shop here, and there are several art galleries. *Wave*, 6-2-27 Roppongi, is a high-tech music store with a computerized record reference system, plus a recording studio, a ticket agency and a small cinema showing foreign art films. *Tokyu Hands*, 12-18 Udagawacho, Shibuya-ku, sells every craft and hobby tool you have ever wanted, including the much-coveted Japanese carpentry tools.

Books You may not find the book you are looking for in a Tokyo bookshop, but you *will* find an interesting and rather idiosyncratic selection, including plenty of books on Japan. The main places for books in English are *Kinokuniya*, 5th floor, 3-17-7 Shinjuku; *Maruzen*, 3rd floor, 2-3-10 Nihonbashi, Chuo-ku; and *Iena*, 3rd floor, 5-6-1 Ginza. The Okura, Imperial and New Otani hotels also have good bookshops. Jimbocho is the area to scour for secondhand books, and you may also find woodblock prints and old maps here. *Sanseido*, 1-1 Jimbocho, has a fine collection of Victorian art and travel books.

Cameras Shinjuku is where everyone goes for cameras. *Yodobashi Camera*, 1-11-1 Nishi-Shinjuku, is the world's largest camera shop, with huge discounts and a tax-free section. *Camera no Sakuraya*, 3-17-2 Shinjuku, is the other big camera shop.

Clothes Japan has recently become something of a fashion mecca, and there is a vast selection of stylish and high quality clothes, at prices ranging from economical to outrageous. Size, however, is a difficulty. Sleeves and trouser legs are often too short, and shoes are almost always tiny. Do not buy anything without trying it on; a packaged shirt, even one with a Western brand name, is likely to be short in the sleeve. Most of the designer fashions are to be found in Shibuya. Issey Miyake, Comme des Garçons and other top designers have boutiques, both men's and women's, in *Parco*, 15-1 Udagawacho, Shibuya-ku, a fashion complex useful for one-stop shopping. *From 1st*, 5-3-10 Minami-Aoyama, Minato-ku, rather more exclusive in atmosphere, houses designer boutiques. *Wako*, in Ginza, is the place to window shop for classic fashions, though only the very wealthy actually buy anything here. *La Forêt*, 1-16-11 Jingumae, Shibuya-ku, is where the trendy Harajuku youngsters buy their fashions, and you may find some stunning designs at economical prices.

Electronic goods For electronic goods, there are more bargains to be found in Akihabara than in the tourist-oriented tax-free shops. Prices here can be as much as 40% below list. *Rajio Kaikan*, 1-15-16 Soto-Kanda, Chiyoda-ku, is a conglomeration of shops selling audio, video and electrical goods. This is one place in Japan where the shopkeepers will bargain. To ensure compatibility, buy only the export model of sophisticated equipment; you can also buy adaptors suitable for each country. Although prices may turn out to be no cheaper than at home, the range of electronic toys in Japan is much wider. To play with the latest audio and video equipment and computers, drop into the *Sony Showroom*, 3-4F Sony Bldg, 5-3-1 Ginza.

Gifts Side by side with Japan's new technology, the old tradition of fine craftsmanship continues. Ginza is the best area for quality arts and crafts.

Begin your search in a department store. *Mitsukoshi* and *Takashimaya*, both in Nihonbashi, have excellent selections of kimonos, and you can pick up the combs and hair pins to go with them in *Matsuzakaya*, in Ginza. For antiques, try the basement of Takashimaya or the *Oriental Bazaar*, 5-9-13 Jingumae, Shibuya-ku. The Ginza *Matsuya* has interesting exhibitions and sales of work by well-known craftsmen. Of the smaller shops, *Takumi*, 8-4-2 Ginza, sells fine ceramics and specializes in Mashiko ware. The finest Japanese handmade paper, used for everything from umbrellas and fans to doors and windows, is in *Haibara*, 2-7-6 Nihonbashi, Chuo-ku. *Heiando*, 3-10-11 Nihonbashi, Chuo-ku, "By appointment to the Imperial Household", has the best traditional lacquerware. Collectors will find moderately-priced woodblock prints at *Matsushita*, 6-3-12 Minami-Aoyama, Shibuya-ku. For pearls, Tokyo's most famous shop is *Mikimoto*, 4-5-5 Ginza, Chuo-ku.

Markets Monthly markets are held in the grounds of some shrines and temples on certain Sundays. You will find plenty of antiques, ceramics and old kimonos, occasionally at bargain prices. There is a market in *Togo Shrine* in Harajuku on the first and fourth Sunday of each month, and at *Nogi Shrine*, near Roppongi, on the second.

Sightseeing

Tokyo is not the best place for sightseeing. If you have a few hours to spare, it is worthwhile forsaking the city and heading out to Kamakura, Nikko or, for a couple of days, to Kyoto. However, although Tokyo has few historic monuments or impressive temples, it does have the finest museums in Japan. Besides the national museums, concentrated in Ueno Park, there are fine private galleries; department stores, too, often have superb exhibitions. For those with limited time, sights not to be missed include Asakusa Kannon Temple in old Edo, Meiji Shrine, the National Museum and the Imperial Palace, with its East Garden. Of the galleries, the Idemitsu has a particularly interesting collection. Most museums and galleries have changing exhibitions and are closed on Mondays. For up-to-date information, consult the local press.

Asakusa Kannon Temple
Officially known as Sensoji, Asakusa Kannon is at the heart of the bustling downtown district of Asakusa. The oldest temple in Tokyo, it was first built in the 7thC to house an image of Kannon, the Buddhist goddess of mercy, which, the story goes, two brothers found in their fishing net. The temple is enormous, with a five-storey pagoda and a huge red lantern, 4m tall, a symbol of Asakusa. The streets around the temple, full of tiny stalls, are always thronged with people. *2-3-1 Asakusa, Taito-ku.*

Goto Art Museum The famous thousand-year-old Genji Monogatari scrolls are displayed for one week in May in this lovely museum set in a hillside garden. For the rest of the year there is a fine collection of Japanese and Chinese paintings, calligraphy and ceramics. *3-9-25 Kaminoge, Setagaya-ku. Open 9.30–4.30; closed Mon.*

Hamarikyu Garden Once the summer villa of the shoguns stood here, but now only the garden – one of the loveliest in Tokyo – is left. This one-time playground of the aristocracy features a tidal pond spanned by three bridges, moon-viewing pavilions and tea houses. *Hamarikyu teien, Chuo-ku. Open 9–4.30; closed Mon.*

Idemitsu Gallery Idemitsu, one of Japan's oil kings, used his fortune to amass a wonderful collection of ceramics, paintings, calligraphy and bronzes, both Japanese and Chinese. His particular passion was the works of the 17th century Zen monk Sengai, and the gallery owns nearly all of them. There is a tranquil lounge with a tea dispenser, where you can sit and gaze over the Imperial Palace, *9F International Bldg, 3-1-1 Marunouchi, Chiyoda-ku. Open 10–5; closed Mon.*

Imperial Palace There is very little to see at the Imperial Palace – top attraction though it is of every itinerary. The official residence of the Emperor, a retiring 80-year-old marine biologist, the Palace itself is open only twice a year, on New Year's Day and April 29th, the Emperor's birthday. Having been rebuilt in ferroconcrete in 1968, it is not, in any case, very impressive. The Imperial Palace East Garden is a spacious and peaceful park with landscaped lawns and flowers. *Chiyoda, Chiyoda-ku. Garden open 9–3; closed Mon and Fri.*

Japan Folkcrafts Museum This fine museum just outside Shibuya houses the collection of well-known folk art patron and author Yanagi Soetsu. There is a changing display of furniture, ceramics and textiles, of outstandingly high quality. The museum itself is a beautiful old wooden house, brought piece by piece from the country and reconstructed here. For craft enthusiasts, this is a must. *4-3-33 Komaba, Meguro-ku. Open Mar–Dec, 10–5; closed Mon.*

Koishikawa Korakuen Garden Designed by Tokugawa Yorifusa in the Edo period, Korakuen is a large and beautiful Japanese garden, with winding streams, arching bridges and a lake full of carp. *1-6-4 Koraku, Bunkyo-ku. Open 9–4.30; closed Mon.*

Meiji Shrine Set in wooded parkland among trees, streams and flowers, Meiji Shrine provides a breath of fresh air and tranquillity in the bustle of the city. It is always full of pilgrims and visitors, particularly in June, when its famed irises bloom. It enshrines the Emperor Meiji (1868-1912). *1-1 Kamizonocho, Yoyogi, Shibuya-ku.*

Nezu Art Museum Set in a beautiful garden with a stream and tea pavilions, the Nezu has an outstanding collection of Japanese paintings and also lacquerware, ceramics and scrolls. *6-5-36 Minami Aoyama, Minato-ku Open 9.30–4.30; closed Mon.*

Okura Shukokan Museum In the grounds of the Okura Hotel, this small museum houses the founder's fine collection of paintings, ceramics, calligraphy and Noh masks. *2-10-3 Toranomon, Minato-ku. Open 10–4; closed Mon.*

Ota Memorial Museum of Art Just off the main Harajuku thoroughfare, the Ota Museum is a quiet Japanese house, with two floors of particularly fine woodblock prints, and a restaurant in the basement. *1-10-10 Jingu-mae, Shibuya-ku. Open 10.30–5.30; closed Mon and from the 25th of each month.*

Riccar Art Museum This tiny museum houses one of the best collections of woodblocks in Japan, which it displays in changing exhibitions. *7F Riccar Bldg, 2-3-6 Ginza. Open 11–6; closed Mon.*

Rikugien Garden A beautifully landscaped garden, Rikugien was laid out in the 17th century around a central lake. With its tea house and miniature mountain, it was a favourite retreat for the Edo aristocracy. *6 Komagome, Bunkyo-ku. Open 9–4.30; closed Mon.*

Tokyo National Museum The largest museum in Japan, the National Museum houses the best collection of Japanese art in the world. Only a small part of the collection is on display at any one time, so it is worth visiting several times. There are also excellent temporary exhibitions. *13-9 Ueno koen, Taito-ku. Open 9–4.30; closed Mon.*

Tokyo National Museum of Modern Art This museum houses an excellent collection of contemporary Japanese art from the Meiji period onwards. Nearby is the Museum's *Crafts Gallery*, with some fine examples of modern ceramics and textiles, attractively displayed. *3 Kitanomaru-koen, Chiyoda-ku. Open 10–5; closed Mon.*

Zojoji Temple Originally built in the 14th century, Zojoji was a Tokugawa family temple, strategically located to protect Edo Castle from dangerous forces, both physical and spiritual. Of the Edo period building, only the main gate remains. *4-7-35 Shiba-koen, Minato-ku.*

Guided tours

The three major companies offering sightseeing tours of Tokyo with English-speaking guides are the *Japan Travel Bureau* ☏ 276 7777, *Fujita Travel Service* ☏ 573 1417 and *Japan Gray Line* ☏ 436 6881. The half- and full-day tours, covering the major sights, are worth taking only if you are pressed for time. Better value are the nightlife tours.

There are also special tours focusing on arts or crafts. Of particular interest are JTB's three full-day "Industrial Tokyo" tours, which take you to factories, computer laboratories and the JAL maintenance base at Haneda.

Out of town

Seasoned Tokyo-dwellers do not travel at the weekend, when the roads are blocked for miles around with traffic, barely moving. If you must travel, take the train; you may have to stand, but you can be certain of arriving in reasonable time.

The Japanese like to repeat the old saying, "Don't say *kekko* until you've seen Nikko." *Kekko* means "splendid", and *Nikko*, 75 miles/120km north of the capital and two hours by train, is truly spectacular. Visitors go to see the *Toshogu Shrine*, built by the Tokugawa shoguns as their mausoleum; but Nikko's mountain setting, with lakes (including the beautiful *Chuzenji*), waterfalls and forests is equally magnificent. Nearer at hand is *Kamakura*, tucked between the mountains and the sea, 30 miles/45km and exactly 1hr on the Yokosuka line from Tokyo Station. For a few years during the 13thC, Kamakura was the capital of Japan, and it still has a certain aristocratic air. Many artists and intellectuals live in Kamakura's pleasant forested hills, among the temples. Avoid the most popular sights: the huge bronze Buddha and Hachiman Shrine. Instead, get off the train one stop before Kamakura, at Kita Kamakura, and wander through the silent Buddhist temples out into the hills. Beyond Kamakura to the south-west is *Hakone*, just over 65 miles/100km from Tokyo, accessible by Bullet Train and the most popular resort area for Tokyoites. The combination of mountains, volcanoes, forests and crater lakes is spectacular. After hiking, riding or boating, you can retreat to one of the hot spring hotels or *ryokan* and immerse yourself in healing sulphuric water. Hakone also boasts the *Open-air Museum*, a fine collection of modern Western and Japanese sculpture. The climbing season for *Mount Fuji*, 65 miles/100km south-west of Tokyo, is July and August. Less arduously, you can visit *Fuji Five Lakes*, which offers good hiking through beautiful countryside. Much closer to the metropolis is *Tokyo Disneyland*, 35–50min by bus from Tokyo Station.

Spectator sports

Baseball is the game closest to the hearts of most young sport-minded businessmen, with rugby just behind. Highlight of the baseball year is not pro baseball but the annual high school tournament in Osaka. It dominates television, and the whole country talks about very little else throughout July and August. Volleyball also has a large following; it is not so long since the Japanese volleyball team was the world's best. Sumo is a bit of an old men's (or old women's) sport, though many resident Westerners become great enthusiasts. Golf is very much a rich man's sport in Japan, and most Japanese restrict themselves to watching it on television.

Baseball Tokyo is the home of five pro baseball teams. The most popular Tokyo team is the Yomiuri Giants, one of the two strongest Central League teams. Tokyo's other Central League team, the Yakult Swallows, are making their way up the league. The Tokyo Lotte Orions and the Seibu Lions, based just outside Tokyo in Saitama, are two successful teams in the less popular Pacific League. The Giants' home field, shared with Pacific League team Nippon Ham Fighters, is the *Korakuen Stadium*, 1-3-61, Korakuen, Bunkyo-ku ☎ 811-2111. The Yakult Swallows are based in the *Jingu Stadium*, Kasumigaoka-cho, Shinjuku-ku ☎ 401 0312.
Tickets for games can be bought on the day or on the preceding Tuesday at the stadium or any Tokyo ticket office. The baseball season is from April to October, with the final game in mid-October. One of the major league American teams visits Japan about once a year and plays a series with a Japanese all-star team; five or six of these games are held in Tokyo. For daily baseball schedules, check the English-language press.
Rugby The top teams are those of the three famous universities, Keio, Waseda and Meiji. The rugby season is very short. The final always takes place in Tokyo, in December or January, at the *National Stadium*, 10 Kasumigaoka-cho, Shinjuku-ku ☎ 469 6081.
Sumo is Japan's *kokugi* or national skill, rather than a mere sport. The *yokozuna*, grand champions, are national heroes. There are sumo tournaments in January, May and September, at the *New Kokugikan*, 1-20 Yokoami, Sumida-ku ☎ 623 5111. Each tournament lasts 15 days and starts on the second Sunday of the month. You will need to reserve well in advance for a good seat. There are usually balcony and bench seats available on the day of the match, or you can stand at the back. Go early for a better seat; most fans arrive late in the day for the most spectacular bouts.

Other sports Tennis, volleyball, basketball and other international sports are keenly followed in Japan, and there are frequent matches, such as the annual Suntory Cup tennis tournaments, featuring international players and teams. The main venue is *Yoyogi National Stadium* ☎ 468 1171, near Harajuku Station.

Keeping fit

In Japan, sporting activity is not simply a matter of keeping fit. Golf, for example, is very much tied up with status. Membership of top golf courses such as the Kawana Hotel Golf Course, Japan's most famous, is restricted to top people; others simply cannot enter. Hence, as an indication of your host company's – and your – importance, you may find yourself, golfer or non-golfer, being whisked off for a compulsory Sunday game. The most valued foreign clients may experience the ultimate sporting excursion, a ride on a private luxury yacht. The possibilities open to those left to their own devices are somewhat more limited.
Golf For inveterate golfers with large expense accounts, *Japan Gray Line* ☎ 433 4801 offers a golf tour to one of Japan's finest private courses, the *Fuji Ace Golf Club* ☎ 503 7931 on the slopes of Mount Fuji, normally open only to members and their guests. There is a pick-up service from major hotels.
Health and sports centres The popular *Clark Hatch Fitness Centre*, 2-1-3 Azabudai, Minato-ku ☎ 584 4092, is oriented towards the visiting foreign executive. It has reciprocal membership arrangements with all other Clark Hatch Clubs. American-run, it has a fully equipped gym and sauna; facilities are open to men only. Training gear and towels are supplied. The women's equivalent of Clark Hatch is the *Sweden Health Centre*, 5F Sweden Centre, 6-11-9 Roppongi ☎ 404 9739, which is, in fact, affiliated with Clark Hatch. There is

a gym and sauna, plus dance and exercise classes. Facilities are open to non-members Jun-Sep on payment of a sizeable monthly fee. There are facilities for visiting executives at the two *Do Sports Plazas*, in Harumi, 5-6-41 Toyosu, Koto-ku ☎ 531 8221, and Shinjuku, Sumitomo Bldg Annex, 2-6-1 Nishi-Shinjuku ☎ 344 1971. These large sports centres have a gym, jogging track, pool, squash courts and sauna.
Jogging The best and most popular jogging course takes you around the moats of the *Imperial Palace* and covers about 3 miles/5km. The *Yoyogi Park* course, about half the length of the Palace course, goes around NHK Television Centre and Yoyogi Stadium. Several of the larger hotels, such as the New Otani and the Tokyo Prince, issue jogging maps.
Massage The best massage in town is at the Capitol Tokyu Hotel. At *Paru Onsen*, 2F Okazaki Bldg, 2-14-13 Shibuya ☎ 409 4882, you can have a massage or *shiatsu* as well as enjoying the Jacuzzi.
Skiing There are overnight buses to the nearest ski slopes and some ski areas can be reached in about 90min by train. Contact the following travel agencies for schedules: *Bell Tour* ☎ 260 6181; *Howa Travel Service* ☎ 342 3271; *Taiyo Recreation Centre* ☎ 295 0041.
Squash Several expatriate groups, such as the American Club and the British Council, have squash clubs. The *Do Sports Plazas* (see *Health and sports centres*) have public courts.
Swimming Public pools are extremely crowded. There are pools in the two *Do Sports Plazas* and in other sports centres. The pools in the following hotels are open, at a fee, to non-residents: Capitol Tokyu, Century Hyatt, Holiday Inn, Keio Plaza, Miyako, New Otani, Okura, Shinagawa Prince, Tokyo Prince. The seaside swimming season is from June to August, and during this period the beaches are packed. At other times you will have the beach to yourself. There are fine beaches on the Boso and Izu peninsulas, and even the beaches of Kamakura, only an hour from Tokyo by train, are relatively clean.
Tennis There is little chance of a game of tennis in Japan. Ever since Crown Prince Akihito met his future wife on a tennis court, there has been a tennis boom in Japan, and courts are booked up months in advance.

Local resources

Business services

The business service centres at the Imperial and the Okura are undoubtedly the best in town and frequently used by non-residents. By far the most useful of the commercial agencies is *Oak Associates* ☎ 354 9502, run by Charlotte Kennedy Takahashi, a long-time Japan resident. Oak also organize useful early morning seminars for business people. *I.S.S.* ☎ 265 7101 and *Manpower Japan* ☎ 582 1761 are large organizations with branches throughout Japan. Other companies used by the local business community include *Alpha Services* ☎ 230 0090, *Best International* ☎ 423 4800, *Chescom International Service* ☎ 341 1111, *Japan Convention Service* ☎ 508 1221, *Kao Co Ltd* ☎ 564 3927, *Summit Service* ☎ 499 0245 and *Tory's Office* ☎ 408 9080.
Photocopying and printing If your hotel will not photocopy for you, go to a camera shop, department store or stationer's, all of which often have photocopying machines; or call *Fuji Xerox Co* ☎ 585 3211. The *Okura Executive Service Centre* ☎ 586 7400 can print your business cards in less than 24hrs. *Nagashima International PR Office* ☎ 504 1111 also prints business cards. For general printing go to *T&T* ☎ 586 3271 or *Hagiwara Printing Co Ltd* ☎ 811 4272.
Interpreters Contact *Oak Associates* (see above) and ask for a personal recommendation. Failing that, try *I.S.S*, *Japan Convention Service*, or

Simul Int'l Inc ☏ 586 8911. These companies also offer translation services.
Secretarial services Use *Temporary Centre Corporation* ☏ 508 1431 or *Tempu staff* ☏ 405 5507.
Translation Consult the *Japan Translation Federation* ☏ 452 9705.
Miscellaneous For catering, Western businessmen go to *André Lecomte* ☏ 475 1770, who is both better and cheaper than hotel caterers; he will also find premises for your function. Chef *André Pachon* ☏ 404 0384 also does catering. The best tailor to go to is *Ricky Sarani* ☏ 582 9741, who will make up a dinner jacket (do not hire one) and do emergency repairs.

Communications

International couriers *DHL Japan, Inc* ☏ 454 0501, *Nippon Express Co Ltd* ☏ 574 1211, *Overseas Courier Service* ☏ 453 8311, *World Courier (Japan)* ☏ 508 9281.
Local messenger services Tokyo's messenger service is rather limited. *Business Cuban* ☏ 476 5671, is reliable and fast.
Post Office The *Central Post Office*, Tokyo Station Plaza, Chiyoda-ku ☏ 284 9527, is open 24hrs for express service. Normal opening hours are 9–7, Mon–Fri; 9–5, Sat. Use *Tokyo International Post Office*, 2-3-3 Otemachi ☏ 241 4891, for sending international parcels or registered letters.
Telex and fax All major hotels provide telex and fax facilities. Otherwise go to *KDD*, International Telegraph Office, 1-8-1 Otemachi, Chiyoda-ku ☏ 270 5111, or one of the business service agencies (see above).

Conference/exhibition centres

Trade fairs and exhibitions are organized by the *Japan Convention Bureau*. The main location for international trade fairs is *Tokyo International Trade Fair Grounds*, 5-3-53 Harumi, Chuo-ku ☏ 533 5311. Fairs are also held at *Convention Centre Tokyo*, Sunshine City ☏ 264 3234, *Tokyo Ryutsu Centre*, 1-1 Heiwa-jima 1-chome, Ota-ku ☏ 767 2162, and the *Tokyo Trade Centre*, 3F World Trade Centre Bldg Annex, Hamamatsucho ☏ 435 5394. Many conferences and smaller exhibitions tend to be held in the major hotels.

Emergencies

Calls to the emergency services – ☏ 119 and ask for the service you require – are answered in Japanese. If you have trouble making yourself understood contact *Tokyo English Lifeline* (TELL ☏ 264 4347 and they will place a call for you.
Bureaux de change Currency desks at the major hotels are open seven days a week, from early until late.
Hospitals Major hotels have lists of hospitals with English-speaking staff and some have medical clinics. The following hospitals and clinics have a 24hr emergency service: *Japan Red Cross Hospital* (Nisseki Iryo Centre), 4-1-22 Hiro, Shibuya-ku ☏ 400 1311, *Tokyo Medical and Surgical Clinic*, 2F 32 Mori Bldg, 3-4-30 Shiba-koen, Minato-ku ☏ 436 3028. There are English-speaking staff at *St Luke's International Hospital* (Seiroka Byoin), 1-10 Akashi-cho, Chuo-ku ☏ 541 5151, *St Mary's International Catholic Hospital* (Seibo Byoin), 2-5-1 Naka-Ochiai, Shinjuku-ku ☏ 951 1111, *Ishikawa Clinic*, 2F Azabu Sakurada Heights, 3-2-7 Nishi Azabu, Minato-ku ☏ 401 6340, and the *International Clinic*, 1-5-9 Azabudai 1-chome, Minato-ku ☏ 582 2646.
Dentists English is spoken at *Besford Dental Office*, 2F 32 Mori Bldg, 3-4-30 Shiba-koen, Minato-ku ☏ 431 4225 and by Dr Yanagisawa ☏ 581 4511.
Pharmacies Hospitals supply drugs. There are no 24hr pharmacies but *Hill Pharmacy*, 4-1-6 Roppongi, Minato-ku ☏ 583 5044, offers to

open specially for out-of-hours emergencies if you phone first (open 8–7; closed Sun). The only pharmacy open on Sundays and holidays is *Koyasu Pharmacy*. Its main branches are at Garden Plaza Hiroo 1F, 4-1-29 Minami Azabu, Minato-ku ☎ 446 4701 (open 10–8 daily, 10–9 in Sept and Oct; closed 2nd and 3rd Tuesday of the month) and Koyasu Bldg 1F, 7-14-7 Roppongi; ☎ 401 8667 (open 8.30–9 Mon–Sat; noon–8pm Sun and hols). There are smaller branches of *Koyasu Pharmacy* in major hotels, including the Hilton, Imperial and Okura. The *American Pharmacy*, Hibiya Park Bldg, 1-8-1 Yurakucho, Chiyoda-ku ☎ 271 4034, fills prescriptions and stocks Western (mainly American) drugs, cosmetics, dental care products, contraceptives and health foods; if you can't find it here, it is probably not available in Japan.

Police In an emergency, go to the nearest *koban*, neighbourhood police box, or dial 110.

Government offices

For information, advice and statistics, the best offices to approach are *JETRO* (see below) and *MITI* (Ministry of International Trade and Industry), 1-3-1 Kasumigaseki, Chiyoda-ku ☎ 501 1511, a monolithic body, but a good source of statistics.

Information sources

Business information The *US Chamber of Commerce*, 7F No 2 Fukide Bldg, 4-1-21 Toranomon, Minato-ku ☎ 433 5381, headed by Herbert Hayde, president of Burroughs Computers, is immensely effective and powerful, particularly in the area of electronics and telecommunications. They will be willing to provide a list of their members – among whom you will find useful contacts – to inquirers of any nationality. Less powerful (though often more useful than the embassies; see *Planning and reference* for embassy addresses) are the other Chambers of Commerce: *Australian*, c/o CPO Box 1096, Tokyo 100-91 ☎ 501 7031; *Belgian*, contact the embassy; *British*, Kowa Daiichi Bldg 3F, 1-11-41 Akasaka, Minato-ku ☎ 505 1734; *Canadian*, C.P.O. Box 2089 or contact the embassy; *French*, French Bank Bldg, 1-1-2 Akasaka, Minato-ku ☎ 587 0061; *German*, Akasaka Tokyu Bldg, 2-14-3 Nagata-cho, Chiyoda-ku ☎ 581 9881; *Netherlands*, Rm 503 Akasaka Q Bldg, 7-9-7 Akasaka, Minato-ku ☎ 586 3701; *Swiss*, c/o Sulzer Brothers (Japan) Ltd, 23F Asahi Tokai Bldg, 2-6-1 Otamachi, Chiyoda-ku ☎ 246 2715. The *Japanese Chamber of Commerce and Industry* (JCCI), 3-2-2 Marunouchi, Chiyoda-ku ☎ 283 7500/7824, and the *Tokyo Chamber of Commerce and Industry*, Tosho Bldg, 3-2-2 Marunouchi, Chiyoda-ku ☎ 283 7610, will also be able to help with information and contacts. The *Japan External Trade Organization* (JETRO) has its headquarters at 2-2-5 Toranomon, Minato-ku ☎ 582 5511; its international lounge has a wide range of business publications, and business advice and information are freely available.

Local media International newspapers are widely available in Tokyo and are more informative than the local English-language ones. Of the latter, the conservative *Japan Times*, run by the Ministry of Foreign Affairs, is the weightiest. The *Asahi Evening News* is the most useful for business information. The liveliest monthlies are *The Magazine*, oriented towards the Western executive community in Tokyo, and *Tokyo Journal*, covering a more male, business-orientated spectrum; it includes the excellent Cityscope, a comprehensive guide to monthly events. Magazines of relevance to business people include *Tokyo Business Today*, *Business Tokyo*, *Japan Economic Journal*, *Japan Foreign Trade Journal* and *Quarterly Forecast of Japan's Economy*. And, of course, everyone reads the *Far East Economic Review*. The *Kyodo News Service*, the Japanese Reuters, transmits a continuous update of current events, received by the business service centres of major hotels. The only English-language radio and television channels are the cable channels *KTYO* (radio) and *JCTV* (television), broadcast in hotels. JCTV, mainly a news service, shows live news from CNN, plus local news, features and documentaries related to business in Japan.

Tourist information Make your first stop the *Tourist Information Centre* (TIC), 1-6-6 Yurakucho, Chiyoda-ku ☎ 502 1461/2, which has knowledgeable English-speaking staff and provides free maps, leaflets and information on current cultural events. For travel assistance, call 502 1461 from anywhere in Tokyo. For recorded information on current happenings, call 503 2911. For general information, contact the *Japan National Tourist Organisation* (JNTO), Tokyo Kotsu Kaikan Bldg, 2-10-1 Yurakucho, Chiyoda-ku ☎ 216 1901. The *Japan Travel Bureau* (JTB), Foreign Tourist Dept, 3F Nittetsu-Nihonbashi Bldg, 1-13-1 Nihonbashi, Chuo-ku ☎ 276 7771 is also helpful. In addition to *Tokyo Journal*, TIC's *Tour Companion* and *Tokyo Weekender* (produced by the local Western community) are useful guides to what's on. There are also two excellent guidebooks to Tokyo, *Tokyo Access* and *Tokyo City Guide*.

Thank-yous

The most prestigious gifts are those gift-wrapped from *Mitsukoshi* ☎ 562 1111. Another good place to go for advice on and purchase of gifts is the *Foreign Customers' Liaison Office* at *Seibu*, in Yurakucho. You can pay here by credit card, and the foreign staff are experienced and helpful. Failing that, the concierge at your hotel will be able to advise. Japanese executives appreciate Scotch whisky (preferably malt) and champagne, while appropriate gifts for resident Westerners might include Japanese tea (Uji tea is the best), Matsuzaka steak (have it sent from a department store) and fruit, such as a large and beautifully packaged melon (see *Shopping*).

FUKUOKA

Area code ☎ 092

Fukuoka is the capital of the large southern island of Kyushu and also its political, economic, cultural and communications centre. Far removed from the influences of Tokyo, it is a flourishing modern city in its own right, with a population of 1.165m and a delightful semitropical climate. It is primarily a business city and a port. The major corporation based in Fukuoka is Nishitetsu, almost a ruling dynasty, which runs a private railway, the buses, a department store and Fukuoka's most prestigious hotel. Japan's major companies and banks are all represented here, and the city's main products are electrical appliances, tools, textiles and foodstuffs. There are American and Korean consulates in the city. Fukuoka's proximity to Asia led to it becoming a leading trading port in ancient times and also a major route through which Chinese culture filtered into Japan, particularly during the Nara and Heian periods (710–1192).

Arriving

From Tokyo or the north you should fly to Fukuoka. From Osaka the train is as convenient unless you are simply changing planes at Itami. By air the journey takes 1hr 45min from Tokyo and 1hr from Osaka. The airport is conveniently near the city centre.

Fukuoka Airport

The main air gateway to Kyushu, Fukuoka Airport consists of an international terminal and two domestic terminals, 5min walk apart. International traffic is mainly with Korea, but there are services from other parts of mainland Asia and the South Pacific. International terminal facilities include: two restaurants, (including Nishitetsu's Grand Chef); VIP lounge; limited range of shops, including duty-free shop; one bank, open whenever a plane arrives. Of the two domestic terminals, Terminal 1 handles traffic to and from Osaka, Nagoya and Sapporo, while Terminal 2 is for Tokyo (Narita) and Okinawa. Several restaurants on landside, open 6.30am–8.15pm, none on airside; VIP lounge; a few shops, including a branch of Iwataya department store, with a limited range of souvenirs; banks open when a plane arrives. Airport information ☎ 621 6059.

City link The airport is only a 10–20min drive from the city centre and even the executive with a modest per diem allowance should take a cab into town. But there are alternatives.
Bus Services depart every 5min for the bus terminal at Hakata Station, where you will have to take another bus or a taxi to reach your hotel.
Car rental Kyushu roads are less crowded than further east, but the road signs are just as foreign. A car might (just) be worthwhile considering if you have business outside Fukuoka. Nippon Rentacar, the main chain operating in Fukuoka, has an office at the airport.

Railway stations

Fukuoka is the last stop to the west on the Bullet Train line. The journey is an awesome 7hrs from Tokyo, and not much cheaper than by plane. Travellers from Osaka and points west usually come by train.
Hakata Station The Bullet Train station is a large modern building surrounded by hotels. A department store, airline offices and the Hakata Post Office are all located here, as well as termini for the buses and subway. Inquiries ☎ 431 3003.

Getting around

Fukuoka is laid out more or less in a grid, which makes it fairly easy to find your way around. The subway connects the city's two transport centres, Hakata Station and Fukuoka Station, where you can change onto the bus, private railway (Nishitetsu, of course) or subway going east. However, Fukuoka is not a large town, nor is it particularly congested. The most convenient ways to get around are on foot or by taxi.

Taxi Fukuoka taxi drivers have the friendly, open nature of Kyushu people and, more importantly, seem to know the major restaurants, hotels and offices.

Walking Distances in the central Tenjin-Nakasu area are not great, and even the raunchiest parts of Nakasu are generally safe.

Subway Fukuoka's sparkling new subway system is clean, smooth, very modern, and – unusually for Japan – not at all crowded. All signs are in English as well as Japanese. From Muromi in the west the line runs into the city past Ohori Park, to Tenjin and Nakasu, and then splits northeast to Kyushu University and southeast down to Hakata Station. The subway is gradually being extended.

Train The train is useful for journeys to the suburbs and out to Kita-Kyushu. JNR local lines from Hakata Station go up and down the coast and inland towards Nagasaki; for Kitakyushu, it is best to take the Bullet Train. The Nishitetsu line begins at Fukuoka Station, in Tenjin, and follows the JNR line through Dazaifu and out to the south.

Bus The *Nishitetsu Bus Company* has terminals at Hakata Station and Fukuoka Station. If you have plenty of time and a good map of Fukuoka to follow your route, travelling by bus is more interesting than the subway.

Driving Driving in Fukuoka is easier than in most other cities. The streets are broadly in a grid and the roads get congested only during rush hours. *Nippon Rentacar* ☏ 622 1885 has offices here.

Area by area

Present-day Fukuoka is divided into two by the Naka River. Hakata, the older, eastern part of the town, was the original port and commercial centre. The castle town of Fukuoka grew up to the west of Hakata in the 17thC, and the two towns amalgamated in 1889. Many businesses are still based in Hakata, but Tenjin, the centre of old Fukuoka, is rapidly developing into the main business area.

Hakata The oldest part of Fukuoka, Hakata includes the port, the Bullet Train station and districts to the east. Much of the commercial and trading activity of the city takes place here, and the Chamber of Commerce and prefectural administrative offices are located in this area.

Tenjin An area of wide streets and modern buildings, Tenjin has grown into the centre of Fukuoka. It is the largest shopping and business centre in Kyushu. Banks, business services, the City Hall and other public offices are here, along with major department stores, a large underground shopping arcade, bus and train terminals and the majestic Nishitetsu Grand Hotel.

Nakasu This island in the Naka River is virtually deserted by day. In the evening, the buildings looming over the maze of streets are bright with neon, and each turns out to be a warren of tiny bars, cabarets, "snacks" and amusement spots. This is the area for soaplands, "fashion massage" and love hotels, and at night it is packed.

The suburbs

Fukuoka is a small city, and the residential suburbs are not far from the city centre. The oldest families live in Daimyo, in what were the samurai areas around the castle. Other wealthy neighbourhoods are out to the west beyond the castle, and the districts of Kiyokawa and Takasago, to the south of Tenjin. The old merchant quarters in Hakata and to the east are rather run-down.

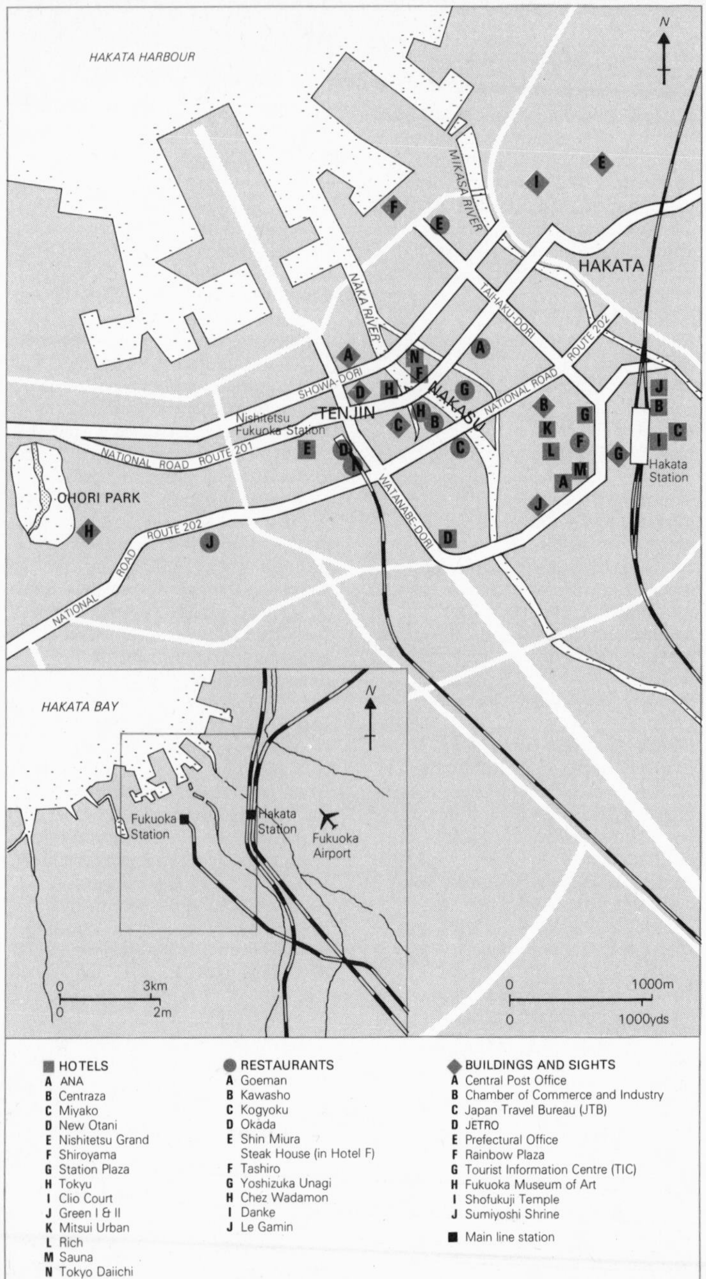
HAKATA HARBOUR
N
MIKASA RIVER
NAKA RIVER
HAKATA
TAIHAKU-DORI
ROUTE 202
SHOWA-DORI
NAKASU
NATIONAL ROAD
TENJIN
Nishitetsu
Fukuoka Station
NATIONAL ROAD ROUTE 201
WATANABE-DORI
Hakata
Station
OHORI PARK
ROUTE 202
NATIONAL ROAD
NATIONAL
HAKATA BAY
Fukuoka
Station
Hakata
Station
Fukuoka
Airport
0
3km
0
2m
0
1000m
0
1000yds
HOTELS
A ANA
B Centraza
C Miyako
D New Otani
E Nishitetsu Grand
F Shiroyama
G Station Plaza
H Tokyu
I Clio Court
J Green I & II
K Mitsui Urban
L Rich
M Sauna
N Tokyo Daiichi
RESTAURANTS
A Goeman
B Kawasho
C Kogyoku
D Okada
E Shin Miura
Steak House (in Hotel F)
F Tashiro
G Yoshizuka Unagi
H Chez Wadamon
I Danke
J Le Gamin
BUILDINGS AND SIGHTS
A Central Post Office
B Chamber of Commerce and Industry
C Japan Travel Bureau (JTB)
D JETRO
E Prefectural Office
F Rainbow Plaza
G Tourist Information Centre (TIC)
H Fukuoka Museum of Art
I Shofukuji Temple
J Sumiyoshi Shrine
Main line station

Hotels

At the top end of the scale among Fukuoka's hotels, the well-known Nishitetsu Grand has age and status, while the New Otani offers many of the conveniences of a modern luxury hotel. None of the hotels in Fukuoka has a business service centre. Hotel-building continues behind the station, where more and more new, glossy hotels are springing up, and Nishitetsu is planning a new hotel near the Grand for 1988.

ANA ¥¥

3-3-3 Hakata-eki-mae, Hakata-ku 812 ☎ 471 7111 TX 722288 • 354 bedrooms, 9 suites, 4 restaurants, 1 bar, 1 coffee shop

One of Fukuoka's older hotels, the ANA has a comfortably faded air. It is immensely popular, and the large, slightly dingy lobby is always crowded. The rooms, all with mini-bar, have views over the Japanese garden, and are spacious and homely, with furniture chosen for comfort, rather than style. Concierge, shops • health club with pool, sauna, training gym, jogging track – open to members and hotel guests • 11 meeting rooms (capacity 20–700).

Centraza ¥

4-23 Chuo-gai, Hakata-ku 812 ☎ 461 0111 TX 724211 • 200 rooms, 1 restaurant, 1 bar, 1 coffee shop

The best of the new hotels behind the station, the Centraza opened in 1985. Although it lacks the character and prestige of the more expensive hotels, it offers modern comfortable accommodation, right by the station, at a reasonable price. The 2-floor restaurant arcade includes a Chinese restaurant and a sushi bar. International calls via hotel switchboard, express check-out, parking difficult • pool, 24hr sauna • 2 meeting rooms (capacity 25–500).

Miyako ¥¥

2-1-1 Hakata-eki Higashi, Hakata-ku 812 ☎ 441 3111 TX 724585 • 260 bedrooms, 9 suites, 2 restaurants, 2 bars, 2 coffee shops

Built in 1972, the squat, cube-like Miyako has an air of solid respectability compared to the garish new hotels all around it. Of the hotels behind the station, this is the choice of most visiting foreign executives. The building has some interesting architectural features, such as long thin bedroom windows, which, though elegant, unfortunately let in very little light. The staff are brisk and efficient. Shopping arcade, parking difficult • 8 meeting rooms (capacity 15-500).

New Otani ¥¥¥

1-1-2 Watanabe-dori, Chuo-ku 810 ☎ 714 1111 TX 726567 • 435 rooms, 6 restaurants, 1 bar, 1 coffee shop

Kyushu's largest hotel, the New Otani combines the facilities of a modern international hotel with a certain Japanese elegance. The lobby is large and impressive, while the bedrooms are tastefully furnished, with a discreetly concealed mini-bar and wide windows overlooking the city. The rooms on the executive floor are particularly spacious. The efficient young concierge is exceptionally well informed and helpful. There is a tea ceremony room, and the hotel's Chinese restaurant has a good reputation locally. Concierge, 2-floor shopping plaza including art gallery, beauty salon • massage salon, pool • 8 meeting rooms (capacity 10-1300).

Nishitetsu Grand ¥¥

2-6-60 Daimyo, Chuo-ku 810 ☎ 771 7171 TX 723351 • Nikko Hotel group • 298 bedrooms, 3 suites, 4 restaurants, 1 bar, 1 coffee shop

This is the best address in Fukuoka. Owned by Nishitetsu, the private railway giant, the Nishitetsu was built in 1969 but is Fukuoka's most famous and most traditional hotel. Its vast lobby is a suitably imposing place to meet one's business contacts. The bedrooms, though recently refurbished and all with mini-bar, have an endearingly old-fashioned air. The location is ideal, at the prosperous Daimyo side of the Tenjin business district. Frequent visitors can join the NGH Club, whose special facilities include discounts, fast check-in and check-out and free parking for members. Express check-out, concierge, restaurant and travel reservations, shops, hairdresser, limited hotel parking • pool • 14 meeting rooms (capacity up to 1200), international conference hall.

Shiroyama ¥
5-3-4 Nakasu, Hakata-ku 810
☏ 281 2211 TX 723219 • 121 bedrooms, 1 suite, 5 restaurants, 2 coffee shops
Situated in the entertainment area of Nakasu, within striking distance of Tenjin, the Shiroyama ("White Mountain") is popular with young Japanese businessmen. Offering views of the river, the elegant all-white rooms, recently refurbished, are equipped with mini-bar and an extra-large desk. The Steak House (see *Restaurants*) is one of Fukuoka's most popular restaurants for business dining. Express check-out, art gallery, parking difficult • sauna, use of nearby sports centre and jogging course • 3 meeting rooms, varying sizes.

Station Plaza ¥
2-1-1 Hakata-eki-mae, Hakata-ku 812
☏ 431 1211 TX 723536 • Royal Hotel group • 245 bedrooms, 3 suites, 2 restaurants, 1 bar
The hotel occupies the top floors of the Asahi Building, opposite Hakata Station. The rooms are a reasonable size for the price; but it is clearly the location that accounts for its popularity with Japanese business travellers. International calls via hotel switchboard, parking difficult • 2 meeting rooms (capacity 30–300).

Tokyu ¥¥
1-16-1 Tenjin, Chuo-ku 810
☏ 781 7111 TX 723295 • 253 bedrooms, 13 suites, 3 restaurants, 1 bar, 1 coffee shop
If you are looking for a base for a few days' working visit, the Tokyu is a good place on balance. On the one hand it lacks prestige and status, the lobby area is distinctly shabby, and the young girls in pink polyester who run it are rather slow and inefficient. But the bedrooms are very spacious and attractively furnished with a Japanese flavour. The location, too, is excellent, mid-way between Nakasu and Tenjin. Beauty salon, pharmacy, travel agent • 6 meeting rooms (capacity 12-300).

OTHER HOTELS

Clio Court ¥ *5-3 Hakata-eki Chuo-gai, Hakata-ku ☏ 472 1111 TX 722312* One of the new hotels just behind Hakata Station, the glitzy Clio Court features an arcade full of boutiques and a revolving restaurant.

Green I and II ¥ *4-4 Hakata-eki Chuo-gai, Hakata-ku ☏ 451 4111 TX 725240* A large business hotel with two buildings, just behind the station.

Mitsui Urban ¥ *2-8-15 Hakata-eki-mae, Hakata-ku ☏ 451 5111 TX 725222* A modest, pleasant hotel, halfway between Hakata Station and Nakasu.

Rich ¥ *3-27-15 Hakata-eki-mae, Hakata-ku ☏ 451 7811 TX 725291* Directly opposite the Mitsui Urban and slightly more upmarket.

Sauna Hotel ¥ *3-3-2 Hakata-eki-mae, Hakata-ku ☏ 451 3535* A capsule hotel, including sauna, next to the ANA.

Tokyo Daiichi ¥ *5-2-8 Nakasu, Hakata-ku ☏ 281 3311 TX 726342* In the heart of Nakasu, close to bars and restaurants, and within walking distance of Tenjin.

Restaurants

Fukuoka businessmen, particularly the older ones, tend to prefer their own fine Fukuoka cuisine; when they patronize the fancy French restaurants it is mainly to impress important guests. The seafood in Fukuoka is outstanding. This is the place for *fugu* (blowfish), a potentially poisonous winter fish, regarded as a great delicacy. It can only be prepared by licensed chefs but, if properly done, it will endanger only your bank balance. It may be served raw, grilled, in a casserole, mixed with rice or as part of a kaiseki meal, and is in season from November to March. In the summer, Fukuoka's eel is a revelation. Tokyo fashions filter slowly through, and even down here you will find knowledgeable young businessmen sampling *nouvelle cuisine.*

JAPANESE

Goemon ¥
Doimachi-ten, 14-27 Kamikawabata, Hakata-ku ☎ *291 0593*
At Goemon they do magical things with tofu, the white bean curd which has recently become a part of Western healthy eating. Order one of the set meals, and you will be presented with a succession of tiny dishes, all containing tofu in different guises and all delicious. This is a modest, unpretentious little restaurant, with a charmingly rustic air. Upstairs there are *tatami* rooms for formal entertaining. Your Japanese colleagues may bring you here, but you will also be welcome on your own. This is a good place for an inexpensive night off.

Kawasho ¥¥¥¥
5-13 Nishi Nakasu, Chuo-ku
☎ *761 0269 • closed 2nd and 4th Sun of month*
The flower arrangements, paintings and even the designs on the curtains change to suit the seasons in this lovely old Japanese house. There is a lively tempura counter downstairs and quiet *tatami* rooms upstairs, each opening onto its own tiny garden with rocks and a pool. Tataki Takehiko, owner and master chef, has been serving fine *kaiseki*, tempura and sashimi here since 1945; he now has 12 young *sous*-chefs working under him. This is one of Fukuoka's most famous restaurants, and Japanese executives reserve well in advance to entertain here.

Kogyoku ¥¥
3-3-9 Haruya-shi, Chuo-ku
☎ *712 5666/751 7447*
Kogyoku is Fukuoka's classiest sushi shop. For an informal meal you can sit downstairs at the counter and point out the fish you want from the glass cabinets. If you come with Japanese colleagues, you will probably be seated upstairs in one of the beautiful private rooms overlooking the river, where your sushi will be accompanied by kaiseki.

Okada ¥¥
B1 Matsushita Watanabe Bldg, 4-10-10 Watanabe-dori, Chuo-ku
☎ *713 0290 • AE DC V*
Okada, by Fukuoka Station in the heart of Tenjin, serves fine teppanyaki to the local businessmen.

Shin Miura ¥¥¥¥¥
21-12 Sekijomachi, Hakata-ku
☎ *291 0821*
Regard it as a mark of the highest esteem if you are invited to this extremely elegant *ryotei.* Shin Miura, housed in a hundred-year-old samurai mansion down by the harbour, is Fukuoka's top restaurant. You will enjoy the attentions of charming kimono-clad ladies, who will prepare the Fukuoka speciality, *mizutaki*, a flavourful stew of chicken and vegetables, cooked at your table.

Steak House ¥¥
9F Shiroyama Hotel, 5-3-4 Nakasu, Hakata-ku ☏ *281 2211* • AE DC V
Perched high above Nakasu, this is one of Fukuoka's smartest restaurants, and *the* place for teppanyaki. At lunchtime, you will need to reserve to be sure of a place along the steel-topped counter, where the chefs, in tall white hats, *sauté* prime Kobe beef. In the evening, young Japanese businessmen dine here with their Western and Japanese colleagues.

Tashiro ¥¥
3-25-25 Hakata-eki-mae, Hakata-ku ☏ *431 5995* • AE DC V
Tashiro's speciality is live seafood, but they will send the fishermen out only if you reserve in advance. There is also fine steak, cooked teppanyaki-style. Tashiro doubles as a bar and is open until 3am. Regular customers – Japanese businessmen form the main clientele – each have their own bottle of whisky kept here.

Yoshizuka Unagi ¥
2-8-27 Nakasu, Chuo-ku ☏ *271 0700* • *closed Mon*
Yoshizuka, a small and unpretentious restaurant facing the river, quite simply serves the best eel in Fukuoka. Locals regard it as the best eel in the world, and Yoshizuka is patronized by local gourmets and well-informed visitors. More formal business entertaining takes place upstairs in the *tatami* rooms. The menu ranges from plain eel with a liberal coating of rich sauce (the exact ingredients are a well-kept secret) to eel kaiseki-style.

NON-JAPANESE

Chez Wadamon ¥¥¥
5-15 Nishi Nakasu, Chuo-ku ☏ *761 2000* • AE DC MC V
Wadamon is where Fukuoka's top executives wine and dine their clients and is a highly suitable place for the Western visitor to return hospitality. The cuisine is French, light and subtle in flavour to suit the Japanese palate, with Nagasaki beef the speciality. The basement rooms are a Japanese evocation of Europe – richly atmospheric, with heavy beams, lamps hung with netting, luxuriant potted plants and ornate china. There are branches of Wadamon in Tokyo's Ginza and Roppongi.

Danke ¥¥
4-9-18 Watanabe-dori, Chuo-ku ☏ *711 0039* • AE DC MC V
Danke is Tenjin's local French restaurant, a favourite of the business community. There are two rooms, suitable for entertaining small groups, with wood-panelled walls, starched white tablecloths and a single rose on each table. Danke is linked to a sake manufacturer and boasts an unusually wide range of sake and French wines at economical prices.

Le Gamin ¥¥
104 Chatlet Succes, 2-4-5 Akasaka, Chuo-ku ☏ *761 2721* • *closed 3rd Tue of month* • AE DC MC V
Both Japanese and Western businessmen are much in evidence at this elegant French restaurant. Young chef Shinji Ebata studied in France, and was at London's prestigious Le Gavroche for three years. His cuisine is a blend of *nouvelle* and traditional French, with plenty of local seafood cooked in an adventurous way. The wine list is one of the best in Fukuoka.

Bars

Nakasu is the nightlife area, not just for Fukuoka, but for the whole of Kyushu. Japanese businessmen like to patronize their locals – two or three bars where they are known and have their labelled bottle of whisky set aside for them – and your Japanese colleagues will no doubt introduce you to theirs.

Cottonfields
1F Egawa Bldg, 2-8-34 Nakasu • AE DC
The local Western community gather

nightly in this tiny bar facing the river. One wall is crammed with shelves full of beer, while another features a large blackboard with the day's menu written on it. Budweiser and spareribs are two of the favourites here.

Sky Bar

14F Nishitetsu Grand Hotel, 2-6-60 Daimyo, Chuo-ku • all major credit cards

This smart hotel bar, with a vista over the lights of the city, is the early evening haunt of the city's executives, both Japanese and Western. It is a good place for a quiet drink and a talk.

Wine House Fujita

4-1-6 Nakasu, Hakata-ku • open 6pm–1am • CB DC

Wine House Fujita has a trendy, upmarket atmosphere, which makes it popular with young Japanese businessmen, particularly exiles from Tokyo. It has a good selection of wines and serves Western food. It is also a comfortable environment for a single woman.

Entertainment

Fukuoka is far removed from the cultural centres of Kyoto and Tokyo. It has its share of visiting performers and musicians, both international and Japanese, though the selection is rather limited. Details of current events are listed in the monthly publication *Rainbow*, and tickets are obtainable through your hotel or from ticket agencies in major department stores. For entertainment, the Fukuokans prefer their lively Kyushu festivals, of which there are many. The major annual festival is the Hakata Gion-Yamagasa, held in July.

Theatre, ballet and music The main venue for performances by visiting theatre and ballet companies and musicians is *Fukuoka Civic Hall*, 1-8-1 Tenjin, Chuo-ku ☏ 711 4111.

Cinema There are a few cinemas in Fukuoka that show English-language movies. German films are shown once a month at the *Nishi Shimin Centre*, 2-2-1 Momochi, Sawara-ku ☏ 831 2321.

Nightclubs Locals boast that Nakasu is the raunchiest bar area in the country, and the foreign businessman is usually unable to avoid being taken on a tour of its nightclubs and bars – some of which are said to be infinitely more salacious than anything in Shinjuku's Kabukicho.

Shopping

Tenjin, with its underground arcades, is the shopping centre of Fukuoka. A wide range of high-quality goods is available, at prices somewhat lower than in Tokyo or Osaka. Look for fine local silks and for porcelain from nearby Arita (a milky-white porcelain with red designs) and Imari (porcelain painted in intricate multicoloured designs). Japanese visitors to Fukuoka buy the famous Hakata dolls.

Department stores *Iwataya*, in Tenjin, is considered to be the best department store, although the venerable *Tamaya*, in Nakasu, is still very popular.

Gifts For old Imari and Arita porcelain look in the department stores and antique shops around Tenjin. *Kukkodo*, Shintencho Arcade, Hakata-ku, has been selling traditional Japanese paper for generations. *Hakusen*, Hakata Station Bldg, 1-1 Chuogai, Hakata-eki, stocks a wide range of Hakata dolls.

Sightseeing

Fukuoka is basically a business city, with little to see. However, there are many interesting sights just outside the city. If you have a weekend to spare, you can explore Kyushu from Fukuoka, or move on to Nagasaki or Kumamoto.

Fukuoka Museum of Art This is one of the largest and best equipped art museums in the country, with a fine collection of paintings and sculpture, including items that belonged to the ruling Kuroda family, and tea ceremony utensils. The museum hosts important visiting exhibitions which change regularly. *1-6 Ohori Park, Chuo-ku ☎ 714 6051. Open 9.30–5; closed Mon.*

Ohori Park Only the gate and a watch tower remain of Fukuoka Castle, built by Lord Kuroda in 1601. The grounds and outer moat now form a large park, with a lake and three small islands linked by bridges. *Ohori Park, Chuo-ku.*

Shofukuji Temple This Zen Buddhist temple was founded in 1195, which makes it the oldest in the country. Its founder, Eisai, also introduced tea to Japan from China. *Okunodo, Gokusho-machi, Hakata-ku.*

Sumiyoshi Shrine Surrounded by cedars and camphor trees, on a hill overlooking the Naka River, Sumiyoshi Shrine is one of Kyushu's oldest, dedicated to the guardian god of sailors. The present buildings date from 1623. *Sumiyoshi, Hakata-ku.*

Guided tours

You can take a sightseeing bus tour, with a commentary (non-stop) in Japanese, around Fukuoka; for enquiries and reservations ☎ 713 5111/2961. There are also guided bus tours of Kyushu.

Out of town

Much of Kyushu is easily accessible from Fukuoka for a weekend trip. *Nagasaki*, with its Meiji period buildings and numerous hostess bars, is 2hrs 45min by limited express. *Kumamoto*'s fine old castle, and *Beppu*, which is noted for its magnificent hot springs, are not much farther. Nearer at hand is *Dazaifu*, 9 miles/14km south of Fukuoka, for centuries the cultural centre and capital of Kyushu. Consecrated to the god of learning, the *Dazaifu-Temmangu Shrine*, is surrounded by plum trees, and is much visited by children who pray for success in examinations. Near the shrine is the fine old *Kanzeonji Temple*. *Karatsu*, an hour's train ride from Fukuoka, is a coastal resort with a 17thC castle; some of Japan's most beautiful pottery is still being produced here. A little farther are *Imari* and *Arita*, where, according to tradition, translucent porcelain was first made. You can study ancient Arita ware in the museum, or perhaps pick up a bargain in the annual sales, held in Imari in early April and Arita in early May.

Spectator sports

Besides the national sport of sumo wrestling, there are sporting events in Hakata Bay, such as yacht races and windsurfing competitions, which excite local interest. For details see *Rainbow*.

Sumo One of the six annual national sumo tournaments is held in Fukuoka in mid-November, at the *International Centre*, 2-2 Chikko-Honmachi, Hakata-ku ☎ 272 1111. There are also amateur sumo matches in *Sumiyoshi Shrine* in early October.

Keeping fit

Golf For those on sizeable expense accounts, there are excellent golf courses in Kyushu. One of the most famous is *Koga*, near Fukuoka ☎ 943 2261. If not invited by colleagues, you can arrange an introduction through your hotel.

Health and sports centres There is a health centre in the ANA Hotel.

Jogging *Ohori Park* is popular with early morning joggers.

Sauna Saunas are the height of fashion in Fukuoka. One of the most popular is *Healthspot 24* in the Centraza Hotel, behind Hakata Station.

Swimming It is best to use the hotel pools if you wish to swim in the city; the Nishitetsu Grand and New Otani have pools. There are several beautiful and clean beaches easily accessible from Fukuoka. *Momoji Matsubara* is 30min by car or 1hr by ferry, while *Niji-no-Matsubara* is near Karatsu.

Local resources

Business services

None of Fukuoka's hotels has a business service centre. Of the commercial companies providing a reasonably wide range of business services, the best are *Manpower Japan* ☏ 741 9531 and *Kao Co* ☏ 481 2561.

Photocopying All hotels provide photocopying services. There are also machines in department stores and camera shops.

Secretarial For secretarial services, try *Temporary Centre Corporation* ☏ 711 1600.

Translation For translation and interpretation, try *Manpower Japan* or *King's Language Services* ☏ 714 4043.

Communications

International couriers The nearest international courier is *DHL* ☏ (093) 581 2129 (Kitakyushu).

Post office The *Hakata Post Office*, 8-1 Hakata-eki, Chuo-gai, Hakata-ku ☏ 431 6381, is at Hakata Station.

Telex and fax All hotels provide telex and fax service. In case of difficulty, contact *KDD* ☏ 474 3352.

Conference/exhibition centres

The nearest exhibition centre is the *West Japan General Exhibition Centre* in Kita-Kyushu (see *Kita-Kyushu*).

Emergencies

Bureaux de change The bureaux de change in the major hotels are open seven days a week, from early until late.

Hospitals In an emergency, call the *Prefectural Emergency Hospital Information Centre* ☏ 471 0099 or the *Municipal Medical Centre for Emergency Services*, Yakuin 2-chome, Chuo-ku ☏ 741 1099.

Pharmacies Prescription drugs are supplied by hospitals.

Police *Fukuoka Prefectural Police Headquarters*, Higashi-koen, Hakata-ku ☏ 641 4141.

Government offices

For enquiries about local government departments and services, contact *Fukuoka Municipal Office*, 1-8-1 Tenjin, Chuo-ku ☏ 711 4111, or *Fukuoka Prefectural Office*, 7-7 Higashi-koen, Hakata-ku ☏ 651 1111. For statistics and information, try the *Fukuoka Department of Commerce and Industry, Tourism Section*, 7-7 Higashi-koen, Hakata-ku ☏ 641 3880.

Information sources

Business information The only Chamber of Commerce in town is the *Fukuoka Chamber of Commerce*, 2-9-28 Hakata-eki-mae, Hakata-ku ☏ 441 1111.

Local media Consult the *Mainichi Daily News* for local information.

Tourist Information The *Tourist Information Centre* (TIC), 2-1 Hakata-eki-Chuogai, Hakata-ku ☏ 473 6696, in Hakata Station, is a useful source of maps, literature and information. You can also call the *Japan Travel Phone* collect; ☏ 106 and ask for *TIC*. The most helpful local travel agent is the *JTB*, Tenjin 1-chome, Chuo-ku ☏ 752 0700. *Fukuoka City International Exchange Centre*, "Rainbow Plaza", c/o Fukuoka Sun Palace, 2-1 Chikko-Honmachi, Hakata-ku ☏ 291 0777, publishes a free monthly newsletter, *Rainbow*, with information on current events, which is available free from the centre and in hotels. They welcome inquiries on any subject; Ms Matsuzaki speaks excellent English.

Thank-yous

Buy your thank-you gifts in *Iwataya* ☏ 721 1111.

HIROSHIMA

Area code ☎ 082

Founded in 1593, Hiroshima was totally destroyed on August 6 1945 by the world's first atomic bomb. In spite of predictions that the area would be unusable for decades, the reconstruction of the city has been rapid and complete. Mazda, Japan's third largest car manufacturer after Toyota and Nissan, dominates the scene, along with Ford, with whom it has close links. Many industries are based around the harbour, where Mitsubishi is developing giant sea-bed oil rigs. Kirin Beer has its main breweries in Hiroshima, and there are offices of most major Japanese companies. Future development plans include the Hiroshima Technopolis, an area of modern technical industries and research centres, and the building of an artificial island in Hiroshima Bay.

Arriving

From Tokyo it is certainly worthwhile flying to Hiroshima, a journey of 90min, as against 5hrs by Bullet Train; from Osaka the Bullet Train takes only 2hrs.

Hiroshima Airport

This small airport handles domestic flights only. Several restaurants, coffee shops and bars on landside, open from 7am–7pm, none on airside; VIP lounge; a few shops selling local delicacies; no banks. Inquiries ☎ 295 5555.

City link The best way to make the 20min (40min in rush hour) journey into the city centre is by taxi.

Bus The express bus goes to the station via the ANA Hotel and the city centre. Buses leave every 5min between 7.45am and 9.30pm.

Car rental Mazda, Toyota, Nissan and Nippon have airport offices.

Hiroshima Station

Local JNR lines, as well as the Bullet Train, stop at this modern and well-organized station. The complex includes a hotel and department store, and there are taxi stands and connections with buses and streetcars. Inquiries ☎ 261 1877.

Getting around

It is usually best to travel by cab, but the city centre is compact and the main hotels, restaurants and offices are within walking distance.

Taxi There are taxi stands at stations and hotels or they can be easily hailed on the streets.

Train *JNR* lines skirt the city and travel out in all directions to the suburbs.

Car rental If you are going outside the city centre, to, for example, the Mazda works or the port, you may find it convenient to drive. The main rental chains have offices in the city.

Streetcar If you have plenty of time, it is not difficult to use the streetcar. The TIC map, available at the station and the airport, has the seven streetcar lines marked on it.

Bus Even more difficult to use than the streetcar, though the network is comprehensive.

Area by area

Although the downtown area is small, Hiroshima is a large, modern city sprawling across the delta of the Ota River. Its long, broad streets are split by six main rivers running to the waterfront. Industries are concentrated to the south of the city, in the direction of the port.

Hachobori is the centre of the city; the major department stores and many offices are here. The business area stretches along the main road to Kamiyacho, where several banks, including the Bank of Hiroshima, are clustered, and down Hondori, lined with insurance companies. To the west of Hondori, on the other side of the river, is the Peace Memorial

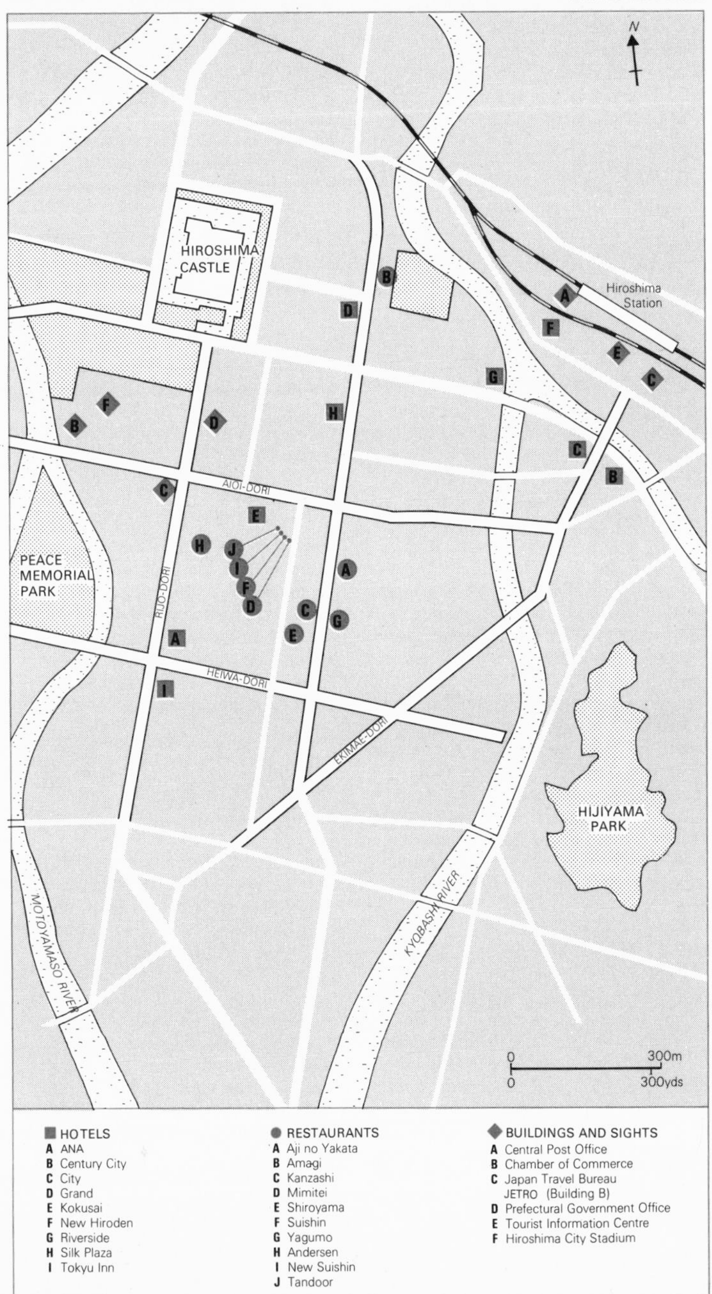
N
HIROSHIMA CASTLE
Hiroshima Station
PEACE MEMORIAL PARK
AIOI-DORI
RIJO-DORI
HEIWA-DORI
EKIMAE-DORI
HIJIYAMA PARK
KYOBASHI RIVER
MOTOYAMASO RIVER
0
300m
0
300yds
HOTELS
A ANA
B Century City
C City
D Grand
E Kokusai
F New Hiroden
G Riverside
H Silk Plaza
I Tokyu Inn
RESTAURANTS
A Aji no Yakata
B Amagi
C Kanzashi
D Mimitei
E Shiroyama
F Suishin
G Yagumo
H Andersen
I New Suishin
J Tandoor
BUILDINGS AND SIGHTS
A Central Post Office
B Chamber of Commerce
C Japan Travel Bureau
JETRO (Building B)
D Prefectural Government Office
E Tourist Information Centre
F Hiroshima City Stadium

Park. East of Hachobori, across Chuo-dori avenue, are Nagarekawa and Yagenbori, a maze of tiny streets full of restaurants and bars. Across the river and east of the main city centre is the station area, at present rather sleazy and reputedly the haunt of the *yakuza* (Japanese Mafia).

The suburbs The smartest suburbs are those in the hills to the north, around Asa and Hijiyama, and to the east, in Higashi-ku.

Hotels

New hotels are springing up in Hiroshima, but the Grand – with the weight of tradition behind it – is still considered the best. The modern ANA comes a close second. Both hotels are used by Ford to house its long-stay overseas executives.

ANA ¥¥

7-20 Naka-machi, Naka-ku 730
☎ 241 1111 TX 652751 • Sheraton • 423 bedrooms, 8 suites, 4 restaurants, 1 bar, 2 coffee shops

Opened in 1983, the ANA, to the south of the main shopping area, near the Peace Park, is a modern luxury hotel. The vast glittering lobby, hung with chandeliers formed of thousands of glass birds, looks out onto a waterfall and rock garden. The bedrooms are less spectacular, but spacious; all have a mini-bar, and those on the top floors have views across to the Inland Sea. The Vega Bar (see *Bars*) is a gathering place for local and visiting executives. The shopping arcade includes a branch of Sogo department store. Concierge, hairdresser • health club with training gym, heated indoor pool and sauna • 10 meeting rooms (capacity 25–600).

Century City ¥

1-1-25 Matoba-cho, Minami-ku 732
☎ 263 3111 TX 653723 • 76 rooms, 5 restaurants, 1 bar, 1 coffee shop

The Century City opened in 1985 directly opposite Hiroshima Station. It is still patronized largely by Japanese, though it deserves discovery by Western business travellers. What it lacks in prestige it makes up for in the quality of the rooms, which are vast, comfortable and tastefully furnished, with mini-bar and views over the river to the hills. The staff are friendly and helpful. 3 meeting rooms.

City ¥

1-4 Kyobashi-cho, Minami-ku 732
☎ 263 5111 TX 652844 • 165 bedrooms, 6 suites, 3 restaurants, 2 bars, 1 coffee shop

The City is directly opposite the station and has a small but regular clientele of Western business travellers. A friendly hotel, it is also the choice of many Japanese. The rooms are large for Japan and pleasantly furnished, with views over the city to the hills and a desk big enough to work on. International calls via hotel switchboard • 2 meeting rooms (capacity up to 150).

Grand ¥¥

4-4 Kami-Hachobori, Naka-ku 730
☎ 227 1313 TX 652666 • 369 bedrooms, 13 suites, 5 restaurants, 1 bar, 1 coffee shop

Secure in its position as Hiroshima's best address, the Grand has an air of quiet dignity. It is located in one of the smarter areas of town, away from the noise and bustle of the city centre. The gracious lobby, looking out onto a waterfall, is normally full of business guests and their clients. The bedrooms, all with mini-bar, are spacious and tastefully furnished, although the view of city streets is rather unappealing. A swimming pool is at the planning stage. The Abeille Bar (see *Bars*) is a popular gathering place for local executives. Concierge, travel and theatre bookings, arcade of shops, hairdresser, shuttle bus service • 15 meeting rooms (capacity 20–620).

Kokusai ¥
3-13 Tate-machi, Naka-ku 730
☎ 248 2323 • 68 bedrooms, 11 suites, 3 restaurants, 2 bars
The Kokusai ("International"), with its top-heavy restaurant tower, is a landmark in the middle of the main Hiroshima shopping area. Its bars, restaurants and meeting rooms are always packed with local and visiting businessmen. Kazuo Fujita, the manager of the (rapidly) revolving Sky Lounge restaurant, spent eight years in England and is friendly and willing to help with contacts. The rooms, sadly, have seen better days. Bowling alley • 5 meeting rooms (capacity up to 500).

OTHER HOTELS
New Hiroden (¥) *14-9 Osuga-cho, Minami-ku 732 ☎ 263 3456* TX *653884*. Near the station, with friendly staff and basic but adequate rooms.
Riverside (¥) *7-14 Kaminobori-cho, Naka-ku 730 ☎ 228 1251* TX *652554*. Across the river from the station, its spacious rooms overlook the river.
Silk Plaza (¥) *14-1 Hachobori, Naka-ku 730 ☎ 227 8111* TX *653753*. Close to the main Hachobori business area, with plenty of character and lively and helpful staff.
Tokyu Inn (¥) *3-17 Komachi, Naka-ku 730 ☎ 244 0109* TX *653841*. Good value; big, attractive rooms.

Restaurants

For business entertaining, the classy restaurants in the ANA and the Grand are the usual choices. If you have an evening to yourself, try the mid-range restaurants on the tenth floor of Sogo or wander into any of the establishments in the backstreets which display a red lantern outside. Hiroshima is famous for its oysters – in season from November to February – and for its sake; ask for *jizake*, "local" sake, rather than one of the nationwide brands.

JAPANESE

Aji no Yakata ¥¥¥
1-3 Shintenchi, Naka-ku ☎ 247 1129 • closed hols • AE DC V
Aji no Yakata is a five-floor restaurant complex in the Nagarekawa bar area. The first three floors specialize in sushi, with fresh fish straight from the Inland Sea, while on the top two floors customers gather around gleaming steel counters to enjoy steak cooked teppanyaki-style. Ford and Mazda's foreign employees frequently dine here with Japanese colleagues.

Amagi ¥¥¥¥
10-10 Kaminobori-cho, Naka-ku ☎ 221 2375 • closed hols
Set in an old samurai mansion in exquisite landscaped gardens, Amagi is Hiroshima's top, and most exclusive, *ryotei*. Company directors and eminent politicians bring their most valued clients here, to feast on the finest *kaiseki* in elegant and refined surroundings.

Kanzashi ¥¥
2-4 Mikawa-cho, Naka-ku ☎ 247 0138 • closed 2nd and 4th Sun of month
This modest restaurant, hidden up a narrow staircase on Chuo-dori, has been serving top-quality tempura to discriminating diners for the last 25 years. Local businessmen gather here after work to enjoy tempura made from the freshest possible ingredients, including *kuruma ebi*, large prawns which are very much alive. There are *tatami* rooms upstairs for business entertaining.

Mimitei ¥¥
6-4 Tatemachi, Naka-ku ☎ 248 0899 • closed hols
Mimitei is celebrated for its

charming female chefs. Clad in red and blue checked aprons, they shout a greeting as you come in and cook the best local Jinseki steak, fried teppanyaki-style on hotplates before you. Sake flows freely, as does whisky and French wine. The customers are mainly businessmen.

Shiroyama ¥
4-13 Mikawa-cho, Naka-ku
☏ 244 2200 • closed Tue
While 80-year-old Mr Shiroyama makes the tofu (bean curd), a job he has been doing for the last 60 years, his son transforms the bland white slabs into a variety of tasty dishes. You can dine in one of the two tiny *tatami* rooms upstairs, or climb onto a stool among the convivial crowd along the counter downstairs. You may meet your Japanese colleagues dining here in informal mood, but are more likely to come across resident Westerners.

Suishin ¥¥
6-7 Tatemachi, Naka-ku ☏ 247 4411 • closed Wed and hols • DC V
This Hiroshima institution has been serving sushi and sashimi, made with fish fresh from the Inland Sea, since the 1950s. Suishin is the place for globefish, stingfish, rock cod and flat fish, as well as oysters and eel. *Kamameshi* – individual rice casseroles – are the house speciality. The downstairs rooms, furnished with tables, are lively; the top three floors of *tatami* rooms are reserved for business entertaining.

Yagumo ¥¥
1-23 Mikawa-cho, Naka-ku
☏ 244 1551 • closed hols • AE DC V
Heavy cast-iron kettles hang from the polished wooden beams of this enormous reconstructed farmhouse. The waitresses, in hand-woven cotton kimonos, serve local specialities like *susugi-nabe*, the Hiroshima equivalent of *shabu shabu*, to a clientele of Japanese executives and, often, their Western guests.

NON-JAPANESE

Andersen ¥¥
7-1 Hondori, Naka-ku ☏ 247 2403 • closed 3rd Tue of month • AE DC V
Andersen is a little corner of Europe in the middle of Hiroshima, appreciated as much by the Japanese for its exotic atmosphere and foods as by homesick Westerners. Mr Tataki, the founder, has his chefs trained in Denmark, and sends there for ingredients; visiting Danes say that the pastries in the shop downstairs are better than the ones back home. Upstairs, on the opposite side of the stairwell from the inexpensive café, there is a fine restaurant serving *nouvelle cuisine*. It is very popular with Hiroshima sophisticates and a highly suitable place to entertain Japanese colleagues.

New Suishin ¥¥¥
6-7 Tatemachi, Naka-ku ☏ 248 2935 • closed Wed and hols • DC V
This smart restaurant is in the basement of Suishin (see earlier). A large proportion of the clientele are businessmen, both Western and Japanese. Each table in the elegant dining room sports a single rose in a cut-glass vase, and the service is equally stylish. Chef Tanaka Tsuneshi's cuisine is traditional French, with a Japanese flair. The wine list is extensive.

Tandoor ¥
3F G House Bldg, 5-7 Tatemachi, Naka-ku ☏ 247 5622 • closed Wed and hols • DC V
The popular Tandoor is Hiroshima's first authentic Indian restaurant. The chefs are Indian, brought over by the owners from a Delhi hotel. Their North Indian cuisine – featuring *nan* (unleavened bread), tandoori meats and meat and vegetarian curries – is relatively mild, to suit Japanese palates. Potted palms, large revolving fans and Indian background music complete the ambience. This is a good place to take Japanese colleagues for an informal meal.

Bars

Estimates of the number of bars in Nagarekawa and Yagenbori vary, from 3,000 upwards; but it is generally agreed that Hiroshima has more per head than any other city in Japan. The most fashionable bars are undoubtedly those in the hotels.

Abeille

B1 Grand Hotel, 4-4 Kami-hachobori, Naka-ku • AE DC V

A favourite of local and visiting executives, this elegant bar, with its distinguished wood-panelled interior, serves an enormous range of cocktails, and features live piano music during the evening. This is a comfortable place for a woman on her own.

Vega

22F ANA Hotel, 7-20 Naka-machi, Naka-ku • AE DC V

This discreet bar at the top of the ANA is a gathering place for local executives. Here you can sip your cocktail or whisky and water while taking in a magnificent view of the city. Single women are welcome.

Wine Bar

3F Zakuro Bldg, 1-15 Horikawa-cho, Naka-ku • DC V

Japanese executives and their American counterparts from Ford and Mitsubishi are among the clientele of this popular wine bar. There is an enormous wine list and a variety of cocktails, and the chef grills steaks behind the counter in the centre of the room.

Wine-ya

3F Kuwamoto Bldg, Horikawa-cho, Naka-ku

For many young executives an evening's drinking begins in this sophisticated wine bar at the quieter end of Namiki-dori. Wine-ya serves 300 different wines, plus a variety of snacks.

Entertainment

The best source of current information on what's on is *Hiroshima Signpost*. Make reservations through your hotel or at Play Guide ticket agencies in major department stores.

Theatre and music Visiting international and Japanese theatre troupes, musicians and orchestras regularly perform in Hiroshima. The main venues are *Yubin Chokin Hall* ☎ 222 2525, *Kosei Nenkin Kaikan* ☎ 243 8881 and *Kenmin Bunka Centre* ☎ 245 2311, Kamiya-cho, Naka-ku.

Nightclubs At night the entire male population of Hiroshima seems to crowd into the narrow neon-lit streets of Nagarekawa and Yagenbori. If your taste runs to lovely hostesses and a live *karaoke* band, *Club Tap*, 11-20 Kanayama-cho, Naka-ku ☎ 243 5525, on Yagenbori, is one of Hiroshima's best venues. For dancing, *Urbis*, 3F Namiki Bldg, Fukuromachi, Naka-ku, a sophisticated disco, is the place to go. *Deck Shoes*, on Nagarekawa, is favoured by the resident Western community.

Shopping

The main shopping area is *Hondori*'s network of paved pedestrian streets and covered arcades. Here you will find many elegant shops and small speciality stores. The fashionable young wander up and down *Namikidori*, dropping into its boutiques, jewellers and cafés. Of the department stores, *Sogo*, at Kamiyacho, is the largest, with the greatest variety of merchandise, while *Fukuya*, at Hachobori, is the oldest, and stocks Paris fashions and other high-class goods. Next door to Fukuya is a branch of *Mitsukoshi*. Local products include writing brushes, clogs, sake and traditional musical instruments.

Sightseeing

The Peace Memorial Park and its museum, sobering reminders of Hiroshima's destruction, draw millions of visitors each year. But there are more cheerful sights both in and not far from the city.

Hiroshima Castle The castle is a 1958 reconstruction of the original built by Terumoto Mori in 1589; it houses a historical museum. *21-1 Motomachi, Naka-ku. Open 9–5.30 (4.30, Oct–Mar).*
Peace Memorial Park North across the river from the Park is the skeletal A-bomb Dome, the ruin of the Chamber of Industry and Commerce which was at the epicentre of the explosion. Within the Park, the *Peace Memorial Museum* has a collection of photographs and exhibits of the destruction, while at the *Peace Memorial Hall*, you can see a half-hour film documenting the horrors of the bombing. *1-3 Nakajima-cho, Naka-ku. Open 9–4.30.*
Shukkeien Garden The ruling Asano lords had their villa here, and the landscaped garden, laid out by tea-ceremony master Munetsutsu Ueda in 1620, was intended to evoke the gardens of Kyoto. It was reconstructed after the war. *2-11 Kaminobori-machi, Naka-ku. Open 9–6 (5, Oct–Mar).*

Guided tours

The *Hiroshima Bus Company* ☏ 261 7104 runs half-day tours of the city, with Japanese commentary only, and full-day tours which include Miyajima. You can also hire a sightseeing taxi with a taped English commentary; contact the *Association of Independent Taxi Drivers* ☏ 283 2311. There are cruises of Hiroshima Bay and day cruises in the Inland Sea, arranged by *Seto Inland Sea Lines* ☏ 255 3344. You can even take a short flight over Hiroshima; contact *Hiroshima Airport* ☏ 231 9131. There are industrial tours of, for example, the Mazda plant, the Kirin brewery and the Hiroshima Mint (the only one outside Tokyo and Osaka); inquire at your hotel or the *TIC*.

Out of town

Even if you have only a few hours to spare, it is worthwhile making the half-hour journey to *Miyajima*, one of Japan's most celebrated beauty spots. On this sacred island is the magnificent *Itsukushima Shrine*, with, apparently floating in the sea, its famous red *torii* gateway.

Spectator sports

Baseball The only sport you need to know about in Hiroshima is baseball. The whole city is fiercely proud of their team, the Hiroshima Toyo Carp, Hiroshima Shimin Kyujo, 5-25 Moto-machi, Naka-ku ☏ 223 2141. This is the only team in Japan sponsored, not by a major company, but by local government. After many unsuccessful years, the Carp broke into the Central League in 1975, and have been national champions several times since. Home games take place at *Hiroshima City Stadium*, Kamiya-cho, Naka-ku.

Keeping fit

Of the hotels, only the ANA has good sports facilities.
Golf There are several comparatively cheap golf courses within an hour's drive of Hiroshima. Inquire at your hotel for details.
Jogging You can jog around the Peace Park or the castle or along one of Hiroshima's many rivers.
Swimming The pool in the ANA is probably the least crowded. If you want to use a public pool go early. These include *Chuo Pool*, 4-41 Moto-machi, Naka-ku ☏ 228 0811; *Yoshijima Indoor Pool*, Konan 5-1-53, Naka-ku ☏ 249 2231; *Prefectural Indoor Pool*, Moto-machi, Naka-ku ☏ 221 7071. For sea bathing head north to the beaches on the Japan Sea; the Seto Inland Sea is heavily polluted.
Tennis There is little chance of getting a court but try *Hiroshima Chuo Tennis Court*, 2-15 Moto-machi, Naka-ku ☏ 221 1463.

Local resources

Business services

Compared to other major Japanese industrial cities, Hiroshima is not well equipped with services for foreign business travellers. None of the Hiroshima hotels has business centres but major hotels will arrange services such as photocopying, printing, secretarial and translation. Otherwise contact *Manpower Japan* ☎ 223 1100, which provides a wide range of business services.

Communications

International couriers *DHL* ☎ 295 6140.
Post office The *Central Post Office*, Hiroshima Station ☎ 245 5318, is open 24hrs for express mail.
Telex and fax Most hotels provide telex and fax facilities. If yours does not, contact *KDD Telecom Hiroshima* ☎ 241 2411.

Conference/exhibition centres

Conferences take place at the ANA and Grand hotels and at the *Yubin Chokin Hall*, the *Kosei Nenkin Kaikan* and the *Sun Plaza*. A large convention hall, the *Kokusai Heiwa Bunka Kaikan*, will open in 1988.

Emergencies

Hospitals In an emergency, call the *Hiroshima Medical Association* ☎ 232 7321. Hiroshima's two main hospitals are the *Municipal Hospital* ☎ 221 2291 and *Funairi Hospital* ☎ 232 6195.
Pharmacies Prescription medicines are supplied by hospitals. There are no 24hr pharmacies.
Police The *Prefectural Police Station* is at Kamiya-cho, Naka-ku ☎ 221 7201.

Government offices

For inquiries about local government departments and services, contact *Hiroshima City Office*, 1-6-34 Kokutaiji-machi, Naka-ku ☎ 245 2111.

Information sources

Business information Close to the A-Bomb Dome, the *Hiroshima Chamber of Commerce and Industry*, 5-44 Moto-machi, Naka-ku 730 ☎ 222 6610 is the biggest of ten local chambers. *JETRO* is housed in the same building.
Local media The most useful English-language newspaper is the *Mainichi Daily News*, published in Osaka. *Hiroshima Signpost*, produced and published by the local Western community, is full of lively articles and reviews and listings of current events.
Tourist information There is a branch of the *Tourist Information Centre* (TIC) in the station ☎ 261 1877 and in the Peace Park Rest House, 1-1 Nakajima-cho, Naka-ku ☎ 247 6738. They will provide maps, information and a free copy of the useful *Tourist's Handbook*. For more detailed information, consult the *Hiroshima City Office, Tourism Section*, 1-6-34 Kokutaiji-machi, Naka-ku ☎ 245 2111. The *JTB* in Hiroshima Station ☎ 262 5588 is also helpful.

Thank-yous

Buy your gifts from *Fukuya* ☎ 246 6111 or *Mitsukoshi* ☎ 244 3111, who will arrange delivery. One of their gift-wrapped packs of brand-name Western foods would be an acceptable present for your Japanese host.

KITA-KYUSHU

Area code ☎ 093

Kita-Kyushu, on the island of Kyushu, is a gigantic industrial city, formed in 1963 by the merger of five formerly independent towns – Kokura, Yahata, Wakamatsu, Moji and Tobata. The area around it, now known as the Kita-Kyushu Industrial Complex, has been Japan's major centre of iron and steel production for centuries. It is the home of the world's largest steel company, the Nippon Steel Corporation. Although heavy industries make up 45% of Kita-Kyushu's total production, the recent trend is towards diversification, and the city's products now include industrial robots, integrated circuits and related products, carbon fibre, nuclear reactor parts and oil drilling equipment. Kita-Kyushu is also an important port, with the only piers for containerized cargo in western Japan.

Arriving

Travellers coming to Kita-Kyushu from Tokyo can take the Bullet Train, a journey of 6hrs 30min, or fly to Fukuoka and make the 23min Bullet Train trip to Kokura.

Kokura Station

Although quite small, with a faintly rustic air, Kokura Station incorporates a shopping arcade. The monorail and streetcar system are within a few minutes' walk.

Getting around

If you are doing business in Kita-Kyushu, you will probably be collected and driven around by your host company. If left to your own devices, you will have to rely on the trains to get from one part of Kita-Kyushu to another. Kokura itself is very small, and you can walk or get around by taxi.

Train There are two major JNR lines in Kita-Kyushu. One travels east and west from Kokura, effectively linking Kita-Kyushu's five towns, while the Nippo line heads along the coast to the south. There are regular departures between 5am and midnight.

Monorail The Hitahikosan Monorail line takes you south out of Kokura town centre down towards the Hiraodai Plateau.

Driving With the aid of a good map, driving is a feasible way of getting around Kita-Kyushu. Good highways link the five towns, and there is a branch of Nippon Rentacar in each.

Area by area

Kokura, the old castle town, is the commercial and cultural centre of the area. It is a charming little town, full of old buildings and a rambling market with stalls of live fish, squeezed between modern thoroughfares lined with office blocks, with the space age monorail arching over all.

Moji Once a small fishing village, Moji is now one of Kyushu's most important commercial ports. It is the nearest point in Kyushu to the main island of Honshu, to which it is linked by a suspension bridge and a railway tunnel.

Tobata is mainly industrial, with fish-processing plants, a Nippon Steel plant and the Shin-kokura power station. Kyushu Institute of Technology is also in Tobata.

Yahata The Yahata district is a centre of chemical engineering and heavy industry. Nippon Steel is based here, as is the Mitsubishi Chemical Plant. Kurosaki, in West Yahata, is a busy shopping area.

Wakamatsu has a large shipping centre, with coal shipping installations, engineering works and shipyards. The Hibikinada Industrial Park is here.

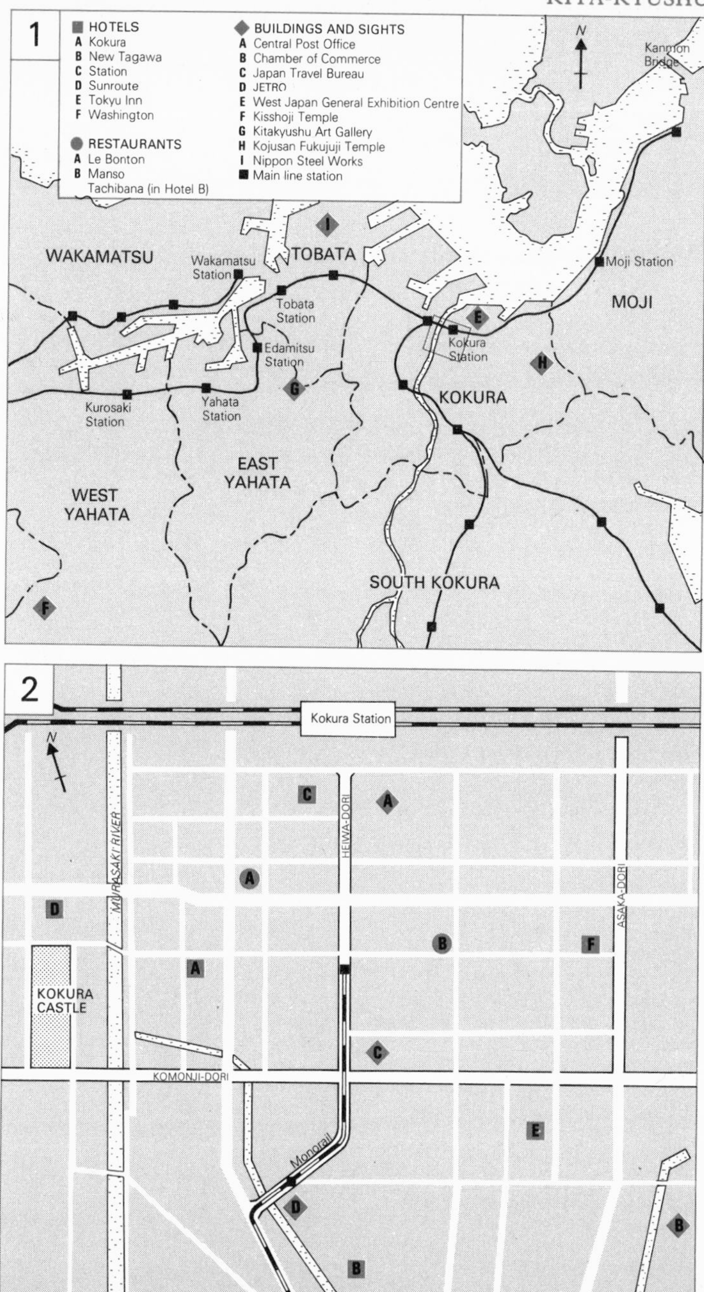
1
HOTELS
A Kokura
B New Tagawa
C Station
D Sunroute
E Tokyu Inn
F Washington
RESTAURANTS
A Le Bonton
B Manso
Tachibana (in Hotel B)
BUILDINGS AND SIGHTS
A Central Post Office
B Chamber of Commerce
C Japan Travel Bureau
D JETRO
E West Japan General Exhibition Centre
F Kisshoji Temple
G Kitakyushu Art Gallery
H Kojusan Fukujuji Temple
I Nippon Steel Works
Main line station
N
Kanmon Bridge
WAKAMATSU
Wakamatsu Station
TOBATA
Tobata Station
Moji Station
MOJI
Edamitsu Station
Kokura Station
KOKURA
Kurosaki Station
Yahata Station
EAST YAHATA
WEST YAHATA
SOUTH KOKURA
2
Kokura Station
HEIWA-DORI
MURASAKI RIVER
ASAKA-DORI
KOKURA CASTLE
KOMONJI-DORI
Monorail

Hotels

Most Western visitors to Kita-Kyushu stay at the New Tagawa or the Kokura. There are also several reliable chain hotels.

Kokura ¥

3-10 Senbamachi, Kokura, Kita-ku 802 ☎ 531 1151 • 101 rooms, 2 restaurants, 1 bar, 2 coffee shops

The Kokura is a large modern international-style hotel, with helpful English-speaking staff. The rooms are big and attractively furnished. Concierge, small shopping arcade • 12 meeting rooms (capacity 10–500).

New Tagawa ¥

3-46 Furusenba-cho, Kokura, Kita-ku 802 ☎ 521 3831 • 94 rooms, 18 suites, 2 restaurants, 1 coffee shop.

The hotel used to be a *ryokan*, and its buildings are dotted around a large and beautiful Japanese garden. Besides the modern hotel building, with its large and comfortable rooms overlooking the garden, there are small traditional wooden Japanese houses where you can stay or simply come and dine (see *Restaurants*). International calls via hotel switchboard • 3 meeting rooms (capacity 25–200).

OTHER HOTELS

Station (¥) *1-1-1 Asano, Kokura, Kita-ku 802 ☎ 521 5031* TX *712411.* By Kokura Station.
Sunroute (¥) *1-2-16 Muromachi, Kokura, Kita-ku 802 ☎ 561 3311* TX *712607.* Beside Kokura Castle.
Tokyu Inn (¥) *8-5 Konya-cho, Kokura, Kita-ku 802 ☎ 521 0109* TX *712690.* One of the best business hotels.
Washington (¥) *1-9-8 Kaji-machi, Kokura, Kita-ku 802 ☎ 531 3111* TX *712606.* Another good business hotel.

Restaurants

There are plenty of restaurants catering to a business clientele, and the city is renowned for fish and seafood.

Le Bonton ¥¥

1-4-12 Uomachi, Kokura, Kita-ku ☎ 521 0035 • AE DC V

Le Bonton has been serving superbly fresh seafood and Matsuzaka beef to a largely business clientele since 1953. Downstairs is a teppanyaki bar, with heavy wooden tables topped with stainless steel plates. On the first floor, both cuisine and ambience are French.

Manso ¥¥

4-14 Kaji-machi 1-chome, Kokura, Kita-ku ☎ 521 8466 • AE V

Manso is the place for fish of the season – *fugu* in winter, turbot in spring. Owner Hiroshi Noda and his assistants grill it, fry it, simmer it, or simply cut it into perfect rectangular slices and serve it raw. Company directors and industrial magnates entertain their clients in Manso's *tatami* rooms.

Tachibana ¥¥

New Tagawa Hotel, 3-46 Furusenba-cho, Kokura, Kita-ku ☎ 521 3831 ext 361 • AE DC V

In the tiny Japanese houses set in the New Tagawa's beautiful landscaped gardens, kimono-clad ladies serve a delicate meal of *kaiseki*. The small rooms on the second floor of the main restaurant are suitable for formal entertaining, and the best place in Kita-Kyushu to entertain your Japanese hosts. The main restaurant itself features fish and steak dishes in a relaxed atmosphere.

Relaxation

Entertainment Kita-Kyushu has a lively folk tradition and many festivals. The Kokura Gion Festival in mid-July is one of Japan's most celebrated.
Shopping The main shopping areas are Kokura and Kurosaki, in West Yahata. Kita-Kyushu's best

department stores are *Izutsuya* and *Tamaya*, in Kokura, and *Sogo*, in Kurosaki.
Sightseeing Worth visiting in or near the city are the *Kisshoji Temple*, the *Kojusan Fukujuji Temple*, *Kokura Castle* and *Kita-Kyushu Art Gallery*. Not far beyond the smokestacks is beautiful mountainous countryside. A few hours away are the mountainous *Kunisaki Peninsula*, full of old temples and stone Buddhas; *Beppu*, a famous hot spring resort; and *Mount Aso*, a spectacular volcano.
Golf *Moji Golf Course* is one of Japan's oldest and best; you will need an introduction.
Hiking The nearest hiking area is *Hiraodai*.
Swimming Along the north shore of Wakamatsu is a long stretch of beautiful beaches. *Waita* is the most popular swimming beach; there are many quieter, cleaner beaches nearby.

Local resources

Business services

There is no provision for business services, nor for translators or interpreters. You will have to rely on your hotel or business associates to provide these.

Communications

International couriers *DHL* ☏ 581 2129.
Post office The *Central Post Office* is at 3-8-1 Kyomachi, Kokura, Kita-ku ☏ 541 3545.
Telex and fax If your hotel is unable to help, the nearest *DHH* ☏ (092) 474 3352 is in Fukuoka.

Conference/exhibition centres

West Japan General Exhibition Centre ☏ 511 6848, *Commercial and Industrial Trade Centre* ☏ 541 1969.

Emergencies

Hospital *Kita-Kyushu Municipal Hospital*, 2-1-1 Bashaku, Kokura, Kita-ku ☏ 541 1831.
Police *Central Municipal Police Station*, 5-1 Journai, Kita-ku ☏ 561 7171.

Government offices

For inquiries about local government offices and services, contact the *Economic Bureau*, Kita-Kyushu City, 1-1 Journai, Kokura, Kita-ku 803 ☏ 582 2062. The *Fukuoka Prefectural Office* will also provide information.

Information sources

Business information The nearest chamber of commerce is in Fukuoka.
Tourist information *JTB*, JTB Bldg, 1-1-1 Sakai-machi, Kokura, Kita-ku ☏ 551 5121. You can also use the *Japan Travel Phone*: ☏ 106 and ask for "Collect call TIC". The *Fukuoka City International Exchange Centre* ☏ (092) 291 0777 is helpful.

Thank-yous

The major department stores are the appropriate places to buy gifts (see *Shopping*).

KOBE

Area code ☎ 078

Kobe is Japan's busiest port, with the largest container capacity in the world. Its industries and commerce are mainly related to the port, and include shipbuilding and iron and steel production. Kobe was one of the first ports to be opened to trade with the West, in 1868. Many Westerners settled here and set up businesses, and a flourishing foreign community grew up. Kobe still has a very international flavour, with a greater density of foreigners than Tokyo, including a large Indian community. Squeezed between the mountains and the sea, Kobe can expand only into the sea. The city's first man-made island, Port Island, opened in the harbour in 1981. Rokko Island, due to be completed in 1989, will be the world's largest artificial island, with residential and industrial areas, cultural facilities and a long beach.

Arriving

The closest airport is Itami (see *Osaka*). The limousine bus to Sannomiya Station departs every 20min between 7am and 9.15pm; journey time is at least 40min.

Railway stations

Shin-Kobe Before boarding the Hikari Bullet Train, check that it stops at Shin-Kobe; some pass straight through. There is a subway link down to Sannomiya Station.
Sannomiya, at the centre of one of Kobe's liveliest shopping areas, houses terminals for the JNR, Hankyu and Hanshin lines from Osaka and Kyoto. The monorail to Port Island starts from here.

Getting around

Kobe is a long, narrow city, with the train lines running east–west through it. North–south transportation is more difficult, but distances in this direction are quite short; walk or take a taxi.
Taxis You should have no trouble hailing a taxi on the street; if you do, stations and hotels are good places to pick one up.
Train The JNR, Hankyu and Hanshin lines connect Rokko and Sannomiya in eastern Kobe with Kobe Station in the west. Check that you are boarding a local train, not a non-stop express.
Monorail The driverless Port Liner leaves Sannomiya every 6min from 5.20am to 11.44pm and takes a circular route around Port Island. Station names and announcements are in English as well as Japanese.
Subway Kobe's subway system, opened in 1985, runs from Shin-Kobe Station west along the city.
Car rental The main rental chains have offices in Kobe. Driving is more trouble than it is worth.

Area by area

The bustling station area of Sannomiya is the heart of Kobe. To the south, running straight down to the port, and lined with trees, is Flower Road. Many hotels and offices and the City Hall are located on this broad boulevard, and the Trade Centre Building is just off it. The main business area extends east, between the railway tracks and the sea, from Flower Road as far as Kobe Station, with most businesses concentrated on Sakaemachi-dori. Over the bridge is Port Island, a futuristic complex of skyscrapers which includes a convention centre, exhibition hall and one of the city's best hotels, the Portopia. To the north of Sannomiya, stretching up the hill, is Kitano, the classiest area of town and an exclusive residential district. Here you will find embassies, consulates, nightclubs, restaurants and streets full of old Western-style houses built by early

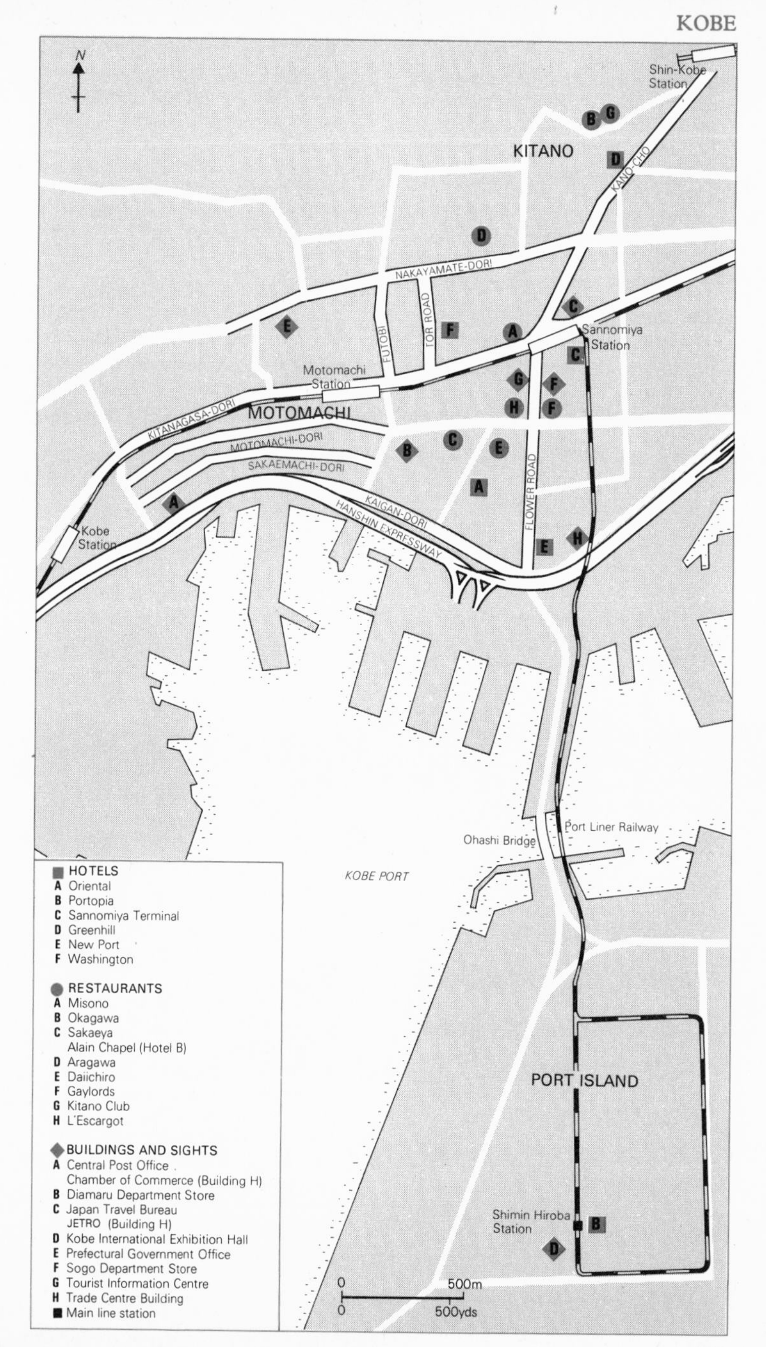
N
Shin-Kobe Station
KITANO
KANO-CHO
NAKAYAMATE-DORI
FUTOBI
TOR ROAD
Sannomiya Station
Motomachi Station
MOTOMACHI
KITANAGASA-DORI
MOTOMACHI-DORI
SAKAEMACHI-DORI
KAIGAN-DORI
HANSHIN EXPRESSWAY
FLOWER ROAD
Kobe Station
Port Liner Railway
Ohashi Bridge
KOBE PORT
PORT ISLAND
Shimin Hiroba Station
0 500m
0 500yds
HOTELS
A Oriental
B Portopia
C Sannomiya Terminal
D Greenhill
E New Port
F Washington
RESTAURANTS
A Misono
B Okagawa
C Sakaeya
Alain Chapel (Hotel B)
D Aragawa
E Daiichiro
F Gaylords
G Kitano Club
H L'Escargot
BUILDINGS AND SIGHTS
A Central Post Office
Chamber of Commerce (Building H)
B Diamaru Department Store
C Japan Travel Bureau
JETRO (Building H)
D Kobe International Exhibition Hall
E Prefectural Government Office
F Sogo Department Store
G Tourist Information Centre
H Trade Centre Building
Main line station

foreign settlers. West of Sannomiya is Motomachi, a smart shopping area. South of here is Kobe's sizeable Chinatown, Nankin-machi.

The suburbs Two of the most exclusive suburbs – where old Japanese families and long-term Western residents have their homes – are Nishinomiya and Ashiya, between Kobe and Osaka. Mikage, between Ashiya and Rokko, is full of up-and-coming young executives, while those who can afford it live on the cool slopes of Mount Rokko, or west of Kobe, near the beaches at Suma.

Hotels

There are not many hotels to choose from in Kobe. The new Portopia on Port Island is Kobe's first hotel of an international standard, while the Oriental is the most prestigious and best of the older hotels. A new luxury hotel, scheduled to open in 1988, is being built near Shin-Kobe station by Daiei, the supermarket chain and builders of the Portopia.

Oriental ¥¥

25 Kyomachi, Chuo-ku 650
☎ 331 8111 ⓉⓍ 5622327 • 204 rooms, 6 restaurants, 1 bar, 1 coffee shop
The first Westerners to come to Kobe stayed at the Oriental Hotel. It is still Kobe's most prestigious, although the old buildings have long since been replaced by modern ones, dating from 1966. The spacious and dignified lobby is a meeting place for the local Japanese community, and many visiting Western executives stay here. Service is impeccable, but the bedrooms, all with mini-bar, are showing signs of age, and are rather cramped and dark. Concierge, arcade of shops • 2 meeting rooms.

Portopia ¥¥

10-1, 6-chome Minatojima, Nakamachi, Chuo-ku 650 ☎ 302 1111 ⓉⓍ 5622112 • 536 rooms, 14 suites, 7 restaurants, 1 bar, 2 coffee shops
The elegant oval-shaped Portopia, the tallest hotel in western Japan, opened in 1981, beside the International Conference Centre on Port Island. It is Kobe's first international-style luxury hotel, and a large proportion of its clientele are businessmen, both Western and Japanese. The striking circular lounge, with chandeliers and a waterfall, is ringed with shops, including an art gallery and branches of Sogo and Mitsukoshi, and there are spectacular views over Kobe and the Inland Sea from the spacious bedrooms, all with mini-bar. The Alain Chapel restaurant (see *Restaurants*) is one of the city's top places for business dining. Pool, gym, tennis courts, jogging track, sauna • secretarial services, 19 meeting rooms (capacity up to 1,500).

Sannomiya Terminal ¥

8-chome Kumoidori 1-2, Chuo-ku 651 ☎ 291 0001 ⓉⓍ 5622131 • 190 rooms, 1 restaurant
A typical station hotel, the Sannomiya Terminal has unusually attractive bedrooms with a view of the Kobe hills. The restaurant Le Chanteclair offers fine French cuisine.

OTHER HOTELS

Greenhill 2 (¥) *2-8-3 Kano-cho, Chuo-ku 650 ☎ 222 0909.* The larger of the two Greenhill hotels, each a few minutes' walk from Shin-Kobe Station, is popular with Westerners. The rooms are a good size.
New Port (¥) *6-3-13 Hamabe-dori, Chuo-ku 651 ☎ 231 4171 ⓉⓍ 5623058.* Convenient for the port and the Kyobashi business area. There is a revolving restaurant on the top floor.
Washington (¥) *2-11-5 Shimayamate-dori, Chuo-ku 650 ☎ 331 6111.* In the main shopping area north of Sannomiya Station.

Restaurants

Japanese businessmen visiting Kobe are always glad of the chance to indulge their taste for foreign food. The city's French, Indian and Chinese restaurants are more famous than its Japanese ones. Kobe beef – the cows are fed on beer and massaged daily – is the tenderest in the world.

JAPANESE

Misono ¥¥¥¥
1-7-6 Kitanagasa-dori, Chuo-ku
☏ *331 2890* • AE DC V
The teppanyaki style of cooking was invented in 1945 by Shigeji Fujioka, the founder of Misono, and this large and impressive restaurant complex still serves only teppanyaki. Each table is topped with a steel hotplate where the chefs fry up succulent slices of prime Kobe beef. The distinguished clientele has included presidents and prime ministers, as well as luminaries of the business world. There are now five Misono restaurants in Japan.

Okagawa ¥¥¥
1-5-10 Kitano-cho, Chuo-ku
☏ *222 3511* • *closed hols* • AE DC V
The Okagawa family has been providing the citizens of Kobe with top-quality sukiyaki and tempura for the last hundred years. Their new restaurant is situated up on the hill, directly below the Kitano Club. They are used to a cosmopolitan clientele here, and there are gaps built in between the tatami and the tempura counter so that the Western executives can stretch their legs. The rooms are decorated in traditional style, with flower arrangements and small rock gardens, and offer a spectacular view of the lights of modern Kobe.

Sakaeya ¥¥¥
2-2-7 Sannomiya-cho, Chuo-ku
☏ *331 5772* • *closed Wed*
Kobe's best tempura is to be found in this tiny rambling house near Motomachi Station. On the ground floor is a counter with space for just ten, where the chef cooks fresh tempura before the customers' eyes. A steep staircase winds past a little stone lantern and wicker fence to the tatami rooms, where Japanese businessmen gather to feast, often bringing with them their Western colleagues. There are no English speakers here, but the chef will hand you a well-thumbed copy of *Eating in Japan* to order from.

NON-JAPANESE

Alain Chapel ¥¥¥¥
31F Portopia Hotel, 10-1, 6-chome Minatojima, Nakamachi, Chuo-ku
☏ *302 1111* • AE DC MC V
One of Kobe's most prestigious restaurants, the Alain Chapel is perched high above the city with views over the Inland Sea, and is the scene of much business entertaining. It features the *nouvelle cuisine* of Michelin 3-star chef Alain Chapel, who comes twice a year from Lyons to oversee the planning of the menu. The wine list is extensive.

Aragawa ¥¥¥¥¥
2-15-18 Nakayamate-dori, Chuo-ku
☏ *221 8547 or 231 3315* • *closed hols* • AE DC V • *reservations essential*
Aragawa is a small and exclusive restaurant in Kitano, specializing in charcoal-grilled steaks of the famous Kobe beef. The red-carpeted rooms are very Western in atmosphere, with heavy beams, wood and brick walls and candles on the white tablecloths. This is where top Western executives entertain their Japanese counterparts.

Daiichiro ¥¥¥
94 Edo-machi, Chuo-ku ☏ *331 0031* • AE DC MC V
For a Chinese restaurant, Daiichiro is unusually restrained in décor. It is

the fine Peking cuisine that draws Japanese businessmen in droves. This is not a place for eating alone. There are four floors, full of small rooms each equipped with a revolving table, where groups of eight to ten ensconce themselves for the evening. Daiichiro's speciality is hors d'oeuvres, and the seafood, straight from the sea, is particularly fine.

Gaylord ¥
B1 Meiji Seimei Bldg, 8-3-7 Isogami-dori, Chuo-ku ☎ *251 4359 • closed hols* • AE DC V
A little corner of the Raj in Japan, Gaylord is probably Japan's oldest Indian restaurant. It is certainly one of the best, and top of the list for many executives, Western or Japanese, visiting Kobe. Chefs and waiters are all Indian, and the food is authentic Punjabi, with – rare in Japan – plenty of vegetarian dishes. The setting is richly Indian, with carved wooden ceiling and tables, red flock walls and Indian music, and the clientele is sophisticated and cosmopolitan.

Kitano Club ¥¥¥¥
1-5-7 Kitano-cho, Chuo-ku
☎ *222 5123 • closed hols* • AE DC V
Set high on the hill in the smartest part of town, with a spectacular view over Kobe, the Kitano Club has long been the place where the sophisticated and wealthy gather. The cuisine is French, but it is the ambience that attracts – the marble pillars, red carpet, heavy draperies and soft piano music. The complex also includes a nightclub (see *Entertainment*) and several shops selling Paris fashions.

L'Escargot ¥¥
1-5-4 Sannomiya-cho, Chuo-ku
☎ *331 5034/1969 • closed hols* • AE DC MC V
Hidden away down a back alley near Sannomiya is a small restaurant which is reputed to serve the finest French food west of Osaka. At both lunch and dinner L'Escargot is crowded with businessmen, Western and Japanese, from nearby offices. Focal point of the elegant basement room is a simple fireplace of grey stone; and the staff are as discreet as the décor. There is a short but imaginative wine list.

Bars

An evening out with Japanese colleagues is likely to begin with a visit to one of the thousands of tiny bars in the streets behind Sannomiya Station, before moving on to dinner or one of Kitano's smart cabarets.

The Attic
Ijinkan Club Bldg, 1-12 Kitano-cho 4-chome, Chuo-ku
Owned by American Marty Kuehnert, the Attic is like a corner of Los Angeles, with plenty of Budweiser, plus the Atticburger, the best burger in Kobe. A good place to meet the local Western community or bring Japanese colleagues.

The Studio
6F Palais de Kitanozaka, 7-11 Kano-cho 4-chome, Chuo-ku
Kobe's Western residents are often to be found lounging in the comfortable armchairs of the Studio, a tiny, intimate bar which feels rather like a private living room. On offer are music, plenty of drink and good food.

Entertainment

For entertainment, Kobe dwellers tend to go to Osaka, a mere 30min by train. Like most Japanese cities, Kobe is stronger on nightlife than culture. For information see *Kansai Time Out* and the Monday edition of the *Mainichi Daily News.*
Ticket agencies Theatre and concert tickets for Osaka as well as Kobe can be bought through your hotel or at Play Guide ticket agencies.
Theatre, cinema and music There is a much wider choice in Osaka, although Kobe has its share of films, concerts and Japanese and

Western theatre. Concerts and theatre often take place at the *Kobe Cultural Hall* ☏ 351 3535.
Nightclubs For nightlife, head for the area north of Sannomiya Station. The bars near the station are fairly sleazy, but up on the hill in Kitano you will find some of western Japan's most sophisticated nightclubs. The *Kitano Club*, 1-5-7 Kitano-cho, Chuo-ku ☏ 222 5123 (see *Restaurants*) is undoubtedly Kobe's best. Both Japanese and Westerners enjoy the classy atmosphere and live music at the *Casablanca Club*, 3-1-6 Kitano-cho, Chuo-ku ☏ 241 0200. Local Westerners as well as fashionable Japanese can be found at *Shekinah*, 8F Palais Kitanozaka Bldg, 4-7-11 Kano-cho, Chuo-ku ☏ 332 0666, and at another of Kobe's most popular discos, the *Vivi en Lee*, Washington Hotel, 2-11-5, Shimo-Yamate-dori, Chuo-ku ☏ 331 6111.

Shopping

Motomachi, with its covered arcades, is the place to go for fashions and quality goods. Among the boutiques there are shops selling cameras, electronic and tax-free goods, handicrafts and fine arts. *Toho Sanoya Honten*, 6-7-3 Motomachi, is a famous old ceramics shop. Sannomiya is a maze of shops, stretching along *Centre-gai* arcade, with, under it, *Santica Town*, a vast network of shops, restaurants and tiny bars. Of Kobe's four department stores, the most popular are *Sogo*, at Sannomiya, and *Daimaru*, at Motomachi. North from Daimaru is Tor Road, lined with restaurants and antique shops. The smart Kitano area has boutiques full of high-class fashions and shops selling luxury goods such as pearls.

Sightseeing

Kobe is beautifully situated between the mountains and the sea, but it has few sights.
Kitano Kobe's main historic area is where the early foreign settlers lived, and streets full of their splendid old houses – including some wonderful examples of eccentric architecture – have been carefully preserved, if rather commercialized, Japanese-style. Many of the houses can be visited.
Kobe City Museum This exceptionally fine municipal museum houses the Namban Art Collection, a fascinating collection of 16th–19th century paintings of Kobe's exotic foreign residents by Japanese artists. *24 Kyo-machi, Chuo-ku. Open 9–4.30; closed Mon.*
Minatogawa Shrine The most famous of Kobe's shrines, Minatogawa, is just north of Kobe Station and is dedicated to the 14th century hero Masashige Kusunoki.
Nada Inveterate sake drinkers will want to make a pilgrimage to Nada, just 6 miles/10km from Sannomiya. You can walk around the fine old breweries with their black wooden walls, or visit one of the museums run by the three major brewers, Hakatsuru, Kikumasamune and Sawanotsuru. *Kikumasamune Memorial Museum, Nozaki Nishimachi 1-chome, Higashi Nada-ku ☏ 851 2275. Open Jan–Mar, 8.30–5; closed Sat and Sun; reservations essential. ☏ 841 4105 (Hakatsuru), ☏ 882 6333 (Sawanotsuru).*

Out of town

The mountain range visible behind Kobe is the Rokko range, of which the highest peak is *Mount Rokko*. There is a cable car to the top, from which you can enjoy views across the city and the Inland Sea to Shikoku Island. On the other side of the peak is Japan's longest ropeway to *Arima Spa*, which can also be reached by bus direct from Sannomiya. Arima is a famous hot spring resort, the oldest in Japan, nestling in a gorge among cherry and maple trees. An hour west of Kobe is the town of *Himeji*, with its castle, the *White Heron*, considered one of the most beautiful in Japan. Well off the tourist track is *Awaji Island*, a short boat ride from

Kobe; there are no sights here, but plenty of countryside. A new bridge links Awaji with *Shikoku*, a lovely island full of spectacular mountains, hot springs and rice paddies.

Spectator sports

There is very little sport in Kobe itself but a wide choice in Osaka.

Baseball *Koshien Stadium*, home of the popular Osaka-based Hanshin Tigers (see *Osaka*) is at Nishinomiya, a Kobe suburb: Naruocho, Nishinomiya ☎ (0798) 47 1041.

Keeping fit

Apart from the one at the Portopia (see *Hotels*), there are no fitness facilities in Kobe hotels. Public facilities are unusually well developed, thanks to the presence of a large international community, and there are outdoor facilities on the top of Mount Rokko. There is plenty of information about sporting activities in *Kansai Time Out*.

Golf Japan's oldest golf course, with 18 holes, constructed in 1903 by Englishman Arthur Groom, is on the summit of *Mount Rokko*.

Health and sports centres *YMCA Fitness Centre*, 2-7-15 Kano-cho, Chuo-ku ☎ 241 7201, and *Mac Sports Club*, 7-8-31 Motoyama Minami-machi, Higashi Nada-ku ☎ 452 1801, are open to non-members for the day; they offer facilities such as weight training, swimming, sauna, gym, tennis courts and jogging track. *Sports World 33*, 10-7 Sannomiya-cho 2-chome, Chuo-ku ☎ 392 3735, is for women only. There is a sauna and a tanning room and classes in dance, yoga and aerobics.

Hiking There are good hiking trails around Kobe's mountain ranges, particularly on *Mount Futatabi*. The popular tracks tend to be crowded.

Jogging The *Kobe Hash Harriers* meet once a week to run. For information, call Bob Smith ☎ (06) 532 3197; for the women's Hash Harriers, call Wilma Shulter ☎ 232 1212 or Mrs Gassman ☎ 222 2993.

Skiing The nearest ski slope is *Mount Rokko Jinko Skiing Area*, Nada-ku ☎ 891 0366. This is a very popular slope, and it is best to ski in the middle of the week. Farther afield, there are ski slopes on *Mount Kannabe* and a new slope on *Mount Hyonosen*. *Taiyo Recreation Centre* ☎ (06) 353 5338 and *Big Tour Osaka Centre* ☎ (06) 363 0451 organize bus trips from Kobe to various ski slopes.

Swimming There are pools in the health clubs. The public pools are cheap but always very crowded: *Hyogo Prefectural Sports Centre Pool*, 1 Hasuike, Nagata-ku ☎ 631 1071; *Port Island Sports Centre Pool*, Port Island ☎ 302 1071. Kobe's *Suma Beach* is popular with young surfers, while *Maiko* and *Shioya* are quieter and somewhat cleaner.

Local resources

Business services

The only hotel business service centre in Kobe is the *Sagawa Express* ☎ 302 1071, in the Portopia Hotel. It is available to non-hotel guests. Otherwise use the local branch of the national companies: *Manpower Japan* ☎ 291 8800, *Kao Co* ☎ 252 1150 and *Temporary Centre Corporation* ☎ 332 0234.

Photocopying and printing Your hotel will arrange photocopying for you. For large quantities, contact *XEROX System Centre* ☎ 251 1701 or *Nice Print* ☎ 332 6918, which also prints namecards. For general printing, use *Daishin Printing Co Ltd* ☎ 302 2700.

Translation and interpreting Call *Kokusai Communications* ☎ 331 6062 (ask for Jo Ash or Jerry Ochs) or *Miss Setsuo Kamiishi* ☎ 842 4571.

Communications

International couriers None operate from Kobe. Use the Osaka couriers.

Post offices *Central Post Office*, 2-1 Sakaemachi-dori 6-chome, Chuo-ku

☎ 351 7011; *Port Post Office*, 118 Ito-cho, Chuo-ku ☎ 331 0701.
Telex and fax Most hotels have telex and fax facilities. If necessary, use the *KDD* ☎ 331 0420.

Conference/exhibition centres

Kobe is second only to Tokyo in the number of international conferences it hosts – more than 450 conferences, trade fairs and exhibitions take place annually. There are a total of 52 conference sites in Kobe. The main conference centre is the *Kobe International Conference Hall*, 9-1 Minatojima-Nakamachi 6-chome, Chuo-ku ☎ 302 5200 (on Port Island). Other important centres are *Kobe Port Terminal Hall*, Minatomachi 4-55, Nakamachi, Chuo-ku ☎ 391 7638; *Kobe Trade Promotion Centre*, Minatojima 6-chome, Chuo-ku ☎ 302 1035; and *Sanbo Hall* 1-32 Hamabe-dori 5-chome, Chuo-ku ☎ 251 3551.

Emergencies

Hospitals The following hospitals have 24hr casualty departments: *Kobe Adventist Hospital*, 8-4-1 Arinodai, Kita-ku ☎ 981 0161; *Kobe Kaisei Hospital*, 11-15 Shinohara-Kitamachi 3-chome, Nada-ku ☎ 871 5201; *Kobe Central Municipal Hospital*, 4-6 Minatojima-Nakamachi, Chuo-ku ☎ 302 4321 (on Port Island). For dental treatment contact *Dr Thomas Ward*, Oriental Dental Clinic, Oriental Ika-Shika Bldg, 4-7 Nakayamate 3-chome, Chuo-ku ☎ 321 2717.
Pharmacies Prescription drugs are supplied by hospitals and doctors. For over-the-counter medicines, most pharmacies are open 10am–8pm. Go to *Shinyaku-do*, Santica Town, 1 Sannomiya-cho 1-chome, Chuo-ku ☎ 391 1778.
Police *Ikuta Police Station* ☎ 331 0044.

Government offices

For inquiries, contact *Kobe City Hall*, 6-5 Kano-cho, Chuo-ku ☎ 331 8181, or *Hyogo Prefectural Office*, 5-10 Shimoyamate-dori, Chuo-ku ☎ 341 7711.

Information sources

Business information *Kobe Chamber of Commerce*, 1-14 Hamabe-dori 5-chome, Chuo-ku ☎ 251 1001. You will probably find the foreign chambers of commerce in Osaka more helpful. The *JETRO* office is at 5-1-14 Hamabe-dori, Chuo-ku ☎ 231 3081.
Local media *Mainichi Daily News*, printed in Osaka, carries information about current events in the Kansai area. The excellent monthly *Kansai Time Out* has articles about Kansai and comprehensive listings of current entertainment and sporting events.
Tourist information There is a small *Tourist Information Office*, 2F Kobe Kotsu Centre Bldg, JNR Sannomiya Station, west exit ☎ 392 0020. At the station there is a helpful branch of the *JTB* ☎ 231 4118. Also try *Kobe International Tourist Association*, 6th floor, International Conference Centre, Port Island ☎ 303 1010; Mrs Shakawa speaks excellent English. *Community House and Information Centre* (CHIC), 6-15 Ikuta-cho 4-chome, Chuo-ku ☎ 242 1043, is run by members of Kobe's foreign community to provide helpful information and support, primarily for Western residents, but also for visiting Westerners. Their publication *Living in Kobe* is full of invaluable information.

Thank-yous

The top department stores are the most suitable place to buy gifts, and they will arrange delivery: *Daimaru* ☎ 331 8121; *Hankyu* ☎ 321 3521; *Mitsukoshi* ☎ 341 3333; *Sogo* ☎ 221 4181. To send flowers within Japan or abroad, contact *Shinko Flower Shop*, 3-1-19 Shimoyamate-dori, Chuo-ku ☎ 331 9221.

KYOTO

Area code ☎ 075

At first sight Kyoto looks like any other Japanese city, all concrete office blocks and traffic-filled streets. Behind this aggressively modern façade, however, lies the Kyoto that most visitors come to see: the ancient capital of Japan and still its cultural centre, a city studded with hundreds of temples, shrines, palaces and gardens, as well as charming little backstreets lined with old wooden houses. If you have time to spare, this is the ideal place to relax for a weekend and discover traditional Japan.

Kyoto was the capital of Japan and the home of the Imperial Family from 794 until 1868; the emperors are still enthroned here in the Imperial Palace. Even when the centre of power moved to Tokyo, Kyoto remained the home of traditional culture and the arts. It is also an important industrial city, producing electrical appliances and precision machines, and the centre of biotechnological research in the Kansai area.

Arriving

The closest airport to Kyoto is Itami (see *Osaka*) from which there is a limousine bus service into the city every 20min during the day, taking 60–90min. From Tokyo the Bullet Train takes just under 3hrs and is quicker and simpler than flying. Osaka is a mere 17min by Bullet Train.

Railway stations

The Bullet Train arrives in Kyoto Station, which is rather far from the city centre. If you are coming from Osaka or Kobe, it is more convenient – and cheaper – to take the Hankyu line to Kawaramachi. From Osaka you can also take the Keihan line to Sanjo Keihan in the city centre.

Kyoto Station The Bullet Train and all JNR lines, including those to and from Osaka and Kobe to the west, Nara to the south and Nagoya to the east, stop at Kyoto Station. The subway line and most buses begin here. The station building itself is quite small, with a department store above it and a cluster of hotels, an underground shopping arcade and more department stores around it. Inquiries ☎ 351 4004.

Kawaramachi The terminus of the Hankyu line, from Osaka, Kawaramachi Station is in the basement of Hankyu department store, in the busiest part of the city, near Gion. Inquiries ☎ 221 1052.

Sanjo Keihan is also in the downtown area, but across the river from Kawaramachi. Change to another train to go on to the Miyako from here. Inquiries ☎ 561 0033.

■ HOTELS		MAP No.
A	ANA	2
B	Fujita	1
C	Grand	2
D	International	2
E	Kyoto	1
F	Miyako	1
G	Royal	1
H	Takaragaike Prince	2
I	Gimmond	1
J	Holiday Inn	2
K	New Hanku	2
L	New Miyako	2
M	Hiiragiya	1
N	Tawaraya	1
O	Yachiyo	1

● RESTAURANTS		
A	Gion Suehiro	1
B	Gontaro	1
C	Junidanya	1
D	Junsei	1
E	Minokichi	1
F	Mishima Tei	1
G	Toriyasu	1
	Yachiyo (Hotel O)	1
H	Yoshikawa Tempura	1
I	Ashiya	2
J	Manyoken	1

◆ BUILDINGS AND SIGHTS		
A	Central Post Office	2
B	Japan Travel Bureau (J.T.B.)	1
C	Kyoto Chamber of Commerce & Industry	2
D	Kyoto Tower	2
E	Prefectural Government Office	2
	Tourist Information Centre (T.I.C.) (Building D)	2
F	Daitokuji Temple	2
G	Ginkakuji Temple	2
H	Heian Shrine	2
I	Katsura Imperial Villa	2
J	Kinkakuji Temple	2
K	Kiyomizu Temple	2
L	Kyoto National Museum	2
M	Nanzenji Temple	2
N	Nijo Castle	2
O	Old Imperial Palace	2
P	Ryoanji Temple	2
Q	Sanjusangendo	2
■	Main line station	

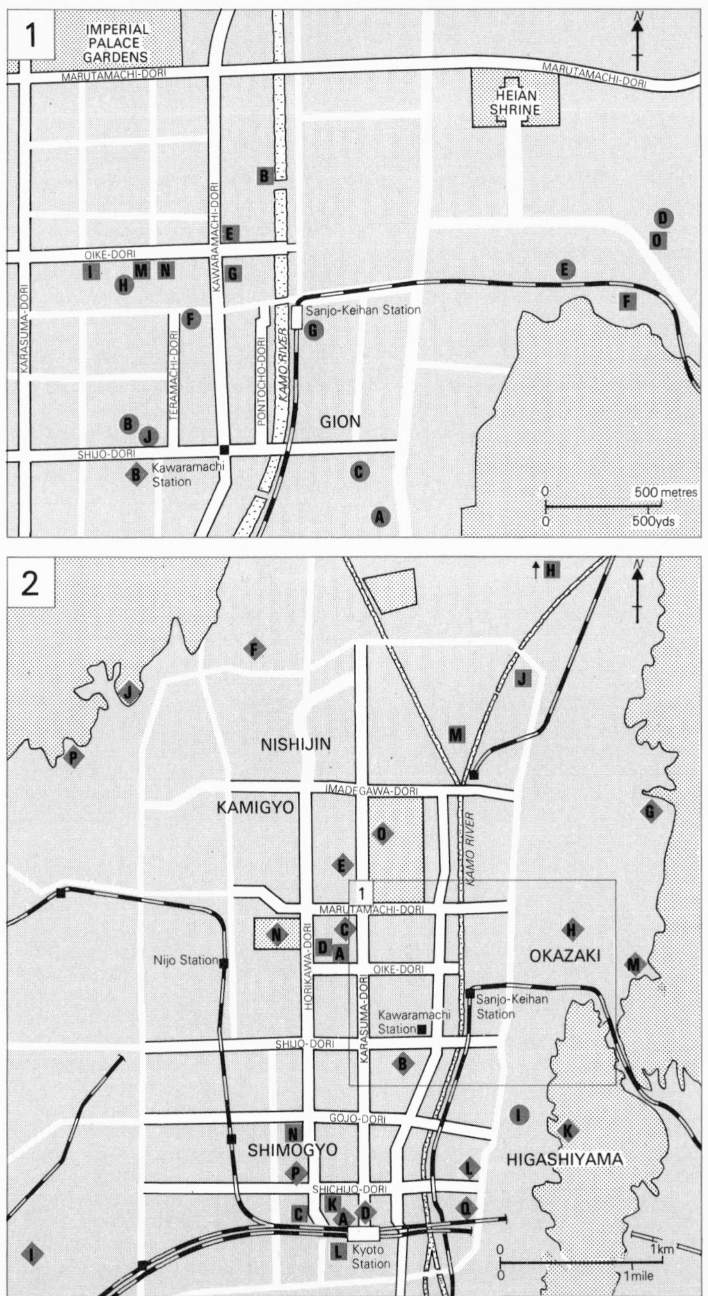
1
IMPERIAL PALACE GARDENS
MARUTAMACHI-DORI
HEIAN SHRINE
KAWARAMACHI-DORI
OIKE-DORI
KARASUMA-DORI
TERAMACHI-DORI
PONTOCHO-DORI
KAMO RIVER
Sanjo-Keihan Station
GION
SHIJO-DORI
Kawaramachi Station
0 500 metres
0 500yds
2
NISHIJIN
IMADEGAWA-DORI
KAMIGYO
KAMO RIVER
MARUTAMACHI-DORI
HORIKAWA-DORI
OIKE-DORI
Nijo Station
OKAZAKI
Sanjo-Keihan Station
Kawaramachi Station
KARASUMA-DORI
SHIJO-DORI
GOJO-DORI
SHIMOGYO
HIGASHIYAMA
SHICHIJO-DORI
Kyoto Station
0 1km
0 1mile

Getting around

Kyoto, like Peking, is laid out in a grid following the classical Chinese model, with nine numbered main streets running east-west, and named north-south avenues. This makes it fairly easy to find your way around, and with the aid of a good map you can take on the bus system. If time is of the essence, taxi is the only choice; but allow plenty of time if you are travelling in the morning or evening rush hours.

Taxi Kyoto has more taxis than anywhere else in Japan, including Tokyo, and you can find one anywhere, at any time of day or night – though like all Japanese taxi drivers, Kyoto drivers sometimes get lost. Of the many taxi companies, light green *Taxis* ☎ 681 3727 and white *MK Company* taxis ☎ 721 4141 are said to be the best.

Bus If you are visiting Kyoto for pleasure rather than business, the bus is a convenient way of getting around except in rush hours. But you will need a map; the simple one on the back of the TIC map of Kyoto shows main routes and bus numbers. Within the city, the fare is the same to every destination; if you are leaving the city, you will have to take a numbered ticket from the dispenser by the door as you enter and pay the fare for that number, as shown on the chart at the front of the bus. To stop the bus, press the small purple buzzer and, as you get off, put the correct fare into the plastic box beside the driver. Although there is usually a change machine for Y50 and Y100 coins beside the box, it is best to have plenty of change.

Train and streetcar There are several railway lines connecting central Kyoto with the suburbs. The Hankyu line, from Osaka, cuts straight across the city to Kawaramachi, while the Keihan line, also from Osaka, becomes a streetcar at Sanjo and trundles past the Miyako and out towards Otsu. The Keifuku streetcar line or the JNR will take you to Arashiyama, and the JNR and Kintetsu lines go down to Nara. To the north of the city, a second Keifuku line goes up towards Mount Hiei and Kurama. In general, the private lines are quicker and cheaper and depart more frequently than the JNR. Apart from the streetcar lines, all the railways have different types of train, including non-stop expresses. If you are travelling locally, check that you do not board the express.

Walking While it is pleasant to walk around the backstreets and between the temples on the east side of the city, you should avoid the main traffic-filled thoroughfares. Distances from one part of the city to another are vast; for example, it would take up to 90min to walk from Kyoto Station to the Imperial Palace.

Subway Kyoto's subway is spotlessly clean, safe and rarely crowded. It runs from the station straight up the middle of the city to Kitaoji and is a rapid and convenient way of getting between the north and south of the city.

Car rental All the main rental chains have offices in Kyoto.

Area by area

Kyoto is a remarkably homogeneous city, bounded by hills on three sides. Although the city does have certain distinct areas, Kyotoites orient themselves by street rather than by neighbourhood. The east-west streets of the Kyoto grid are conveniently numbered, from Shichijo, "Seven", down by the station, through Gojo, "Five", and Sanjo, "Three", up to Nijo (as in the castle), "Two".

City centre Bounded by Shijo to the south, Karasuma to the west, Oike-dori to the north and the river to the east, this is an area full of traffic, crowds and modern shops, including the main department stores. Hidden behind the main streets are tiny backstreets of old wooden houses. Running between Kawaramachi and the river is Pontocho, lined with restaurants. To the north of the shopping area is

Oike-dori, a wide boulevard running from the Kyoto Hotel to Nijo Station. This is the main business section of the city. Offices of various companies including airlines, the Kyoto Chamber of Commerce and the City Hall are here.

Kamigyo and the north The northern part of town is mainly residential: row after row of narrow streets lined with wooden houses and tiny corner shops. The bright lights and *pachinko* parlours are limited to the main roads that cut across it. Here you will find the Imperial Palace, many famous temples such as Kinkakuji and Ryoanji, and, to the east, Kyoto University. Nishijin, to the west, is the centre of silk weaving. Farther out into the northern suburbs is Takaragaike, home of the Kyoto International Conference Hall.

Higashiyama and the east Across Shijo Bridge, to the east of Kawaramachi, is Gion, the traditional entertainment area. Its narrow streets are lined with old houses, many of which are restaurants or geisha quarters. To the east of Gion, stretching the length of the city, is Higashiyama, "East Mountain", a tranquil area popular with walkers. Some of Kyoto's most beautiful temples are here, from Ginkakuji in the north, through Nanzenji, to Kiyomizu. Tucked in near Nanzenji is the Miyako hotel. In nearby Okazaki is a small cultural centre, with museums and Noh theatres.

Shimogyo and the south The area around Kyoto Station and stretching up Karasuma is Kyoto's second main shopping area, rather dusty and traffic-filled, which also includes hotels, temples and the Kyoto National Museum. To the south is Fushimi, home of Fushimi sake (one of Japan's finest) and Kyoto's main industrial centre.

Western Kyoto The western part of Kyoto is a somewhat bleak residential area.

The suburbs Because of its hills, Kyoto does not have many suburbs, but they are smarter than the city itself. Many of the older families live around the northern edges, in Kitano and Kinugasa. Ohara and Kurama, to the north, are also full of wealthy families, as is Arashiyama – a popular tourist spot full of rushing streams and wooded hills – to the west.

Hotels

Kyoto's hotels, like the city, have a certain mellow charm. Of the Western-style hotels, the choice ranges from the legendary Miyako to modern luxury hotels like the ANA and the Takaragaike Prince. For the ultimate in Japanese hospitality, Kyoto's *ryokan* (see *Planning and Reference: Hotels*) are the best in the country.

ANA ¥¥¥

Nijo Castle-mae, Horikawa-dori, Nakagyo-ku 604 ☎ 231 1155 • 288 rooms, 14 suites, 4 restaurants, 1 bar, 1 coffee shop

Opened in 1986, the ANA is Kyoto's newest hotel and the first to provide a wide range of modern facilities, such as business services. It is well up to ANA standards, with a luxurious lobby area looking out onto a waterfall and Japanese garden. The rooms are a good size, decorated in cool greens or dusty pinks, each with a mini-bar and large leather-topped desk. The staff are helpful and eager to please. Concierge, travel desk, arcade of shops • sauna, pool, massage, jogging, special arrangements with nearby tennis and golf clubs • secretarial services, 10 meeting rooms (capacity 180–1,500).

Fujita ¥¥¥

Kamogawa-Nijo, Nakagyo-ku 604 ☎ 222 1511 TX 5422571 • 191 rooms, 4 suites, 6 restaurants, 2 bars

Situated just north of the city centre,

the Fujita has a distinctive style. The main block stretches along the riverside; next to it is a small Japanese house, a replica of Baron Fujita's 1907 villa, housing two steak restaurants. The peaceful lobby looks out onto a waterfall and a Japanese garden, with mandarin ducks and black carp. The bedrooms have a Japanese atmosphere, with woodblock prints, large plants and sliding paper windows looking across the river to Higashiyama. Japanese television only. Concierge, theatre and travel reservations, arcade of shops, shuttle bus to airport • 9 meeting rooms (capacity 15–150).

Grand ¥¥
Shiokoji, Horikawa, Shimogyo-ku 600 ☎ 341 2311 TX 5422551 • Royal Hotel Osaka • 553 rooms, 21 suites, 8 restaurants, 3 bars, 2 coffee shops
The Grand is a vast, solid hotel, offering old-fashioned comforts and service. It is rather far from the action, in a grim section of town, directly above the railway tracks, but convenient for the airport bus which departs from here. With the exception of a business service centre, it has every conceivable facility, including conference rooms with moveable stages and audiovisual equipment. The bedrooms are small and simply furnished, with paper screens over the windows; all rooms are soundproofed. Concierge, travel booking, arcade of shops • heated indoor pool, sauna (men only) • 18 meeting rooms (capacity 10–800)

International ¥¥
284 Nijo Aburanokoji, Nakagyo-ku 604 ☎ 222 1111 TX 5422158 • Fujita • 332 rooms, 3 restaurants, 2 bars, 2 coffee shops
Opposite Nijo Castle and beside the new ANA, the International has long been popular with both business travellers and tourists. The lobby, built around a Japanese garden, is always crowded and bustling. The rooms have a spectacular view over the castle and are appropriately Japanese in style, with paper doors and windows. Concierge, travel and theatre bookings, shops • pool • 13 meeting rooms (capacity 10–450).

Kyoto ¥¥
Kawaramachi-Oike, Nakagyo-ku 604 ☎ 211 5111 TX 5422126 • Nikko • 495 rooms, 12 suites, 7 restaurants, 2 bars
Second only to the Miyako, the Kyoto is a popular, modern hotel with every luxury. It is right in the centre of the city, close to shopping and sightseeing areas. The rooms are small but attractively furnished, and all have a mini-bar and are soundproofed; the rooms in the newer building are more spacious. Service is brisk and efficient. Concierge, shops, hairdresser • 11 meeting rooms (capacity 30–1,000).

Miyako ¥¥¥¥
Sanjo Keage, Higashiyama-ku 605 ☎ 771 7111 TX 5422132 • 445 rooms, 10 suites, 4 restaurants, 1 bar, 2 coffee shops
Undoubtedly Kyoto's best hotel, the gracious Miyako is where visiting royalty and presidents invariably stay. It has the patina of centuries of tradition and service, combined with every modern luxury. The elegant bedrooms, all with mini-bar, are decorated in pale brocades and marble, and have views over shrines, temples and palaces. For the complete Japanese experience, you can stay in one of the tiny traditional wood and paper houses, set on the hillside in the 16-acre landscaped gardens. The tatami rooms, with sliding screens and sunken wooden baths, also have central heating, extra mattresses, shower and television. A fitness centre will open in spring 1988. Concierge, travel and theatre bookings, shops, hairdresser, barber, limousine bus to Itami airport • 4 pools, sauna, steam bath, sunken bath, massage, concessionary rates at nearby golf course and tennis courts • 11 meeting rooms (capacity 40–900).

Royal ¥¥
Kawaramachi Sanjo, Nakagyo-ku 604
☎ *223 1234* ⓉⓍ *5422888* • *Friendship*
• *387 rooms, 7 suites, 8 restaurants,*
2 bars, 1 coffee shop
The Royal is probably the best located of all the Kyoto hotels, directly on the main Kawaramachi-dori. The lobby is rather dismal, but the rooms are light and airy, with remote-control cable TV and comfortable furnishings. Ask for one of the twin rooms, which look out over the city. Concierge, theatre and travel bookings, shops • 16 meeting rooms (capacity 25–250).

Ryokan Hiiragiya ¥¥¥¥¥
Anegakoji, Fuya-cho, Nakagyo-ku 604
☎ *221 1136* ⓉⓍ *5432045* • *33 rooms*
Hiiragiya is the most famous and Westernized of Kyoto's *ryokans.* It is a rambling Japanese house, more than 100 years old, with a beautiful garden with mossy stone lantern, maple trees and a stream full of carp. Each of the spacious rooms has a modern Western-style bathroom. Hiiragiya is efficiently run by its uniformed, English-speaking staff, which gives it the atmosphere almost of a hotel in the guise of a *ryokan.* International calls through hotel switchboard • banquet hall.

Takaragaike Prince ¥¥¥¥¥
Takaragaike, Sakyo-ku 606
☎ *712 1111* ⓉⓍ *5423261* • *295 bedrooms, 35 suites, 3 restaurants, 1 bar*
Kyoto's new Prince hotel opened in 1986 in the north of the city, adjacent to the International Conference Hall. The striking circular building is set in a beautiful Japanese garden, and the spacious rooms are all equipped with mini-bar. 24hr room service, concierge • 8 meeting rooms.

Tawaraya ¥¥¥¥¥
Fuya-cho, Oike-sagaru, Nakagyo-ku 604 ☎ *211 5566* ⓉⓍ *5423273* • *19 rooms*
The Okazaki family has kept an inn here for the last 300 years, making this the oldest *ryokan* in Kyoto. It is also one of the most expensive hotels in Japan. The present building, dating from 1850, is a maze of winding passages and sliding doors opening on to tiny gardens. The rooms are cool, spacious and silent; the only concession to modernity is the bathroom, with its Western toilet. Japanese television only • international calls via hotel switchboard.

Yachiyo ¥¥¥¥¥
Nanzenji, Sakyo-ku 606 ☎ *771 4148*
ⓉⓍ *5423238* • *22 rooms, 3 suites, 1 restaurant*
Beyond the wooden entrance hall is a maze of dark corridors and stairways crisscrossing the labyrinthine two-floored Japanese house. The tatami rooms are all different. Most have Japanese-style bathrooms, with a deep sunken wooden bath. Japanese television only • international calls via hotel switchboard • travel and theatre bookings.

OTHER HOTELS

Gimmond (¥) *Takakura Oike-dori, Nakagyo-ku 604* ☎ *221 4111* ⓉⓍ *5423 219.* Functional and friendly, near offices, shops and transport.
Holiday Inn (¥¥) *36 Nishiraki-cho, Takano, Sakyo-ku 606* ☎ *721 3131* ⓉⓍ *5422251.* In northern Kyoto; lots of sports facilities.
New Hankyu (¥) *Shiokoji-shinmachi, Shimogyo-ku 600* ☎ *343 5300* ⓉⓍ *5423142.* Opposite Kyoto Station.
New Miyako (¥¥) *Hachijo-guchi, Minami-ku 601* ☎ *661 7111* ⓉⓍ *5423211.* An enormous modern hotel just behind the station.
Prince (¥) *43 Matsubara-cho, Shimogamo, Sakyo-ku 606* ☎ *781 4141* ⓉⓍ *5422611.* Small, in northern Kyoto.
Tokyu (¥¥¥) *Gojo-sagaru, Horikawa-dori, Shimogyo-ku 600* ☎ *341 2411* ⓉⓍ *5422459.* Just north of the station.

Restaurants

Although Kyoto has its share of fine Western restaurants, it is really the place to master the intricacies of Japanese cuisine. In the backstreets of Pontocho and Gion, you will find plenty of little restaurants selling moderately priced everyday fare, while for business entertaining, Kyoto's oldest, grandest and most expensive restaurants serve the best *kaiseki* in the country. Some of the finest food in the city is to be found in the temple restaurants, where you can dine on *shojin ryori* – mainly vegetarian – cuisine and try some tofu (bean curd) dishes.

JAPANESE

Gion Suehiro ¥¥¥
570-46 Gion-machi-minamigawa, Higashiyama-ku ☎ *541 1337-9 • closed hols •* AE DC MC
Gion is where the geisha learn their trade, and at Gion Suehiro you will be served and entertained by *maiko*, youthful trainee geisha. Your Japanese colleagues are likely to bring you to this highly popular restaurant, which epitomizes what most Japanese believe to be the Westerner's image of Japan. You will dine on *shabu shabu*, sukiyaki, *kaiseki* or even snapping turtle, depending on the season.

Gontaro ¥
Shijo-agaru, Fuyacho-dori, Nakagyo-ku ☎ *221 5810 • closed Wed and hols*
Gontaro has been preparing and serving hand-made noodles since 1910, and the little restaurant with its rough wooden tables and indigo-blue cushions is always packed. The plump, jolly proprietress greets every customer, some of whom have been coming for decades. The formula has been so successful that there are now several branches. Gontaro will be too cheap for your Japanese colleagues; you should come here for a wonderful meal on a night off.

Junidanya ¥¥¥
570-128 Gion-machi-minami, Higashiyama-ku ☎ *561 1655 • closed Thu and hols •* AE DC MC V *• reservations essential*
This charming old building in Gion is more like a small folkcraft museum than a restaurant. There is no menu. The only dish is *shabu shabu*, made from the finest Omi beef, served in a long, low, wood-beamed room cluttered with old chests, Munakata prints, Hamada pots and Kuroda lacquerware. Every night the restaurant is full. There is a cheaper branch of Junidanya just around the corner.

Junsei ¥¥
60 Kusakawa-cho, Nanzenji, Sakyo-ku ☎ *761 2311 • closed hols •* AE DC MC V
Inside the grounds of Nanzenji Temple are many restaurants serving simmered bean curd (*yudofu*) and other dishes typical of Buddhist cuisine. One of the oldest, most famous and most popular is Junsei. Built in 1834 as a medical school, it consists of 17 rooms spread through a beautiful Japanese garden, complete with the original herb gardens. You can dine cheaply in the vast main dining hall or entertain, as many Japanese executives do, in one of the small private rooms, overlooking the trickling streams, bamboo groves and carp-filled ponds.

Minokichi ¥¥¥¥
Dobutsuenmae-dori, Sanjo-agaru, Sakyo-ku ☎ *771 4185 • closed hols •* AE DC MC V
Minokichi is just down the road from the Miyako hotel. It first opened its doors in 1716, and its exquisite *kaiseki* dishes, served on the finest porcelain, have been famous ever since, though more robust dishes, such as *shabu shabu* or tempura have been introduced specially to suit

Western tastes. Top politicians and company directors often entertain in the private tatami rooms.

Mishima Tei ¥¥¥
Sanjo-Teramachi, Nakagyo-ku
☎ 221 0804 • closed hols • AE DC
In the heart of Kyoto, at the end of Teramachi shopping arcade, is a huge wooden house, three storeys tall. Mishima Tei opened as a butcher's and meat restaurant in 1873, when meat was still an exotic delicacy, and its sukiyaki, *mizutaki* (with chicken) and *oil yaki* (fried beefsteak) are famous. The house itself is a warren of tiny tatami rooms, each different, with woven bamboo ceilings and hanging screens. The rooms are often used for formal entertaining.

Toriyasu ¥¥
Shimbashi-agaru, Nawate-dori, Higashiyama-ku ☎ 561 7203 • closed Mon and hols
Toriyasu sells chicken – not just any chicken, but Tamba chicken, the best. Even the little wicker basket that holds your steaming towel is chicken-shaped. You can have chicken skewered on a stick (*yakitori*), simmered in a casserole (*mizutaki*), made into tempura or served in a box. Sit downstairs and enjoy the riotous company along the counter, or, for more serious business entertaining, take one of the tatami rooms upstairs.

Yachiyo ¥
Nanzenji, Sakyo-ku ☎ 7711 4148 • AE DC MC V
Yachiyo is a famous old *ryokan* (see *Hotels*), but it also has a small tea room and restaurant just inside the gates to Nanzenji Temple, where visitors can dine on simple Kyoto cuisine, served in a beautiful lacquered box.

Yoshikawa Tempura ¥¥
Tominokoji, Oike-sagaru, Nakagyo-ku 604 ☎ 221 5544/0052 • closed Sun and hols • AE DC MC V
Of Kyoto's myriad tempura restaurants, Yoshikawa Tempura is said to be the best. You thread your way down a narrow alley beside a tall wicker fence, and slide open a wooden door to enter the tiny restaurant. There is room for just 12 around the polished pine bench, where the young chef creates light-as-air tempura, serving each piping-hot morsel directly onto your plate. The clientele is largely professional. For more formal entertaining, there are rooms in the Yoshikawa Ryokan, of which the tempura corner is a part, and here you can dine on tempura *kaiseki.*

NON-JAPANESE

Ashiya ¥¥¥
4-172-13 Kiyomizu, Matsubara, Higashiyama-ku ☎ 541 7961 • closed Mon and hols • AE DC V
Down a side alley on the way to Kiyomizu Temple, Ashiya was started by American Bob Strickland in 1965. It has been one of the smartest Kyoto dining spots ever since, and is a suitable place to entertain Japanese colleagues. Dinner in the beautifully restored hundred-year-old inn begins with drinks (including genuine American-style martinis) in the upstairs gallery where the works of local artists are displayed. Downstairs, customers dine on the finest Kobe and Omi beefsteak, cooked teppanyaki style.

Manyoken ¥¥¥
Fuyacho, Shijo, Shimogyo-ku
☎ 221 1022 • closed 2nd and 4th Tue of each month • AE DC MC V
Manyoken is greatly celebrated as Kyoto's oldest and most famous Western-style restaurant. Since its opening in 1910, it has served classic French cuisine to generations of customers, including royalty and presidents. The opulent décor, with plush red carpets, curving marble staircases and massive chandeliers, is much admired by the Japanese, as is the formality of the service. There is an extensive list of fine wines.

Bars

Kyoto's bar area is Pontocho. Some bars are forbiddingly traditional and very pricey; others are downright sleazy. Never enter a bar that employs a pavement tout. On a hot summer evening, those overlooking the river are pleasantly cool. Important business decisions continue to be made down in Gion, in Japan's only remaining geisha quarters. Japanese businessmen are well used to the phenomenal cost of a geisha evening; fortunately, it is considered an improper way for foreigners to entertain their Japanese colleagues.

Rosenthal

Sanjo-sagaru-nishi, Kawaramachi-dori, Nakagyo-ku • AE DC V
Rosenthal, Kyoto's oldest beer hall, is very popular with the city's foreign community.

Wine River

Takoyakushi-higashi, Kawaramachi, Nakagyo-ku • AE DC V
Fashionable young Japanese gather in Wine River, a bar which has a sophisticated wine list, interesting snacks and good music.

Entertainment

Kyoto has been the cultural centre of Japan for a thousand years, and the entertainment available ranges from the most traditional, such as Noh theatre and geisha parties, to the most modern. At dusk you can see geisha and trainee geisha (*maiko*) hurrying to work through Gion and Pontocho.

For current information on entertainment, look at the notice board at the TIC, or check the *Kyoto Monthly Guide*, *Kansai Time Out*, *Kaleidoscope Kyoto* or the *Mainichi Daily News*. Most cultural activities in Kyoto take place between October and May. Make reservations through your hotel or at Play Guide ticket agencies in major department stores.
Theatre Kyoto is the home of the ancient, aristocratic and ritualistic *Noh* drama; translations of the most popular Noh plays are available in Maruzen and other bookshops stocking foreign books. Performances, held on Saturdays and Sundays for about 3hrs, usually consist of three Noh plays interspersed with two *kyogen* comic interludes. The main Noh theatres are *Kanze Kaikan*, 44 Okazaki, Enshoji-cho, Sakyo-ku; *Kongo Noh Gakudo*, Shijo-agaru, Muromachi-dori, Nakagyo-ku; and *Oe Noh Gakudo*, Yanaginobamba-higashi-iru, Oshikoji-dori, Nakagyo-ku. If you are in Kyoto in June, do not miss *Takigi Noh*, "Torchlight Noh", in the spectacular grounds of the Heian shrine.

All the *Kabuki* stars come up from Tokyo in December, and do a series of gala performances at the *Minami-za*, Nakano-cho, Shijo Ohashi-higashi-zume, Higashiyama-ku.

Maiko (apprentice geisha) perform "cherry dances" throughout April at the *Kobu Kaburenjo*, Gion, Higashiyama-ku. You can see geisha dances in spring and autumn at the *Pontocho Kaburenjo*, Sanjo-agaru, Pontocho-dori, Nakagyo-ku. At *Gion Corner*, Hanamikoji Shijo-sagaru, Gion, between March and November, there is a twice-nightly geisha show for tourists that includes traditional arts such as *bunraku*, *kyogen*, tea ceremony and *koto*.
Cinema Plenty of cinemas show foreign films, mainly English-language.
Music The choice of music ranges from traditional Japanese through Western classical to rock at Kyoto's six concert halls.
Nightclubs Nightlife in Kyoto is rather subdued and comes to an end at 11.30. The lights stay on a little longer at the sophisticated *Maharaja Discotheque Saloon*, 2F Fuji Kanko Bldg, 574 Gion-machi minami-gawa, Higashiyama-ku.

Shopping

Kyoto is the place to buy traditional arts and handicrafts, such as Nishijin silk, Kiyomizu porcelain, lacquerware, elegant dolls, screens, fans and bronzes. For expensive but top-quality goods, visit the arcades of the Miyako, Kyoto and International hotels. For window shopping the area around Kawaramachi and the river, between Sanjo and Shijo, is a warren of arcades and little lanes full of interesting shops. Teramachi, a few blocks in from Kawaramachi, is lined with dark old houses, including *Ippodo*, the best place to buy tea-ceremony tea, and curio and antique shops. Ninnenzaka and Sannenzaka, on the way to Kiyomizu, are full of little pottery and handicraft shops.

Department stores Kyoto's best department stores are *Takashimaya* and *Hankyu*, both at Shijo Kawaramachi, and *Daimaru*, on Shijo.

Gifts There are many shops selling Kyoto handicrafts in the main shopping street along *Kawaramachi* between Shijo and Oike-dori, and on the two covered arcades parallel to Kawaramachi to the west. For a less commercialized atmosphere, take a leisurely stroll around *Ninnenzaka* and *Sannenzaka*, near Kiyomizu Temple. The tour buses always stop at the *Kyoto Handicraft Centre*, Kumano Jinja Higashi, Sakyo-ku. Here you can watch craftsmen at work and buy their products, including silk, dolls, woodblock prints, lacquerware and pottery. You could also try the *Kyoto Craft Centre*, 275 Gion-machi-kitagawa, Higashiyama-ku, which also features craftsmen at work, and the basement shop in the *Kyoto Museum of Traditional Industry*, Nijo-dori, Okazaki, Sakyo-ku. Kyoto also has some outstanding specialist shops. The most famous doll shop in Japan is *Tanakaya*, Shijo Yanaginobamba, Shimogyo-ku. For fans, go to *Miyawaki Baisen-an*, Tominokoji-nishi, Rokkaku-dori, Nakagyo-ku, and for cloisonné to *Inaba Cloisonné*, Shirakawa-bashi, Sanjo-dori, Higashiyama-ku.

Antiques Kyoto is full of antique shops, mainly very expensive. The arcades of the top hotels have goods of an assured quality at high prices, and you can be certain at least of high prices in the little antique shops along *Shinmonzen* and *Furumonzen*, between Sanjo and Shijo, and down *Teramachi*. For pottery and curios, wander the small streets around Kiyomizu Temple.

Markets There are markets at the *YWCA Thrift Shop* on the third Saturday of each month, and at *Toji Temple* on the 21st and *Kitano Shrine* on the 25th of each month. Go early for the best selection.

Sightseeing

It would be a hopeless task to attempt to see all of Kyoto's 1,650 Buddhist temples, 400 Shinto shrines, 60 temple gardens, 3 palaces and half a dozen museums. The best approach is simply to stroll through a chosen area, such as northern Kyoto or Higashiyama, where you will discover tiny temples well off the tourist track, as well as some of the more important ones. You will, however, need to make arrangements in advance to see four of Kyoto's most famous sights – the three palaces (the Old Imperial Palace, Katsura and the Shugakuin) and Saihoji, the Moss Temple. Make sure you do so, through your hotel or any JNTO (Tourist Office) or JTB office, as soon as you arrive in Kyoto, at the very latest. Most temples and shrines are open from 9 to 5. To avoid other tourists it is best to make an early start.

Daitokuji Temple You could spend half a day simply wandering through the grounds of Daitokuji, a functioning Zen temple in the north of Kyoto. Of its many small sub-temples, eight are open to the public. Koto-in and Zuiho-in have classic Zen gardens and fine works of art. *Daitokuji, Kita-ku.*

Ginkakuji Temple The Silver Pavilion was built in 1489 as the retreat of the shogun Yoshimasa Ashikaga. A devotee of the tea ceremony, he had a tiny house constructed for it here, the first in Japan. The garden, designed for moon-viewing, was built by the great Soami. After the shogun's death, the villa became a temple. *Ginkakuji, Sakyo-ku.*

Heian Shrine The most famous of Kyoto's shrines, built in 1895, is a model of the old Imperial Palace. Its grounds are particularly beautiful at cherry blossom time. *Okazaki, Higashiyama-ku.*

Katsura Imperial Villa It is well worth the trouble of getting a pass to see the Katsura Imperial Villa. Built for a brother of the Emperor, and completed in 1624, the magnificent villa took 27 years to build, and is considered one of the pinnacles of Japanese architecture. Tea houses, moon-viewing pavilions and lakes with tiny islands are scattered around the grounds, which were designed by the great Kobori Enshu and are considered the most perfect of all Japanese gardens. *Katsura Rikyu, Nishikyo-ku. Closed Sat pm, Sun and hols.*

Kinkakuji Temple The Golden Pavilion, one of Kyoto's most famous and beautiful temples, is completely covered in gold leaf and exquisitely set in a small lake. It was originally built by Yoshimitsu, the third Ashikaga shogun, in 1397. The pavilion was burned to the ground by a mad priest in 1950 and rebuilt exactly as before. *Kinugasa, Kita-ku.*

Kiyomizu Temple This magnificent temple, jutting out of the hillside supported on great wooden pillars, was built in 1633. There are spectacular views of the city from its balcony. *Kiyomizu-dera, Higashiyama-ku.*

Kyoto National Museum The ideal place for a rainy day, this is one of Japan's best museums, with a fine collection of paintings, pottery, lacquerware and armour. *527 Chayamachi, Higashiyama-ku. Open 9–4.30; closed Mon.*

Nanzenji Temple There are 12 sub-temples in this vast complex, noted for the 16thC paintings on its sliding doors and a beautiful garden of white sand and rocks. *Okazaki, Higashiyama-ku.*

Nijo Castle Built in 1603, Nijo Castle was the Kyoto residence of the first great Tokugawa shogun, Ieyasu. While enjoying a lavish lifestyle in this opulent villa, surrounded by priceless works of art, the shogun was ever mindful of security. The "nightingale floors" of the corridors creak under the lightest tread, to warn the guards of any intruders. In Ieyasu's time there were no trees in the magnificent landscaped gardens, for the falling leaves reminded him of death. *Nijo-jo, Nakagyo-ku.*

Nishi Honganji The little-known Nishi Honganji, main temple of the Jodo Shinshu Buddhist sect, was originally built as an imperial palace and is one of Kyoto's finest temples. Ask to be shown the beautiful painted wooden screens and old Noh theatre inside the temple. *Shimogyo-ku.*

Old Imperial Palace The original palace of the emperors, farther to the northwest, was razed by fire in 1788, and the present palace dates from 1854. To join a tour (10am and 2pm), arrive 20min beforehand with your passport. *Kamigyo-ku. Closed Sat afternoon, Sun and hols.*

Ryoanji Temple Arrive very early, before the crowds, to savour the tranquillity of this most famous of Zen gardens. *Ukyo-ku.*

Saihoji Temple You will have to reserve in advance and pay a sizeable fee to enter Saihoji, the Moss Temple. The temple and garden, with its heart-shaped pond and hundred varieties of moss, were designed in 1339 by Muso Kokushi. *Saihoji, 56 Kamigatani, Matsuo, Nishikyo-ku.*

Sanjusangendo This popular temple houses 1,001 images of Kannon, the thousand-armed goddess of mercy, clustered around a large image carved in 1254. *Higashiyama-ku.*

Shugakuin Imperial Villa Set in

the hills overlooking the city, the Shugakuin has beautiful and extensive gardens dotted with pavilions and tea-ceremony rooms. It was built in 1629 as a retirement villa for the Emperor Gomizuno-o. You will have to make an appointment to join a tour. *Sakyo-ku. Closed Sat pm, Sun and hols.*

Walking routes

The most satisfying way to get to know Kyoto is to explore small parts of it on foot. You can get detailed walking maps at the Tourist Information Centre.

Higashiyama There is a pleasant walk from Kiyomizu Temple through winding lanes across Maruyama Park to Heian Shrine, taking about an hour.

The Philosopher's Path Beginning at Ginkakuji, follow the philosopher's footsteps along the canal lined with cherry trees to Nanzenji, a 50min walk.

Kinkakuji and Ryoanji This 40min walk will take you through northern Kyoto's tree-lined backstreets and into two of its most beautiful temples.

Arashiyama Take a circular route around Arashiyama to enjoy its temples, hills and rushing river – a walk of about 80min.

Ohara Allow half a day to visit this lovely country area. A gentle stroll around the *Jakko-in* and *Sanzen-in temples*, with their sad and romantic history, will take 2hrs.

Guided tours

There are ten half-day bus tours, with English-speaking guides and a pick-up service from main hotels, which cover some of Kyoto's major sights; you can also combine a morning and an afternoon tour. For information and reservations, contact *JTB* ☎ 361 7241, *Fujita Travel Service* ☎ 222 0121 or *Kinki Nippon Tourist* ☎ 222 1224. There are also tours of the Inaba cloisonné workshops and the Yuzen silk-dyeing centre.

Spectator sports

Rugby The only sport at which Kyoto shines is rugby. Kyoto's *Doshisha University* team is the best team in Japan, and there are annual matches in December and January at the team's home ground, *Hanazono Stadium.*

Keeping fit

There are limited keep-fit and sporting opportunities in Kyoto itself, but more in the nearby countryside and around Lake Biwa. Of the Kyoto hotels, the Holiday Inn has by far the best sporting facilities, most of which are open to non-residents for a fee.

Cycling There is a 6-mile/10km cycling course around Arashiyama and Sagano, starting from Hankyu Arashiyama Station. Rent a bicycle at *Cycpick*, Hankyu Arashiyama ☎ 882 1111, or *Keihan Rent-a-cycle*, Togetsukyo Arashiyama ☎ 861 1656.

Health and sports centres There is a well-equipped health centre in the Holiday Inn. Of the public health centres, the following are open to non-members or have a nominal membership fee. *Kampol Kyoto*, 13 Shuurishiki-cho, Matsugasaki, Sakyo-ku ☎ 721 3111, has a gym and sauna. *Kyoto City Sports*, 23 Shironokoshi, Shimotoba, Fushimi-ku ☎ 621 8188, is a vast sports centre with a gym, a 100m indoor running track, racquetball and tennis courts, swimming pools, a sauna and a hot-spring bath. Kyoto's classiest health centre is *Act One*, 2F Gondolia-Mibu Bldg, 53 Mibuboujyo-cho, Nakaggo-ku ☎ 841 1596, which offers weight training, a gym, and a personal fitness programme.

Hiking There is good hiking in the mountains that surround Kyoto. The nearest is *Mount Hiei*, in the northeast, and there are also hiking courses in Biwako Valley. Check *Kansai Time Out* for monthly hikes organized by the *Kansai Ramblers.*

Jogging In the morning there are plenty of joggers along the banks of

the Kamo, Takano and Katsura rivers. Kyoto's tree-lined back streets are ideal for joggers, and you can also jog around Nijo Castle.
Skiing The nearest ski slopes are in the mountains to the west of Lake Biwa, at *Biwako Valley* ☎ (06) 343 1271, *Hirasan* ☎ (07759) 6 1068, and, farther north, at *Hakodateyama* ☎ (0740) 22 2486. Buses bound for the ski areas pick up in Kyoto; contact *Taiyo Recreation Centre* ☎ (06) 353 5338 or *Big Tour Osaka Centre* ☎ (06) 363 0451.
Swimming There are indoor pools in the ANA, Grand, International and Miyako hotels and in the Holiday Inn. The public pools are, as everywhere, very crowded. For outdoor swimming, go to Lake Biwa, the largest freshwater lake in Japan, or head north to the relatively clean beaches along the Japan Sea coast.
Tennis Try the Holiday Inn, or book well in advance at the *Ohara Green Tennis Club* Ueno-cho, Ohara, Sakyo-ku 50 ☎ 744 2461, open to non-members.
Windsurfing Contact *All Kansai Windsurfing* ☎ (0775) 79 0333 or *Biwako Adventure Sports* ☎ (0775) 72 1254 if you want to windsurf on Lake Biwa.

Local resources

Business services

The only formal business service centre is at the ANA; but all the major hotels will make every effort to meet your requirements. A company providing a wide range of business services is the Kyoto branch of *Manpower Japan* ☎ 241 2030.
Photocopying and printing You can arrange photocopying or printing through your hotel. Some department stores, camera shops and stationers have photocopyers.
Secretarial For secretarial assistance, try *Career Staff* ☎ 255 5691.
Translation For translators and interpreters go to *Kita English Centre* ☎ 492 1682.

Communications

International couriers *DHL* ☎ 661 7255.
Post office The *Central Post Office*, Kyoto Station, Shimogyo-ku, is open 24hrs. Inquiries ☎ 365 2471.
Telex and fax All major hotels provide telex and fax facilities. Otherwise go to *Manpower Japan* (see above) or *KDD Telecom Kyoto*, 338 Tominaga-cho, Matsubara-agaru 2-chome, Kawaramachi-dori, Shimogyo-ku ☎ 341 2733.

Conference/exhibition centres

The *Kyoto International Conference Hall*, Takaragaike, Sakyo-ku 606 ☎ 791 3111 is one of the largest and most fully equipped international convention centres in Asia. Smaller exhibitions and trade fairs are held at *Kyoto Sangyo Kaikan*, Shijo-dori, Karasumaru Nishi-iru, Shimogyo-ku ☎ 211 4506.

Emergencies

Bureaux de change The bureaux de change in the major hotels are open seven days a week, from early until late.
Hospitals The following hospitals provide emergency service at night and on holidays and weekends; you will be accepted only if you arrive by ambulance: *Kyoto First Red Cross Hospital*, 15-749 Honmachi, Higashiyama-ku ☎ 561 1121; *Kyoto Second Red Cross Hospital*, Marutamachi-sagaru, Kamanza-dori, Kamikyo-ku ☎ 231 5171; and *Kyoto Prefectural University of Medicine Hospital*, Hirokoji, Kawaramachi-dori, Kamikyo-ku ☎ 231 2311. There are two American doctors at the *Japan Baptist Hospital*, 47 Yamanomoto-cho, Kitashirakawa, Sakyo-ku ☎ 781 5191. For emergency dental service, contact *Kyoto Prefecture Emergency Dental Clinic*, 33 Gosho Tamachi, Murasakino, Kita-ku ☎ 441 7174; their south Kyoto clinic is at Imamachi, Fushimi-ku ☎ 622 3000.
Pharmacies Prescription drugs are

issued only by hospitals. There are no 24hr pharmacies.
Police *Kyoto Prefectural Police* ☏ 441 8580. In an emergency ☏ 110.

Government offices

For inquiries about local government departments and services, contact the *Kyoto City Government*, Kyoto Kaikan, Okazaki, Sakyo-ku ☏ 771 6051.

Information sources

Business information *Kyoto Chamber of Commerce*, Ebisugawa-agaru, Karasuma-dori, Nakagyo-ku ☏ 231 0181.
Local media Many international newspapers are available in Kyoto. Of the five locally produced English-language papers, the *Mainichi Daily News*, based in Osaka, carries news and information relevant to Kansai and is the most useful. The lively monthly *Kansai Time Out* has articles on Kyoto and listings of local events. The only English-language television is the cable news channel transmitted to major hotels.
Tourist Information The staff at the Kyoto *Tourist Information Office*, Kyoto Tower Bldg, Higashi-Shiokoji-cho, Shimogyo-ku ☏ 371 5649, are extremely efficient, knowledgeable and friendly and will load you down with maps, literature and information; they will also make hotel reservations. They have a bulletin board of the week's events and publish the very useful free *Kyoto Monthly Guide*. For the Japan Travel Phone, a TIC service, ☏ 371 5649 within Kyoto, and for the TIC recorded information service ☏ 361 2911. The monthly *Kaleidoscope Kyoto* also lists current happenings. For enjoyment as well as information, read *Kyoto, a Contemplative Guide*.

Thank-yous

Uji tea is the standard gift to buy in Kyoto. Buy it beautifully gift-wrapped from *Takashimaya*, who will also deliver, or, for the ultimate in finesse, from *Ippodo*, Teramachi, Nakagyo-ku, Japan's best tea shop.

NAGOYA

Area code ☏ 052

Japan's fourth largest city and third largest port lies in the middle of the Tokyo-Hiroshima megalopolis and is the only stop on the Hikari Bullet Train between Tokyo and Kyoto. Nagoya is a prosperous commercial and industrial city, with a population of over 2m. Heavy industries – primarily automobile manufacture, plus the production of rolling stock, chemicals and textiles – thrive alongside traditional light industries such as ceramics, for which this area has been famous since the 12th century. Advanced technological plants are now under development, and coastal waters are being reclaimed to meet the need for more industrial land.

Japan's three great historical warlords (see *Sightseeing*) hailed from this area, and the city grew up around their strongholds and around the great castle which Tokugawa Ieyasu built here in 1612 for his son. In the 1930s Nagoya became a centre of the aircraft and munitions industries, and in consequence was completely flattened in World War II. It has since regained its former prosperity and is currently expanding its cultural and conference facilities and extending the subway in preparation for 1989, when the city celebrates its hundredth anniversary.

Arriving

Travellers arriving from Hong Kong, Seoul and Manila have the option of flying direct to Nagoya; and it is also worthwhile flying from more distant parts of Japan. From Tokyo it is quicker and simpler to take the Bullet Train.

Kamaki Airport

In terms of importance and size, Kamaki is third after Tokyo's Narita and Osaka's Itami. The small amount of international traffic that passes through is handled quickly and efficiently, and there are flights to all major Japanese cities. A variety of restaurants, coffee shops and bars are open until 8pm on landside, but such facilities are very limited on airside; executive lounge, shops selling local foods and souvenirs, of interest mainly to Japanese travellers, and one bank. For information ☏ (0568) 28 1221.

City link If you have little luggage or are staying near the station, the bus is a reasonably fast and convenient way of getting into the city. Unless you are being met, taxi is the only sensible alternative.

Bus The bus to Meitetsu Bus Centre, near Nagoya Station, departs every 15min, and takes about 40min; allow 55–60min in rush hour.

Taxi A taxi is more convenient than the bus, but only a little quicker and much more expensive.

Car rental It is difficult to find your way from Kamaki to Nagoya, and if you plan to drive in the city, it is better to pick up a car in town. At Kamaki there are branches of Japan Rentacar, Nippon and Mazda.

Railway stations

The Bullet Train takes 2 hours from Tokyo, 50min from Kyoto and just over an hour from Osaka.

Nagoya Station The station is enormous and the Bullet Train tracks are inconveniently located on the far side, away from the city centre. The JNR lines out to the suburbs depart from here, as does the Kintetsu line and the Meitetsu line (though this is difficult to find). The station area itself is a hive of activity, with five hotels and three department stores within a few minutes' walk. Inquiries ☏ 551 8111.

Getting around

After Nagoya's total destruction in the war, it was rebuilt in a neat grid, with wide boulevards dividing the town into areas. As a result, it is particularly easy to find your way around the central district on foot. Unless you want to go somewhere very out-of-the-way, you will find the subway system and taxis the most convenient modes of transport.

Taxi Taxis are plentiful, and the drivers are fairly efficient at finding their way around. There are always taxis waiting in the ranks at the station and outside the major hotels, but you should have no problem flagging them down on the streets.

Subway Nagoya's subways are fast and comfortable, but extremely crowded during the morning and evening rush hours. A very useful map in English is available from the Tourist Information Centre (TIC). There are three lines, one of which links the station to Fushimi and Sakae, the main interchanges. The station names are marked in English, and platforms are indicated by the destination of the train. If you are making more than five journeys, it is worthwhile buying a one-day pass, which can be used on buses as well as the subway; buy one at any main subway station. To relieve the current pressure on the subway system, a new line from Nakamura Kuyakusho via the station out to Imaike (just north of the present east-west line) will open in 1989.

Train Of the train lines out to the suburbs, the private Kintetsu and Meitetsu lines are cheaper, more frequent and more comfortable than the JNR lines.

Limousine *Teisan Auto Company* ☏ 911 1351 and *Tokyu Shachi Bus* ☏ 913 1111 offer cars with drivers, a few of whom speak some English.

Driving Although the streets are wide and straight, they tend to be congested, particularly at rush hour, and parking is a problem. If you want to drive, the main car rental chains have branches in the city.

Bus Nagoya has an extensive bus system, best avoided unless you can read Japanese.

Area by area

In spite of its modern grid plan, Nagoya is still an old castle town. The former samurais' neighbourhood, now simply the wealthier section of town, lies just outside the castle wall, with the "pleasure quarters" a respectable distance away. Until recently, the station formed the boundary of the main city, but now the urban sprawl beyond is being transformed into an area of offices and hotels.

Fushimi An area of soaring office blocks and wide boulevards, Fushimi is the business centre of this primarily business city. Here, alongside Nagoya's top city hotel, the Kanko, you will find branches of the major banks, including the Bank of Japan, and offices of local and national corporations. The Nagoya Chamber of Commerce and Industry is to the south.

Sakae Here, too, are offices spreading up and down the wide and green Hisaya-Odori, "Park Way", which runs north–south through the city. But most people come for the shops, restaurants, bars, cabarets and cinemas, and at night Sakae is the place to be.

Nagoya Castle area This is where the samurai families used to live, well removed from the hustle and bustle of the city centre. Among the old houses and sleek residences are exclusive *ryotei* and the city and prefectural government buildings.

The suburbs Many of Nagoya's wealthiest families live in the cool hills along the eastern edge of the city, in the Motoyama-Yamate district, near Nagoya University. This is an area of parks and greenery, including Higashiyama Botanical Gardens. Many people commute into Nagoya from Ichinomiya and Inuyama, smart residential towns a short train ride to the north.

Hotels

Nagoya seems to be enjoying a spate of hotel-building, although none of the new hotels around the station poses a threat to the standing of the grand old Castle and Kanko. The biggest Tokyu yet will open in Toshincho in late 1987, with an enormous convention hall and a sports centre. And a new Hilton will open near the Kanko in 1988. As from late 1986, Nagoya hotels have been able to receive English-language television; CNN news is now broadcast direct from Nagoya, not Tokyo.

Castle ¥¥
3-19 Hinokuchi-cho, Nishi-ku 451
☏ 521 2121 TX 4452988 • 247 rooms, 5 suites, 4 restaurants, 2 bars, 1 coffee shop
Nagoya's grandest (but not its oldest) hotel stretches along the moat-side, directly opposite Nagoya Castle. The bedrooms, all with mini-bar, are huge and attractively furnished; all but the single rooms have views of the castle. There are original oil paintings in each room and in the lobby. The top-floor restaurant and bar, with their views of the castle, floodlit at night, are classy and popular, and Rosen (see *Bars*) is where many executives, both Japanese and Western, meet after work for a civilized drink. Concierge, theatre and travel bookings, shops including florist, beauty salon • outdoor pool • secretarial services, 9 meeting rooms (capacity 30–1,000).

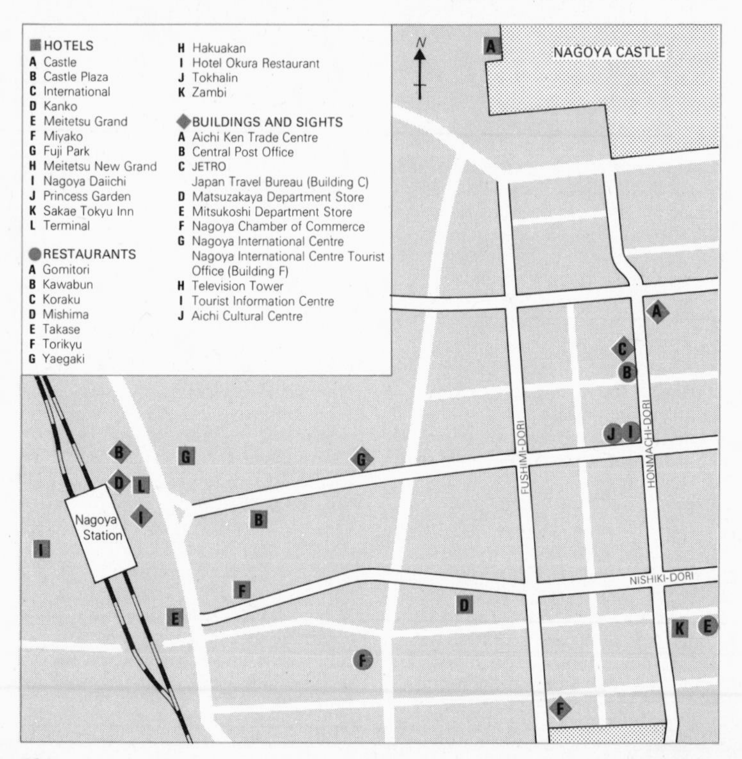

Castle Plaza ¥
4-3-25 Mei-eki, Nakamura-ku 450
☎ 582 2121 TX 59678 • 263 rooms, 4 restaurants, 1 bar
While top executives stay at the Castle, the Castle Plaza caters for their junior colleagues. It is one of Nagoya's newer hotels and is convenient for the station. The rooms are neat and reasonably spacious, and there is an excellent range of sporting facilities. Arcade of shops • health club with pool, jogging tracks, gym and sauna • 10 meeting rooms (capacity 40–450).

International ¥¥
3-23-3 Nishiki, Naka-ku 460
☎ 961 3111 TX 4443720 • 259 rooms, 4 suites, 5 restaurants, 1 bar, 2 coffee shops
Long popular with business travellers, the conveniently located International recently completed a major programme of refurbishment. The lobby is now graciously decorated in tones of gold and dark brown, with elegant antique-style furnishings. There are several types of single room, including spacious rooms on the executive floor and large bright singles redecorated in dazzling lime greens and yellows. Avoid the cheapest singles, which are very dark. Concierge, travel bookings, shops, beauty salon • 16 meeting rooms.

Kanko ¥¥
1-19-30 Nishiki, Naka-ku 460
☎ 231 7711 TX 4427413 • JAL • 496 rooms, 9 suites, 5 restaurants, 2 bars, 1 coffee shop
The 19-storey Kanko is ideally located in the middle of the Fushimi business area, equidistant from the

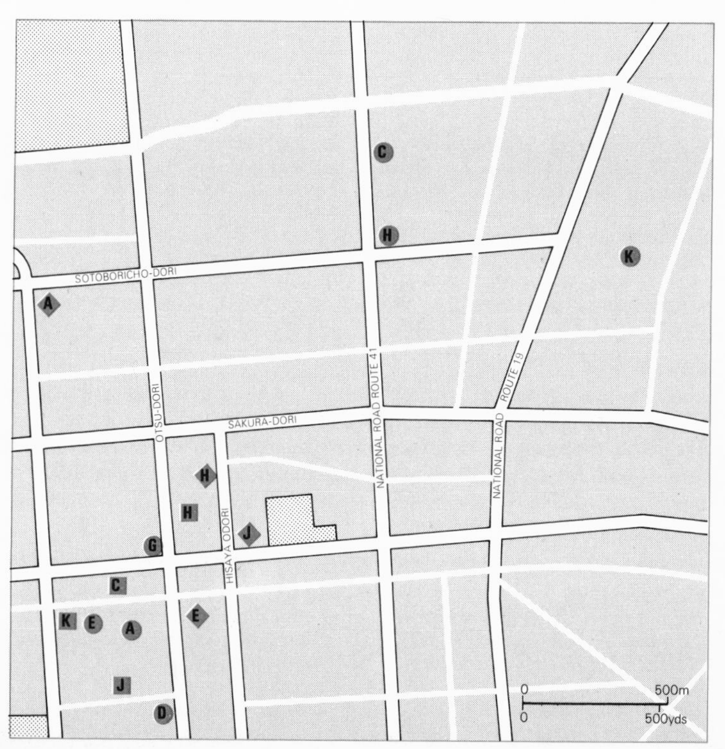

station and Sakae. There has been a Kanko here since 1936, which makes it the oldest of the city's hotels. The bedrooms all have huge windows and window seats and are comfortably furnished with many individual touches. A good proportion of the guests are foreign, mainly business travellers. International calls via hotel operator, arcade of shops, hairdresser • discounted rates at nearby health club • 11 meeting rooms (capacity 50–3,000).

Meitetsu Grand ¥
1-2-4 Mei-eki, Nakamura-ku 450 ☎ 582 2211 TX 4422031 • 242 rooms, 3 restaurants, 1 bar
The Meitetsu, on the top floors of a department store a few minutes' walk from the station, is popular with Japanese business travellers. The public areas look down over the city, and the bedrooms are attractive and spacious for the price. International calls via hotel operator • meeting rooms (capacity up to 500)

Miyako ¥¥
4-9-10 Mei-eki, Nakamura-ku 450 ☎ 571 3211 TX 4422086 • 398 rooms, 2 suites, 3 restaurants, 1 bar, 2 coffee shops
The tranquil Miyako, just around the corner from the station, is popular with visiting international artists and musicians as well as businessmen. The rooms are large, light and soundproofed, with a big desk, and the service is up to the Miyako's usual high standards. Arcade of shops, beauty salon • 13 meeting rooms (capacity 25–800)

OTHER HOTELS

Daiichi (¥) *3-27-5 Mei-eki, Nakamura-ku 450 ☎ 581 4411 TX 9517269.* One of the cluster of new hotels around the station, this is unusually attractive.
Fuji Park (¥) *3-15-30 Nishiki, Naka-ku 460 ☎ 962 2289 TX 4444489.* A small, quiet, pleasant hotel, in the heart of Sakae.
Meitetsu New Grand (¥) *6-9 Tsubaki-cho, Nakamura-ku 453 ☎ 452 5511 TX 4432803.* The first hotel in the developing area at the back of Nagoya station, very close to the Bullet Train exit.
Princess Garden (¥) *3-13-31 Sakae, Naka-ku 460 ☎ 262 4111 TX 4422355.* In the heart of Sakae and a favourite of travelling Japanese executives.
Sakae Tokyu Inn (¥) *3-1-8 Sakae, Naka-ku 460 ☎ 251 0109 TX 4422550.* One of Nagoya's newest hotels, midway between Fushimi and Sakae.
Terminal (¥) *1-2-1 Mei-eki, Nakamura-ku 450 ☎ 561 3751 TX 4457263.* Right inside the station, the ageing Terminal is still popular, although its fading rooms offer little competition to the glamorous new hotels nearby.

Restaurants

Nagoya has plenty of restaurants to cater for its large business community, ranging from exclusive *ryotei* in the suburbs out towards the castle, to the small restaurants lining the streets around Sakae, where you stop off for a quick bite before moving on to a bar. *Cochin*, Nagoya chicken, is considered the best in Japan and is the speciality of several of Nagoya's finest restaurants.

JAPANESE

Gomitori ¥
Princess Odori Sakae Daiei Minami 77, Sakae 3, Chuo-ku ☎ 241 0041
Gomitori is like a cluttered old antique shop, crammed with dusty wooden sculptures and with sake bottles, dried gourds, ancient clocks and torn paper lanterns. You perch at the counter and order food by the skewerful. Specialities include grilled sparrows, grilled frogs, locust and anglerfish liver, as well as less alarming delicacies.

Kawabun ¥¥¥¥¥
2-12-19 Marunouchi, Naka-ku
☏ 231 1381
The somewhat run-down exterior of this venerable *ryotei* – located in a dusty backstreet behind the Hotel Okura Restaurant – belies its true status. Entry to its tatami rooms is restricted to the city's leaders and top executives and their guests. If your host does you the honour of bringing you here, you will dine on kaiseki, featuring, of course, Nagoya chicken, in the most elegant of surroundings.

Koraku ¥¥¥¥¥
3-3 Chikara-machi, Higashi-ku
☏ 931 3472
To enter Koraku you go through a thatched gate, up a winding path of mossy stepping stones, past a tea-house to your left, around a brushwood fence, and arrive at the imposing entrance of this ancient samurai mansion, where you are greeted by ladies in kimonos. If you are not with one of their distinguished regular customers, this is as far as you will get, for Koraku is one of Nagoya's most exclusive *ryotei*. The highly privileged can discover whether the chicken dishes here are truly, as claimed, the best in Nagoya.

Mishima ¥¥
3-27-4 Sakae, Naka-ku ☏ 242 0828
At Mishima, the humble sardine becomes a delicacy. Every dish in this elegant restaurant, in a lovely old Japanese house, contains sardines – raw, grilled, simmered, or brought to the table resting on a fragrant leaf of the *ho* tree, on a flaming charcoal brazier. Mishima is highly esteemed, and often used for business dinners.

Takase ¥¥
B2 Nikko Shoken Bldg, 3-2-3 Sakae, Naka-ku ☏ 263 4137 • closed Sun
Owner chef Hideo Takase produces some of Nagoya's finest tempura in this small basement restaurant midway between Fushimi and Sakae. His fish and seafood are of the highest quality and completely fresh; you can watch them swimming in an aquarium until the very last second. To accompany tempura, he offers not only the standard sake and whisky, but also a selection of French wines. Businessmen make up the majority of the customers and frequently entertain here.

Torikyu ¥¥
1-1-15 Mei-eki Minami, Nakamura-ku
☏ 541 1888 • closed Sun
Torikyu is a fine and famous restaurant which welcomes all comers. It backs onto the river, and in the old days customers used to arrive by boat. The food here is chicken, raw, grilled, in a casserole, or in kaiseki. You may well come here in a party with Japanese colleagues and take over one of the spacious tatami rooms overlooking the river.

Yaegaki ¥¥
3-17-28 Nishiki, Naka-ku ☏ 951 3250 • closed Sun • AE
Among the concrete office blocks and glass-fronted shops in Sakae is a small Japanese house of wood and bamboo, built around a garden. Here Saburo Usami makes what many consider in the finest tempura in central Japan, continuing the tradition begun by his grandfather 60 years ago. Top executives and politicians figure among the distinguished clientele, which also includes Kabuki stars such as Shoroko and Baiko. Be sure to sit at the round table, which the chef, seated inside, revolves to serve four different groups of guests in turn.

NON-JAPANESE

Hakuakan ¥¥¥¥
B1 Yokota Bldg, 2-28-24 Izumi, Higashi-ku ☏ 931 1569 • closed Mon • AE • reservations essential
At Hakuakan, which means "white house", everything, from the heavy chandeliers to the ornate period furniture and cabinets full of porcelain, is French. Chef Ijima

spent two years in Alsace, and his classic and *nouvelle* cooking is highly rated, not only by the business community but by the local French, many of whom entertain their Japanese colleagues here.

Hotel Okura Restaurant ¥¥¥

25F Tokyo Kaijo Bldg, 2-2-19 Marunouchi, Naka-ku ☎ 201 3201 • AE DC V • reservations essential

This may be Nagoya's top Western restaurant for quality and is certainly top for prestige. Chief executives wine and dine each other here, and it is an appropriate place to return hospitality. Chef Tsuneo Fukuda hails from the Tokyo Okura, and the menu – unusually adventurous for Nagoya – covers all the major European cuisines. The wine list is equally eclectic.

Tokhalin ¥¥¥

25F Tokyo Kaijo Bldg, 2-2-19 Marunouchi, Naka-ku ☎ 201 3201 • AE DC V • reservations essential

Much of Nagoya's business entertaining takes place within the private rooms of Tokhalin. Among other Cantonese delights, chef Ryo Juno (from Hong Kong) prepares whole roast piglet (which must be ordered a week in advance), braised deer tail and bear paw. The flavours are simpler and the food less oily than usual, in deference to the Japanese taste for blander foods.

Zambi ¥¥

7-17 Daikan-cho, Higashi-ku ☎ 936 4511-3 • closed 2nd and 4th Sun of month • AE DC

Zambi is a sophisticated restaurant bar, dark and atmospheric, with log walls, potted palms and spotlights, hidden inside a Japanese house in the suburbs. Late in the evening Nagoya's international community gathers here to drink, talk and eat snacks. Zambi is open until 2am, and businessmen drop in for steaks and seafood, plus a liberal dose of alcohol. There is live piano music as the night draws on.

Bars

At night, having had a token drink in a sober hotel bar, everyone drifts towards the bright lights of Sakae.

Gaslight

10F Daini Washington Hotel, 3-12-22 Nishiki, Naka-ku

The Gaslight, in the centre of the lively Nishiki area, is the favourite of young Japanese businessmen, who meet here before moving on to the sleazier dives of Sakae. You can have roast beef here, to accompany your whisky.

Igirisuya

B1 Fujita Bldg, 1-5-8 Sakae, Naka-ku

Igirisuya means "English house" and this popular bar in the heart of Fushimi is decked out like a British pub, with large oak beams, wood panelling, candles, and even a bust of Shakespeare. The fare includes pizza and Japanese whisky, and the clientele is equally cosmopolitan.

Rosen

Castle Hotel, 3-19 Hinokuchi-cho, Nishi-ku • AE DC MC V

Many high-powered discussions are concluded and vital decisions made in the deep leather armchairs around the well-spaced tables of the Rosen – which also offers a view across a carp-filled pond to the castle. The atmosphere is more like that of a gentlemen's club than a bar; and even the barman adopts hushed tones.

Entertainment

Nagoya is the cultural centre of the area, and visiting performers usually stop here on their way to Kyoto and Osaka from Tokyo. Many performances take place at the *Aichi Cultural Centre*, which is being enlarged in anticipation of the 1989 celebrations. The TIC's excellent monthly *Nagoya Calendar* will keep you up to date with what's on. Make reservations through your hotel or at Play Guide ticket agencies in major department stores.

Theatre, ballet and opera In any given month your choice of drama and dance at one of Nagoya's seven theatres might range from Ibsen to the Paris Opera to Ennosuke and his Kabuki troupe up from Tokyo.
Cinema Most of Nagoya's many foreign films are English or American.
Music There is plenty of choice in Nagoya for everyone, from those who want to hear the *Yomiuri Nikkyo Orchestra* playing Stravinsky to lovers of sitar. The main venue for concerts is the *Aichi Cultural Centre*, Sakae.
Nightclubs Your Japanese colleagues will probably plan a full programme of evening activities for you. In the unlikely event of finding yourself at a loose end in Nagoya, you will meet fellow Westerners at the highly respectable *Playboy Club*, 12F Imaike Bldg, 5-1-5 Imaike Chikusaku; single women will also feel comfortable here. In the *Three Aces*, in the basement of the same building, there are low lights, soft music and charming hostesses to ply you with drink. The *Mikado*, Iriecho, Naka-ku, is a vast, glittering cabaret, Nagoya's most popular, where you can dine on sushi or even join in the floorshow.

Shopping

The region around Nagoya is rich in traditions and handicrafts. Look for Seto pottery, handmade paper from Mino, paper lanterns and oiled paper umbrellas from Gifu, lacquerware and woodcarving from Takayama, and cloisonné, intricately tie-dyed fabric (*shibori*) and Noritake china from Nagoya itself. Most of the major shops are clustered around Sakae, where there is an underground warren of shopping arcades. There is a second smaller shopping centre around and under Nagoya Station.
Department stores Nagoya has six department stores, including two branches of *Matsuzakaya* and two of *Mitsukoshi. Meitetsu*, above Nagoya Meitetsu Station, is associated with the Nagoya-based private railway line and has branches throughout the region.
Electrical goods *Radio Centre Ameyoko Bldg*, 3-30-86 Osu, Naka-ku, is a miniature version of Tokyo's Akihabara, packed with camera and electrical shops; you may pick up some bargains here.
Gifts To get some idea of the exceptionally fine local handcrafts available in Nagoya, begin by looking at the extensive selection in any of the major department stores. Jewellery made of pearls from the nearby Ise peninsula are sold by *K Mikimoto Co*, Chunichi Bldg, 4-1-1 Sakae, Naka-ku. For the best china, go direct to *Noritake Sales Ltd*, 2-1 Shinsakae, Naka-ku, and for cloisonné to *Ando Cloisonné*, 3-27-17 Sakae, Naka-ku. The craft shops in the arcades also have good selections.

Sightseeing

Many of the great battles of Japanese history took place in this region, and Japan's most famous warlords, Oda Nobunaga, Toyotomi Hideyoshi and Tokugawa Ieyasu, all came from in or around Nagoya. Most of Nagoya's vestiges of grandeur were destroyed in World War II, but the surrounding area is rich in interest and historical remains.
Atsuta Shrine Atsuta Shrine, to the south of the city, is the home of the Sacred Grass-Mowing Sword (one of the emperor's three pieces of regalia) and one of Japan's three holiest shrines. It was founded in the 3rd century, and the great wooden buildings stand in glades of towering cedars.
Nagoya Castle The high point of most tours of the city is the castle. The present castle, sadly, is a 1959 ferroconcrete copy of Tokugawa Ieyasu's original, built for his son Yoshinao in 1612, which was destroyed in the war. Even so, it is magnificent, set in beautiful grounds, and it houses a fine collection of art treasures from the

old palace. *Open 9.30–4.30.*
Tokugawa Art Museum Built on the site of the Tokugawa mansion, the museum contains a splendid collection of Japanese paintings, ceramics, lacquerware and prints, amassed by the Tokugawa family. *Shindekimachi, Higashi-ku. Open 10–4; closed Mon.*

Guided tours
Half- and full-day tours of the city, covering the major sights, with a commentary in Japanese only, can be booked through the TIC or *Nagoya Yuran Bus* ☎ 561 4036. Be sure to reserve in advance if you want to take the popular *Industrial Tour*, every Friday, which visits factories such as Ando Cloisonné, Arimatsu Shibori (tie-dyeing) and Noritake (china); you can also visit these and other factories privately.

Out of town
Both *Kyoto* and *Nara* are a comfortable day trip from Nagoya, though each is well worth a longer visit. Nagoya is also a convenient base from which to visit *Ise*, the most important shrine in Japan. This has been a holy place for well over a thousand years, although the vast wooden buildings that you see are ceremonially rebuilt every 20 years (the last time was in 1973). If you have half a day to spare, visit *Inuyama*, 19 miles/30km from Nagoya, and see Japan's oldest surviving castle, built in 1440. Just down the road from Inuyama is *Meiji Mura*, a marvellous collection of buildings from the Meiji (1868–1912) era.

Spectator sports
Baseball Nagoya's Chunichi Dragons are a Central League team. Reserve well in advance to see them play on their home ground, *Nagoya Stadium* ☎ 351 5171/2222.
Sumo The sumo giants do battle at the *Aichi Prefectural Gymnasium*, 1-1 Ninomaru, Naka-ku ☎ 971 2516, in July.

Keeping fit
Golf The *Forest Park* course in Kasugai, 12 miles/18km north of Nagoya, is open to the public ☎ (056) 153 1551. Towards Ise is the *Shima* course ☎ (059) 947 3256, where you play on a sandy beach under pine trees.
Health and sports centres Of the hotels, only the Castle Plaza and the new Sakae Tokyu Inn have health clubs. *Nagoya Sports Centre*, 1-60 Monzen-cho, Naka-ku ☎ 321 1591, has a wide range of facilities, including a skating rink, and is open to non-members. *Tsuyuhashi Sports Centre*, 14-1 Tsuyuhashi 2-chome, Nakagawa-ku ☎ 362 4411, and *Nagoya Shampia Sports Centre*, 6-27 Shirogane 3-chome, Showa-ku ☎ 871 4611, are a little farther out; both have heated pools.
Jogging The best area for jogging is around Nagoya Castle and Meijo Park; the longest course here is 3 miles/4.6km long.
Swimming Outdoor pools, both public and the one in the Castle Hotel, are open during July and August only. There are indoor pools at the Castle Plaza Hotel and in the sports centres.
Tennis There is more chance of a game of tennis in Nagoya than in Tokyo, although the odds are still against it. Try the *Odaka Ryokuchi* courts, Odaka-cho, Midori-ku ☎ 622 2282, *Obata Ryokuchi* courts, Obata, Moriyama-ku ☎ 791 9492, or the *Shonai koen* courts, Nazuka-cho, Nishi-ku ☎ 522 8381.

Local resources
Business services
Of the hotels, only the Castle has even rudimentary business service facilities. There are branches of *Manpower Japan* ☎ 962 7771 and *Kao Co* ☎ 571 4131, nationwide companies providing a reasonably wide range of business services.
Photocopying and printing All major hotels provide photocopying and will arrange for printing services; otherwise contact

International Translation and Printing Ltd ☏ 571 5611.
Secretarial For secretarial services contact *Career Staff* ☏ 962 2228, *Temporary Centre Corporation* ☏ 586 4525 or *Tempstaff* ☏ 951 2357.
Translation *Manpower Japan, International Translation and Printing* and *ASI* ☏ 671 0358 will provide translators. For interpreters, the people to contact are *Manpower Japan* or *TS International Co* ☏ 951 2357.

Communications

International couriers *DHL* ☏ 571 1455
Post offices *Nagoya Central Post Office*, Nagoya Station ☏ 564 2101, is open 24hrs.
Telex and fax All hotels provide telex and fax services; otherwise go to *KDD Nagoya* ☏ 203 3311.

Conference/exhibition centres

Conferences are generally held either in a hotel or at the *Nagoya International Centre*, 1-47-1 Nagono, Nakamura-ku ☏ 581 5678. The main exhibition halls are *Nagoya Trade and Industry Centre*, 6-3 Fukiage 2-chome, Chikusa-ku ☏ 753 2111, *Nagoya International Exhibition Hall*, 2-2 Kinjo Futo, Minato-ku ☏ 398 1771, and *Aichi-ken Trade Centre*, 3-1-6 Marunouchi, Naka-ku ☏ 231 6351. For inquiries contact *Nagoya Convention and Visitors' Bureau*, 31-12 Sakae 2-chome, Naka-ku ☏ 201 5733.

Emergencies

Hospitals 170 hospitals and 989 clinics take part in Nagoya's 24hr medical care system. In an emergency ☏ 119 for an ambulance or call the *Medical Care Information Centre* ☏ 263 1133, who will tell you the nearest hospital available. *Ishikai Emergency Clinic*, 4-38 Aoi 1-chome, Higashi-ku ☏ 937 7821, is open on weekends and holidays.
Pharmacies Hospitals supply prescription drugs.
Police *Aichi Prefectural Police Headquarters* ☏ 951 1611.

Government offices

For inquiries about local government departments and services, contact *Nagoya City Office*, 1-1 San-no-maru 3-chome, Naka-ku ☏ 961 1111; for information on the prefecture, *Aichi Prefectural Government Office* ☏ 951 1611.

Information sources

Business information The *Nagoya Chamber of Commerce*, 10-19 Sakae 2-chome, Naka-ku ☏ 221 7211 will provide information and help with contacts in relevant trade or manufacturers' associations. *JETRO*, 2-4-7 Marunouchi, Naka-ku ☏ 211 4517, is also helpful for information, assistance and contacts.
Local media Of the five local English-language newspapers, the *Mainichi Daily News*, based in Osaka, has news and information related to Nagoya and central Japan.
Tourist information The most useful source of information and assistance is the *Nagoya International Centre* 47-1 Nagono 1-chome, Nakamura-ku ☏ 581 5678, staffed largely by resident Westerners, who are available daily to help visitors or telephone callers, from 9am to 9pm. They publish the excellent *Nagoya Calendar* (see *Entertainment*). The *TIC*, Nagoya Station ☏ 541 4301, will provide maps, information, suggestions and several monthly guides, including *Nagoya Eyes* and *Nagoya Avenues.* To call TIC collect ☏ 106 and ask for "Collect call TIC". Of the travel agencies, the *JTB*, Matsuzakaya department store, Nagoya Station ☏ 563 0041 is the most helpful.

Thank-yous

The most suitable places to buy gifts are the prestigious department stores, *Mitsukoshi* and *Matsuzakaya*, either of which will pack the gift beautifully and deliver it.

OSAKA

Area code ☏ 06

The standard greeting in Osaka is "Mo kari makka?" – "Making any money?" Osaka is Japan's business capital, a mammoth commercial and industrial city; the whole conurbation has a population of 22m (2.9m in the city itself), making it the second largest city in the world. A quarter of the country's industrial output is produced here, including textiles, iron and steel; the airport and docks handle 40% of total exports. Home of Japan's pharmaceutical industry, it is a leader in the development of up-to-the-minute biotechnology. Osaka was founded by the 16th-century warlord Hideyoshi, who, wise to the importance of commerce, made it a city of merchants, forcing them to live here and giving special privileges to the wealthiest. The great business and banking dynasties – Sumitomo, Itochu, Marubeni, Sanwa and Daiwa – all have their roots here. The city is currently being transformed by the 21st Century Plan, an ambitious series of projects which includes a new offshore international airport due to open in 1992, the biggest convention hall in the Kansai area and the development of Osaka Business Park near the castle.

Arriving

Experienced business travellers often prefer to fly direct to Osaka rather than to Tokyo, in spite of Itami's limited landing times, conclude their business there and fly on to Haneda, thus avoiding the long trek in from Tokyo's Narita.

Osaka International (Itami) Airport

Japan's second international airport, Itami handles flights direct from Europe, North America and Asia as well as via Tokyo, with connections to every other major Japanese city. Landing is permitted only between 6am and 9pm. Good range of restaurants, coffee shops, bars; some useful shops selling luxury goods, souvenirs; several banks, all closing by 7.30pm.

Nearby hotels *Osaka Airport*, 3F Osaka Airport Bldg, 3-555 Nishimachi, Hotarugaike, Toyonaka 560 ☏ 855 4621 ⓉⓍ 5286125 • Hankyu. *Senri Hankyu*, 2-chome Higashi-machi, Shin Senri, Toyonaka 565 ☏ 872 2211; one of the best airport hotels in Japan, 5min from Itami.

City link There is no rail link between Itami and Osaka. The best way to get into the city is by bus or taxi; some hotels provide a shuttle bus service.

Bus The limousine bus leaves Itami every 7–8min between 7am and 9.30pm. The journey takes about 30min, but allow twice that in rush hour. Buses stop at the major hotels and stations, where it is easy to get a taxi.

Taxi A taxi direct to your hotel will save a little time, but the cost is much higher.

Car rental Nippon Rentacar has a branch at the airport.

Railway stations

Although it is worthwhile flying from Tokyo, Osaka is accessible by train from most major cities.

Shin Osaka This large modern station, slightly to the north of Osaka, is the Bullet Train station, connected to Umeda and points south by subway (the Midosuji line) and rail.

Osaka An enormous complex, recently renovated, this station houses department stores, hotels and an underground shopping arcade, as well as the main JNR lines to Kyoto and Kobe. It is very close to Umeda, for the Midosuji subway line, and to Hankyu and Hanshin Umeda stations.

Getting around

Although Osaka is almost as congested as Tokyo, the subway is frequent, quick and easy to use and, particularly in rush hours, preferable to taxis.

Subway Osaka's subways are rapid, efficient, and apparently designed with the Western traveller in mind. Maps of the subway system are widely available, and every station name is given in English as well as Japanese. There are six subway lines, distinguished by colour, which crisscross the city. Services run every 4min (more frequently in rush hour) between 5.30am and 11.45pm. The most useful, the Midosuji line, links the Umeda Station complex with Shin Osaka and the three other main city stations, Shinsaibashi, Namba and Tennoji. If you are making more than seven journeys within the city, it is worth buying a one-day pass, which covers subways and buses and is available in main ticket offices and JTB.

Train Of the five private railway lines, the most useful are the Hankyu and Hanshin lines from Umeda, which serve northern Osaka and go on to Kobe. The Hankyu and Keihan lines go to Kyoto, and the Kintetsu line from Namba goes out through Nipponbashi towards Nara. There are stopping, semi-express and express trains, marked as such and identified in different colours on the station timetables. JNR lines loop the city and also link Umeda with the port.

Taxi Taxis are available throughout the city. Osaka taxi drivers are said to be friendlier than those in Tokyo, but they are just as unlikely to know the way.

Walking Accurate walking maps are widely available, but distances can be deceptive – Osaka is an enormous city.

Bus Buses are plentiful but difficult to use; bus stops are marked in Japanese only.

Car rental The main rental chains all have offices in Osaka, but unless your business takes you outside the central city area, it is better not to drive. Osaka is congested, especially at rush hours, and parking is difficult.

Area by area

At present the main business and commercial areas are in Yodoyabashi and Hommachi, on Midosuji-dori, a wide boulevard lined with gingko trees which runs down the centre of Osaka, linking north (Kita) and south (Minami); but many companies are already buying up office space in Osaka Business Park, the business area of the future, currently being developed near the castle. Running from north to south, the main areas are as follows.

Umeda The area around the Osaka Umeda station complex is full of skyscrapers and wide dusty roads congested with traffic. The main concentration of hotels is here, together with office blocks and department stores. There is also a vast underground shopping arcade, nearly 2miles/3km long. Umeda has plenty of restaurants, bars and nightclubs, of the smarter, more fashionable variety, as well as more colourful nightlife down the side streets.

Nakanoshima Located over the bridge south of Umeda, this small island contains the Bank of Japan, a leading newspaper (the *Asahi Shimbun*), Osaka's top hotel (the Royal), the International Trade Centre, the Festival Hall, the science faculties of the university and offices of several businesses and international corporations.

Yodoyabashi and Hommachi Straddling Kita and Minami is Osaka's business area, extending from Yodoyabashi (across the bridge from Nakanoshima) down Midosuji-dori and eastwards into Hommachi.

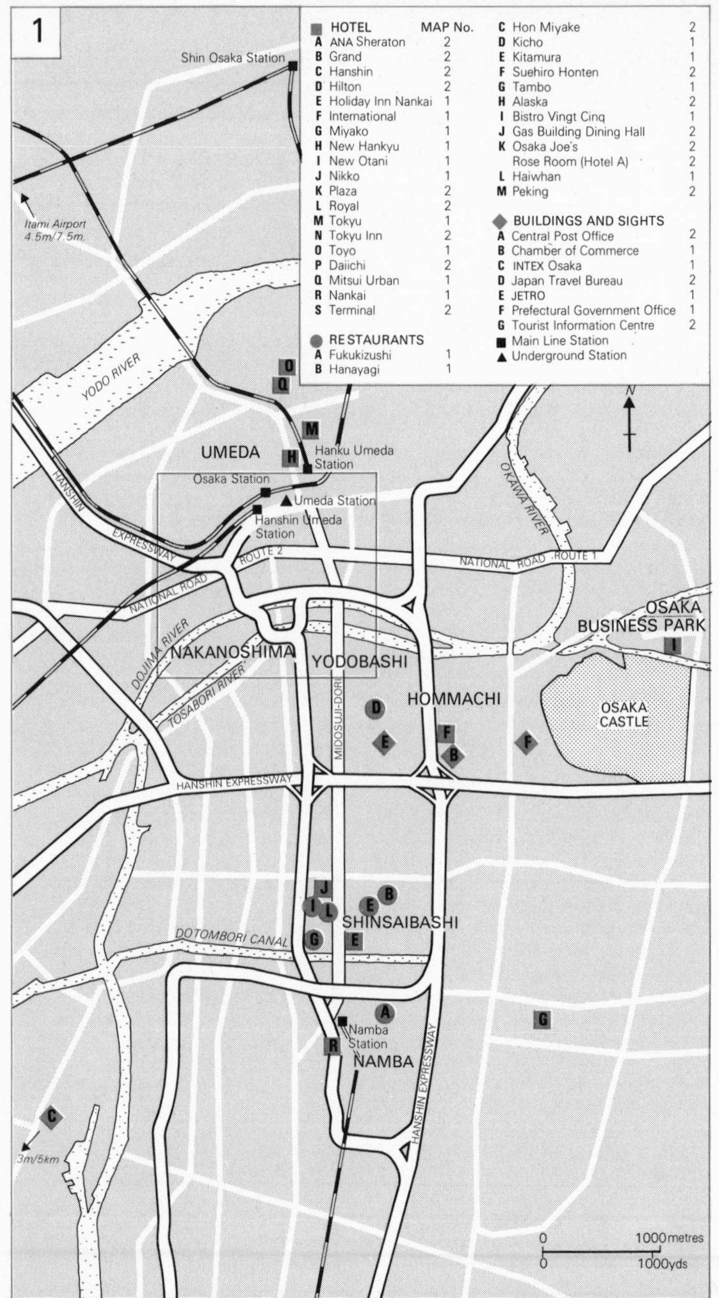
1
HOTEL MAP No.
A ANA Sheraton 2
B Grand 2
C Hanshin 2
D Hilton 2
E Holiday Inn Nankai 1
F International 1
G Miyako 1
H New Hankyu 1
I New Otani 1
J Nikko 1
K Plaza 2
L Royal 2
M Tokyu 1
N Tokyu Inn 2
O Toyo 1
P Daiichi 2
Q Mitsui Urban 1
R Nankai 1
S Terminal 2
RESTAURANTS
A Fukukizushi 1
B Hanayagi 1
C Hon Miyake 2
D Kicho 1
E Kitamura 1
F Suehiro Honten 2
G Tambo 1
H Alaska 2
I Bistro Vingt Cinq 1
J Gas Building Dining Hall 2
K Osaka Joe's 2
Rose Room (Hotel A) 2
L Haiwhan 1
M Peking 2
BUILDINGS AND SIGHTS
A Central Post Office 2
B Chamber of Commerce 1
C INTEX Osaka 1
D Japan Travel Bureau 2
E JETRO 1
F Prefectural Government Office 1
G Tourist Information Centre 2
Main Line Station
Underground Station
Shin Osaka Station
Itami Airport 4.5m/7.5m.
YODO RIVER
UMEDA
Hanku Umeda Station
Osaka Station
Umeda Station
Hanshin Umeda Station
HANSHIN EXPRESSWAY
ROUTE 2
NATIONAL ROAD
NATIONAL ROAD ROUTE 1
OKAWA RIVER
OSAKA BUSINESS PARK
DOJIMA RIVER
NAKANOSHIMA
YODOBASHI
TOSABORI RIVER
HOMMACHI
OSAKA CASTLE
MIDOSUJI-DORI
HANSHIN EXPRESSWAY
SHINSAIBASHI
DOTOMBORI CANAL
Namba Station
NAMBA
HANSHIN EXPRESSWAY
3m/5km
0 1000metres
0 1000yds
N

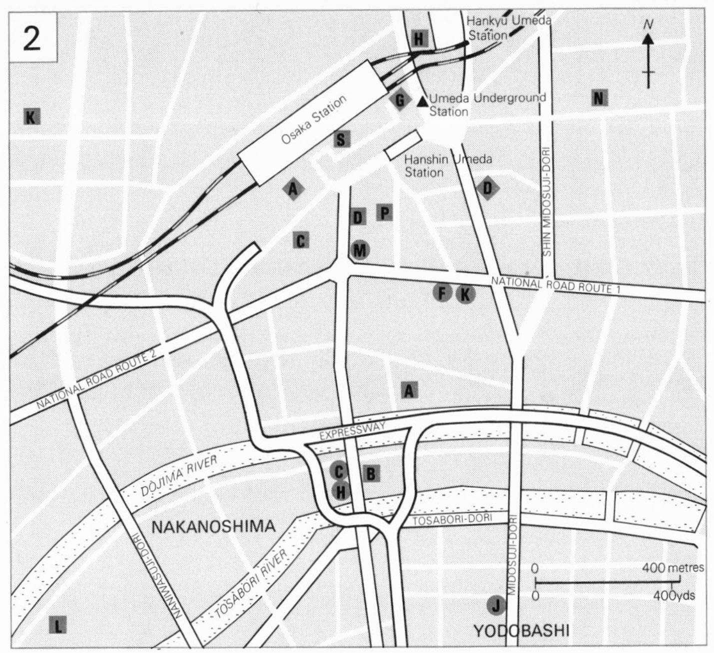

The main concentration of banks and businesses is in Hommachi; these include the head offices of major trading companies such as Marubeni, Sumitomo, Nissho Iwai and C. Itoh. The Osaka Chamber of Commerce and Industry and the Foreign Trade Institute are in this area.

Osaka Castle The main administrative and prefectural offices are to the east of Hommachi, next to Osaka Castle. On the other side of the castle, a large triangular bomb site is being developed into Osaka Business Park.

Shinsaibashi Just south of Hommachi, around the Nikko Hotel, is Shinsaibashi, Osaka's main shopping area; behind the department stores on Midosuji-dori stretch a network of covered arcades and tiny streets full of restaurants (including some of the finest in Osaka), boutiques and speciality shops. The streets are laid out in a grid, bordered by Midosuji-dori and Dotombori, making it easy to find your way around.

Dotombori Full of neon lights and tiny restaurants, this is the place to come for Osaka's famed nightlife; here pleasure-seeking Osakans used to bankrupt themselves.

Namba Around Namba Station is a maze of lively, cluttered alleys, full of drinking spots, tiny restaurants and soaplands massage parlours. In the middle of all this you can also find department stores, theatres and a vast underground shopping arcade. Farther south you will find the Shin Sekai pleasure quarters, one of Japan's most famous.

The suburbs

Most Osakans commute to work from the suburbs. The pleasantest and smartest suburbs are those to the north and northeast of the city: Toyonaka and Senri near Itami airport, and Ibaraki, along the Hankyu line towards Kyoto. Many top executives live farther out still, in Minoo.

Hotels

Top companies still put their executives in the Royal or the Plaza, but the plethora of de luxe international-style hotels, such as the Nikko, ANA, Hilton and New Otani, which have opened recently in Osaka as part of its 21st Century Plan, has given the business traveller a much wider choice.

ANA-Sheraton ¥¥¥
1-3-1 Dojimahama, Kita-ku 530
☎ 347 1112 TX 5236884 • 474 rooms, 26 suites, 6 restaurants, 3 bars, 1 coffee shop
A new American-style de luxe hotel, opened October 1984, in the commercial area of north Osaka. The lobby is somewhat over-extravagant in décor, but the rooms, all with mini-bar, are ample and comfortable. Sally Yagi, in the business centre, provides all the services of a personal secretary for visiting foreign executives. The Rose Room (see *Restaurants*) is a favourite among foreign businessmen and diplomats for its *nouvelle cuisine.* 24hr room service, express check-out, concierge and travel desk, arcade of shops, hairdresser, florist, shuttle bus to Osaka Station and airport limousine terminal • sauna, pool • business service centre with many facilities, 11 meeting rooms (capacity 15–800).

Grand ¥¥¥
2-3-18 Nakanoshima, Kita-ku 530
☎ 202 1212 TX 5222301 • Royal Hotels • 345 rooms, 13 suites, 3 restaurants, 1 bar, 1 coffee shop
The Grand was once Osaka's best and retains a reputation for excellent service. Sadly, it is now looking much the worse for wear, although it still has a following among artists and musicians as well as businessmen, undeterred by its cramped rooms and general air of faded grandeur. The location is exceptionally convenient, next to the Yodoyabashi commercial area. Concierge, travel and theatre reservations, express check-out, limited hotel parking, shuttle bus to Osaka Station • 2 meeting rooms (capacity 10–20).

Hanshin ¥¥
3-30 Umeda 2-chome, Kita-ku 530
☎ 344 1661 TX 5234269 • Inter Japan • 243 rooms, 8 restaurants, 2 bars, 3 coffee shops
The Hanshin occupies the top floors of a large office block close to Osaka Station, and the clientele is mainly businessmen. The rooms are small but attractively furnished in the Japanese mode, with paper screens that slide over the windows. A particularly pleasant mid-range hotel. Shuttle bus to airport • sauna • 6 meeting rooms.

Hilton ¥¥¥¥
3 Umeda 1-8-85 chome, Kita-ku 530
☎ 344 4511 TX 5242201 • 475 rooms, 78 suites, 4 restaurants, 1 bar, 3 coffee shops/tea lounges
Opened in September 1986, the elegant new Hilton is the first de luxe international-class hotel to join the cluster of hotels around Osaka Station. The spacious rooms, pleasantly Japanese in décor, are each equipped with a mini-bar. There are three executive floors, with express check-in and a private lounge. 24hr room service, concierge, arcade of shops, hairdresser, pharmacy • health club with gym and sauna, indoor pool, tennis court • business service centre with extensive facilities, 19 meeting rooms (capacity 20–1,000).

Holiday Inn Nankai ¥¥
28-1 Kyuzaemon-cho, Minami-ku 542
☎ 213 8281 TX 5222939 • 228 rooms, 2 suites, 4 restaurants, 2 bars
Probably the only good mid-range hotel in south Osaka, the Holiday Inn is a safe, if unimaginative, option, and there are plenty of Western guests, both business

travellers and tourists. The rooms are a good size. Arcade of shops, limited hotel parking, shuttle bus to airport • pool • 2 meeting rooms.

International ¥¥
58 Hashizume-cho, Uchihonmachi, Higashi-ku 540 ☏ 941 2661 TX 5293415 • 391 rooms, 3 suites, 5 restaurants, 1 bar, 1 coffee shop
The International is a large, friendly business hotel situated in the midst of offices in the Hommachi business district and used by the major companies (such as Marubeni and C. Itoh) to house their long-term foreign staff. It offers functional, reasonably priced accommodation, very close to the Hanshin expressway. Concierge, travel and theatre bookings • 12 meeting rooms (capacity 6–1,500).

Miyako ¥¥
1-55 Uehommachi 6-chome, Tennoji-ku 543 ☏ 773 1111 TX 7733322 • Kintetsu • 608 rooms, 9 restaurants, 1 bar, 4 coffee shops
Located slightly off the beaten track, the Miyako is a glossy new de luxe hotel. Rooms, complete with closed-circuit video, are pleasant and spacious, particularly those on the executive floor, which has a private lounge, express check-in and secretarial services. Service is brisk and somewhat impersonal. 24hr room service, concierge and information service; shops, beauty salon • health club with indoor pool, squash courts, gym • business service centre with limited facilities, 20 meeting rooms (capacity up to 3,000).

New Hankyu ¥¥
1-1-35 Shibata, Kita-ku 530 ☏ 372 5101 TX 5233245 • 1,029 rooms, 13 restaurants, 4 bars, 6 coffee shops/tea lounges
Very much a business hotel, conveniently located at Umeda Station, the New Hankyu is big and impersonal, but efficient and much used by Japanese businessmen. Its two basement arcades house restaurants, coffee shops and bars. Limited hotel parking • pool, sauna • 1 meeting room (capacity 1,100).

New Otani ¥¥¥
1-4-1-chome, Shiromi, Higashi-ku 540 ☏ 941 1111 TX J63068 • 597 rooms, 13 suites, 16 restaurants, 4 bars
One of Osaka's newest hotels (opened September 1986), and the first to serve Osaka Business Park, the New Otani is a de luxe hotel which functions almost as a mini-city, providing quality shops and restaurants for the area. Designed particularly for the business traveller. Concierge, medical clinic • private fitness club with gym and sauna, tennis courts, indoor and outdoor pools • business service centre with extensive facilities, 19 meeting rooms (capacity up to 4,000).

Nikko ¥¥¥
7 Nishino-cho, Daihoji-machi, Minami-ku 542 ☏ 244 1111 TX 5227575 • 643 rooms, 8 suites, 4 restaurants, 2 bars, 2 coffee shops
Towering above the business and entertainment area of Shinsaibashi, the Nikko, a gleaming white, modern luxury hotel, is undoubtedly the best in south Osaka. Foreign staff (currently Benedicte Plaige, from France) help with guest relations, and there are romantic rooms designed by Hanae Mori, the Japanese fashion and interior designer, as well as executive suites with a more masculine decor. Les Célébrités (French) and Benkei (Japanese) are useful restaurants, and Jet Stream (see *Bars*) is a popular bar. The Samba Club (see *Entertainment*) is one of Osaka's most sophisticated discos. 24hr room service, concierge and travel desk, arcade of shops, JAL office • secretarial services, meeting rooms.

Plaza ¥¥¥¥
2-2-49 Oyodo-Minami, Oyodo-ku 531 ☏ 453 1111 TX 5245557 • 533 rooms, 14 suites, 5 restaurants, 5 bars, 1 coffee shop

A de luxe hotel with a relaxed, understated style, located in the commercial area of north Osaka, the Plaza is many business travellers' favourite. Service is friendly and efficient, and the rooms are spacious. There are extra-large corner rooms in the executive suites. Le Rendezvous, renowned for its French cuisine "après la cuisine" of Louis Outhier, is a popular restaurant for business dining. 24hr room service, express check-out, concierge and travel desk, arcade of shops, hairdresser, shuttle bus to Osaka Station • outdoor pool • secretarial services, 20 meeting rooms (capacity 10–1,500).

Royal ¥¥¥
3-68, 5-chome, Nakanoshima, Kita-ku 530 ☎ *448 1121* TX *5245407 • 1,420 rooms, 65 suites, 7 bars, 12 restaurants, 2 coffee shops*
The Royal is considered by many to be Osaka's best hotel and is certainly one of its most prestigious. It is enormous, with a spectacularly imposing lobby, overlooking a Japanese garden. The bedrooms, all sound-proofed and air-conditioned, are more restrained and businesslike. The Royal Tower rooms on the top three floors of the executive tower offer more space and luxury. In the basement are branches of two extremely famous Japanese restaurants, Kicho and Nadaman (see *Restaurants*) and also branches of luxury and department stores. The Cellar Bar (see *Bars*) is a favourite gathering place. Concierge and travel desk, hotel bus to airport and Yodoyabashi subway station • health club with indoor pool, gym, sauna • business service centre with extensive facilities, 58 meeting rooms (capacity up to 6,000).

OTHER HOTELS
Daiichi (¥¥) *1-9-20 Umeda, Kita-ku 530* ☎ *341 4411* TX *5234423.* Distinctive round orange skyscraper very near Osaka Station, terminal for airport bus.
Mitsui Urban (¥) *3-18-8 Toyosaki, Oyodo-ku 531* ☎ *374 1111* TX *5233701.* Close to Nakatsu station; particularly pleasant for the price.
Nankai (¥) *17-11 Namba Naka 1-chome, Naniwa-ku 556* ☎ *649 1521.* Budget hotel in south Osaka, close to Namba Station.
Terminal (¥¥) *3-1-1 Umeda, Kita-ku 530* ☎ *344 1235* TX *5233738.* Above Osaka Station, convenient for business and shopping.
Tokyu (¥¥) *7-20 Chaya-machi, Kita-ku 530* ☎ *373 2411* TX *5236751.* The best of the hotels to the north of Osaka Station, this is one of the better Tokyus and has a pool.
Tokyu Inn (¥¥) *2-1 Doyamacho, Kita-ku 530* ☎ *315 0109* TX *5422704.* Modestly priced, but a sizeable walk from Umeda Station.
Toyo (¥¥) *16-19 Toyosaki 3-chome, Oyodo-ku 531* ☎ *372 8181* TX *5233886.* Superior business hotel above Nakatsu subway station.

Restaurants

While Kyotoites are said to spend all their money on kimonos, Osakans traditionally bankrupt themselves for food, making Osaka the home of fine dining (the most ruinously expensive restaurant in Japan, Kicho, is in Osaka). Much expense-account dining takes place in the smart restaurants of Kita, but for a meal after work with colleagues, Japanese executives are likely to head for the noisy little eateries along Dotombori. Few dishes are pure Osakan, but Osaka has excellent sashimi.

JAPANESE
Fukukizushi ¥¥¥¥
1-19-6 Nipponbashi, Minami-ku ☎ *632 0865 • closed Sun L, Mon and hols • AE • reservations essential for private rooms*
Hidden away down a side street near Nipponbashi subway station in south

Osaka is one of the city's finest sushi shops. Yamamoto Kanji, carrying on the tradition begun by his family 80 years ago, slices up top-quality local fish behind the long wooden counter, while in front regulars, mainly local businessmen, rub shoulders with company directors and their foreign guests. Although there are no English speakers here, there is an English menu. Fixed price menu available at less than half the price of à la carte.

Hanayagi ¥¥¥
22 Higashi Shimizu-machi, Minami-ku ☎ 271 8028 • closed Tue and hols • no reservations
Despite its modest exterior, Hanayagi has a reputation as being one of the best tempura restaurants in Kansai. Only 12 at a time can fit along the unpolished wooden counter, but turnover is rapid and it is worth the wait.

Hon Miyake ¥¥
10F Asahi Bldg, 3-2-4 Nakanoshima, Kita-ku ☎ 231 3188 • closed Sun and hols
In the middle of the Nakanoshima commercial area, on the tenth floor of an office block, is a little old Japanese restaurant, founded 80 years ago. You follow a cobbled path past a small garden with bamboos and a stone basin, to a tiny Japanese house, where a very old kimono-clad lady serves up the finest sukiyaki, *shabu shabu* and *butteryaki* (beef sautéed in butter). Hon Miyake is one of Osaka's more famous restaurants, and a popular choice for business entertaining.

Kicho
3-23 Koraibashi, Higashi-ku ☎ 231 1937
Prime Minister Nakasone's favourite, Kicho is said to be Japan's best restaurant. You will not get in except by personal invitation; regard it as a mark of the highest esteem to be brought here. You will dine on the finest *kaiseki* cuisine in an atmosphere impeccably Japanese, served with the utmost finesse by kimono-clad ladies. No bill will be presented, but you may be sure that the meal will make a sizeable dent in your host's account. There are more accessible branches of Kicho in several top hotels.

Kitamura ¥¥
46 Higashi Shimizu-machi, Minami-ku ☎ 245 4129 • closed Sun and hols • AE DC MC V • reservations essential
This venerable sukiyaki restaurant was founded in 1881, and still occupies the same large and beautiful old Japanese house in a small alley just off Midosuji Avenue in Shinsaibashi. The ambience is intensely Japanese, quiet and refined, with a tiny garden containing bamboos and a stone basin, and austere tatami rooms. The owner, Mr Kitamura, welcomes Western guests, whether alone or with Japanese colleagues. A popular choice among Japanese for business entertaining.

Suehiro Honten ¥¥
1-11-11 Sonezaki Shinchi, Kita-ku ☎ 341 1638 • closed Dec 31–Jan 3 • AE DC V
This is the original Suehiro, founded 76 years ago, where *shabu shabu* was invented in 1959. It now spreads over five floors in a quiet, spacious new restaurant near Osaka Station. The owner, Kiyoshi Miyake, is a well-known patron of the arts and crafts, and you dine surrounded by Munakata prints, off fine handmade pottery. An Osaka institution.

Tambo ¥
B1 Shouzan Bldg, 22 Minami Iwaya-cho 1-chome, Minami-ku ☎ 211 8759 • closed Tue • no reservations
On their night off, Japanese businessmen are to be found enjoying excellent food and plenty of sake in little eateries down dark alleys, with a red lantern hanging outside. Tambo's red lantern is enormous, and the greeting given to guests is raucous.

In the stone-floored basement room, you can sit at the counter and point out vegetables and meat to be skewered and grilled over charcoal, or by the old country-style open hearth, and enjoy fine traditional cuisine at amazingly low prices.

NON-JAPANESE

Alaska ¥¥¥¥
13F Asahi Shimbun Bldg, Nakanoshima 3-chome, Kita-ku ☎ *231 1351 • closed Sun and hols • AE DC MC V*
One of the first Osaka restaurants to serve European-style food, the dignified red-carpeted Alaska, with its views over surrounding Nakanoshima, is the natural choice of many Japanese executives for entertaining business clients. The menu is Japanized European, with plenty of steak – solid, unimaginative, but well prepared. Charcoal-broiled Kobe beef is the speciality, and there is an extensive wine list. A cheaper set menu is available.

Bistro Vingt Cinq ¥¥¥
25 Taihoji-machi. 25 Nishino-cho, Minami-ku ☎ *245 6223 • closed 3rd Sun of month and hols • AE DC MC V*
Chef Hara Yoshikata's *nouvelle cuisine* is outstanding, and Westerners, including the local French, are much in evidence at this smart and fashionable bistro, just around the corner from the Nikko Hotel. The room, decorated in classical style, is small, but tables are widely spaced and the atmosphere is intimate. In the evening the clientele consists largely of businessmen, both Japanese and Western. A respectable wine list of mainly French wines.

Gas Building ¥¥¥
8F Gas Bldg, 5-1 Hirano-machi, Higashi-ku ☎ *231 0901 or 1064 • closed Sun and hols • V • reservations essential for lunch*
Squeezed in between banks and trading companies on Midosuji, the Gas Building Dining Hall has been an Osaka institution since before the war. At lunchtime it is always packed with businessmen. The four-course lunch menu, featuring steak, is excellent value, and the cooking, though uninspired, is acceptable.

Haiwhan ¥¥¥¥
11F Midosuji Bldg, 8 Nishi Shimizu-machi, Minami-ku ☎ *281 0080 • closed Dec 30–Jan 1 • AE DC MC V • reservations for private rooms*
Almost next to the Nikko Hotel, this is a celebrated Cantonese seafood restaurant, popular among Japanese businessmen, who use the many small private rooms for entertaining. The décor is extravagantly ornate, with carved wooden tables, luxuriant foliage, stone lions and copper and bronze screens. A huge tank of fish occupies the centre of the room. Live prawns are the speciality. Less expensive set menus available.

Osaka Joe's ¥¥¥
2F IM Excellence Bldg, 1-11-20 Sonezaki-shinchi, Kita-ku ☎ *344 0124 • AE CB DC MC V • no reservations*
A more restrained version of its counterpart, Miami Joe's in Florida, Osaka Joe's stone crab restaurant is quiet, classy and very American in atmosphere, with dark wood panelling, stained glass and discreet lighting – an impressive place to entertain a few Japanese colleagues. Stone crabs are hard to find outside Florida and well worth tasting. There is a reasonable wine list, dominated by American wines.

Peking ¥¥
12F Osaka Ekimae Daiichi Bldg, 1-3-1 Umeda, Kita-ku ☎ *341 4071 • closed Dec 30–Jan 3*
One of the best and most popular Chinese restaurants in the city and conveniently close to Osaka Station. The décor is sumptuous but tasteful, with carved stone screens, chests inlaid with mother-of-pearl and huge vases. There are small private rooms for business entertaining, and inexpensive menus for groups.

Rose Room ¥¥¥¥
ANA-Sheraton Hotel Osaka, 1-3-1 Dojimahama, Kita-ku ☎ *347 1112*
• *closed Sun L and hols* • AE DC MC V
• *reservations essential*
This elegant hotel restaurant is one of Osaka's best. Chef Yokota Tomoyoshi was apprenticed at Maxim's in Paris and has already won two stars in *Guruma*, the Japanese equivalent of the *Michelin Guide*, for his classic and light French cuisine. He likes to meet the guests and recommend particular wines from the extensive list. The spacious dining room with rose motif décor is suitable for business entertaining; your fellow guests will include top-level foreign and Japanese executives and diplomats.

Bars

For an evening's serious drinking with Japanese colleagues, the smart bars in Kita are the place to go. South Osaka's bars are considerably more relaxed. Most of the bars listed open at 5pm and close around midnight; few accept credit cards.

Cellar Bar
B1 Royal Hotel, 5-3 Nakanoshima, Kita-ku • *all major credit cards*
The classiest of the hotel bars, with a dignified, old-world style, this is the place to invite your Japanese colleagues. Famous for its charming hostesses.

Cellar Bar Williams
B1 Tamaki Bldg, 25 Unagidani-Nakano-cho, Minami-ku
A quiet, classy bar in Shinsaibashi, Cellar Bar Williams sports beamed ceilings and waiters in tuxedos. Not as fashionable as it was a few years ago, but still very pleasant.

Jet Stream
32F Nikko Hotel, 7 Nishinocho, Daihoji-machi, Minami-ku • *all major credit cards*
Stylish new bar at the top of the Nikko Hotel, with a streamlined design like the inside of a jumbo jet. There are live jazz bands and visits from famous singers.

Pig and Whistle
43 Sakamiya-cho, 22 Soemon, Minami-ku
Fight your way to the bar in this very British pub. Located amid the neon of Dotombori, the Pig and Whistle offers darts, dominoes, beer and fried chicken and is a favourite gathering place of Western businessmen.

Scotch Bank
B1 Fukuhara Bldg, 44 Tatamiyamachi, Minami-ku
This basement bar in Shinsaibashi features an entire wall of named bottles of whisky. The style is fashionable high tech, and there is live piano music. Plenty of Western customers, including single women.

Sherlock Holmes
B1 Osaka Ekimae Daiichi Bldg, 1-3-1 Umeda, Kita-ku
A low-key pub in north Osaka, highly recommended by resident Westerners.

Entertainment

Osaka is the home of Bunraku, the puppet theatre, and also of the pleasure quarters of Shin Sekai, famed throughout Japan. Most entertainment is centred in the lively Sennichimae area, in the south – worth a stroll, particularly at night. For current information see the *Mainichi Daily News*, *Kansai Time Out*, *Japan Visitor's Guide*, *Meet Osaka* and *Tour Companion* – the last three available free in hotels. Make reservations through your hotel or at Play Guide ticket agencies in major department stores.
Theatre *Bunraku* is performed twice a day during January, April, July and October at the *Asahiza Theatre*, 2-18 Dotombori 1-chome, Minami-ku. The puppeteer to see is Yoshida Tamao, a living national treasure. The *Kabuki* stars perform in Osaka

once a year, in May, at the *Shin Kabukiza Theatre*, 3-25 Namba 4-chome, Minami-ku. The theatre also shows modern Japanese dramas.
Cinema Several cinemas show English, American and Continental films – see local press for current details.
Music Regular concerts of both traditional Japanese and Western music are held at the *Festival Hall* 2-3-18 Nakanoshima, Kita-ku, and the *Symphony Hall* 2-chome Oyodo-minami, Oyodo-ku.
Nightclubs Kita's nightclubs are smart and expensive; for a wild night out, Minami is the area to head for. Most hotels provide a complimentary "key" to enter the *Playboy Club*, 13F Sumitomo Nakanoshima Bldg, 3-2-18 Nakanoshima, Kita-ku ☏ 448 5271. The most fashionable disco in Kita, full of smart young Japanese, is *St Tropez*, 5F Nippo Dojima Centre, 1-3-9 Dojima, Kita-ku ☏ 345 0131. Another sophisticated disco is the *Samba Club*, B2 Nikko Hotel, 7 Nishinocho, Daihojimachi, Minami-ku ☏ 244 1111. At *Club Maiko*, B1 V.O. Bldg, Kitashinchi Hondori, Kita-ku ☏ 344 2913, you will be entertained by *maiko*, trainee geisha, as you dine.

Shopping

For high-quality goods, try Shinsaibashi – the classiest shopping area, with covered arcades and marble pavements – or the shopping arcades of the major hotels; the Royal and the Plaza arcades are reputable but expensive. The Acty Osaka Building, above Osaka Station, houses branches of well-known shops, and under Umeda and Namba are vast underground shopping complexes. Goods to look out for include cloisonné, cameras, electronic goods, pearls, silk and watches.
Department stores Osaka has nine major department stores, including the Osaka-based *Hankyu* and *Hanshin*. *Takashimaya* in Namba, *Daimaru* and *Sogo* in Shinsaibashi and *Mitsukoshi* in Koraibashi are considered to be the best.
Cameras Plenty of bargain camera shops. One of *Doi Camera*'s seven branches is at 20 Okawacho, Higashi-ku. *Kawahara Camera*, 2-2-30 Umeda, Kita-ku, is well established, and has an enormous stock.
Electrical goods Nipponbashi-suji, south of Nipponbashi Station, is the area for electrical goods, with more than 300 shops. *Toa Denka*, 4-11-6 Nipponbashi, Naniwa-ku, specializes in tax-free goods for foreigners.
Pearls Many Osaka shops specialize in pearls from the nearby Ise peninsula. The following shops offer international guarantees: *Mikimoto*, 1F Shin-Hankyu Bldg, 1-12-39 Umeda, Kita-ku, and *Tasaki Shinju*, 1F Namba City Main Bldg, 5-1-60 Namba, Minami-ku.

Sightseeing

Osaka has a long history and the castle is worth seeing, although the original buildings have long since been destroyed and replaced by modern reconstructions.
Fujita Art Museum In a splendid setting in the railway tycoon Baron Fujita's former mansion, the Fujita Art Museum is his collection of Japanese and Chinese paintings, ceramics and calligraphy, and one of Japan's best private museums. *10-32 Amijima-cho, Miyakojima-ku. Open Mar–Jun, Sep–Dec, 9.30–4.30; closed Mon.*
Museum of Oriental Ceramics The first museum in the world designed specifically for viewing ceramics, with an exceptionally fine collection of Chinese and Korean ware. Situated in Nakanoshima. *1-1 Nakanoshima, Kita-ku. Open 9.30–5; closed Mon.*
National Museum of Ethnology A celebrated and lively new museum with exhibits and videos. *Expo Memorial Park, Suita. Open 10–5; closed Wed.*
Osaka Castle Hideyoshi's original castle, built in 1583, was a great fortified city, 7 miles/11km around;

the present castle is a 1931 ferroconcrete reconstruction (inaccurate, according to the Japanese press), set in extensive grounds. *Kyobashi, Higashi-ku. Open May–Sep, 9–8.30; Oct–Apr, 9–5.*

Shitennoji Temple Founded in 593, the temple is the oldest in Japan; the present temple is a modern reconstruction, but the abbot's chamber in the main sanctuary and the stone *torii* (sacred gate) are the originals. *Tennoji-ku. Open 8.30–4.*

Sumiyoshi Shrine A faithful 1810 reconstruction of the shrine founded in 202 to the guardian deity of the sea, who protects the port of Osaka. *Sumiyoshi-koen. Open 6am–5.*

Temmangu Shrine The site of Osaka's most spectacular annual festival (in July), Tenjin Matsuri, Temmangu was built in 949 to enshrine Sugawara Michizane, the great calligrapher who is now the god of scholars; students pray here for exam success. *Minami Morimachi. Open 9.30–5.*

Guided tours

There are five different half-day tours, circling the city and covering various sights; commentary in Japanese only. Make reservations through: *Osaka Municipal Bus* ☎ 311 2995; *Tourist Information Office* ☎ 345 2189; or *JTB* ☎ 344 0022. There are industrial tours of, for example, a brewery, car factory, broadcasting centre, the Mint and the port, in March, April, July, August and October, for ten days each month. Individual companies such as Matsushita Electric, Suntory and Asahi Breweries also arrange tours, sometimes with English-speaking guides. Book through your hotel, *JTB* or the *tourist office.*

Out of town

To the north of Osaka are the two old capitals, *Nara* and *Kyoto*, the latter less than an hour away by train and top of every traveller's list. To the south, and easily accessible for a weekend trip, is an area of surprisingly remote and wild countryside. *Mount Yoshino*, less than 2hrs from Osaka on the Kansai line, is famous for its cherry blossoms and is crowded in April. It offers fine views, old temples and good hiking throughout the summer. *Mount Koya*, 3hrs by train from Namba, is the main centre of the Shingon Buddhist sect, the largest sect in Japan. The flat top of the mountain is covered with temples, and many famous people are buried in the mile-long avenue of mausoleums. The train ride from Osaka is spectacular. If you stay in a temple, expect superlative vegetarian fare, and a 5am alarm call to prayers – given on a gong.

Spectator sports

Baseball Osaka has two major league teams, the Hanshin and the Hankyu, backed by the Osaka-based railway/department store chains. The annual high school baseball tournaments, which the whole nation follows avidly, take place in July in the *Nissei Stadium*, 2-1-55 Morinomiya Chuo, Higashi-ku ☎ 941 5505.

Sumo Sumo comes to Osaka in March, and all of Osaka crowds to the *Prefectural Gymnasium*, 2 Shinkawamachi, Naniwa-ku ☎ 631 0120.

Keeping fit

There are plenty of public keep-fit facilities in Osaka, but they tend to be very crowded; hotel facilities are more comfortable.

Cycling There are two cycle tracks in Osaka: *Kansai Cycle Sports Centre* is 2 miles/3km long; *Sakai City Bicycle Road* is slightly shorter.

Health and sports centres The Royal, New Otani, Hilton and Miyako hotels have health clubs, open to members and hotel guests, which include a fitness centre/gymnasium with instructors and a swimming pool. Several hotels have saunas. *New Japan Sauna*, B3 Toyo Hotel, 3-16-19 Toyosaki, Oyodo-ku ☏ 372 8181, is a famous sauna complex with a gymnasium; for men only. The *Dotombori New Japan Sauna*, 2-3-28 Dotombori, Minami-ku ☏ 211 0832, is open to men and women and includes pools, massage rooms and a beauty salon, as well as a sauna, but no gym. *The Prefectural Gymnasium*, 2 Shinkawamachi, Naniwa-ku ☏ 631 0120, has facilities for basketball, volleyball and judo, as well as a gym.

Jogging Nakanoshima Park, in the business area, is full of joggers in the morning; a jogging map is available from the ANA-Sheraton Hotel. The Nikko Hotel provides a jogging map for south Osaka.

Skiing During the short skiing season, special trains run from Osaka to the ski slopes of Mount Kannabe (Hyogo Prefecture) and Mount Daisen (Tottori Prefecture).

Swimming If you want to brave a public pool, go early in the morning. *Osaka Municipal Pool*, 1-1-21 Ogimachi, Kita-ku ☏ 312 8121.

Tennis There are courts at the Hilton, Miyako and New Otani hotels. Public courts are always booked up.

Local resources

Business services

The best business centre is run by Sally Yagi in the ANA Hotel and is frequently used by non-hotel guests. In general the hotel business centres (also in the Royal, New Otani and Hilton) are better than commercial agencies. All hotels provide photocopying, telex and fax services and most will arrange secretaries, translators or interpreters as required. Companies providing a wide range of business services are *I.S.S.*(Royal Hotel) ☏ 441 2090, *Manpower Japan* ☏ 222 6300, *Kao Co Ltd* ☏ 344 4520 and *Temporary Centre Corporation* ☏ 204 1431.

Secretarial and translation *Kokusai Shinko IBP* ☏ 266 1901 (ask for Raymond Sweat), *Kansai Manpower* ☏ 538 0515, *Career Staff Co Ltd* ☏ 251 5631.

Communications

It is easier to send an important document or package abroad than to another city in Japan; outside of Tokyo the domestic courier network is limited and unreliable.

International couriers *DHL Japan Inc* ☏ 445 8151, *Overseas Courier Service* ☏ 473 2631, *World Courier Japan* ☏ 365 9670.

Post office *Osaka Central Post Office*, 3-2 Umeda, Kita-ku ☏ 347 8034

Telex and fax Almost all hotels offer telex and fax facilities. Otherwise, use the *KDD* at Shinhanshin Bldg, Umeda, Kita-ku ☏ 343 2571 and Mitsui Bldg, Nakanoshima ☏ 441 5496; also for international phone calls and telegrams.

Conference/exhibition centres

INTEX OSAKA, 1-12 Nanko-kita 1-chome, Suminoe-ku 559 ☏ 612 3773, was opened in 1985 as part of Osaka's 21st Century Plan; annual international trade fairs are held here, organized by the Osaka International Trade Fair Commission. The previous centre, the *Minato Fair Ground*, 1-5 Tanaka 3-chome, Minato-ku ☏ 573 5381, is still in use. Other centres include *Osaka Foreign Trade Institute*, Otemai Usami Bldg, Tanimadi 2-chome 36, Higashi-ku 540 ☏ 942 2251; *Osaka International Trade Centre*, 3-51 Nakanoshima 5-chome, Kita-ku 530 ☏ 441 9131; and *Osaka Merchandise Mart*, 1-7 Kyobashi, Higashi-ku 540 ☏ 943 2020.

Emergencies

Hospitals The following hospitals have English-speaking staff: *Yodogawa Christian Hospital*, 2-chome Higashi Yodogawa-ku ☏ 322 2250, *Osaka National Hospital* Hoenzaka-cho, Higashi-ku ☏ 942 1331. For dental treatment try

the *Osaka University Dental Clinic*, Kita-ku ☏ 943 6521.
Pharmacies Drugs are available in hospitals. There are no 24hr pharmacies.
Police *Osaka Prefectural Police Headquarters*, 9 Otemaeno-cho, Higashi-ku ☏ 943 1234. There are English-speaking staff at *Sonezaki Police Station* ☏ 315 1234.

Government offices

Osaka Municipal Centre for Business and Trade ☏ 262 3261. *Osaka Municipal Office*, 3-20 Nakanoshima 1-chome, Kita-ku 530 ☏ 208 8181.

Information sources

Business information *British Chamber of Commerce*, c/o Price Waterhouse and Co, Osaka Centre Bldg, 68-3 Kita Kyutaro-machi 4-chome, Higashi-ku 540 ☏ 252 6791. *German Chamber of Commerce and Industry*, 23F Nakanoshima Centre Bldg, 2-27 Nakanoshima 6-chome, Kita-ku 530 ☏ 447 0021. There are also Indian and Korean Chambers of Commerce in Osaka. *Osaka Chamber of Commerce and Industry*, Uchihommachi, 58-7 Hashizume-cho, Higashi-ku 540 ☏ 944 6412, may be willing to help provide contacts. *JETRO*, 4F Bingomachi no Miura Bldg, 1-51 Bingomachi, Higashi-ku ☏ 203 3601.
Local media The *Mainichi Daily News*, based in Osaka, covers Kansai as well as national news. *Kansai Time Out* is a monthly magazine produced in Kobe, with features on life in Kansai and listings of films, exhibitions, etc.
Tourist information *Osaka Tourist Information Office*, 1-1 Umeda 3-chome (Osaka Station, East Exit) ☏ 345 2189, has information on sightseeing, accommodation and transport. For more detailed information and literature, contact the *Osaka Tourist Association, Trade and Tourist Dept*, Osaka Municipal Office, 4F Sumintomo Seimei Yodayabashi Bldg, 27 Okawa Cho Higashi-ku ☏ 208 8955. The Association produces three monthly publications – *Tour Companion, Meet Osaka* and *Japan Visitor's Guide*, which are available free; also available at major hotels.

Thank-yous

The top department stores are the appropriate place to buy a gift, and they will arrange delivery: *Takashimaya* ☏ 631 1101; *Daimaru* ☏ 271 1231; *Mitsukoshi* ☏ 203 1331; *Sogo* ☏ 281 3111.

SAPPORO

Area code ☎ 011

Sapporo is the capital of Hokkaido, Japan's "Last Frontier". A large island to the north of Honshu (the main island), Hokkaido was settled by the Japanese as late as 1869. With 22% of the country's total land area, it still has only 5% of the population, the majority pioneering Japanese, plus a few original inhabitants, the Ainu, Gilyak and Oroke. Hokkaido's spacious rolling pastures supply much of Japan's food. The main products include potatoes, sweet corn, wheat, beans and almost all of the country's dairy produce. Fishing and forestry are other key industries. More than 70% of the land is under timber, and the annual lumber production is a quarter of the nation's total. Sapporo is Hokkaido's main link with the outside world, and is the island's cultural, economic and political centre, and a focal point for winter sports.

Arriving

Although it is possible to get to Sapporo by ferry or train (a gruelling 17hrs 30min from Tokyo), most visitors fly in. From Tokyo the journey takes 1hr 30min and from Osaka 1hr 45min. The Tohoku Bullet Train line will soon be extended to Sapporo, cutting the train journey from Tokyo to just under 6hrs.

Chitose Airport

Chitose is a large, efficient, modern airport, handling one flight weekly from Honolulu and regular domestic flights. There are 24 flights a day from Tokyo, plus flights from major Japanese cities. Facilities include a good range of restaurants (open 7am–8pm) on landside, none on airside; a non-smoking VIP lounge; plenty of shops with limited local goods; a bank open Mon–Fri 9am–3pm, Sat–noon. JAL Cargo Services ☎ (0123) 26 0111. Airport information ☎ (0123) 23 0111 or (0123) 41 2111.

Nearby hotels *Nikko*, 4-4-4 Honcho, Chitose-shi 066 ☎ (0123) 22 1121 TX 949959. *Airport*, 6 Chiyoda-cho, Chitose-shi 066 ☎ (0123) 26 1155. *Chitoseya*, 2-17 Nishiki-cho, Chitose-shi 066 ☎ (0123) 23 2811.

City link The 45min taxi ride is the simplest route to Sapporo but there are alternatives.

Bus JAL and ANA operate bus services which depart at about 15min intervals, but only during plane arrival times. The bus stops at major hotels, reaching the station 1hr 10min after departure.

Train If you are staying near the station, or have little luggage, you might take the train. Departure times are shown in the airport, and the station is a few minutes' walk. The local train takes 50min, and the express 35min.

Car rental If you plan to drive in Sapporo, it is sensible to rent a car at the airport. There are branches of Budget, Nippon, Nissan, Toyota and Mitsubishi.

Getting around

Sapporo is conveniently laid out in a regular grid. Above and below Odori Park the streets are respectively numbered north (*kita*) and south (*minami*). Either side of Soseigawa Canal they are numbered east (*higashi*) and west (*nishi*). Although it is easy to find your way around, it is less easy to locate a particular place from the address. For example, 4 Nishi Kita-2 (west 4, north 2) refers to several blocks, and it is helpful to know the name of the building. The best way of getting around, apart from taxi, is a combination of subway and walking.

Subway Sapporo's subway, which opened in 1972, runs smoothly and quietly on huge rubber tyres. There

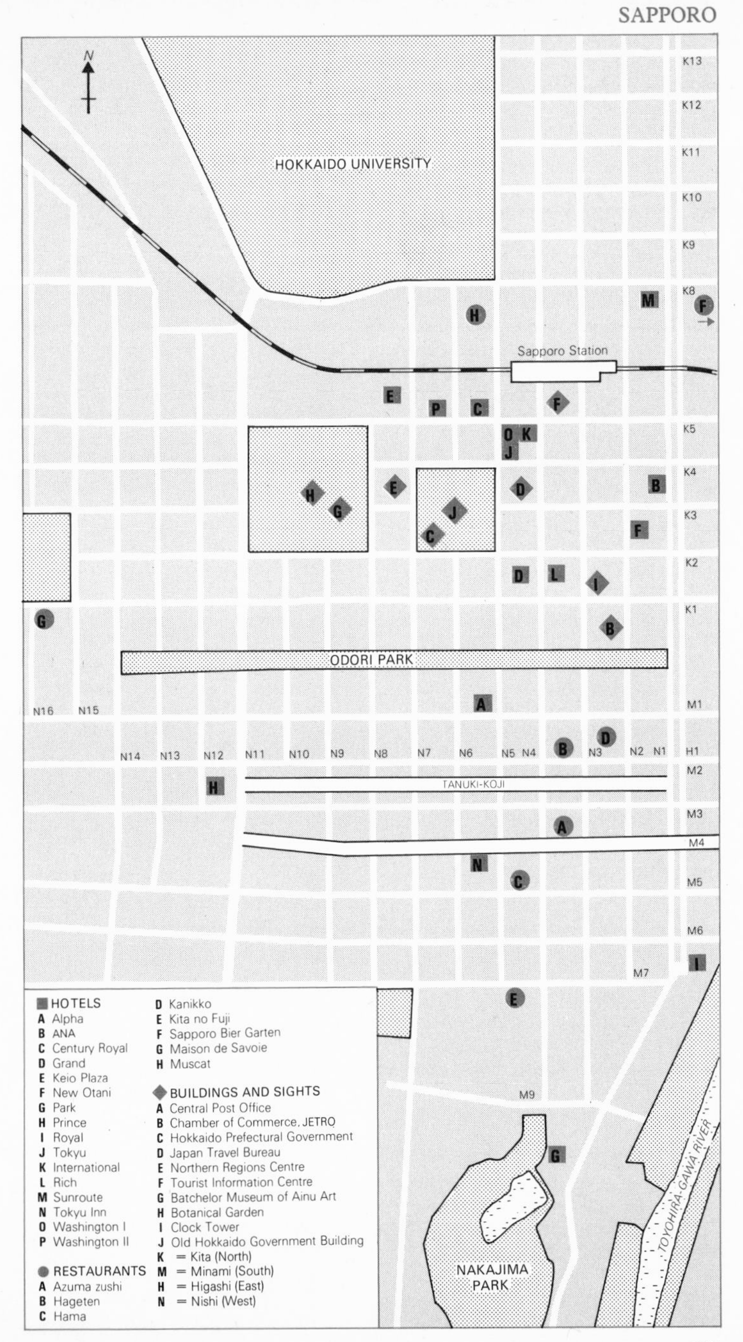
N
HOKKAIDO UNIVERSITY
Sapporo Station
ODORI PARK
TANUKI-KOJI
NAKAJIMA PARK
TOYOHIRA-GAWA RIVER
K13
K12
K11
K10
K9
K8
K5
K4
K3
K2
K1
M1
H1
M2
M3
M4
M5
M6
M7
M9
N16 N15
N14 N13 N12 N11 N10 N9 N8 N7 N6 N5 N4 N3 N2 N1
HOTELS
A Alpha
B ANA
C Century Royal
D Grand
E Keio Plaza
F New Otani
G Park
H Prince
I Royal
J Tokyu
K International
L Rich
M Sunroute
N Tokyu Inn
O Washington I
P Washington II
RESTAURANTS
A Azuma zushi
B Hageten
C Hama
D Kanikko
E Kita no Fuji
F Sapporo Bier Garten
G Maison de Savoie
H Muscat
BUILDINGS AND SIGHTS
A Central Post Office
B Chamber of Commerce, JETRO
C Hokkaido Prefectural Government
D Japan Travel Bureau
E Northern Regions Centre
F Tourist Information Centre
G Batchelor Museum of Ainu Art
H Botanical Garden
I Clock Tower
J Old Hokkaido Government Building
K = Kita (North)
M = Minami (South)
H = Higashi (East)
N = Nishi (West)

are two lines, which intersect at Odori. The north-south Nanboku Line passes through the station, Odori, Susukino and Nakajima Park; the east-west Tozai Line runs from the suburbs under Odori Park. Subway maps at stations and on ticket machines are in English and Japanese. Green ticket machines are for subway tickets only; tickets from yellow machines allow you to transfer onto the bus or streetcar. For more than five journeys, get a one-day pass (available at Sapporo JNR Station and Odori subway station), which may be used on subways, buses and streetcars.

Driving If you want to try driving in Japan, Sapporo is the place to do it. The roads are wide, not too crowded, and the grid system makes navigation easy. Outside the city, on Hokkaido's broad highways, driving is the ideal way to travel. The main rental chains have offices in the city.

Streetcar If you have time, the bumpy streetcar does a long loop around the south of the city, from Odori back to Susukino, and is useful for out-of-the-way places.

Train JNR lines run out to the suburbs from Sapporo Station.

Bus The extensive bus network is best avoided unless you are feeling adventurous.

Area by area

At the city's centre is *Odori Park*, a long, narrow expanse of lawns and fountains. The main business area extends from here north to the station: full of modern offices, hotels and banks, it is often called "Little Tokyo". The Prefectural Assembly and Sapporo's top hotel, the Grand, are here. North of the station are the grounds of Hokkaido University. The main shopping area stretches south of Odori Park, while under the park is a vast shopping arcade. Farther south is *Susukino*, the bar and restaurant area, and beyond that *Nakajima Park.*

The suburbs

The better residential areas are around Maruyama, in the hills west of the city. The most exclusive district is Miyanomori, farther to the west.

Hotels

The Grand, opened in 1934, is Sapporo's oldest and finest Western-style hotel. More recent competitors include the Park and the Royal, both built in 1964, and many newer hotels, some of them built for the 1972 Winter Olympics. High season in Sapporo is from May to October, at the New Year and during the February Snow Festival. Room rates drop by as much as 60% during the off-season.

Alpha ¥¥¥

5 Nishi, Minami-1, Chuo-ku 060
☎ 221 2333 TX 935345 • Okura • 145 bedrooms, 2 suites, 4 restaurants, 2 bars, 1 coffee shop/tea room

A relatively small hotel right in the centre of the city, the Alpha is very popular with visiting foreign executives. It offers the fine service to be expected of an Okura hotel, with a distinct individual style. The rooms are spacious, designed for living in, not just sleeping, with elegant rattan furniture. There is a cinema and the Sapporo branch of the Playboy Club, which doubles as a spaghetti house by day. La Rouge (see *Bars*) is the best bar in town. Concierge, beauty salon, limited hotel parking • pool, sauna • 4 meeting rooms (capacity 10–500).

ANA ¥¥

1 Nishi, Kita-3, Chuo-ku 060
☎ 221 4411 TX 934712 • 468 bedrooms, 2 suites, 4 restaurants, 1 bar, 1 coffee shop

This is not one of the better ANAs.

The lobby is small and cluttered, but has a lounge (rare in Japan) with a fireplace. The rooms are cramped but acceptable, with a desk and views over the city. Shopping arcade • sauna • 7 meeting rooms (varying capacities).

Century Royal ¥¥
5 Nishi, Kita-5, Chuo-ku 060
☎ 221 2121 TX 934439 • 327 bedrooms, 9 suites, 3 restaurants, 2 bars, 1 coffee shop
Near the station, this is a solid, respectable hotel showing signs of age. It is popular with Japanese business travellers. The rooms are vast and full of old-fashioned furniture. The revolving restaurant offers good views. Limited hotel parking • 10 meeting rooms (capacity 4–240).

Grand ¥¥
4 Nishi, Kita-1, Chuo-ku 060
☎ 261 3311 TX 932613 • Nikko • 569 bedrooms, 16 suites, 4 restaurants, 4 bars, 2 coffee shops
The Grand easily outclasses Sapporo's other hotels. Redecorated in 1986, it is a mini-city of four linked buildings, which are extremely elegant throughout. Most rooms have views over the city or onto the Japanese gardens. On the Executive Floor there is a small business salon with a secretary and an attractive lounge. The many fine restaurants and bars include the Old Saloon 1934 (see *Bars*), where executives gather in the evening. The excellent arcade has a branch of Mitsukoshi. Concierge, theatre and travel booking, arcade of shops, beauty salon • men's sauna • secretarial services, 21 meeting rooms (capacity 30–800).

Keio Plaza ¥¥
7-2 Nishi, Kita-5, Chuo-ku 060
☎ 271 0111 TX 933271 • 517 bedrooms, 8 suites, 7 restaurants, 2 bars, 2 coffee shops
The Keio Plaza was conceived on a grand scale, with the visiting foreign executive in mind, and offers many of the amenities of an international hotel. The lobby is an impressive place to meet clients, and the rooms are furnished for comfort. Concierge, travel bookings, car rental, shops, hairdresser, medical centre • health club with gym, sauna, massage room, pool • 13 meeting rooms (capacity 14–2,000).

New Otani ¥¥
1-1 Nishi, Kita-2, Chuo-ku 060
☎ 222 1111 TX 933650 • 340 rooms, 1 restaurant, 1 bar, 1 coffee shop
In a developing area near the station, the New Otani has a restrained but classy air, and is one of the more impressive places to stay. The lobby is elegant and the rooms carefully designed to make the most of the limited space. The staff – especially the concierge – are helpful and friendly. Concierge, shops • 7 meeting rooms (varying capacities).

Park ¥¥
3 Nishi, Minami-10, Chuo-ku 064
☎ 511 3131 TX 932264 • 227 rooms, 3 restaurants, 1 bar, 2 coffee shops
A subway ride from the city centre, the Park is a large and gracious hotel, overlooking Nakajima Park and its lake. The lobby is impressive, and the rooms spacious and tastefully designed. The staff are courteous and efficient. Ask for a room on the park side. Concierge, shops, beauty salon • 18 meeting rooms (capacity 10–1,000).

Prince ¥¥
11 Nishi, Minami-2, Chuo-ku 060
☎ 241 1111 TX 933949 • 345 rooms, 5 restaurants, 1 bar, 1 coffee shop
In the business district to the west of town, close to the mountains, the Prince is favoured by Japanese business travellers and sportsmen. Both lobby and rooms are rather idiosyncratic, with dark red carpets and ornate brocaded furniture. The staff are friendly and efficient and the concierge very helpful. A small business service centre is planned for

the near future. 24hr room service, concierge, small shop, hotel bus to winter ski slopes • reduced rates at hotel's golf course • 21 meeting rooms (capacity 20–1,000).

Royal ¥
1 Higashi, Minami-7, Chuo-ku 060 ☎ 511 2121 ⓉⓍ 932330 • 88 bedrooms, 6 suites, 2 restaurants, 1 bar, 1 coffee shop
Within walking distance of Susukino, the Royal is a small and friendly hotel. The rooms, refurbished in 1986, are spacious and quiet. The helpful manager, Toshihiko Abe, speaks good English and can provide business contacts and information. Concierge, travel bookings, hotel parking • concessionary rates at local golf club • 10 meeting rooms.

Tokyu ¥¥
4-1 Nishi, Kita-4, Chuo-ku 060 ☎ 231 5611 ⓉⓍ 934510 • 261 bedrooms, 2 suites, 2 restaurants, 1 bar, 1 coffee shop
A few minutes' walk from the station, the Tokyu is not one of Sapporo's top addresses. The lobby is looking a little shabby, but the rooms, decorated in the usual Tokyu style, are homely and spacious. Shopping arcade, florist, limited hotel parking • 6 meeting rooms (capacity 15–500).

OTHER HOTELS
International ¥ *4 Nishi, Kita-4, Chuo-ku 060 ☎ 222 3811 ⓉⓍ 933780* Opposite the station, it houses the ANA offices.
Rich ¥ *3-3-10 Nishi, Kita-1, Chuo-ku 060 ☎ 231 7891* A business hotel 5min walk from the station.
Sunroute ¥ *1 Nishi, Kita-7, Kita-ku 060 ☎ 737 8111 ⓉⓍ 932202* A very pleasant budget hotel on the wrong side of the tracks, 3min walk from the station.
Tokyu Inn ¥ *1-5 Nishi, Minami-4, Chuo-ku 064 ☎ 531 0109 ⓉⓍ 935301* At the centre of the Susukino entertainment district.
Washington I ¥ *1-4 Nishi, Kita-4, Chuo-ku 060 ☎ 251 3211* A large hotel opposite the station.
Washington II ¥ *6 Nishi, Kita-5, Chuo-ku 060 ☎ 222 3311* 4min walk from the station.

Restaurants

Like everything else in Hokkaido, business dinners are more relaxed than in mainland Japan; far from nibbling at tiny morsels of *kaiseki*, you will find yourself confronted with gigantic feasts. You can dine on lamb or beef from Hokkaido's luxuriant pastures, or on hairy crab, huge salmon or scallops, fresh from its coasts. To wash it all down, there is plenty of Sapporo beer, said to be the best in Japan.

JAPANESE
Azuma zushi ¥
3 Nishi, Minami-4, Chuo-ku ☎ 261 7161 • closed 3rd Tue of month • AE V
Located in the heart of Susukino, Azuma zushi first opened as a small sushi shop in 1890. Now, run by the founder's great-great-grandson, it has expanded into a vast four-floor restaurant, serving the best and cheapest sushi in Sapporo. Lunchtime and evenings, the pine counters and *tatami* rooms are packed with noisy groups of Japanese businessmen, often accompanied by Western colleagues. As well as sushi, Azuma zushi serves local seafood.

Hageten ¥
B1 Kataoka Bldg, 3 Nishi, Minami-2, Chuo-ku ☎ 271 2018 • closed Mon
Hage means "bald" and *ten* is short for "tempura" – a reference both to the menu and to the physical appearance of the founder and of his

grandson and successor, Mr Yanno. Highly recommended by the top hotels, Hageten serves many kinds of Japanese food, but the speciality is, of course, tempura, freshly cooked before your eyes. The clientele is largely professional, both Japanese and Western.

Hama ¥¥¥¥
3F No 8 Polestar Bldg, 4 Nishi, Minami-5, Chuo-ku ☎ *512 2541* • AE DC V
Much of Sapporo's top-level business entertaining goes on among the Roman statues and potted palms of Steak House Hama. Discreet tuxedoed waiters serve the distinguished clientele with best Kobe beef, cooked teppanyaki-style on steel plates at the table. The classical décor extends to the bar, where there is an enormous range of pre- and post-prandial liquors. This is a highly appropriate place to return hospitality.

Kanikko ¥
B1 Togashi Bldg, 2 Nishi, Minami-2, Chuo-ku ☎ *231 4080* • AE V
Enormous hairy crabs are caught between April and November around Shiretoko, in the farthest reaches of Hokkaido. At Kanikko you can eat them raw, baked, boiled, stuffed and fried, or minced and made into dumplings. There are tables and chairs for informal meals and *tatami* rooms for business dinners.

Kita no Fuji ¥¥
1F Keikyu Plaza, 4 Nishi, Minami-7, Chuo-ku ☎ *512 5484*
Kita no Fuji is the name of the sumo wrestler who owns this restaurant, and if you come here in August you can shake his enormous hand. Among the Japanese business community, this is a favourite place for celebrations and other formal dinners. To reach the dining rooms you walk around a full-size sumo ring. The restaurant serves *Chanko* – enormous casseroles heaped with giant prawns, crabs and scallops. This is the food that makes sumo wrestlers huge.

Sapporo Bier Garten ¥
9 Higashi, Kita-6, Higashi-ku ☎ *742 1531*
This beautiful old red-brick 19thC brewery, with its towering chimney, is packed out daily with feasting Japanese businessmen; you are very unlikely to be brought here for a meal. As well as beer, served in great mugfuls, the speciality of the house is Genghis Khan, heaps of Hokkaido lamb and vegetables grilled on a cast-iron plate at your table. For a few thousand yen, you are set loose for two hours to eat and drink as much as you can.

NON-JAPANESE

Maison de Savoie ¥¥
Odori Haim, 15 Nishi, Kita-1, Chuo-ku ☎ *643 5580* • *closed Mon* • AE DC
It is almost worth a special trip to Sapporo for Takashi Ohara's cooking. Mr Ohara spent ten years in France, studying mainly with Michel Guérard, and cooks *nouvelle* and traditional French cuisine, both superbly. There is an enormous and carefully chosen wine list, one of the best in Japan. The small, quiet dining room is extremely elegant, and there is a patio outside for warm summer days. The clientele includes local French residents and professional people; your Japanese hosts will be flattered if you entertain them here. There is also an excellent value five-course set lunch.

Muscat ¥
ST Residence Koei, 5 Nishi, Kita-6, Kita-ku ☎ *727 3100* • AE DC V
Muscat opened in 1955 and quickly established a reputation for the best Western food in Hokkaido. The foreign executives who used to patronize it have yet to find it in its new location on the other side of the tracks. Meanwhile it continues to delight the local business community with its excellent and economical French food.

Bars

Any Japanese executive on a trip to Sapporo is likely to be teased that what he is really interested in is the pleasures of Susukino. With 3,700 bars, restaurants, cabarets, nightclubs and strip joints, Susukino is said to be the liveliest nightlife area north of Tokyo. The hotel bars offer a more civilized alternative to Susukino's backstreets.

La Rouge

Alpha Hotel, 5 Nishi, Minami-1, Chuo-ku • *AE DC V*

The refined and classy La Rouge is where the city's top executives keep their bottles of whisky, chosen from 20 varieties available. It is also a favourite meeting place for Westerners, both resident and visiting. To accompany the drinks, there is a short menu of steaks, including Canadian prime.

Lorelei

B1 Keiai Bldg, 4 Nishi, Minami-4, Chuo-ku • *AE DC V*

In this popular beer cellar in the heart of Susukino, waiters in embroidered alpine waistcoats serve *rösti*, German potatoes and Sapporo beer. This is where local executives come to relax, and the resident German community is also in evidence. As night draws on, a band with violins and accordions may strike up German folk songs.

Old Saloon 1934

Grand Hotel, 4-Nishi, Kita-1, Chuo-ku • *AE DC V*

Many high-powered discussions are concluded around the tables of this dignified and comfortable bar, over a whisky and water or one of the enormous selection of cocktails.

Entertainment

In spite of its sizeable foreign population, Sapporo still feels a little like a frontier town. Visiting Japanese and overseas entertainers provide some culture but, apart from Susukino's colourful nightlife, local activities seem to be largely restricted to sports and the ever-popular Snow Festival. For current information, check *The Monthly Hokkaido* or *What's on in Sapporo*, or enquire at TIC or your hotel.

Ticket agencies Reserve tickets through your hotel or at Play Guide ticket agencies in major stores.

Theatre, cinema and music Japanese and international theatre companies, orchestras and rock bands often perform in Sapporo. *Mitsukoshi Cinema*, in the Alpha Hotel, shows English-language films.

Nightclubs To compensate for the lack of cultural activities, Sapporo has an enormous variety of nightlife. Before being dragged off to Susukino's more decadent establishments by your Japanese colleagues, you may wish to try the *Playboy Club* in the Alpha Hotel, a smart gathering place for executives, both male and female. In Susukino, the vast and glittering *Emperor*, Aoki Bldg, 2 Nishi, Minami-4 ☏ 511 0458, claims to be Hokkaido's top cabaret and the playground of the rich and famous. It offers live entertainment, *karaoke* and English-speaking hostesses. As for discos, *Maharajah*, 4F Suzuran Bldg, 4 Nishi, Minami-4 ☏ 261 8866, used to be rated Sapporo's best, and is still very popular. The smart set flock to *Exing*, 8F Dai-san Green Bldg, 3 Nishi, Minami-4 ☏ 511 3434, to nibble sushi and dance among Art Nouveau sculptures.

Shopping

Sapporo is the island's capital, and the quality of its shops reflects this. Several of the best Tokyo stores, including *Mitsukoshi*, *Parco* and the excellent bookshops *Maruzen* and *Kinokuniya* have branches here. These and other high-class shops are clustered at the east end of Odori Park, around Odori subway station. Sprawling for several blocks under the park is an underground shopping arcade, essential during the long, snowbound winter. There is another vast underground mall in the station area. *Tanuki-koji*, "Badger Alley", is a seven-block-long covered arcade parallel to Odori Park, a few blocks south. It is crammed with restaurants and shops, including antique, craft and tax-free shops. You can see the full range of Hokkaido crafts – especially wood carvings – at *Hokkaido Boeki Bussan Shinkokai*; *Seibansha*, 4 Nishi, Minami-7, has a particularly fine selection.

Sightseeing

Sapporo has few historic sights. Its main attractions are the fascinating relics of the Ainu culture and the wide open spaces of Hokkaido, which are nearby.

Batchelor Museum of Ainu Artifacts Dr John Batchelor, an English clergyman who lived here in the late 19thC, collected 20,000 Ainu and Gilyak artifacts, ranging from embroidered costumes to canoes. The collection is in the old wooden house that was Batchelor's home. *Botanical Garden. For opening times see below.*

Botanical Garden Around the pleasant lawns of the spacious Botanical Garden, a favourite place for strolling, are planted more than 4,000 varieties of Hokkaido plants. *8 Nishi, Kita-3. Open May–Sep, 9–4, Oct –3.30; closed Mon.*

Clock Tower The small white wooden Clock Tower was built in 1878 and now houses a museum of local history. *2 Nishi, Kita-1. Open 9–4; closed Mon.*

Hokkaido Museum of Modern Art This dramatic modern building houses a collection of modern Japanese art and hosts visiting exhibitions. *17 Nishi, Kita-1. Open 10–5; closed Mon.*

Mount Moiwa Mount Moiwa is Sapporo's nearest mountain, with views over the city and, on a fine day, across to the centre of Hokkaido.

Nakajima Park Nakajima Park, a beautiful park to the south of the city, contains a landscaped Japanese garden, a teahouse and a manor house which was once used by the Imperial family.

Old Hokkaido Government Building Familiarly known as the Red Brick Building, this is a stately Victorian mansion surrounded by lawns. *6 Nishi, Kita-3. Open 8.30–5.30, Sat –1.30; closed Sun.*

Guided tours

There are seven half-day bus tours covering sights within the city, run by the *Municipal Bus Company* ☎ 221 8875. *Chuo Bus* ☎ 251 8141 and *JTB* ☎ 241 5851 have day trips to scenic areas. *Sapporo Beer Company* ☎ 741 9191 and *Snow Brand Dairy Products Museum* ☎ 748 2289 are open to visitors.

Out of town

Hokkaido's spectacular mountains, steaming hot springs, lakes and rolling plains are within easy reach. If you have only half a day to spare, *Shikotsu-Toya National Park*, 45 miles/70km southwest of Sapporo, will give you a taste of Hokkaido's glories, although, as a popular tourist spot, it is fairly tamed. Within the park are Lake Toya, a circular volcanic lake, mountains, forests and volcanoes. Of the park's hot springs, *Noboribetsu* is one of the most famous in Japan. Its "Hell Valley" is a cauldron of boiling streams and sulphurous fumes but you can bathe in comfort at the spa. If you have a weekend free, head for the wildernesses east of Sapporo. The ugly town of Asahigawa is just over an hour on the express train from Sapporo: hire a car there or in Sapporo and head into *Daisetsuzan National Park*, Hokkaido's most spectacular, with five soaring mountains, ravines and spas, including the popular *Sounkyo*. Farther east, *Akan National Park* has volcanoes, forests and three magnificent lakes.

Spectator sports

Winter sports Sapporo made its name by staging the 1972 Winter

Olympics. In 1986 it hosted the first Winter Asian Games, and there is an annual International Ski Marathon in February. The *Teine Olympia Ski Ground*, Mount Teine ☎ 681 3191, is the main location for alpine, bobsled and toboggan events. Ski-jumping events take place at the 90m *Okurayama Ski Jump*, Maruyama Park, and there is a summer jump tournament every August at the neighbouring 70m *Miyanomori Ski Jump*, also in Maruyama Park.

Baseball June to August is the time for pro baseball; games take place in *Maruyama Baseball Stadium*, Maruyama Park ☎ 641 3015.

Keeping fit

Many of Hokkaido's visitors come here specifically for the sporting opportunities, and locals, too, are great sport enthusiasts. In winter you can take advantage of being near Japan's best ski slopes; the closest are only 30min drive away. Hokkaido's summers are pleasantly cool compared to the rest of Japan, and many Japanese come here for the hiking and mountain climbing.

Golf The rolling fields of Hokkaido are perfect for golf, and there are plenty of courses within easy reach of Sapporo – generally cheaper and less exclusive than on Honshu. As always, it is best to be introduced by your hotel or by colleagues. The 27-hole course at *Teine Olympia*, Mount Teine ☎ 681 3191 is especially popular. The sports-oriented Prince Hotel ☎ 241 1111 has its own course, the 36-hole *Sapporo-Hiroshima*, open to non-hotel guests.

Health and sports centres Of the hotels, the Keio Plaza has a health club with a gym and sauna, and the Grand, Alpha and ANA all have saunas. There is a large public sports centre with a pool in *Nakajima Park*. *ESPO*, 4-chome Plaza, 4 Nishi Minami-1 ☎ 251 6111, is a ten-floor 24hr sauna with boutiques, hairdressers, dance classes and a snack bar. It is very much *the* place to go.

Hiking There is plenty of superb hiking around Sapporo. If time is short, stroll up *Hitsujigaoka* or *Mount Maruyama*. For more taxing hikes, head for the *national parks* (see *Sightseeing*).

Jogging You can jog around *Odori Park* if you watch out for traffic, but it is better to join the students in the vast grounds of *Hokkaido University*.

Mountain climbing Nearest to Sapporo is *Mount Moiwa*. For serious climbing, the *national parks* (see *Sightseeing*) are the place.

Skiing Japan's best slopes are in Hokkaido. Those nearest to Sapporo are *Maruyama Park*, *Mount Moiwa* and *Mount Arai*. A little farther afield, *Teine Olympia*, Mount Teine ☎ 681 3191, the site of the 1972 Winter Olympics, is the most famous and therefore very crowded. *Niseko* and *Furano* are slightly farther still, and also popular. The Prince chain has hotels in all the ski resorts, and there are direct buses from the Sapporo Prince. The skiing season is from late November to mid-April.

Swimming There are pools in the Alpha and Keio Plaza, and a public pool in *Nakajima Sports Centre*.

Tennis Sapporo's tennis courts are not crowded or expensive. There are many courts in *Toyohiragawa*; reserve through your hotel.

Local resources

Business services

At present none of the Sapporo hotels has a business service centre, although the *Prince* is planning one. The *Grand* offers secretarial services. Nationwide companies providing business services are *Manpower Japan* ☎ 222 4881 and *Kao Co* ☎ 222 5661.

Photocopying and printing Arrange through your hotel or one of the business service companies. Some department stores, camera shops and stationers have photocopiers.

Secretarial Contact a business service company or *Career Staff* ☎ 221 0681, *Temporary Centre Corporation* ☎ 241 2171 or *Tempstaff* ☎ 222 5817.

Translation *TS International Co* ☏ 222 5817 provides interpreters; *Manpower Japan* has both translators and interpreters.

Communications

International couriers *Nippon Express Co*, 3-1-7 Odori Chiazashi, Chuo-ku ☏ 241 4764.
Post office *Sapporo Central Post Office*, 1 Higashi, Kita-6, is open Mon–Fri 9–7, Sat–5, Sun–12.30.
Telex and fax Major hotels offer both, as does *KDD Telecom Sapporo*, 5 Nishi, Kita-4 ☏ 241 6802.

Conference/exhibition centres

The main venues for conferences and exhibitions in Sapporo are the Alpha and Grand hotels and the *Northern Regions Centre*, 7 Nishi, Kita-3 ☏ 221 7840.

Emergencies

Bureaux de change Go to the major hotels, whose efficient services are open 7 days a week, from early until late.
Hospitals For an ambulance ☏ 119. The best hospitals in Sapporo are the *City General*, 9 Nishi, Kita-1 ☏ 261 2281, and the *Hokkaido University Hospital*, 5 Nishi, Kita-14 ☏ 716 1161. The *Emergency Dental Clinic*, 10 Nishi, Minami-7 ☏ 511 7774, is open in the evenings from 7–11.
Pharmacies Prescription drugs are supplied by hospitals.
Police In an emergency, dial 110 or go to the nearest *koban* (neighbourhood police box) or *Sapporo Central Police Station*, 5 Nishi, Kita-1 ☏ 241 3201.

Government offices

For municipal inquiries contact *City Hall*, 2 Nishi, Kita-1 ☏ 211 2032; for prefectural matters, *Hokkaido Government*, 6 Nishi, Kita-3 ☏ 231 4111. *JETRO*, 6F Hokkaido Keizai Centre, 2 Nishi, Kita-1 ☏ 261 7434/231 1122 ext 263, is a helpful source of advice and statistics.

Information sources

Business information *Junior Chamber Incorporated*, Keizai Centre, 2 Nishi, Kita-1 ☏ 231 1122.
Local media The *Mainichi Daily News* and *Japan Times* are the most useful of the Japanese English-language newspapers. For international news, foreign papers can be found in large bookshops and hotels.
Tourist information The *Tourist Information Centre*, B1 Sapporo Station ☏ 251 0828, is a source of essential information, maps and pamphlets. The *JTB*, 4 Nishi, Kita-3 ☏ 241 6201, is also helpful. To call TIC direct, ☏ 106 and ask for "collect call TIC". For detailed information and statistics, contact *Tourism Department, City of Sapporo* ☏ 211 2376 or *Sapporo Tourist Association* ☏ 211 3341, both at City Hall, 2 Nishi, Kita-1. *Hokkaido Tourist Association*, Keizai Centre Bldg, 2 Nishi, Kita-1 ☏ 231 0941, is the place for information on the whole of Hokkaido. *The Monthly Hokkaido* and *What's on in Sapporo* are useful guides to current events.

Thank-yous

For gifts, go to the top department stores, *Mitsukoshi* ☏ 271 3311 and *Matsuzakaya* ☏ 531 1111.

YOKOHAMA

Area code ☎ 045

For centuries a small fishing village, Yokohama rose to prominence as Japan's gateway to the West. After the centuries of isolation ended in the mid-19th century, it was through the port of Yokohama that foreign merchandise, technology and ideas poured into the country. Foreign traders, diplomats and businessmen were allowed to settle here and formed a large community. Today, Yokohama retains its international flavour. It is Japan's largest trading port and third largest city, with a population of nearly 3m. It is also a commercial and industrial metropolis, with shipbuilding, engineering, automobile and petrochemical plants in the factory zone along the shore, and offices of many major international corporations. The city is now engaged in a major land reclamation project, the New Port City Plan. By the 21st century a large area of the harbour will be reclaimed, and a convention centre, housing, offices and cultural facilities will be built there.

Arriving

From Narita there is a half-hourly limousine bus service to Yokohama City Air Terminal, but it is probably as quick to make your way into Tokyo and take the train out. The entire journey will take more than 2 hours during rush hours. From Haneda either bus or taxi is a good way of making the 30min journey. Buses to YCAT and Yokohama Station depart every few minutes.

Railway stations

Travellers arriving from Tokyo should avoid the Bullet Train and take the Yokosuka (the fastest), Tokkaido or Keihin Tohoku lines direct to Yokohama Station. The Keihin Tohoku line will take you on to Kannai, the main business centre, and Ishikawa-cho. The private Toyoko line (as always, cheaper and faster than the JNR) connects Shibuya with Yokohama.

Shin-Yokohama Station, the Bullet Train station, is 5 miles/8km from Yokohama. Travellers coming from Nagoya and points west will arrive here. Change to the Yokohama line for the 7min journey to Yokohama Station.

Yokohama Station This vast complex leads directly into Takashimaya. There are several excellent restaurants here, including a branch of Tempura Tenichi. The station is the communications centre for the city, housing the bus terminal and subway line, as well as the JNR, Toyoko and Sotetsu lines.

Getting around

Getting to Kannai, which is likely to be your centre of operations, is a quick train journey from other points in Yokohama. From the station, most destinations are a short walk or an easy taxi ride away. There are good maps available, and it is easy to find your way around.

Train The Keihin Tohoku and Yokohama lines, from platform 3 of Yokohama Station, go to Sakuragicho, Kannai and Ishikawa-cho, and on west to Ofuna. Buy the cheapest ticket from the machine.

Taxis Hailing a cab on the street is easy. In the middle of the day it may be quicker to walk.

Subway There is a subway line from Yokohama to Kaminagaya, passing through Sakuragicho and Kannai, but it is fairly difficult to locate the subway in the busy maze of Yokohama Station.

Bus Even for old Yokohama hands, the buses are confusing.

Driving Driving through Yokohama's congested streets is not advisable. Nippon, Rentacar and Japaren have branches in the city.

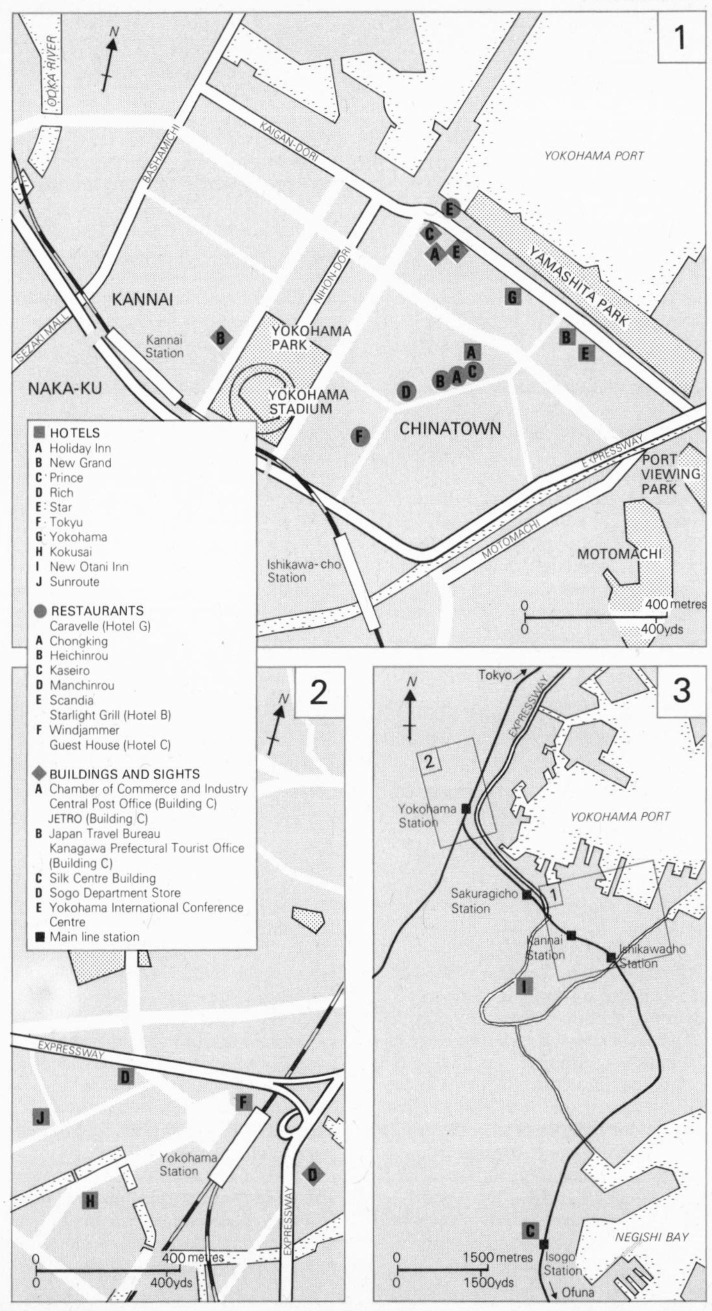
1
YOKOHAMA PORT
ŌOKA RIVER
KAIGAN-DORI
BASHAMICHI
NIHON-DORI
YAMASHITA PARK
KANNAI
ISEZAKI MALL
Kannai Station
YOKOHAMA PARK
YOKOHAMA STADIUM
NAKA-KU
CHINATOWN
EXPRESSWAY
PORT VIEWING PARK
MOTOMACHI
Ishikawa-cho Station
0 400 metres
0 400yds
HOTELS
A Holiday Inn
B New Grand
C Prince
D Rich
E Star
F Tokyu
G Yokohama
H Kokusai
I New Otani Inn
J Sunroute
RESTAURANTS
Caravelle (Hotel G)
A Chongking
B Heichinrou
C Kaseiro
D Manchinrou
E Scandia
Starlight Grill (Hotel B)
F Windjammer
Guest House (Hotel C)
BUILDINGS AND SIGHTS
A Chamber of Commerce and Industry
Central Post Office (Building C)
JETRO (Building C)
B Japan Travel Bureau
Kanagawa Prefectural Tourist Office (Building C)
C Silk Centre Building
D Sogo Department Store
E Yokohama International Conference Centre
Main line station
2
EXPRESSWAY
Yokohama Station
0 400 metres
0 400yds
3
Tokyo
EXPRESSWAY
Yokohama Station
YOKOHAMA PORT
Sakuragicho Station
Kannai Station
Ishikawacho Station
NEGISHI BAY
Isogo Station
Ofuna
0 1500 metres
0 1500yds

Area by area

Yokohama's wilderness of factories, office blocks and housing complexes extends north to merge with Kawasaki and Tokyo. To the south it lightens gradually beyond Totsuka and Ofuna. The hub of this sprawling mass is the Kannai area, with Yokohama Station as a secondary focus.

Yokohama Station area Around Yokohama's smart new station complex is a glossy shopping and entertainment area, with arcades, both under and overground, cinemas, and department stores, including Takashimaya, Mitsukoshi and the vast new Sogo.

Kannai means "within the barrier" and it was in this part of Naka-ku that foreigners were constrained to live. Foreign consulates are still located in this area, which has since become Yokohama's business centre. The square bounded by Kannai Station, Bashamichi shopping centre, the harbour and Nihon Odori boulevard contains the City Hall, airline offices, banks, hotels and the head office of the prefectural newspaper, the *Kanagawa Shimbun.* Many major national and international companies have offices here, particularly shipping companies such as Nippon Yusen, Eastern Shipping and Swires. Along Nihon Odori, the wide boulevard stretching from Yokohama Park to the harbour, are the Bank of Japan, the law courts and the prefectural offices. Just east are Yokohama's famous and colourful Chinatown and the fashionable shops of Motomachi.

The suburbs

Yokohama itself serves as a vast suburb, a "bedtown" of Tokyo, with one in ten of its citizens commuting to Tokyo to work. Those who can afford it live beyond Yokohama's urban sprawl, among the hills of Kamakura, farther down the Miura peninsula in Zushi, or out to the west in Fujisawa and Chigasaki.

Hotels

Yokohama's hotels have a lot of character. Some, particularly the still-prestigious New Grand, retain vestiges of the glamour that enticed foreign tourists by the boatload in the prewar years, though others can only be described as running colourfully to seed. For business travellers looking for a centrally located, modern luxury hotel, The Hotel Yokohama is the place to stay.

Holiday Inn ¥¥¥

77 Yamashita-cho, Naka-ku 231
☎ 681 3311 TX 3822758 • 185 bedrooms, 1 suite, 3 restaurants, 1 bar

The large Holiday Inn, with its cylindrical tower, is located close to the business district, on the edge of Chinatown, and the owner and many of the staff and customers are Chinese. While the ornate lobby with its inlaid stone floor feels distinctly Chinese, the bedrooms are decorated in standard Holiday Inn style and, apart from the view of Chinese neon shop signs, could be anywhere in the world. Hairdresser • pool, ladies' sauna • 1 meeting room (capacity 500).

New Grand ¥¥¥

10 Yamashita-cho, Naka-ku 231
☎ 681 1841 TX 3823411 • 191 bedrooms, 4 suites, 1 restaurant, 1 bar, 1 coffee shop

The New Grand, dating from 1869, is Yokohama's oldest hotel; the present building – a monolithic pile sprawling along the waterfront – was designed in 1927 by Watanabe Gin. Before the war, when Yokohama was the premier port of call for international travellers, the Grand was where they stayed, and in 1945 General MacArthur made it his headquarters. Miraculously, it remains largely intact – from the stone pillars with intricate Art Nouveau designs in the lobby, to the ornate headboards in the bedrooms and the huge European baths. The Starlight Grill and Sea Guardian bar (see *Restaurants* and *Bars*) are gathering places for Yokohama's top executives. Shops, florist, hairdresser • secretarial services, 7 meeting rooms.

Prince ¥¥¥
13-1 Isogo 3-chome, Isogo-ku 235
☎ 753 2211 • 36 rooms, 4 restaurants, 1 bar
Isogo is an industrial area 10min by train from central Yokohama, and the Prince is where its many companies house visitors. The hotel occupies the beautiful grounds of a former prince's palace. The old palace itself, with its layers of curving roofs and pagoda-like spire, perched on the very top of the hill, is now a stately restaurant (see *Restaurants*). Every room in the small, friendly hotel opposite has a balcony overlooking the garden. 24hr room service, concierge • outdoor pool • 11 meeting rooms (capacity up to 600).

Rich ¥¥
1-11-3 Kitasaiwai, Nishi-ku 220
☎ 312 2111 TX 3823761 • 204 bedrooms, 12 suites, 4 restaurants, 1 bar, 2 coffee shops
Of the hotels in the station area, the Rich is generally considered to be the best. The rooms are a good size and attractively furnished, all with balconies (unfortunately overlooking a busy road). There is even a tea ceremony room and small Japanese garden. No room service, international calls via hotel operator • 6 meeting rooms.

Star ¥
11 Yamashita-cho, Naka-ku 231
☎ 651 3111 TX 3823578 • 126 bedrooms, 2 restaurants, 1 bar, 1 coffee shop
One of Yokohama's newest hotels, the Star is squeezed in next to the New Grand, facing Yamashita Park. Several Australian companies house their visiting executives in its attractive, rather flowery rooms. Each room has a balcony overlooking the park and the harbour. No room service, international calls via hotel operator • 2 meeting rooms (capacity up to 50).

The Hotel Yokohama ¥¥¥
6-1 Yamashita-cho, Naka-ku 231
☎ 662 1321 TX 3822061 • Nikko • 165 bedrooms, 5 suites, 2 restaurants, 2 bars, 2 coffee shops
Many foreign travellers choose this modern luxury hotel. The American Consulate used to stand here, and its venerable chandelier hangs over the gleaming marble lobby. The bedrooms are a good size and well furnished; it is worthwhile paying a little extra for a room overlooking the sea. Caravelle (see *Restaurants*) is one of Yokohama's smartest French restaurants. Florist, beauty salon • 9 meeting rooms (capacity 8–350).

Tokyu ¥¥¥
1-1-12 Minami-Saiwai, Nishi-ku 220
☎ 311 1682 TX 3822264 • 211 bedrooms, 8 suites, 4 restaurants, 2 bars, 1 coffee shop
The Tokyu is in a prime location, right beside the station, and it is always crowded. The rooms are adequate but very small; take a semi-double rather than a single. Beauty salon • 10 meeting rooms (capacity 16–165).

OTHER HOTELS

Kokusai (¥) *2-16 Minami-saiwai, Nishi-ku 220 ☎ 311 1311 TX 3822536.* Superior business hotel near station.
New Otani Inn (¥) *4-81 Sueyoshi-cho, Naka-ku 231 ☎ 252 1311 TX 3823651.* Member of an excellent chain, a few minutes' subway ride from Yokohama station, in the Isezaki shopping area.
Sunroute (¥) *2-9-1 Kita Saiwai, Nishi-ku 220 ☎ 314 3111 TX 3823632.* A reliable chain hotel, 7min walk from Yokohama Station.

Restaurants

For an important dinner, many visiting businessmen, both Japanese and Western, play safe and go to the grand old Tokyo establishments half an hour away by train. However, Yokohama has many fine restaurants, patronized by the local business community. Most are in Chinatown and along the Bund (now Kaigan-dori), the old European area.

JAPANESE

Guest House ¥¥
Prince Hotel, 3-13-1 Isogo, Isogo-ku
☎ *753 2211* • AE DC MC V
If you want to eat Japanese in Yokohama, the Guest House of the Prince Hotel is the place to do it. Red carpeted stone steps lead to the entrance of this beautiful old building, which was once a prince's palace. Bowing waiters wearing black suits show you into the drawing room, where, drink in hand, you gaze out over exquisite landscaped gardens. Up a massive curving staircase are the dining rooms, both *tatami* and Western-style with crisp white tablecloths and brocade Regency chairs. Here you dine on *kaiseki*, fit for a prince.

NON-JAPANESE

Caravelle ¥¥¥
F13 The Hotel Yokohama, 6-1 Yamashita-cho, Naka-ku ☎ *662 1321*
• AE DC MC V
Much expense account dining goes on at the Caravelle, with its spectacular views over the harbour and live piano music. The cuisine is French, and fish and seafood are the specialities. A good place to entertain Japanese colleagues.

Chongking ¥¥
164 Yamashita-cho, Naka-ku
☎ *641 8288*
Gourmets in search of genuine Szechuan cuisine travel down from Tokyo to dine at Chongking, Chinatown's only Szechuan restaurant. The emphasis is on food rather than atmosphere, and the décor is austere by Chinese standards. Local businessmen often entertain clients here.

Heichinrou ¥¥
149 Yamashita-cho, Naka-ku
☎ *681 3001* • AE DC V
Chinatown's oldest and most celebrated restaurant, Heichinrou celebrated its hundredth anniversary by having a facelift. Its splendid new seven-floor building opened in April 1986 and makes a striking contrast to the surrounding clutter of Chinese restaurants, junk shops and cookie stalls. The regular clientele seem to like the elegant interiors with their spotlights and tasteful Chinese motifs, and the Cantonese cuisine remains superlative.

Kaseiro ¥¥
164 Yamashita-cho, Naka-ku
☎ *661 0661*
Kaseiro's atmosphere is best described as high-class Chinese. The thick red carpets are top quality, and the pale gold walls are adorned, not with extravagent carvings, but with tasteful framed black and white ink paintings. The Peking cuisine is the best in Chinatown, and the *tatami* rooms upstairs are much used for business entertaining.

Manchinrou ¥¥
153 Yamashita-cho, Naka-ku
☎ *681 4004*
Manchinrou is a Chinatown institution, with all the colour and flamboyance of Hong Kong. Ladies in red and gold silk *cheongsam* lead you past screens carved with dragons to the vast dining rooms full of ornate wooden panelling and hung with red paper lanterns. Here Western and Japanese businessmen, as well as Chinese families, crowd in for *yum cha* at lunchtime or feast on Cantonese delights prepared by the

23 Chinese chefs, ranging from sautéed frogs to bear's paw and whole roast piglet. Upstairs is a maze of *tatami* rooms with tiny Japanese gardens for formal dining.

Scandia ¥¥
1-1 Kaigan-dori, Naka-ku
☎ 201 2262 • closed Sun L
Japanese love the European atmosphere of Scandia, with its high ceilings, heavy draperies and wooden carvings. It is famous for its smorgasbord and serves French as well as Scandinavian dishes. The clientele is largely professional; this is a highly appropriate place to return hospitality.

Starlight Grill ¥¥¥
5F Hotel New Grand, 10 Yamashita-cho, Naka-ku ☎ 681 1841 • AE DC MC V
In the days when fashionable and wealthy Europeans strolled the streets of Yokohama, they used to dine at the top of the New Grand, looking out over the harbour. Today the restaurant, with its tasselled gold draperies and courteous white-jacketed waiters, still preserves the atmosphere of Old World gentility, making this a very suitable place to entertain Japanese colleagues. The cuisine is still French, though the chef is now Japanese, and there is an extensive wine list.

Windjammer ¥¥
215 Yamashita-cho, Naka-ku
☎ 661 0462 • closed Mon • AE DC MC V
American Jim Stockwell started Windjammer around 1970. It has since changed from a San Francisco-style dinner restaurant to French, serving traditional and *nouvelle* cuisine, but continues to be one of the most popular gathering places for Westerners, both resident and visiting. Many of the regular Japanese clientele came here first as guests of Western colleagues. The interior, with its curved wooden roof, is designed like the inside of a ship, and the atmosphere is quiet and congenial. (See also *Bars.*)

Bars

Yokohama has little nightlife of its own to compete with the bright lights of Tokyo, 30min up the line. The main bar area stretches from Sakuragicho to Kannai, but it caters mainly to foreign sailors. More civilized drinking can be found along Yamashita-cho.

Cable Car
200 Yamashita-cho, Naka-ku • AE DC MC V
Cable Car is the latest venture of Jim Stockwell, founder of Windjammer. The bar stretches the length of the enormously long and narrow room, designed to look like the inside of a San Francisco cable car. This is a suitable place to come either with Japanese colleagues, who enjoy the American atmosphere, or alone.

Sea Guardian
Hotel New Grand, 10 Yamashita-cho, Naka-ku • AE DC MC V
Once the haunt of fashionable young men-about-town, the Sea Guardian, Yokohama's most distinguished hotel bar, is now the gathering place of the city's top executives and their Western colleagues.

Windjammer
215 Yamashita-cho, Naka-ku • AE DC MC V
Windjammer is where Yokohama's resident Westerners come to relax and fashionable Japanese come to mingle with them. Like the restaurant upstairs (see *Restaurants*) it is designed to resemble the inside of a ship, with closely packed tables and plenty of atmosphere. There is jazz late in the evening.

Entertainment

With Tokyo just up the road, Yokohama's cultural facilities are inevitably limited.

Theatre, cinema and music Visiting international and Japanese performers frequently make their way down to Yokohama. The main venues are in the Kannai area and

around Yokohama Station. Several cinemas show English-language films.
Nightclubs Yokohama's most popular nightspot is *Cowbell*, 12F Yokohama Centre Bldg, 3-33 Masago-cho, Naka-ku; you can dine and dance until 4am.

Shopping

Most of Yokohama's glossiest shops are clustered in the arcades around and under the station. At the west exit are the prestigious department stores *Mitsukoshi* and *Takashimaya*, along with the popular *Joinus*, several shops selling high fashion, and a branch of the bargain camera chain, *Yodobashi Camera*. The shopping area to the east of the station is a more recent development, given a considerable fillip in 1985 by the opening of the vast new *Sogo*, one of the largest department stores in the world. Yokohama's other major department store is *Matsuzakaya*, in the Isezaki-cho shopping mall. Isezaki is the area in which to look for souvenirs and tax-free goods. Over beyond Chinatown, Motomachi is where the foreigners used to shop. It is now full of boutiques and antique shops.

Sightseeing

Chinatown is worth exploring and there are panoramic views of the port from the Port Viewing Park up on the Bluffs. The monuments, shrines and museums of Kamakura are only half an hour away.
Sankeien Garden Sankeien is an outstandingly beautiful Japanese garden, laid out by Tomitaro Hara, a millionaire silk merchant, at the turn of the century. Dotted around the grounds are some fine old buildings brought from all over the country, including one of the shoguns' villas, a 17thC tea house and an old thatched farmhouse. *293 Honmoku-sannotani, Naka-ku. Open 9am–4pm*
Silk Centre Silk was the main export of the port of Yokohama, and the fascinating museum in the Silk Centre records the history of silk in Japan. The Centre also houses the Tourist Information Centre and the offices of many of the major shipping companies. *1 Yamashita-cho, Naka-ku.*

Spectator sports

Baseball The main sporting event in Yokohama is baseball. *Yokohama Stadium*, Yokohama Park, Naka-ku ☎ 641 1421, was built to house the city's team, the Taiyo Whales and opened in 1978. The Whales are a Central League team.

Keeping fit

The first keep-fit facilities in Yokohama were built by its foreign residents – mainly the British, who could not endure the idea of going without a game of cricket. The Yokohama Country and Athletic Club (YCAC), which opened its doors in 1870, provided them with a pitch and continues to thrive.
Health and sports centres None of the Yokohama hotels has a sports centre. Of the public facilities, the venerable *YCAC*, 11-1 Yaguchidai, Naka-ku ☎ 623 8121, is the classiest. The *Yokohama Cultural and Athletic Hall*, 2-7 Huro-cho, Naka-ku ☎ 641 5741, is an indoor gym.
Jogging In the morning you can jog in Yamashita or Yokohama parks. There is an annual men's marathon in mid-November.
Swimming Besides the pools in the Prince Hotel and Holiday Inn, there are public pools in parks throughout the city. The most central is *Motomachi Park Pool*, 15 Nihon Odori, Naka-ku ☎ 661 0691. If you prefer a beach, head for the *Miura Peninsula*, rather than *Kamakura Beach*, which is fairly dirty.

Local resources

Business services

Among the Yokohama hotels, only the New Grand provides basic secretarial services. Of the commercial companies providing a reasonably wide range of business services the best are *Manpower Japan* ☏ 314 1222, *Kao Co* ☏ 319 8635 and *Temporary Centre Corporation* ☏ 681 0781.

Photocopying and printing All hotels provide photocopying services and will arrange printing for you. There are also photocopying machines in department stores and camera shops.

Translation Go to *JES* ☏ 313 3721. You can find an interpreter through *TS International Co* ☏ 314 6608.

Communications

International couriers *DHL* ☏ 201 1022.

Post offices The *Central Post Office*, Yokohama Station east exit ☏ 461 1385, is open longer than standard hours.

Telex and fax All hotels provide telex and fax services. In case of difficulty, contact *KDD Yokohama* ☏ 671 8051.

Conference/exhibition centres

Yokohama International Conference Centre, which opened in 1977, is administered by *Yokohama Association for International Communications and Exchanges*, 3F Sangyo Boeki Centre Bldg, 2 Yamashita-cho, Naka-ku ☏ 671 7128/7151.

Emergencies

Hospitals *Saiseikai Kanagawa-ken Hospital*, 6-6 Tomiya-cho, Kanagawa-ku ☏ 432 1111, has a 24hr casualty department, as does *Washinzaka Hospital*, 169 Yamate-cho, Naka-ku ☏ 623 7688. There are also a large number of English and German-speaking doctors in Yokohama; ask at your hotel. There are no dentists offering 24hr emergency treatment, but several who speak English or German. To call an ambulance ☏ 119.

Pharmacies Prescription drugs are supplied by hospitals. There are no 24hr pharmacies.

Police *Yamate Police Station* ☏ 623 0110 (ask for the Foreign Affairs Department).

Government offices

For enquiries about local government departments and services, contact *International Relations Division, the City of Yokohama* ☏ 671 2079.

Information sources

Business Information The *Yokohama Chamber of Commerce*, 2 Yamashita-cho, Naka-ku ☏ 671 7411, will provide information and help with contacts, as will *JETRO*, Silk Centre Bldg, 1 Yamashita-cho, Naka-ku ☏ 641 4990/3254.

Local media International and locally-produced newspapers are available in Yokohama. The *Mainichi English Weekly* also offers an English telephone service for an update on current news ☏ 322 1819. JCTV can be received in Yokohama; resident Westerners recommend *FM Radio Yokohama* (84.7mHz) for the British and American charts with no chat.

Tourist Information The *Yokohama Municipal Tourist Association*, Silk Centre, 1 Yamashita-cho, Naka-ku ☏ 641 5824/651 2688, provides maps, leaflets and assistance in English. Also helpful is *Yokohama Association for International Communications and Exchanges* (YOKE), 3F Sangyo Boeki Centre, 2 Yamashita-cho, Naka-ku ☏ 671 7128; its aim is to promote exchange of information between Japan and abroad, and to assist foreigners in Japan. YOKE publishes the monthly *Yokohama Echo*, which provides information on current cultural and sporting events. There is also a *Tour Companion* published by TIC, dealing specifically with events in Yokohama and Kamakura.

Thank-yous

An appropriate thank-you would be a gift-wrapped item from *Mitsukoshi* ☏ 312 1111, *Takashimaya* ☏ 311 5111 or *Sogo* ☏ 465 2111. To send flowers contact *Misugi Florist* ☏ 641 1187 or *Florist Sakata* ☏ 453 1120.

Planning and Reference

Entry details

The following requirements and regulations apply to visitors regardless of port of entry.

Documentation

Passports Required by all visitors and it must be carried at all times; those from New Zealand and most of Western Europe and South America need nothing else for short stays.
Visas Japan has mutual agreements with over 40 states. British, Irish, French, Swiss, West German and Austrian passport-holders can stay up to 180 days without visas. Most other West Europeans and South Americans can stay for up to 60 days, and New Zealanders for up to 30. US and Australian passport holders have to apply for a 60-day visa from a Japanese embassy or consulate but are exempted from the fee and should experience little delay. After entry, 60-day visas can usually be extended twice at an immigration office, up to a maximum of 180 days.
Health regulations Certificates of vaccination are needed only if entering from an area where typhoid and cholera are endemic. Those travelling via South-east Asia with stopovers en route should check the inoculation requirements of the countries concerned.
Driving licence If you intend to drive in Japan you will need an international driving licence.

Customs regulations

Personal effects and portable professional equipment not intended for sale are free from duty. Items, such as samples, can be sent separately by mail but a customs declaration form from your post office should be shown to customs officials on your arrival and to the Japanese post office upon collection. Parcels without a customs declaration are subject to duty.

Things you cannot bring in freely include pornography (defined as illustrations showing pubic hair, ie most men's magazines); some drugs; firearms and explosives; and some fresh foods, particularly fruit and vegetables from tropical countries. If travelling with prescribed drugs, carry a copy of the prescription or a doctor's certificate.
Customs allowances The duty-free allowances are: three 76cl bottles of alcoholic beverages; 400 cigarettes *or* 100 cigars *or* 500g of tobacco, *or* any combination with a combined weight of 500g; 57 grammes/2 fl oz of perfume; 2 watches worth less than Y30,000 each, including any in current use; and any other goods up to a total value of Y100,000.

Climate

Japan is a long, thin, mountainous archipelago and climate varies considerably, depending on latitude, topography and ocean currents. There are four main climatic regions.
The Pacific Coast region comprises Shikoku, northern Kyushu and eastern Honshu, including Tokyo, Nagoya, Kyoto, Osaka and Kobe. Summers are hot and humid, with temperatures consistently over 80°F. Summer officially lasts from June 1 to September 1 but the warm weather often continues to the end of October; wear light clothing and take extra shirts or blouses – you may need to shower several times a day. Winter temperatures in Tokyo can be very cold, similar to those in New York or Vienna. It often freezes but heavy snowfalls are uncommon. Annual rainfall is around 150cm. Spring and autumn are wettest but there is also a short rainy season, *tsuyu*, beginning in mid-June and continuing into July. Winter is the driest season.
The Japan Sea region, to the west of Honshu, is characterized by severe

winter snowfalls. Snow reaches depths of over 3m in places, making travel almost impossible.
Hokkaido, in the north, has bitterly cold winters, short, late springs and early autumns. It escapes the June rainy season and summer temperatures are 70–75°F.
Southern Kyushu is sub-tropical, with cool winters, hot, humid summers and an early spring and autumn. The rainy season begins at the end of May and continues through June. September is the season of typhoons.

Holidays

There are three periods to avoid in planning a business trip to Japan; the New Year (Dec 28–Jan 5), Golden Week (Apr 29–May 5) and Obon (a week in mid-August) when families visit the graves of their ancestors. At these times, hotels and trains are filled to capacity and most businesses and many restaurants and shops are closed. During the other national public holidays listed below, banks and many offices are closed but much else remains open.
Jan 1 *Gantan* (New Year's Day)
Jan 15 *Seijin-no-Hi* (Adults' Day)
Feb 11 *Kenkoku kinen-bi* (National Foundation Day)
Mar 20 *Shunbun-no-Hi* (Spring Equinox)
Apr 29 *Tenno Tanjobi* (Emperor's Birthday)
May 3 *Kempo kinen-bi* (Constitution Memorial Day)
May 5 *Kodomo-no-Hi* (Children's Day)
Sep 15 *Keiro-no-Hi* (Respect for the Aged Day)
Sep 23 *Shubun-no-Hi* (Autumn Equinox)
Oct 10 *Taiiku-no-Hi* (Health and Sports Day)
Nov 3 *Bunka-no-Hi* (Culture Day)
Nov 23 *Kinro kansha-no-Hi* (Labour Thanksgiving Day)

Information sources

In your own country

Business information In capital cities your government agencies are good sources of information. The *Japanese Embassy* will also provide background information and addresses for other organizations. The *Japanese Chamber of Commerce and Industry* and the *Japan External Trade Organization* (*JETRO*) have information on the economy, business and market entry.
Tourist information The *Japan National Tourist Organization* (*JNTO*) has offices around the world giving information on travel, accommodation, culture and sightseeing. Other contact points are *Japan Airlines* (*JAL*) and the *Japan Travel Bureau* (*JTB*), a private agency specializing in travel to and accommodation in Japan.

Money

Japan is very much a cash economy. Personal cheques are rare and credit cards have only recently become generally acceptable.

Local currency

Japan's unit of currency is the yen (¥). Coins used are 1, 5, 10, 50, 100 and 500 yen (though the Y1 piece is becoming rare). Banknotes are issued in denominations of 500, 1,000, 5,000 and 10,000 yen. Only yen may legally be spent in Japan; unlike the rest of Asia, US dollars are not accepted in cash transactions.
Acceptable currencies The currencies of most European countries and those of the USA, Canada, Australia and Hong Kong can be exchanged. However, the currencies of Taiwan and Korea will not be exchanged in Japan.

You can convert yen into foreign currency before leaving, but only US dollars are readily available. There is no limit on the amount of yen which can be taken out of Japan.
Traveller's cheques are the safest way to carry your money, although in Japan this should be weighed against the low incidence of crime and the time it can take to cash the

cheques. Yen cheques are more convenient than those denominated in other currencies as they can be cashed at major hotels and at big city stores that have a large foreign clientele. Outside the cities, only yen traveller's cheques will be readily changed by a bank.

Credit and charge cards
American Express (AE), Carte Blanche (CB), Diners Club (DC), MasterCard/Access (MC) and Visa (V) are accepted in the major hotels and Western restaurants and in high quality shops. Cards cannot be relied on to the exclusion of cash. Outside the main cities credit cards are often not acceptable, even by hotels, and you should check this when making reservations.

Changing money

On presentation of your passport, currency and traveller's cheques can be exchanged during office hours at the international airports, at banks that have a foreign exchange desk and at most major hotels, whose facilities are usually quicker and are open longer. Banks offer the best rate of exchange.

Banks

Most banks have a separate foreign exchange department, which is usually upstairs. Show your passport and you will be given a number and asked to wait in line. It can be a long wait. A number of foreign banks have one or more branches in Tokyo. Banking hours are Mon to Fri, 9–3; Sat, 9–12; all banks close on the 2nd Sat of the month.

Tipping

No tipping is the rule throughout Japan. If you really want to give money, put it in an envelope; this makes it a gift rather than a tip. If you wish to reward for exceptional personal service, a small token from your home country would be warmly received, though not expected; a sincere "thank you" (*domo arigato*) is all that is really required. Most hotel, bar and restaurant bills include a service charge. At airports and major stations, there is a fixed charge for baggage handling (between Y100 and Y250 per piece). Tariffs are always clearly displayed.

Getting there

Japan is well served by international flights. From Europe it is a long haul, although the introduction of some direct flights has cut the journey time from London, for example, to 11 hours. Most European flights still break the journey at Moscow, Hong Kong or Anchorage. Direct flights from New York take around 15 hours. Departing passengers must pay an airport tax of Y2,000.

Gateway airports

Most scheduled flights land at Tokyo's Narita Airport.
Narita This busy international airport, 40 miles/60km north-east of Tokyo, is served by most international carriers. Allow 2hrs plus to transfer to Tokyo's Haneda Airport for a domestic flight.
Haneda China Airlines is the only international airline which lands here. Situated to the south-west of Tokyo, Haneda is now the main domestic air terminal.
Osaka Regular flights arrive from Los Angeles, Hong Kong, Singapore, Bangkok and other Asian cities. The airport is convenient for Kyoto.
Nagoya Direct flights arrive from Hong Kong, Seoul and Manila.
Others Kagoshima on Kyushu has direct flights from Hong Kong, Singapore and several other Asian cities. Kumamoto (also on Kyushu) receives flights from Korea. A limited number of flights arrive at Niigata on Honshu, Fukuoka on Kyushu and Naha on Okinawa.

Getting around

For inter-city journeys executives travel either by train or by air. Flying, though more expensive, is the best option on longer trips, such as that from Tokyo to Fukuoka, or to cities not served by the Bullet Train. Driving is rarely a viable option.

Within cities, taxis are most convenient, although in the rush hour the subway may be quicker.

By air

There is a well-developed internal air network. The major carriers are Japan Airlines (JAL), All Nippon Airways (ANA) and Toa Domestic Airlines (TDA). Most major cities have an airport, although for Kyoto you have to fly to Osaka. Tickets can be purchased at all major travel agents in Japan. There are no discount tickets for internal routes, nor is there any type of air pass.

Train

The Japan National Railways (JNR) runs one of the most efficient and comprehensive railway networks in the world. Trains are frequent, punctual and spotlessly clean, and are categorized on the basis of speed. Fastest of all is the *Shinkansen* or Bullet Train, covering the 730 miles/1177km between Tokyo and Fukuoka in under 7 hours. Other trains include limited express (*tokkyu*), express (*kyuko*), rapid (*kaisoku*) and local (*futsu*). Private railway companies run slightly cheaper suburban services from major cities.

Fares are calculated according to distance, with surcharges on all journeys except on rapid and local trains.

Seat reservations are advised on long distance trains, particularly at weekends and on national holidays. Reservations cannot be made more than one month prior to the date of travel.

Tickets for short rides are sold from vending machines. If in doubt about the correct fare, buy the cheapest ticket and pay the difference at the Fare Adjustment Office at your destination. For longer journeys, ordinary and Green Car (first class) tickets can be purchased from the Travel Service Centres at stations or from travel agents. There is a range of discount tickets; fares depend on the day of travel, distance and length of stay.

Rail pass Foreign visitors can buy a Japan Rail Pass for ordinary or first class travel, which offers unlimited journeys at substantial savings for periods of 7, 14 or 21 days. The pass can be purchased only *outside Japan*, through a JAL office or authorized travel agency. They will issue a voucher to be exchanged for a pass in Japan.

Facilities Long-distance trains have dining or buffet cars with a wide range of fare. *Ekiben* – lunch boxes of Japanese food – and a good selection of snacks and drinks are available on most trains and on station platforms. Smoking is prohibited on commuter trains. Other trains have cars or seats allocated for smokers. *Shinkansen* trains are equipped with coin-operated telephones.

Information The Japan National Tourist Organization (JNTO) produces a condensed railway timetable summarizing all JNR's services and fares. The Travel Information and Service Centres at major stations will reserve tickets and supply information.

Taxi

Taxis are plentiful, clean and air-conditioned. Few drivers speak English and most have only a patchy knowledge of their city. Ask your hotel porter to brief the driver and to write down your destination in Japanese. For the return journey, carry matches or headed paper from the hotel to show to the driver. Allow plenty of time for your journey.

Hailing a cab Use your outstretched arm, fingers pointing slightly down; never whistle. When it's raining, or at night, you will see people hailing cabs with two, three or four fingers raised, indicating that they will pay that number of times the normal fare. Cabs show a red light when free, yellow when answering a radio or telephone call (20% surcharge) and green when the night surcharge is payable (20% surcharge between 11pm and 5am). Fares are on a meter that measures time and distance; expressway tolls are added. Drivers operate the passenger door by automatic control; stand clear as it opens and do not try to open or close it yourself.

Subway

Tokyo, Osaka, Nagoya, Yokohama, Fukuoka and Sapporo have extensive subway systems. Tickets are sold from vending machines at the stations. If you are unsure of the fare buy a minimum fare ticket (Y120) and pay the balance to the guard on the ticket barrier at your destination. There is no smoking on subway trains.

Driving

Car rental is rarely worthwhile because of the poor road system, traffic congestion and parking problems. However, if you plan an extended stay and have friends to help with the directions, contact one of the larger car rental chains. The car itself, rather than the driver, will usually already be insured, but check this. Drinking and driving is illegal, and the law is strictly enforced.

Roads Traffic jams are common during rush hours, weekends and holidays. The Japanese drive on the left and use conventional international road signs. The speed limit on expressways is usually 100kmph, on highways 60kmph, on most other roads 40kmph and in the cities 30kmph.

The *Japan Automobile Federation* (JAF) has reciprocal agreements with most automobile associations throughout the world; it produces a booklet giving details about Japanese traffic laws. Contact JAF at 3-5-8, Shiba-koen, Minato-ku, Tokyo ☎ (03) 264 2834.

Bus

City buses are frequent but often follow tortuous routes and display destinations only in Japanese. They offer a leisurely method of sightseeing and orientation, but should not be relied on for getting to a business appointment.

Hotels

The mid-1980s have seen an ambitious programme of hotel building. The number of hotels with at least rudimentary business service centres is increasing rapidly, and many hotels which do not yet have executive floors are planning them. However, the most prestigious and expensive hotel in town is likely to be the oldest, and this is where all high-ranking executives – or those who want to be seen as such – will be expected to stay. Choice of hotel is crucial to the impression you create in Japan, and money spent on high-priced accommodation should be seen as a worthwhile investment. Outside Tokyo, most hotels still cater largely to the needs of Japanese rather than Western business travellers; service is excellent but rooms are often cramped.

Styles and standards

Western-style Most business travellers (including the Japanese) stay in Western-style hotels. Service is always impeccable, and at the top end of the scale standards are very high. The new luxury hotels provide better business-support services than the older, higher status hotels and are gradually acquiring more prestige.

Japanese-style Every hotel has a few Japanese rooms, largely unfurnished except for the beautiful straw tatami mats on the floor on which your bedding is laid out at night, and a deep Japanese bath. A *ryokan*, or Japanese-style inn, offers a relaxing and highly aesthetic experience. Your tatami-matted room, complete with television, will probably overlook a Japanese garden of stones and moss. The price of the room includes meals, served in your room by your personal maid; there is no restaurant or bar. A *ryokan* is ideal for a weekend off but is not suitable for working in.

Business and budget hotels The traveller on a tight budget can follow the lead of many Japanese businessmen and use a business hotel. These are designed for sleeping, not working, and do not offer the facilities of a full-scale hotel. The majority of the rooms are singles and are extremely small.

The accommodation

Public areas Lobbies are vast and often extravagantly splendid, if somewhat vulgar. There is usually no lounge as such, but there will be at least one coffee shop or tea lounge suitable for an informal discussion. Hotel restaurants are often the most highly-rated places to eat in town, while the hotel bar is a favoured meeting place for local businessmen. Most hotels have shops or a shopping arcade, sometimes with branches of major department and luxury stores.

Bedrooms The standard hotel bedroom could charitably be described as compact; very few are big enough to work in comfortably. Most business travellers prefer a twin or double room at a reduced price for single occupation. From some hotels you may have to make international calls via the front desk.

Prices

In a luxury Tokyo hotel, you can expect to pay more than Y17,000 a night for a single room (exclusive of meals), and in the best hotels you will be paying as much as Y23,000. Prices are considerably lower outside Tokyo; budget for Y10,000 for a single in a top hotel. A room in a business hotel will cost Y8–9,000 in Tokyo, Y5–7,000 elsewhere. A 10% tax and 10% service charge will be added to your total bill (including meals and drinks at the hotel). *Ryokans* vary widely in price, but are generally more expensive than other hotels; the average cost is Y30,000 per head, inclusive of dinner and breakfast.

Few hotels offer corporate rates but many offer special executive packages, at an inclusive price which covers extras such as breakfast.

Making reservations

You should make reservations at least a week in advance. During the busy holiday periods – New Year, Golden Week in May and the first two weeks of August – hotels are fully booked weeks, if not months, beforehand. Reservations can be made directly by telephone or, for the larger chains, through booking offices in the USA and Europe.

Major hotel chains

Many Japanese hotels belong to chains. The major airlines, ANA and JAL, are opening enormous luxury hotels in every city. The established chains, from Hilton at the top, through Prince, down to Tokyu, are also building bigger and better hotels.

ANA *ANA Enterprises Ltd, Kasumigaseki Bldg, 3-2-5 Kasumigaseki, Chiyoda-ku, Tokyo 100* ☎ *(03) 580 2591/281 0311.* USA ☎ *New York (212) 466-1188.* UK ☎ *London (01) 583 0272.*

ANA (All Nippon Airways) opened several super-deluxe hotels in 1986, bringing their total of non-resort Japanese hotels to 13. These hotels are built on the American scale, with abundant luxury but little Japanese charm, and offer every conceivable service, including business service centres and foreign staff.

Daiichi *1-2-6 Shinbashi, Minato-ku, Tokyo* ☎ *(03) 501 5161.*

Popular among Japanese businessmen on a tight budget, these superior business hotels have tiny, cramped rooms but are conveniently situated near the business and entertainment areas of major cities.

Hilton *6-6-2 Nishi-Shinjuku, Shinjuku-ku, Tokyo 160* ☎ *(03) 344 5111/262 8981.* USA ☎ *New York*

(212) 697-9370. UK ☏ *London (01) 379 6277.*
Hilton has hotels in Tokyo and Osaka, and one planned for 1988 in Nagoya. All are up to the usual Hilton standards and are well suited to the international traveller, with executive floors and comprehensive business service centres. The EBS (Executive Business Service) Programme ensures preferential reservations, express check-out, and use of special business facilities.
Miyako (Kintetsu chain) *1-1-50 Shiroganedai, Minato-ku, Tokyo 108* ☏ *(03) 447 3111.*
The 15 Miyako hotels, mostly in the Osaka/Kyoto area, vary widely in standard, from Kyoto's finest hotel to rather run-of-the-mill first class hotels. One can, however, expect excellent service and a certain quiet dignity from any Miyako hotel.
New Otani *4-1 Kioi-cho, Chiyoda-ku, Tokyo 100* ☏ *(03) 265 1111.* USA (toll-free) ☏ *(800) 252-0797.* UK ☏ *London (01) 731 4231/3.*
Any New Otani can be confidently assumed to be one of the best hotels in town, unfailingly elegant in décor, with efficient and pleasant staff. It will often be the immediate choice of visiting foreign executives. In addition to Tokyo's enormous New Otani, there are 13 others, including some budget New Otani Inns. The New Otani Club offers preferential reservations and discounts.
Nikko *2F Daiichi Koda bldg, 2-4-10 Yaesu, Chuo-ku, Tokyo 104* ☏ *(03) 281 0783.* USA (toll-free) ☏ *(800) 221-4862.*
Japan Airlines has built only a few Nikko hotels as yet, of a style and standard similar to the ANA hotels; but many of the best hotels in Japan come under the umbrella of Nikko Hotels International, bookable through JAL.
Prince *8F Prince Promenade PePe, 1-30-1 Kabuki-cho, Shinjuku-ku, Tokyo 160* ☏ *(03) 209 8686.* USA (toll-free) ☏ *(800) 223-2094.* UK ☏ *London (01) 370 3484.*
Prince hotels are all different, and include some of the most spectacular modern architecture in Japan. Standards vary widely; the Tokyo, Akasaka and Takanawa Prince hotels are among the best in Tokyo, but others are definitely second rate. There are preferential rates and privileges for members of the Prince Club International.
Tokyu *6-6 Koji-machi, Chiyoda-ku, Tokyo 102* ☏ *(03) 264 4436.* USA (toll-free) ☏ *(800) 822-0016.* UK ☏ *London (01) 493 2585.*
Every major city has a Tokyu hotel, built to a pattern several years ago and looking a little the worse for wear, but with a comfortably familiar décor and good service at a reasonable price. Apart from the Capitol Tokyu – considered by some to be the best hotel in Tokyo – the 18 Tokyu hotels are first class rather than deluxe.

Business hotel chains

The following chains have a good reputation among Japanese businessmen and offer cheap, good quality accommodation throughout Japan, at a consistent standard.
Tokyu Inn ☏ *(03) 406 0109.* Very pleasant business hotels, to be found in every major city.
Mitsui Urban ☏ *(03) 279 5711.* Has one of the best reputations among business hotel chains.
Sunroute ☏ *(03) 375 3211.* An extremely economical chain with about 50 small, friendly hotels, including four in Tokyo; the rooms, though small, are pleasant.

Our recommended hotels

The hotels which we have selected are of a consistently high standard, conveniently located for the major business areas of each city, and particularly suitable for travelling foreign executives. We have included hotels ranging in style and price from the top hotels of each city, including some of the world's best, down to cheaper but reliable hotels designed specifically for the business traveller.

Standard facilities

Almost all hotels have at least one restaurant and a bar. Unless otherwise stated, the following facilities are standard at all hotels given full entries.

Credit cards Major credit cards are accepted. Check when booking.

Facilities Central heating; air conditioning; western bed and furniture, including desk; attached bathroom with a bath and/or a shower and a Western toilet; television; radio; direct dial telephone; refrigerator; tea-making facilities; cotton dressing gown and slippers.

Services Room service (24-hr service is unusual); laundry service.

Shops Several shops, including a gift shop.

Additional facilities

Good hotels will have an English-speaking concierge to make travel, restaurant and entertainment bookings. Massages are often available, conducted by a little old lady in your room. Many bedrooms have a mini-bar. Hotel parking is often very limited.

Sports facilities Many top hotels have indoor or outdoor pools and a sauna. A few have health clubs with gyms, whose facilities are available to hotel guests at special rates.

Business facilities

As yet few Japanese hotels have full business service centres. Unless otherwise stated, all hotels given full entries offer telex, fax and photocopying at the front desk. Other facilities – often open to non-hotel guests – are as follows.

Secretarial services This usually means a desk operated by a secretarial firm. They generally provide typing, translation and interpreting. Word processing, typewriter rental and business card printing may be available. All services are at expensive Japanese commercial rates.

Business service centre with limited facilities A small centre provided by the hotel for the use of hotel guests. Facilities similar to those offered by secretarial firms are usually complimentary or offered at discounted rates.

Business service centre with extensive facilities A centre based in a sizeable lounge, equipped with a library of business reference books and a variety of facilities, likely to include a photocopier, a Kyodo News Service printer, typewriters and word processors. There will be high calibre secretarial assistance, which will include introductions to business contacts and business consultancy, as well as normal secretarial services. Meeting rooms with audiovisual and simultaneous translation facilities are usually available.

Meeting rooms Most hotels have at least one large meeting room, used for banquets and conventions. Many also have smaller rooms suitable for business meetings.

Other hotels

Most hotels under this heading are economy hotels which are members of business hotel chains (see earlier). They are usually located near the station and business areas. Rooms, all with small private bathroom, will be cramped but pleasant. There is usually no room service and international calls must be made via the hotel switchboard. Shops are limited and rooms will not have a refrigerated mini-bar.

Price band system

The price symbols used in the *City by city* section have the following meanings:

¥ up to Y8,000
¥¥ Y8,000 to Y12,000
¥¥¥ Y12,000 to Y16,000
¥¥¥¥ Y16,000 to Y20,000
¥¥¥¥¥ over Y20,000

Restaurants

Eating out plays a pivotal role in cementing a Japanese business relationship. The meal will begin formally with toasts and speeches, and may end somewhat informally after quantities of sake have been consumed. You may be certain that the restaurant has considerable local prestige, and that your host is well known there. The bill may not be presented, but will be discreetly added to his account.

The range of restaurants

In selecting a restaurant, matters such as status and expense come well before the quality of the cuisine; it would not do to take an important guest to a restaurant that offered superb cuisine at a moderate price. Many of the most expensive restaurants are in hotels, and this is where much business entertaining takes place. *Ryotei* are the classiest traditional restaurants, patronized by politicians and businessmen, and are highly exclusive and expensive. You cannot reserve a room unless you are introduced by a regular patron.

In Tokyo, with its 77,000 restaurants, you can probably dine better than anywhere else in the world, on any cuisine you fancy. Outside Tokyo, you are likely to be eating Japanese (including the local specialities), Chinese and hotel French, although fine French restaurants are springing up in the most unlikely places.

For status and cost, French cuisine still holds sway, and is the safest bet for entertaining your hosts. The Japanese frequently entertain in Chinese restaurants, which have small private rooms with revolving tables and are particularly suitable for parties. Foreign cuisines are usually adapted to Japanese tastes, and can be disappointingly bland, especially in hotels. For a working lunch, it is worthwhile remembering that a Japanese meal takes less than an hour to serve and eat.

Prices An excellent meal at a small local restaurant will cost Y1,000–Y1,500, whereas business entertaining can cost Y10–40,000 a head. All restaurants offer a set lunch which is extremely good value, often a fraction of the cost of the same meal in the evening. Service charge and tax (about 10% each) will be added to your bill in larger restaurants and hotel restaurants.
Opening hours Meals are taken early; lunch will be from 12–2pm, and dinner around 6 or 7pm. Outside Tokyo, most restaurants are closed by 9pm.

Japanese cuisine

You may be faced with a plate of raw crab's brain or a dish of large prawns, very much alive, and your Japanese hosts will be impressed if you can down them without flinching. But generally Japanese food does not make such demands.

Traditional Japanese cuisine is the inspiration for *nouvelle cuisine*, designed to delight, and only incidentally to fill the stomach. The chef composes each dish like a picture, and you are expected to pause and admire before eating. Simple, natural flavours are preferred, and ingredients of the highest quality, particularly fish, are often served raw. The meal usually ends with rice, pickled vegetables and miso soup made from soya bean paste.

The following are the main Japanese cuisines and dishes that you are likely to encounter.
Fugu is blowfish, whose liver contains a poison which causes instant death. It can be prepared only by licensed chefs. It is considered one of the great delicacies and is commensurately expensive. Fugu restaurants serve fugu sashimi – transparently thin slices of fugu spread out like a flower – and fugu simmered with vegetables. The season is November to March.
Kaiseki-ryori is the cuisine of the *ryotei*, although also served, less

expensively, in more accessible establishments. It is Japan's *haute cuisine*. A *kaiseki* meal is a succession of minuscule works of gastronomic art, including portions of raw and charcoal-grilled fish, a delicately flavoured soup and fresh vegetables. The china, surroundings and service are invariably beautiful.

Sashimi is the choicest parts of the best quality fish, sliced just before eating and served with soy sauce mixed with a little stingingly hot *wasabi* (a form of horseradish). It appears in most Japanese meals. Sometimes the fish's head, tail and skeleton are decoratively served with its finely sliced flesh.

Sukiyaki, shabu shabu Until the end of the last century, meat-eating was taboo in Japan, and both sukiyaki (the finest beef, sliced paper-thin, sautéed at table with a rich sauce) and shabu shabu (slices of beef swished in boiling broth) are recent inventions.

Sushi The best sushi is made from the finest rice, lightly flavoured with vinegar, topped with a slice of fresh raw fish. Sushi is a meal in itself, served in sushi bars. Hold the sushi with your fingers, with the fish underneath, and dip it lightly in soy sauce before eating. There are delicious alternatives such as *hamachi* (young yellowtail), *katsuo* (bonito), *hotategai* (scallop), *ama-ebi* (raw shrimp), *uni* (sea urchin roe) and *anago* (grilled conger eel).

Tempura is seafood and vegetables deep-fried in a light, crisp batter. It should be freshly made before your eyes and eaten immediately, dipped in a light sauce.

Teppanyaki A teppanyaki restaurant is a Japanese steak house. Customers sit around a large counter topped with a gleaming steel plate, on which the chefs fry prime steaks and vegetables to your taste.

Unagi Freshwater eel, grilled over charcoal and brushed with a sweet sauce, is a rich and succulent dish, served in summer for its purported energy-giving and aphrodisiac properties.

Yakitori is a favourite snack of the Japanese businessman on his way home. It is chunks of chicken (including the gizzard, liver and tongue) grilled on bamboo skewers over charcoal and basted with a rich sauce.

Our recommended restaurants

The restaurants selected for each city have been chosen with the needs of the business traveller in mind. They offer a variety of cuisines for different occasions. They include top restaurants which you are unlikely to visit independently but to which you may be invited; restaurants oriented towards business entertaining, where you can confidently take your Japanese colleagues; and restaurants to be visited for their cuisine and ambience. Among our restaurants are those generally agreed to be the best in town, as well as the more idiosyncratic favourites of Western executives. All have an excellent reputation for both their cuisine and their service. They are convenient for the major hotels and business areas, and, importantly, it is usually possible to communicate without speaking Japanese.

All restaurants accept major credit cards, except in the few cases noted. You will usually find a public telephone, although it is seldom quiet or private. Some restaurants are closed on Mondays, and Friday nights are often busy. Most restaurants close over New Year (Dec 31–Jan 3). Reservations are always recommended, especially for entertaining.

Price band system

The price symbols used in the *City by city* section have the following meanings:

¥ up to Y4,000
¥¥ Y4,000 to Y8,000
¥¥¥ Y8,000 to Y12,000
¥¥¥¥ Y12,000 to Y16,000
¥¥¥¥¥ over Y16,000

Bars

Alcohol plays a major part in offsetting the stresses of the executive lifestyle. A recent survey showed that two-thirds of Japanese men get drunk at least once a week and one in eight does so daily. The Japanese are very tolerant of even extreme drunkenness. The most common toast in Japanese bars is "*Kampai*".

Solo drinkers should head for their hotel bars, away from compulsory sing-alongs, hidden extras and students practising their English.

Women will feel most comfortable in hotel, *nomiya* and *karaoke* bars. Beer halls and hostess clubs tend to be all-male preserves. In recent years there has been a dramatic increase in the number of women drinking. All female groups are not uncommon.

Opening hours Bars open from midday to the early hours. Alcohol is on unrestricted sale from restaurants, shops and vending machines.

Five types of bar

Hostess clubs are expensive. The services of the hostess who pours your drink will go on the bill. Characterized by low lighting, soft music and pleasant décor, hostess bars are frequented by those in the upper echelons of business.

Hotel bars are popular places to meet colleagues for an after-work cocktail. Bars in the older prestigious hotels have great charm and atmosphere, while those in the modern hotels tend to be more functional. Tariffs are usually displayed in English.

Nomiya are cheaper, ethnic bars. Lively, noisy and popular with the young, they are easily recognized by the red lantern hanging outside. Their décor is simple and the drinks are limited mainly to sake and beer. Many display tariffs in Japanese only.

Karaoke bars can be either Western or Japanese in style. Customers are invited to take the microphone (you usually have little

Understanding sake

Sake, pronounced "sah-kay", is the national drink. It is a potent rice wine that is served in bars and restaurants, either hot or cold, in thimble-sized cups called *sakazuki* and poured from a small clay vessel known as a *tokkuri*. It can seem deceptively innocuous.

Sake has no vintage years; it is best drunk young, within three months of being bottled, or at the longest within the year. The purest sake is *junmaishu*; *honjoshu* is also fine sake. *Sanbaizoshu* is the lowest quality. In a restaurant you will probably be served *amakuchi*, sweet sake; connoisseurs demand *karakuchi*, dry sake.

Reading a sake label Most sake bottles have a small oval label on the neck. At the top is the grade: *nikyu* (second grade), *ikkyu* (first grade) or *tokkyu* (special). This is not a sure guide to quality, since sharp brewers may label their special as second grade to avoid tax. In the middle of the label is the alcohol content, and at the bottom the ingredients: the shorter the list, the better the quality.

Regional sakes The best of the country's 2,500 breweries are reckoned to be in the west and north, although most people swear by their local sake. Sake from the ancient port of Nada is said to be "masculine", clean and vigorous to the palate. Fushimi, to the south of Kyoto, produces a delicately "feminine" sake. Akita in the north and Hiroshima also produce excellent sake.

Recommended sakes The best brands are Tamano-hikari, Taruhei and Uragasumi. For the connoisseur, the following are excellent (regions in brackets). Dry: Madonoume (Saga). Sweet: Goshun (Osaka). Complex: Shikizakura (Tochigi), Kikuhime (Ishikawa), Hira Izumi (Akita).

choice) and sing a favourite song accompanied by a backing tape. It is useful to have a Frank Sinatra or Beatles standard in your repertoire.
Beer halls are popular for company outings and are frequently overrun with inebriated businessmen. Many department stores turn their roofs into beer gardens in summer.

Popular drinks

Locally brewed lager beers account for 70% of the alcohol consumed in Japan. Local and imported wines, however, are expensive and are rarely available in bars.
Mizuwari (whisky diluted 1:6 with water and ice) is popular in business circles, especially where there are foreigners to impress. Great snobbery attaches to different grades of imported whisky (Chivas Regal is reckoned the top brand). Show appreciation.
Shochu is a potent spirit, usually distilled from rice or sweet potatoes. The best *shochu* is said to come from the warmer regions of Japan and is known as *awamori*.

Shopping

An enormous range of products are on sale in Japan, from antique kimonos to the latest in hi-tech. But it is not the place to look for bargains. If you can find what you want at home, it is probably as cheap as in Tokyo. Tax-free centres offer goods to foreign shoppers; show your passport for discounts of 10–20%. The same, or greater, reductions can often be found in the discount shops, which also offer a wider choice.

The brand-name stores in hotel arcades are invariably expensive. For leisure shopping use the department and ordinary stores, as the Japanese do. Shops stay open between 10 and 6 (some stay open later) and close one day a week. Most are open on a Sunday.

Department stores

Not just places to shop, department stores include restaurants, travel agencies and even art galleries. When buying a gift, remember that the wrapping and the name on the paper often say more than the gift.
Daimaru A popular chain selling high quality goods at sensible prices.
Hankyu Based in Osaka, Hankyu is expanding. A fairly down-market range of goods.
Matsuzakaya has a staid, rather unexciting image.
Mitsukoshi Undoubtedly the most prestigious store; the only place to buy an important gift.
Seibu The most innovative of the chains with a wide range of goods. Its new Tokyo store has a section devoted to foreigners' needs.
Sogo A well-established but unexciting chain, Sogo has modernized its image with the largest department store in the world, in Yokohama.
Takashiyama Mitsukoshi's only rival so far as prestige is concerned, and with many more branches – 19.

Local information

The first person to try is the concierge in your hotel. Some are famous for their endless funds of up-to-date information. They provide good maps and give directions, as well as recommending the best restaurants in town.
Tourist Information Centres (TIC) in Tokyo and Kyoto have well-informed, multilingual staff. They produce free maps and monthly publications on entertainment, sightseeing and festivals. They are also willing to make phone calls and hotel reservations. In other cities the TIC may be less useful, although staff will speak some languages and supply an English map of the city. TIC is closed on Sundays.
Japan Travel Phone For information and assistance in English you can dial 106 and ask for "Collect call TIC". In Tokyo ☎ 502 1461, and in Kyoto ☎ 371 5649. The service is available 9–5 throughout the year.

Japan Travel Bureau JTB has branches throughout the country. They are often a useful source of information, and are invaluable for making reservations and purchasing tickets.

Public lavatories

There are toilets in hotels, restaurants, department stores and (best avoided) stations, usually clearly indicated by a symbol of a man or woman. They may be Western-style or designed for squatting, Japanese-style. If there are several cubicles, there will be a separate queue for each. Knock on a closed door – an answering knock indicates that it is occupied. Toilet paper may not be provided, so carry tissues.

Crime

Japan's crime rate is low and its detection rate high. Both men and women can feel safe almost everywhere, even at night (but avoid dock areas and sleazier night-life districts). Hotel staff, taxi drivers and even complete strangers go to extraordinary lengths to trace owners of mislaid cameras and umbrellas.
The police Standards are high in police recruitment, training, discipline and morale. Police expect and get widespread public co-operation and know their "beat" to a degree some Westerners would find intrusive. They are more concerned with order than with law and can and do exercise considerable personal discretion when deciding whether or not to invoke the law. Police boxes (*koban*) can be found every kilometre or so in urban areas and, subject to limitations of language, visitors can generally be confident of courteous assistance.

Hotel staff are very trustworthy but it is wise, nevertheless, to consign valuables to the hotel safe. Car doors should be locked if you leave the vehicle out of direct sight.

If you are arrested

Japanese law requires that an arrested person be charged or released "as soon as possible" and, in any case, within 24 hours. An arrested person will usually wish to contact his or her embassy and Japanese authorities are likely to cooperate since consular presence will probably make their task easier. The authorities may well be content with a stern warning if the matter is a minor one or where some practical restitution can be made. If discussing restitution, take care not to look as though you are trying to buy your way out or offer a bribe. If a serious crime is involved an accused person may at least be comforted to know that several leading British and US law firms have close links with Japanese counterparts (see *The law*).

Embassies

All the embassies listed below are in Tokyo (telephone code 03).
Australia 2-1-14 Mita, Minato-ku, 108 ☏ 453 0251/9
Austria 1-1-20, Moto Azabu, Minato-ku, 106 ☏ 451 8281/3
Belgium 5 Niban-cho, Chiyoda-ku, 102 ☏ 262 0191/5
Canada 7-3-38 Akasaka, Minato-ku, 107 ☏ 408 2101/8
Denmark 29-6 Sangaku-cho, Shibuya-ku, 150 ☏ 496 3001
Finland 3-5-39 Minami Azabu, Minato-ku, 106 ☏ 442 2231
France 4-11-44 Minami Azabu, Minato-ku, 106 ☏ 473 0171
Germany, West 4-5-10 Minami Azabu, Minato-ku, 106 ☏ 473 0151
Greece 3-16-30 Nishi Azabu, Minato-ku, 106 ☏ 403 0871
Ireland No. 25 Kowa Bldg, 8-7 Sanban-cho, Chiyoda-ku, 102 ☏ 263 0695
Italy 2-5-4 Mita, Minato-ku, 108 ☏ 453 5291/6
Netherlands 3-6-3 Shiba Koen, Minato-ku, 105 ☏ 431 5126/9
New Zealand 20-40 Kamiyama-cho, Shibuya-ku, 150 ☏ 467 2271
Norway 5-12-2 Minami Azabu, Minato-ku, 106 ☏ 440 2611

Portugal Olympia Annex 304, 305, 306, 6-31-21 Jingumae, Shibuya-ku, 150 ☏ 400 7907
Spain 1-3-29 Roppongi, Minato-ku, 106 ☏ 583 8531/3
Sweden 1-10-3 Roppongi, Minato-ku, 106 ☏ 582 6981/9
Switzerland 5-9-12 Minami Azabu, Minato-ku, 106 ☏ 473 1021
United Kingdom 1 Ichiban-cho, Chiyoda-ku, 102 ☏ 265 5511
United States 1-10-5 Akasaka, Minato-ku, 107 ☏ 583 7141
Yugoslavia 4-7-24 Kita Shinagawa, Shinagawa-ku, 140 ☏ 447 3571/3

Health care

Japan offers health care of a very high standard. Most Japanese citizens are under the National Health Insurance scheme introduced in 1961. Visitors to Japan should always take out comprehensive medical and dental insurance to avoid the high fees charged for treatment.

Western medicine is the most common form of treatment, although alternatives such as Chinese medicine (*kampo yaku*), acupuncture and Japanese acupressure massage (*shiatsu*) are available. Mineral baths (*onsen*) are also thought to have curative properties.

If you fall ill

Your first recourse should be to the hotel doctor or to one of the reputable English-speaking clinics which provide emergency cover with a doctor on call (see *City by city*). Help can also be obtained by calling Tokyo English Life Line (TELL) ☏ (03) 264 4347. TELL will make emergency arrangements or be able to refer you to a reputable doctor.

Pharmacies Most pharmacies sell medicines produced and packaged in Japan with names and instructions in Japanese. Western brand-name drugs are available only from specialist pharmacies (see *City by city* for details). Many large hotels have a pharmacy selling Western drugs. In Tokyo there are pharmacies at the following hotels: Hilton, Imperial, Okura, Pacific, Shinjuku Washington, and the Takanawa Prince.

Doctors Most ailments and injuries are dealt with by hospital doctors. You can visit a hospital clinic (*byoin*) as an out-patient but it is unwise to do so unless you are with a Japanese-speaker or have been referred by an English-speaking doctor. Hospitals vary markedly in atmosphere and décor; nursing standards are low compared to the West, and administrative staff are often less than helpful. Long queues are the norm.

Private specialist clinics, however, are of a high standard and are equipped with up-to-date medical technology.

Some big-city hospitals have English-speaking staff (see *City by city* for details). Apart from these hospitals, most doctors can speak some English. *The Tourist's Handbook* – free from JNTO or the TIC – has a bilingual section on emergencies and illnesses which may be helpful.

If you fall ill at your hotel, they will usually make the necessary arrangements and add the cost of treatment to your bill. Otherwise you may need to pay doctors in cash, reclaiming the money from your insurers.

Dentists are very expensive and are highly qualified. Western-style surgeries have ultra modern equipment. For a complete list of dentists, including those who speak English, contact the TIC offices in the major cities.

Emergencies If you need urgent treatment, go to a doctor in the out-patient department of your nearest hospital. If it is a dire emergency and you are not at your hotel or with Japanese colleagues, find a Japanese speaker. Emergency calls are answered in Japanese and it is unusual to find anyone who speaks English. To call an ambulance dial 119 and state which service you require; better still, call TELL.

Communications

Telex and fax services are widely available and the telephone and postal systems are of a high standard, though not cheap. Two useful information sources are the *Japan Yellow Pages* ☎ (03) 239 3501 and the *Japan Times Directory* ☎ (03) 453 5311.

Telephones

Phones are operated by Nippon Telegraph and Telephone Company (NTT). Local calls (Y10 for 3mins) may be made on pink, red or blue phones. For long distance and international calls use yellow or green ones. Green ones take telephone cards.

Making a call Insert coins (Y10 for local calls, otherwise Y100). The dial tone is a continuous hum. "Beep" means you are running out of money. Engaged is a "bao-bao" noise. Unused coins (but not fractions of Y100) are returned at the end of the call. The Japanese answer calls with "moshi-moshi" but "Hai, X desu" ("Yes, this is X"), is also common.

Cutting costs Long distance (over 60km) calls cost 40% less from 7pm to 8am and from 6am to 9pm on Sundays and holidays. From 9pm to 6am calls over 320km are 50% cheaper.

International calls are handled by Kokusai Denshin Denwa (KDD). Calls can be made from KDD offices in major cities, as well as from other phones (see *International dialling codes*). KDD operators use American English, so say "collect", not "reverse charges", and "zero", not "nought". Most countries can be dialled direct.

Emergency calls Police is 110 and Fire and Ambulance 119, but these services operate in Japanese only. Use Tokyo English Life Line ☎ (03) 264 4347.

Telegrams can be written in Roman script and handed in at post offices and railway stations. International telegrams can be sent from KDD offices, some post offices and larger hotels and always from the Central Post Office in front of Tokyo Station, where there are English-speaking staff. After midnight use KDD offices in Tokyo, Kyoto and Osaka or ☎ (03) 344 5151.

Telex and fax

Both services are widespread in hotels and offices; larger places will have both domestic and international facilities. KDD offices (see *City by city*) provide public facilities.

Mail

Post offices (*yubin kyoku*) are indicated by the symbol of a red capital T with a bar over it, which is also used in addresses to denote a postal district (written in the top right-hand corner of the envelope). All post offices open 9–5 weekdays and 9–12.30 Saturdays but close on the second Saturday of each month. There are 24-hour post offices in Tokyo, Kyoto and Osaka and post offices in some other cities are open late (see *City by city*). Hotels usually sell stamps and air letters.

Mail boxes are red and free-standing. In Tokyo they often have two slots: the right-hand one is for city mail only.

Rates vary for ordinary and first class. Express, registered delivery and advice of delivery services are available. Overseas charges vary by zone. There are special rates for printed matter.

Deliveries First class letters usually take one day. Letters for Europe and North America take four or five days. *Poste restante* services are operated by the Japanese Post Office and by American Express.

Parcels Overseas packages (up to 10kg weight and 1 metre long) must be sent from main post offices. Department stores are usually happy to post bulky purchases.

Couriers There are excellent internal and external courier services. Much of Japan's traffic in letters and packets is handled by private carriers, such as Yamato, who offer guaranteed delivery times.

International dialling codes

Operator-connected calls
You can make station-to-station, person-to-person, collect, credit card or conference calls. There are no discount rates on operator-connected calls.
Operator ☎ 0056
Directory inquiries ☎ 0056
Direct dialling is cheapest. Discount rates apply at the following Japanese times: 5am–8am, 7pm–11pm 20% cheaper; 11pm–5am 40% cheaper. On Sundays all calls are at discount rates: 5am–11pm 20% cheaper; 11pm–5am 40% cheaper. Before dialling the country's code, dial 001.

Areas	Country Code	Time differences
Alaska	1	(-18~-19)
Algeria	213	(-8)
Argentina	54	(-12)
Australia	61	(-1~+1)
Austria	43	(-8)
Bahrain	973	(-6)
Belgium	32	(-8)
Bolivia	591	(-13)
Brazil	55	(-12~-14)
Burma	95	(-2.30)
Canada	1	(-12.30~-18)
Canary Islands	34	(-9)
Chile	56	(-13)
Colombia	57	(-14)
Costa Rica	506	(-15)
Cyprus (Rep. of)	357	(-7)
Czechoslovakia	42	(-8)
Denmark	45	(-8)
Ecuador	593	(-14)
Egypt	20	(-7)
El Salvador	503	(-15)
Fiji	679	(+3)
Finland	358	(-7)
France	33	(-8)
Germany (Dem. Rep.)	37	(-8)
Germany (Fed. Rep.)	49	(-8)
Gibraltar	350	(-8)
Greece	30	(-7)
Guatemala	502	(-15)
Guyana	592	(-12)
Hawaii	1	(-19)
Honduras	504	(-15)
Hong Kong	852	(-1)
Iceland	354	(-9)
India	91	(-3.30)
Indonesia	62	(-2~±0)
Iran	98	(-5.30)
Iraq	964	(-6)
Ireland	353	(-9)
Israel	972	(-7)
Italy	39	(-8)
Ivory Coast	225	(-9)
Jordan	962	(-7)
Kenya	254	(-6)
Korea (Rep. of)	82	(±0)
Kuwait	965	(-6)
Lesotho	266	(-7)
Liechtenstein	41	(-8)
Luxembourg	352	(-8)
Macao	853	(-1)
Madagascar	261	(-6)
Madeira	351	(-9)
Malawi	265	(-7)
Malaysia	60	(-1)
Malta	356	(-8)
Mexico	52	(-15~-17)
Monaco	33	(-8)
Morocco	212	(-9)
Mozambique	258	(-7)
Namibia	264	(-7)
Netherlands	31	(-8)
New Zealand	64	(+3)
Nicaragua	505	(-15)
Nigeria	234	(-8)
Niger	227	(-8)
Norway	47	(-8)
Oman	968	(-5)
Pakistan	92	(-4)
Panama	507	(-14)
Papua New Guinea	675	(+1)
Paraguay	595	(-13)
Philippines	63	(-1)
Poland	48	(-8)
Portugal	351	(-9)
Qatar	974	(-6)
Romania	40	(-7)
San Marino	39	(-8)
Saudi Arabia	966	(-6)
Singapore	65	(-1)
South Africa	27	(-7)
Spain	34	(-8)
Sri Lanka	94	(-3.30)
Sweden	46	(-8)
Switzerland	41	(-8)
Taiwan	886	(-1)
Tanzania	255	(-6)
Thailand	66	(-2)
Tunisia	216	(-8)
Turkey	90	(-7)
Uganda	256	(-6)
United Arab Emirates	971	(-5)
United Kingdom	44	(-9)
Uruguay	598	(-12)
USA (Mainland)	1	(-14~-17)
USSR	7	(-6~+4)
Vatican	39	(-8)
Venezuela	58	(-13)
Yemen	967	(-6)
Yugoslavia	38	(-8)
Zambia	260	(-7)

Conversion charts

Japan has embraced the metric system almost totally (dual imperial/metric markings on packaging are generally not acceptable). Currency, distances, lengths, weights, liquid capacity, temperature and large measurements of area (hectares) are all metric. However, S.I. units are not widely understood, sizes for shoes and clothing differ from those used in the West, and years are sometimes enumerated from the start of the Emperor's reign: Showa 61 = 1987.

The main traditional measurements still commonly in use are those for floor area. The tatami is based on the straw floor mat of that name, and is used for domestic room measurements. The tsubo is used for office areas or whole apartments.

1 tatami = 1.8 × 0.9 meters = 1.62 square meters.

1 tsubo = 3.3 square meters.

Temperature

°F	32	40	50	60	70	75	85	95	105	140	175	212
°C	0	5	10	15	20	25	30	35	40	60	80	100

Length

centimeters (cm)	cm or in	inches (in)
2.54	=in 1 cm=	0.394
5.08	2	0.787
7.62	3	1.181
10.16	4	1.575
12.70	5	1.969
15.24	6	2.362
17.78	7	2.756
20.32	8	3.150
22.86	9	3.543
25.40	10	3.937
50.80	20	7.874
76.20	30	11.811
101.60	40	15.748
127.00	50	19.685

Mass (weight)

kilograms (kg)	kg or lb	pounds (lb)
0.454	=lb 1 kg=	2.205
0.907	2	4.409
1.361	3	6.614
1.814	4	8.819
2.268	5	11.023
2.722	6	13.228
3.175	7	15.432
3.629	8	17.637
4.082	9	19.842
4.536	10	22.046
9.072	20	44.092
13.608	30	66.139
18.144	40	88.185
22.680	50	110.231

Distance

kilometers (km)	km or miles	miles
1.609	=mi 1 km=	0.621
3.219	2	1.243
4.828	3	1.864
6.437	4	2.485
8.047	5	3.107
9.656	6	3.728
11.265	7	4.350
12.875	8	4.971
14.484	9	5.592
16.093	10	6.214
32.187	20	12.427
48.280	30	18.641
64.374	40	24.855
80.467	50	31.069

Volume

liters (l)	liters or US galls	US galls
3.79	=l 1 gall=	0.26
7.58	2	0.52
11.37	3	0.78
15.16	4	1.04
18.95	5	1.30
22.74	6	1.56
26.53	7	1.82
30.32	8	2.08
34.11	9	2.34
37.90	10	2.60
75.80	20	5.20
113.70	30	7.80
151.60	40	10.40
189.50	50	13.00

Background reading

General Surveys

The Sun at Noon Dick Wilson (Hamish Hamilton, 1986).
The Japanese E.O. Reischauer (Harvard University Press, 1979).
Japan As Number One: Lessons for America Ezra Vogel (HUP, 1979).
Japan Today W.H. Forbis (Harper & Row, 1975).

The Economic Scene

Asia's New Giant. How the Japanese Economy Works Hugh Patrick and Henry Rosovsky (eds) (Brookings Institution, 1976).
Japan in the World Economy Saburo Okita (Japan Foundation, 1975).

The Industrial Scene

Management and Worker: The Japanese Solution James C. Abegglen (Kodansha, 1976).
Industrial Organization in Japan R. Caves and M. Uekusa (Brookings Institution, 1976).
Japan's Multinational Enterprises M.Y. Yoshino (HUP, 1976).
British Factory-Japanese Factory Ronald Dore (George Allen & Unwin, 1973).

The Political Scene

Politics in Modern Japan: Development and Organization Koichi Kishimoto (Japan Echo, 1978).
Policymaking in Contemporary Japan T.J. Pempel (ed) (Cornell University Press, 1977).
Political Change in Japan T. Tsurutani (Longman, 1977).
Japan: Divided Politics in a Growth Economy J.A.A. Stockwin (Norton, 1975).

The Business Scene

Kaisha; The Japanese Corporation James C. Abegglen and George Stalk Jr (Harper & Row, 1986).
The Japanese Company Rodney Clark (Yale University Press, 1979).
Japan's Public Policy Companies Chalmers Johnson (American Enterprise Institute, 1978).
From Bonsai to Levis George Fields (Macmillan, 1983).
Marketing Opportunities in Japan Dentsu Inc (McGraw-Hill, 1978).
Current Legal Aspects of Doing Business in Japan and East Asia John O. Haley (ed) (American Bar Association, 1978).
Introduction to Japanese Law Yosiyuki Noda (ed) (Tokyo University, 1976).

Business Awareness

Corporate Strategies in Japan K. Odaka, R. Grondine, S. Mizushima (Longman, 1985).
Doing Business in Japan JETRO (Gakuseisha, 1984).
The Art of Japanese Management R. Pascale and A. Athos (Penguin, 1981).

Cultural Awareness

History *Japan vs Europe: A History of Misunderstanding* Endymion Wilkinson (Penguin, 1983).
The Development of Japanese Business 1600–1973 J. Hirchmeier and T. Yui (George Allen & Unwin, 1979).
East Asia: Tradition and Transformation J.K. Fairbank, E.O. Reischauer, A.M. Craig (Houghton Mifflin, 1973).
Culture *A Japanese Mirror. Heroes and Villains of Japanese Culture* Ian Buruma (Penguin, 1984).
Japan: A Comparative View A.M. Craig (Princeton University Press, 1979).
The Anatomy of Dependence Takeo Doi (Kodansha, 1973).
Japanese Society Chie Nakane (Penguin, 1973).
Manners and customs *Simple Etiquette in Japan* Helmut Morsbach (Paul Norbury Publications, 1984).
Land of the Rising Yen George Mikes (Penguin, 1972).
Japan Unmasked Ichiro Kawasaki (Tuttle, 1969).
Language *Hugo's Japanese* (Hugo's Language Books, 1986).
Survival Characters (Institute of Linguists, 1986).
Japanese Business Glossary Mitsubishi Corp. (Oriental Economist, 1983).

Index

Abe, Shintaro 38
accountants 68–9
accounting principles 51
addresses, understanding 106
address, forms of 81
advertising 70–1
agents, distribution 75
agriculture 12
Agriculture Ministry 40
aid, foreign 15
airports 236
Ajinomoto 35
allowances, company 55
Amersham International 34
annuity insurance 62
Anti-Monopoly Act (1947) 44
applications software 25
arbitration (*chusai*) 63
Ark Hills complex 108, 118
arrest, in case of 246
Asahi Evening News 88
Asahi Shimbun 88
ASEAN 42
Ashikaga 90
attorneys (*bengoshi*) 64; patent 66
audit corporations (*kansa hojin*) 68–9; addresses 67
automation 26–7; car industry 23

balance of payments 16
Bank of Japan 56, 61
Bank of Yokohama 58
banking, VANs in 29
bankruptcy 48
banks 57–8; information on companies 51; using 236
Banque National de Paris 58
bars 244
bathing 105
Bender, Matthew: *Doing Business in Japan* 66
benefits: fringe 55; sickness 62
biotechnology 19, 31
Boehringer Mannheim 34
body language 103–4
bond markets 60
bonuses 55
branch office (*shiten*) 51
Braun 34
brokers, foreign 59
Buddhism 89, 94
bureaucrats 40–1; in business 45
bus, travelling by 238
business 44–75; awareness 76–88; framework 48–51; government and 44–5; power in 46–7
Business Accounting Deliberation Council 68
Business Japan 88
business law 65–6; international 64

C.Itoh 50
Cabinet 36, 37
CAD/CAM (computer-aided design/computer-aided manufacturing) 26, 27
camera/recorder, compact 24
cameras 18
capital: intensity in industry 18; net exporter 17
car industry 18, 22–3, 26–7, 49
carbon fibre, polyacrylonitrile (PAN) 30
cards, business (*meishi*) 80–1, 83
cars, company 55
cartels 45, 49
Caterpillar Tractor 34
cell fusion 31
cellular radio 28
Center for the Inducement of Industry to Rural Areas 61
ceramics 30
chairman (*kaicho*) 78
chambers of commerce 51
chemicals industry, heavy 21
cheques, travellers' 235
China 9, 23, 42, 89
Christianity 90
Chukakuha 43
Citicorp 58
city banks, assets (1985) 57
Civil Code 64
civil service 40–1; control in business 44–5
climate 234
Coca Cola 34
colleges, technical 97
commercial banks 57
Commercial Code 68
commissions 60
commodities markets 60
communications 28–9, 248
compact discs (CDs) 24
compact video 24
companies: foreign 34–5; ownership 48–9; setting up 50–1; size 48; Top ten 32–3; types 50
company law 51
competition: domestic 9; international 19
computers 18, 25, 29
confidentiality 65–6
Confucian ethics 90, 96
Constitution 36, 43, 63
consumer laws 65
Consumer Products Safety Law (1973) 65
contracts, business 64–5
conversation 102–5
copiers 18
corporate attitudes 48
corporate hierarchies 78
corporate networks 49–50
corporation tax 14
corporations 49; public 15
courts 63
credit banks, long-term 57
credit cards 236
crime 246
cuisine 242–3
cultural awareness 89–102
culture 93
currency 14, 235
customs regulations 73, 234

Dai-ichi Kangyo 57
Daily Yomiuri 88
Daiwa Securities 59
data communications 29
databases, computer 29
decision-making 78
defence 37, 43; expenditure 15
Defence Agency 43
deficit financing 14
Democratic Socialist Party 39
dentists 247
department stores 75, 245
deregulation 14; telecommunications 28
design applications 65
dialling codes, international 249
Diamond's Economic Journal Industria 88
Diet, the 36, 41
digitization of telecommunications 28
directories, company 88
directors, non-executive (*Sodanyaku*) 78
disclosure requirements, company 51
discrimination, wage 54–5
distribution 75
diversification 19
doctors 247
Doi, Takako 39
Doing Business in Japan (Bender) 66
Domei (Japan Confederation of Labour) 39, 54
Dow Chemical 35
dress, for business 84; general 104
drinking 76, 79, 83, 244–5
driving 234, 238
dual economy 49
Dunlop 34, 35

earthquakes 10, 62
EC 42; protectionism 24

Economic Planning Agency 40
economy 8–9
Edo (or Tokugawa) period 90–1
education 8, 15, 96–7
Education Ministry 40
elections 36–7; 1986 results 39
electoral reform 37
electrical equipment industry 26
electroceramics 18, 30
Electronic Buyers' Guide 88
electronics 19; components 18, 25; consumer 18, 24
embassies 51, 74, 246
emergencies 247
emigration 13
Emperor 36, 89
employers, pointers for prospective 53
employment 52–5; effect of automation on 27
employment law 53
energy 10–12
entertainment 86
entertainment allowances 51, 77
entry requirements 234
Equal Employment Opportunities Law 52, 53
Eurobond market 59
Europe 42; trade restrictions 18
examinations 96–7
executive, the 36–7
expenditure; national 15; public 14
Export-Import Bank 41
exports: top ten 17; voluntary restraints 23

"face" 48
facsimile machines 18, 28; *see also* fax
factory, setting up a 61
Fair Trade Commission (FTC) 44–5, 71
family 95
family firms 49
fax 248
fermentation techniques 31
finance 37; institutions 56; sources of 61
Finance, Ministry of 9, 40, 41, 56
finances, national 14–15
Fiscal Investment and Loan Plan (FILP) 14
fiscal policy 14
fisheries 12
Foreign Affairs, Ministry of 41
foreign banks 58
foreign companies, listing on TSE 60
forestry 12
Formosa 91
fraud 69
Fuji Bank 88
Fuji Xerox 34
Fukuda faction 38
Fukuoka 10, 148–57
futures trading 60

General Account 14
gifts 87
Gotoh, Noboru 47
government 36–7; assistance to business 45; flexibility 19; intervention in finance 56

hardware, computer 25
health care 247
Health and Welfare, Ministry of 44
Heian period 89
Hideyoshi 90
hierarchy 78
high technology: centres 45; industries 18, 24–30
Hiragana 98
Hiraiwa, Gaishi 47
Hirohito 89, 92
Hiroshima 158–65
history 89–92; important events 92
Hitachi 32
Hokkaido 10
Hokkaido-Tohuko Development Finance Public Corporation 61
holidays 77; national 235
Honda 19
Honda, Soichiro 8
Honshu 10
hospitality 85–7
hotels 238–41; *see also* under Cities
hours, business 76–7
House of Councillors 36
House of Hardy 34
House of Representatives 36
hurricanes 10

IBM Japan 34, 51
Ieyasu, Tokugawa 90
immigration 13
imports 16–17; dependence on 10–12; quotas 72
Inayama, Yoshihiro 47
income, national 14–15
income tax 14, 55
incorporation 51
Industrial Bank of Japan 57, 88
industrial centres 106
industrial groups (*keiretsu gaisha*) 50
industrial property rights 65
industry 18–19, 34–5; companies 20–33
inflation 14
information, business: background 251; retrieval of economic 29; sources 235
Information Network Systems (INS) 28
insurance 62
intelligence services 43
interest rates 56
international alignments 42
interpreters, use of 81–2, 99
investigators, private (*koshinsho*) 51
investment 18–19; capital 58; foreign direct 8, 34, 72; portfolios 62
invitations 85–7
Ishibashi, Masashi 38–9
Ishihara, Takashi 47
islands 10
Izvestia 88

Japan Airlines 237, 239
Japan Automobile Federation 238
Japan Business Directory 88
Japan Cable Television (JCTV) 88
Japan Communist Party 39
Japan Company Handbook 88
Japan Development Bank 41, 45, 61
Japan Economic Almanac 88
Japan Economic Journal 88
Japan Economic Yearbook 88
Japan Electronics Almanac 88
Japan External Trade Organization (JETRO) 45, 74, 235
Japan Federation of Bar Associations (*Nichibenren*) 64
Japan Industrial Location Center 61
Japan Key Technology Center (JKTC) 31
Japan National Railways 15, 44
Japan National Tourist Organization 235
Japan Regional Development Corporation 61
Japan Salt and Tobacco 44
Japan Seaman's Union 54
Japan Socialist Party 38–9
Japan Times 88
Japan Travel Bureau 235, 245

Japanese Chamber of Commerce and Industry 235
Japanese Companies Consolidated Data 88
Japanese Embassy 235
Japanese Institute of Certified Public Accountants 68
Japanese Securities and Exchange Law, (Article 65) 56, 58
JAPIO (Japan Patent Information Online) 29
JETRO (Japan External Trade Organization) 45, 74, 235
JICST (Japan Centre of Science and Technology) 29
joint ventures 34, 51; in new materials 30
Journal of Japanese Trade and Industry 88
judiciary 37
juku (private crammers) 96–7

Kamakura period 89–90
Kanji 98
Kansai, plain of (Kyoto-Osaka) 10
Kanto, plain of (Tokyo) 10
Katakana 98
Katakura 48
Keidanren (Federation of Economic Organizations) 44, 46–7, 74
Keidanren Review on Japanese Economy 88
Keio University 97
Keizai Doyukai (Japan Committee for Economic Development) 44, 47
Keizai Koho Center 46, 88
Kita-Kyushu 166–9
Kobe 170–7
Kokusai Denshin Denwa (KDD) 28
Komeito 39
Komoto faction 38
Korea 90, 91
Korea, South 23; shipbuilding 20
Kublai Khan 90
Kurile Islands 10
Kyoto (historically Heian) 89, 90, 178–91
Kyoto University 97
Kyushu 10

labour costs 54–5
labour force 13
labour relations 52–5
Labour Relations Adjustment Law 53
Labour Standards Law 53
land: reform 8; scarcity 10; use 12–13
language 98–101
LaserDisk system 24
lavatories, public 105, 246
law 63–7; employment 53; firms' addresses 67
lawyers 63–4; using 66
legislature 36
leisure 95
liaison office 50
Liberal Democratic Party (LDP) 9, 36, 37, 38, 44, 46, 91
liberalization 17, 41, 56; of telecommunications 29
life insurance 62
literacy 8
litigation 63
living, standard of 94
local government 15, 37; aid for business 45
local information 245
locating places 99
Long Term Credit Bank 57, 88
lunches, business 83

MacArthur, General 91
mail 248
Mainichi Daily News 88
Mainichi Shimbun 88
management, middle 78
Manchuria 91
manners 102–5
maps of Japan 11, 107
marketing, direct 71
markets 59–60; entry to 72–4
Marubeni 50
materials: composite 30; new 30
Matsushita, Konosuke 32
media, business 88
meetings, business 80–3
Meiji Restoration 91
metals, amorphous 30
militarism 91
Minamoto 89
ministers, power of 40
ministries 9, 40–1
Mita, Katsushige 32
MITI; Industrial Location Guidance Division 45
MITI; software development programme 25
MITI *Handbook* 45
MITI (Ministry of International Trade and Industry) 9, 18–19, 21, 22, 40, 41, 44–5; address 61
Mitsubishi 50, 91
Mitsubishi Heavy Industries 32
Mitsubishi Trust and Banking 58
Mitsui 50, 91
Miyazawa, Kiichi 38
monetary policy 14
money 235–6
Mongols 90
monopoly legislation 44, 45
Morita, Akio 8, 48
motorcycle industry 18
Muromachi period 90
myths about Japan 8–9

Nagoya 192–201
Nagoya Sogo Bank 29
Nakasone 37; faction 38
Narita Airport 43
national debt 14
NCR 34
NEC 33
NEEDS database 29
nemawashi (consensus-building) 78
Nestlé 34
network, old-boy (*gakubatsu*) 97
Newpis Ltd 48
news retrieval service 29
newspapers 88
NEXIS database 29
Nichibenren 64, 66
Nihon Keizai Shimbun 29, 88
Nikkeiren (Japan Federation of Employers' Associations) 47
Nikko Securities 59
Nippon Credit Bank 57
Nippon Electric Co (NEC) 34
Nippon Kokan (NKK) 33
Nippon Steel 32
Nippon Telegraph and Telephone Corporation (NTT) 28, 29, 44
Nissan Motor 32
Nissho (Japan Chamber of Commerce and Industry) 47, 74
"no", avoid use of 82, 102
Nobunaga, Oda 90, 92
Nomura International Finance 59
Nomura Securities 59
NTT, *see* Nippon Telegraph and Telephone Corporation

Occupation 91
OEM (original equipment manufacture) 27
Office of Trade Ombudsman 73
offshore banking 58
oil crises 20, 21
Okinawa 10
optical fibres 28
Organization of the Government of Japan 45

Osaka 202–15
Osaka Securities Exchange 60
Otsuki, Bunpei 47

Pacific Basin Economic Council 47
Pacific War 8, 91
pacifism 36, 43, 91
partners, checking out 51
partnership companies (*goshi gaisha* or *gomei gaisha*) 50
party politics 38–9
passports 234
patents 65; law 64
PATOLIS database 29
PBXs (private branch exchanges), digital 28
peace constitution 91
pension funds 62
peripheral devices, CAD/CAM 27
personal computers (PCs) 25, 29
petrochemicals 21
pharmaceutical companies 31
pharmacies 247
phrases, useful 98–101
plastics, engineering 30
Plaza Agreement (1985) 17, 72
police 43, 246
Police Agency 43
Police Reserve Force 43
politeness 83
politics 36–43; party 38–9
population 13, 91
Postal Savings Bank 14
Posts and Telecommunications, Ministry of 28
power, reins of 40–1
Pravda 88
president, company (*shacho*) 78
price controls 44
prime minister 37, 40
private limited companies (*yugen gaisha*) 50
privatization 44
Procter & Gamble 35
protectionism 12, 19, 72
Protein Engineering Research Institute 31
public limited liability company (*kabushiki kaisha* or *kk*) 50
public sector 44
punctuality 81

R&D 19; funding 61
radio 70
rank, business 78
rationalization, forced in chemical industry 21
raw materials 10
recombinant DNA 31
recruitment 52–3; for life 52
"red bonds" 14
redundancies 53
regional banks 57
Regional Development Laws 61
regions 10
religion 94
reports, company 69
research offices (*chosa jimusho*) 51
resources 10–13, 91
restaurants 242–3; *see also* under Cities
Retail Distribution in Japan (Dodwell) 75
retail outlets 75
rice prices 12
ringi-sho (decision–requesting circular) 78
riots 43
roads 22, 238
robot production (1971–86) 27
robotics 18, 26–7
Rodime 34
Rolls Royce 34
Romaji 98
Russia 8, 91; *see also* USSR
Ryukyus 10

Saito, Eishiro 47
sake 244
salaries, executive 55
samurai 90–1; bonds 60
Sanken (Industrial Issues Study Council) 47
Sapporo 216–25
satellites, communication 28
savings 56
schools 96–7
Science and Technology Agency 40
scripts 98
Sears Roebuck 60
securities dealing, and banks 56–60
Securities and Exchange Laws 68
securities market 59
security, national 43
Self Defence Forces 43
self-employment (*jiei gyosha*) 50
semiconductor industry 18
seniority 40, 78
service sector, employment 13
setting up a company 50–1
shareholding 48–9, 59–60
Shikoku 10
Shinto 91
shipbuilding 18, 20
shushin (moral education) 97
shoes, removing 105
shoguns 89–90; bonds 60
shopping 245
Shoshu Buddhist sect 39
Silicon Valley, Japan's 10
skill base 13
social life 77
Société Générale 58
software, computer 25
sogo shosa 50, 74, 75
Sohyo (General Council of Trade Unions) 38, 54
Soichiro, Honda 48
Soka Gakkai 39
sole proprietorships (*hitori kaisha*) 50
Soseki, Natsume 91
sponsorship 71
standards, technical and certification procedures 72
statutory examiners (*kansayaku*) 68–9, 78
steel industry 18
stock market 59–60
subsidiaries, wholly owned (*genchi hojin*) 51
subway, travelling by 106, 238
Sumitomo 50, 91
Sumitomo Metal Industries 33
Sumitomo Rubber Industries 35
Supreme Court 36, 37, 63
sushi bonds 60
Suzuki faction 38

Taira 89
takeovers 48
Takeshita, Noboru 38
Tanaka 37; faction 38
targeting 18; biotechnology 31
tariffs 72
tax: corporation 51; laws 69; personal 55; reform debate 15
taxation: direct 14; indirect 15
taxi, travelling by 106, 237
teachers' union (*Nikkyso*) 54
technology 19
Technopolis programme (MITI) 61
telecommunications 28; deregulation 25, 28
telephone calls 248
television: advertising 70; cable 71; high-definition 24; integrated 24
telex 248
tenders, government 72
Texas Instruments 34
textile industry 18
tipping 236

toilets, public 105, 246
Tokugawa (or Edo period) 90–1
Tokyo Business Today 88
Tokyo Commodity Exchange 60
Tokyo English Lifeline 247
Tokyo (historically Edo) 90–1, 108–47
Tokyo Stock Exchange (TSE) 17, 56, 59–60
Tokyo University 40, 45, 97
Toshiba 33
Tourist Information Centres 245
Toyota Motor 32
trade, international 16–18
trade mark law 65
Trade Union Law 53
trading companies; general (*sogo shosha*) 74; specialized (*senmon shosha*) 74
trading partners 16–17
train travel 237
training, in-house by corporations 97
Transport, Ministry of 20
travel: to Japan 236; within Japan 106, 236–8
trust banks 58
TV, cable 88

UN 42
underemployment 13, 52
unemployment 13, 52
unions 38, 53–4
United Social Democratic Party 39
universities 97
USA: trade restrictions 18
USA 42; CAD/CAM companies 27; defence assistance 15, 43; technological competition 19
USSR 9, 42

value added networks (VANs) 25, 28, 29
VCRs (video cassette recorders) 24
venture capital 61
VHD (video high density) 24
video cassette recorders 18
videodiscs 24
visas 234
Volkswagen 22, 23

wage bargaining (*shunto*) 54
wage rates 18
Warburg, S.G. 58
Waseda University 97
weather 84
welfare 14; company 15; public spending 15
Western industrial weakness 18
whaling 12
women: in business 79; dress 84; safety 104; wage discrimination 54–5; in workforce 13, 79
work ethic 77
workers 76
World Bank 42
written word 98

Yamaichi Securities 59
yen 9, 17, 19, 37
Yen Eurobonds 60
Yokohama 226–33
Yomiuri Shimbun 88
Yukio, Mishima 91

zaikai 46
Zen culture 90